Cocaine Hoppers

Cocaine Hoppers

Nigerian International Cocaine Trafficking

Jude Roys Oboh

LEXINGTON BOOKS
Lanham • Boulder • New York • London

Published by Lexington Books
An imprint of The Rowman & Littlefield Publishing Group, Inc.
4501 Forbes Boulevard, Suite 200, Lanham, Maryland 20706
www.rowman.com

6 Tinworth Street, London SE11 5AL, United Kingdom

British Library Cataloguing in Publication Information Available

Library of Congress Cataloging-in-Publication Data

Names: Oboh, Jude, 1955- author.
Title: Cocaine hoppers : Nigerian international cocaine trafficking / Jude Oboh.
Description: Lanham : Lexington Books, [2021] | Includes bibliographical references and
    index. | Summary: "This lively, theoretically grounded study examines the new trend
    of traffickers dominating the illicit cocaine trade through West Africa to destinations
    across the globe to provide an account of Nigerian involvement in international drug
    trafficking as it has never been divulged before"—Provided by publisher.
Identifiers: LCCN 2021028353 (print) | LCCN 2021028354 (ebook) |
    ISBN 9781793637277 (cloth) | ISBN 9781793637284 (epub) |
    ISBN 9781793637291 (pbk)
Subjects: LCSH: Cocaine industry—Nigeria. | Drug traffic—Nigeria.
Classification: LCC HV5810 .O26 2021 (print) | LCC HV5810 (ebook) |
    DDC 362.29/809669—dc23
LC record available at https://lccn.loc.gov/2021028353
LC ebook record available at https://lccn.loc.gov/2021028354

To Amaka, Fia and RJay Oboh

Contents

List of Figures and Tables   ix

Acknowledgments   xi

List of Abbreviations   xiii

Introduction   1

1   The Emergence of Cocaine in Nigeria   17

2   "State Crisis" and Fostering Cocaine Culture   45

3   Cultural Factors Motivating Nigerian Cocaine Trafficking   85

4   The Structure and Modus Operandi of Nigerian Cocaine
        Traffickers   107

5   The Brazil Connection   139

6   Cocaine Hoppers and the Culture of Cocaine Trade and
        Consumption in China   173

7   Involvement in Southeast Asia, the United States, the United
        Kingdom, and the Netherlands   223

8   Controlling International Cocaine Hoppers in Nigeria, Brazil,
        China, and Indonesia   243

9   Findings and Conclusion   273

Bibliography   285

Index   339

About the Author   359

List of Figures and Tables

FIGURES

Figure 0.1 X-Ray Picture of Male Courier Showing Swallowed
            Cocaine Pellets   2
Figure 0.2 X-Ray Picture of Female Courier Showing Swallowed
            Cocaine Pellets   3
Figure 0.3 Picture of Cocaine Pellets   4
Figure 6.1 Picture of Nigerian Cocaine Traffickers' Violence
            (Guangzhou)   216

TABLES

Table 4.1   Destination of Drug Couriers Arrested by NDLEA in
            2011 at MMI Airport in Lagos   129
Table 4.2   Schiphol Airport Amsterdam: Data Drugs Couriers,
            Nigeria 2011   130

Acknowledgments

I decided to transition from agricultural engineering after years of working for the FAO-United Nations to the study of criminology in large part because of pressing developmental concerns in Africa, particularly Nigeria. It has been a long road to realize this work, and I am deeply indebted to the writers and researchers who laid the groundwork in this field.

First and foremost, I am immensely grateful to the people who assisted me in this work, without which it would never have been possible. I am deeply obliged to my mentors, Dina Siegel and Damian Zaitch, for their ardent supervision and support. Thank you for convincing me to pursue ethnographic fieldwork activities, but more importantly, for instilling in me the self-confidence and critical reflection needed to undertake such a daunting task. I am very appreciative to Ebbe Obi of University of Chattanooga, Tennessee, for his hearty encouragement, critical reflection, counseling, and careful reading of my text. I thank you all for your unabated willingness to respond to my inquiries at all times. I am greatly indebted to Henk van de Bunt of Erasmus University, Rotterdam and Frank Bovenkerk of Utrecht University; each passionately gave me crucial belief, confidence, and motivation to see beyond my doubts and the sometimes negative image of Nigeria.

I owe an immeasurable debt to many Nigerians and their families, both in Nigeria and abroad, whom I met during my visits and fieldwork. I thank them profoundly for narrating their stories and sharing their experiences with me. This work would not have been possible without their tremendous contributions. Thank you for sharing your stories and for the bonds of friendship forged through this process.

This was truly a global project. In Brazil, a special thank you is due to Andréa Rocha, Marisa Feffermann, Maria Alice Pollo Araujo, Lilian Ratto, Maria Isabel, Carmen Silvia de Moraes Barros, and Richard. I am very appreciative for your vigorous support and encouragement. I remain thankful to Michiel Princen, Bob Vreeman, and the entire team of *Bureau Financieel Economische Recherche* in Amsterdam. In China, my distinct appreciation goes to Peter Tervoort, Li Kwai-wah Steve, and Mathews Gordon of Chinese University, and Wing Lo of City University of Hong Kong for their assistance and critical views. I would like to express my gratitude to Ryan Lee, Junxion Wang, Zhuo Cheng, and in particular Jian Bang Hong for their care, translation, and great hospitality. In Malaysia, I thank Eze ndi Igbo and friends for their assistance at all times. In Italy, and other countries in Europe, countless people shared extensive knowledge with me and helped make this work a reality; in particular, my friends Gabrio Filonzi, Daniel Agiddi, Ify Ijeoma, Emmanuel Heinzpeter, Andy Ndukuba, James Udom, Fidel Dayo, and Richard Adebambo. In the Netherlands, I profited enormously from friends and colleagues, especially Willem Janssen, Gerry, Julien and Nasha Desbarida, Alphonse Muambi, and Andre da Silver. I thank you for your encouragement. My gratitude also goes to friends and their families in the United States, especially Ben Koffie Nassar of International Monetary Fund Washington and Anthony Agbenyega of Illinois State University. I remain appreciative for your assistance and critical reflections.

I also must express my gratefulness to my family members and relations who have encouraged me all through this study. I am grateful to my best friend Monique Maaswinkel for her endless support and patience in making this work a reality. Mo, good on you! My special appreciation to Uchenna and Mary Rose for their efforts and support. Furthermore, I wish to thank Agatha in Australia; Hyman, Albertus, and Magnus in the United States; and Mark and Eleonora in China for their enormous encouragement. Finally, I am obliged to my late parents Michael Eziakonwa Oboh and Patricia Urewuchi Oboh for my excitement for education and social awareness. I deeply appreciate that they gave me more than what a son can look forward to.

List of Abbreviations

BBC	British Broadcasting Corporation
BRL	Brazil Reals
CFR	Council on Foreign Relations
CIA	Central Intelligence Agency
CNY	Chinese Yuan
CRDA	Central Registry of Drug Abuse
CSIS	Center for Strategic and International Studies
DEA	Drug Enforcement Administration
EFCC	Economic and Financial Crimes Commission
EIR	Executive Intelligence Review
EMCDDA	European Monitoring Centre for Drugs and Drug Addiction
EU	European Union
FAO	Food and Agriculture Organization of the United Nations
FBI	Federal Bureau of Investigation
HRW	Human Rights Watch
IANS	Institute for Applied Network Security
IARD	International Alliance for Responsible Drinking
IBA	International Bar Association
IBGE	Instituto Brasileiro de Geografia e Estatística
ICCPR	International Covenant on Civil and Political Rights
ILO	International Labour Organization
IMF	International Monetary Fund
INCB	International Narcotics Control Board
INCSR	International Narcotics Control Strategy Report
KMar.	Royal Netherlands *Marechaussee* (Dutch Military Police)
KPK	Corruption Eradication Commission (in Indonesia)
MMIA	Murtala Mohammed International Airport

MNF	*Monkey No Fine*
MYR	Malaysian Ringgit
NAFDAC	National Agency for Food and Drug Administration and Control
Naija	Nigeria
Naijas	Nigerians
NDCMP	National Drug Control Master Plan
NDLEA	National Drug Law Enforcement Agency
n.d.	Not Dated
NPE	National Policy on Education
NSRP	Nigeria Stability and Reconciliation Programme
OEC	Observatory of Economic Complexity
OECD	Organisation for Economic Co-operation and Development
Oga	Boss
OGD	World Geopolitics of Drugs
ONCB	Office of the Narcotics Control Board
OSAC	Overseas Security Advisory Council
Oxfam	Oxford Committee for Famine Relief
PCC	Primeiro Comando da Capital
PFC	Penitenciária Feminina da Capital
PSB	Public Security Bureau
RAD	Rockefeller Foundation-Aspen Institute Diaspora Program
SEA	Southeast Asia
SP	São Paulo
TNI	The Transnational Institute
UI	University of Ibadan
UK	United Kingdom
UNCOVA	A Nigeria-Based News Portal
UNDP	United Nations Development Programme
UNECA	United Nations Economic Commission for Africa
UNHRC	United Nations Human Rights Council
UNICEF	United Nations International Children's Emergency Fund
UNODC	United Nations Office on Drugs and Crime
USA	United States of America
VOA	Voice of America
WACD	West Africa Commission on Drugs
Wahala	Trouble/problem
WCDDC	White Cloud District Detention Centre
WHO	World Health Organization
Yeye	Useless

Introduction

The purpose of this research is to explore the role Nigerians have played in international cocaine trafficking in the past decades. That role is twofold. First, Nigeria has become a transit nation and a consumer country. Second, Nigerians live all over the world. They have become more involved in international trade than ever before. They are distributing cocaine to markets in Nigeria and internationally. Nigeria turned into a consumer country when Nigerians became brokers of Latin American cocaine. Its geographic location directly across the Atlantic Ocean encouraged easy transportation from South America into the country. Nigeria's historical connection with Brazil through the slave trade helped to consolidate Nigerians' participation in the international cocaine trade. In effect, Nigeria became a consumer country because of the involvement of Nigerians in international trade, and international trade facilitates the illicit cocaine trade.

This feedback loop is one of the reasons Nigerians are so successful in the international cocaine trade. Brazil and China are two countries where Nigerian traffickers are prominent. On the one hand, Brazil is very important because it is a major exporter nation of cocaine at this moment (United Nations Office on Drugs and Crime [UNODC] 2018). Although Brazil does not produce it, cocaine is moved in from the three main producers, Bolivia, Peru, and Colombia, and Brazil exports it to the world. On the other hand, the centrality of China is that in recent times, Nigerian traders were sought out by their Chinese business partners to come to China for long-term business relationships. However, while luring legitimate Nigerian traders, China also attracted illicit cocaine traffickers. As the illegal trade grew, Nigerian traffickers discovered that there was a new and growing market.

According to the Nigerian National Drug Law Enforcement Agency (NDLEA 2017) and the National Drug Control Master Plan 2015–2019

1

(NDCMP), drug trafficking is thriving in Nigeria. Technological changes have enabled Nigerian cocaine traffickers to establish a worldwide through globalization, from cocaine production and transit countries in South America to consumer destinations around the world. Some Nigerian international cocaine traffickers see their activity simply as an advantageous trade opportunity based on the market forces of covert demand and supply. The potential for huge profits attracts individuals across all ethnic groups, professions, ages, and races. So successful are Nigerian traffickers that they have been credited with popularizing the deployment of couriers who swallow cocaine balls, as shown in the figures 0.1, 02, and 0.3 below.

Nigerian cocaine trafficking poses challenges to democratic governance, political stability, and human security in Africa. According to the UNODC (2016), the past decades have witnessed a new trend in international cocaine trafficking: the increasing role of West Africa, especially Nigeria, in trafficking cocaine between South America to Europe and other countries. The International Narcotics Control Strategy Report (INCSR) stated: "Nigerian

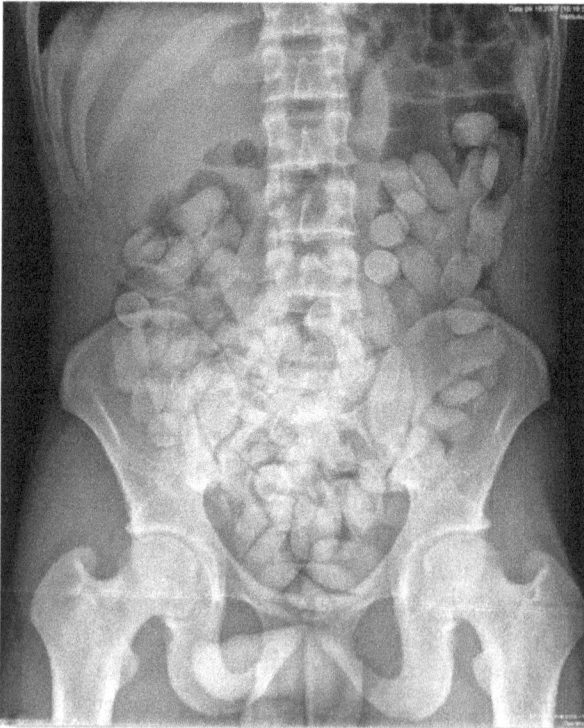

Figure 0.1   X-Ray Picture of Male Courier Showing Swallowed Cocaine Pellets. *Source*: Royal Netherlands Marechaussee, 2011.

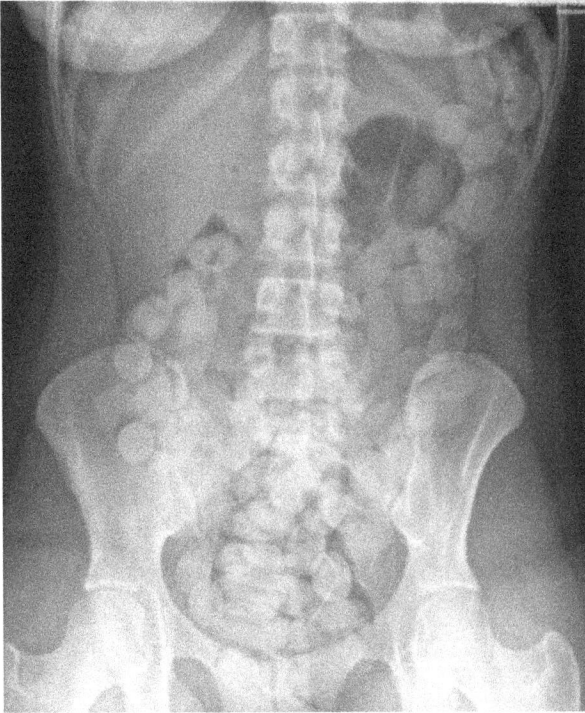

Figure 0.2 X-Ray Picture of Female Courier Showing Swallowed Cocaine Pellets.
Source: Royal Netherlands Marechaussee, 2011.

organized criminal networks remain a major factor in moving cocaine and heroin worldwide, and have begun to produce and traffic methamphetamine to and around Southeast Asia". They also engage in financial fraud targeting U.S. citizens (INCSR 2016, 233).

Nigeria has a history of instability and unrest, making it a ripe territory for the rising drug trade. Financial problems and poverty, endemic bribery and corruption, crimes committed by those in power, the absence of role models, and the strain of the "Nigerian Dream" (Oboh 2016) all play a role in the development of trafficking culture. The Nigerian state crisis created a criminogenic situation that made the illicit cocaine trade either attractive or necessary for some of its people. Nigerian cocaine traffickers, in targeting a large financial profit or "the big catch" as traffickers call it, exploit the blurred relationship between legal and illegal business. In turn, this environment has fostered a pervasive "reverse social capital," wherein criminality as a means to achieve wealth has become the driving force of social networks, connections, and associations in and among all sections of society. Nevertheless, despite profitability for those involved in international cocaine trafficking, there is no comparison

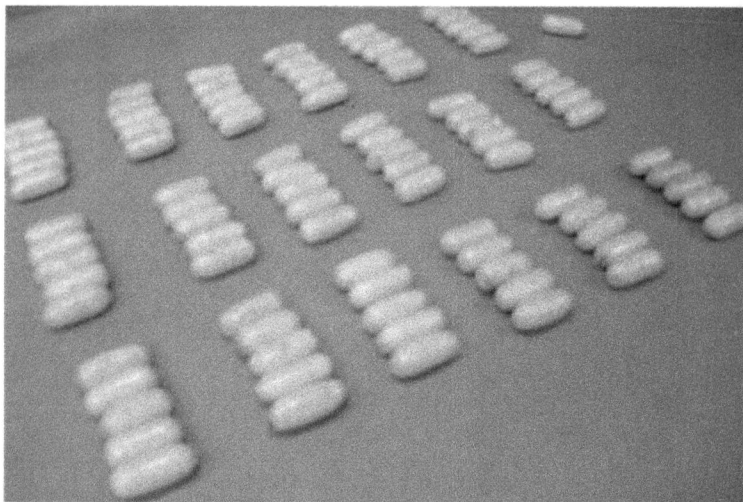

Figure 0.3   Picture of Cocaine Pellets. *Source*: Royal Netherlands Marechaussee, 2011.

or justification to be made for its devastating long-term effects both in Nigeria and abroad.

The former president of Nigeria, Goodluck Jonathan, identified the drug trade as one of the most pressing concerns for the country in his declaration against the adverse impact of illicit cultivation, trafficking, production, and abuse of drugs in Nigeria (NDCMP 2015–2019, 1; INCSR 2016).

In the Nigerian news media, reports of South American cocaine seizures and individuals arrested in connection with cocaine trafficking are common. For instance, between January and March 2016, the NDLEA at the Nigerian Murtala Mohammed International Airport (MMIA) in Lagos arrested 30 drug traffickers (26 males and four females) and confiscated 100.545 kilograms of narcotic drugs, valued at USD1.6 million. In the same year, the antidrug control agency received a total of 204 Nigerians, made up of 197 males and seven females, deported on drug-related offenses. Illicit drug money confiscated included about EUR300,000 and USD90,000, among other currencies (NDLEA 2016/2017).

Nigeria topped the list of the countries involved in drug trafficking and drug use in West Africa, and the list of drug couriers arrested in Europe (National Assembly Press 2016). It is estimated that about 170,000 Nigerians are in prisons in foreign countries as noted by *The Sun* (2018). A key consequence of the modern drug wars is growth in prison population, which draws from the war on crime that President Nixon declared in 1971 (Nixon 1971). The Criminal Justice System (CJS) has failed to implement policies that stand a good chance of reducing crime, to treat as crime the harmful acts of the rich and powerful, and to eliminate political bias in criminal justice itself. The growth in prison population is a result of the focus on one-on-one crime of the poor, reflected in the "Carnival Mirror." The Pyrrhic defeat theory argues that the persistence of this failing CJS yields benefits to those in positions of power that it amounts to a victory for them (Reiman and Leighton 2017).

However, figures derived from drug seizures, deportations, and imprisonment provide an imperfect picture of the whole. Studies of drug trafficking are scarce both in Nigeria and internationally (Bunt et al. 2014; Bovenkerk et al. 2003). This is mainly due to the difficulty of researching a covert activity. There is little information on drug trafficking, because this type of crime depends on detection by authorities (Van de Bunt et al. 2014; Oboh 2011).

Conversely, the "dazzling" or fictitious figures in official statistic of crime could be used to interrogate many of the truth-claims that animate the oppressive-repressive policing of popular culture and counter-hegemonic cultural activism (Agozino 2003, 215). The errors in criminal records include exclusion and incompleteness as well as inclusion and superfluity. We don't know the number of false criminal convictions. Most by far remain hidden—false convictions far outnumber exonerations—and we have too little information to estimate that hidden figure (Gross, Possley and Stephens 2017, 10).

Bovenkerk et al. (2003) found in a similar study on drug traffickers in the Netherlands that "dark numbers"—crime that is neither reported nor recorded by law enforcement agencies—are by definition difficult to trace; thus, calculations in such cases are even more problematic. First, no study of any sort has yet been conducted specifically on Nigerian involvement in international cocaine trafficking. Second, the number of illegal Nigerian migrants in Brazil, China, United Kingdom, and the United States, for instance, is a matter of rough estimation. Third, secrecy, flexibility, and imprecise information exchange lie at the core of any drug transaction. In other words, the number of Nigerians involved in this destructive global trade remains uncertain.

This work seeks to provide insight into a new trend in international cocaine trafficking that presents a serious threat to lives and security to West Africa and the world at large. Transit countries too easily become cocaine consumers, as is evidenced in Brazil and Mexico. Nigeria is not an exception.

It is easy to point fingers at criminals in Nigeria and the diaspora as being solely responsible for choosing profits over ethics. However, this research suggests that the Nigerian state crisis has caused systemic factors resulting in an environment where cocaine trafficking is for some the only potential source of income or escape from poverty. The reasons for the Nigerian role in international trafficking are more complex than is currently acknowledged. On the one hand, millions of innocent Nigerians are victims of humiliations and distrust worldwide; on the other hand, some Nigerians are indeed party to cocaine trafficking networks and the violence associated with them. Therefore, the role of Nigerians in international cocaine trafficking must be analyzed from a more comprehensive and multifaceted perspective, examining the multiple factors that continue to drive so many into this dangerous business.

Given the complexity of the issue, this book aims to examine in-depth Nigerian involvement in the cocaine business. The guiding research questions are as follows:

1. What is the role of Nigerians in the international cocaine trade?
2. What are the mechanisms behind the success of Nigerians in the global cocaine trade?
3. What is the degree of Nigerian involvement in its primary cocaine export country (Brazil) and in destination countries globally, including the United States, United Kingdom, Indonesia, and China, and how can this involvement be explained?

In trying to bridge this knowledge gap, this work cannot provide a singular "solution" to the problem, but it will contribute to the debate by providing insights into the role of Nigerians in international cocaine trafficking. This work will trace Nigerian traffickers' efforts in Brazil, as well as their increasing activity in China. In contrast to Brazil, which has a historic connection with Nigeria and Africa as a whole, China represents a new market for new traffickers. In this respect, they have posed considerable challenges to law enforcement agents and society in cities such as Guangzhou and beyond.

Anthropological and criminological studies point out the importance of fieldwork, observation, and data collection in gathering information close to the source to provide the most comprehensive understanding (Decorte and Zaitch 2016). Therefore, each chapter will deal with one of the significant contributing factors of Nigerian involvement in the cocaine trade. Although this research on Nigerian drug trafficking is directly related to the study of criminology, I was born and raised there, and issues related to developments in Nigeria have always been part of my daily observations. Consequently, while this study is grounded in theoretical and empirical research, it is also informed by my personal experiences with people affected by cocaine trafficking both in Nigeria and abroad.

METHODOLOGY

This work was initially based on the fact that much is known about Nigeria as a country; however, very little information is available on the involvement of Nigerians in the cocaine trade and who the Nigerian traffickers are. The general belief is that they follow the standard model of organized cartels or criminal gangs and are headed by drug barons who work in partnership with South American cartels.

Consequently, the academic world has largely relied on the information derived from the media or law enforcement but not from firsthand observations and accounts. Therefore, scholars only have limited insight into Nigerian involvement in the illicit international cocaine business.

In this regard, my research method was implemented in line with the anthropology and sociology of deviance carried out by interviewing and observing participants in the criminogenic environment. Hence, it was based principally on various qualitative data the author received rather than collected, because of ethical and technical reasons, in Nigeria and abroad, including the Netherlands, Malaysia, China, Hong Kong, and Brazil. Agozino (1995) noted in "Methodological Issues" that, ethically, data collection tends to presume the powerlessness of the source, whereas data reception recognizes the autonomy of the subject. He posits that data collection is nearly impossible due to the autonomous agency of the source and so assumes that the only thing social scientists should and can aspire to is data reception (57).

This work builds on qualitative methods consisting of almost 20 years of work experience and regular observations as part of my daily activities, rather than detached analysis of policy reports, and years of informal conversations and in-depth interviews with members of the six categories of Nigerian drug traffickers. Instrumental in this area is triangulation of the interviews, observation, and analysis to foster the validity (King et al. 1994). Years of experience observing the subjects made contradictions evident between real behavior and verbal claims, as will be detailed later. These were the materials used for the general information on Nigeria and theoretical concepts on crime to establish a sound analysis of the Nigerian case and to acquire insight into the viewpoints and experiences of Nigerian international cocaine traffickers.

Interviews, observations, and the analysis of the secondary data resulted in ample data to respond to the research questions.

In addition to participant observation, open interviews were conducted for gathering information during fieldwork in various countries. Lagos was the best place to begin this research since it is the commercial heart of business in Nigeria. Social networks brought me into contact with direct and indirect participants of Nigerian cocaine trafficking. On the whole, I surveyed several different countries and varied suitable places. I conducted open and in-depth interviews with more than 250 people on the subject. Interviewees ranged from several direct actors, convicted individuals in prisons, and other informants. Additionally, acquaintances and relatives of cocaine traffickers in Nigeria, the Netherlands, Italy, England, Germany, Malaysia, Hong

Kong, China, and Brazil were sources of information. The purpose was to pool together various direct and indirect actors in terms of the background of members of the Nigerian international cocaine trafficking.

Also useful were personal ties in the country, which allowed entry into various settings also frequented by those involved in cocaine trafficking. These included bars, restaurants, dance clubs, fundraising activities, traditional weddings, churches, markets, retail stores, offices, private homes, village chiefs, traditional rulers, and so on. On most occasions with Nigerians in Nigeria or in the diaspora, issues related to Nigeria's problems were always discussed, and Nigerians' involvement in cocaine trafficking was no exception. As a vital instrument, "a theme list assisted to allow the respondents to chat liberally, as well as to cover all relevant issues" (Noaks and Wincup 2004, 79–80). The content of the discussions was also a criterion for selection. A detailed inventory of subjects resulted in varied opinions concerning the dynamics of Nigerian cocaine trafficking, as well as other popular topics.

Interviews developed into more open conversations in the course of the fieldwork, allowing a certain degree of flexibility within the structure of the work for respondents to express their views extensively. Conversations and interviews lasted about three to four hours on average. Follow-up conversations resulted in further meetings in Nigeria, the Netherlands, Italy, United Kingdom, the United States, Brazil, Malaysia, China, and other countries. Looking at the extensive nature of the Nigerian international cocaine trafficking, I made a selection of useful occasions and sub-forums for the fieldwork.

The selection criteria concerned when to travel to a particular country, when the in-depth interviews and conversations took place, as well as their content and duration. I used a theoretical, purposive sampling technique to pool direct and indirect actors in terms of the background of members of the Nigerian international cocaine trafficking, conducting progressive interviews with selected participants and then analyzing them. "Theoretical sampling continued, moving back and forth between sampling, data collection, and analysis, until I reached data saturation, or the point at which the researcher fails to collect new information with subsequent interviews" (Statistics Solutions 2019).

This made it possible to compare divergent views and experiences. We seek to provide an assessment that can illuminate the attraction to cocaine trafficking and thwart preconceptions vis-à-vis ethnicity, age, religion, profession, and the willingness to take part in illicit trade. The snowball method engaged respondents through existing trust relations who otherwise could have been unreachable or may have declined to participate.

Nigerian international cocaine trafficking is a borderless activity involving individuals across all ethnic groups in Nigeria. Participant ages ranged from 16 to over 70 years old; however, the majority of respondents were between 25 and 40 years old. The respondents' level of education varied from primary and high school levels to academic institutions. Of course, such a diverse group requires more data to reach saturation (Mortelmans 2010). In this project, data streaming observations and informal conversation analysis compensate for the relatively limited number of interviews. Furthermore, in harmony with the requirement for saturation, the final interviews did not lead to novel information but substantiated the initial finding.

Concerning drug trafficking from a formal state perspective, law enforcement officials from the various countries were interviewed. Likewise, several other experts working with the CJS, including criminologists specializing in drug trafficking, criminal justice lawyers, and specialized journalists, were interviewed. I interviewed professional court interpreters in various countries such as Germany, England, Italy, and the Netherlands. Because of its commercial importance, good infrastructure, and location, the Netherlands is a critical cocaine transit hub and a consumer country. About 20 years of work experience with the Dutch CJS and immigration provided the writer with broad experience on the nature of Nigerian involvement in the illicit cocaine business in the country and extensive networks globally. It also gave the writer opportunity for interaction with law enforcement agents in other parts of the world.

For this research, I used various methods for note-taking during the interviews and observations. Daily recorded notes of observations, interviews, and experiences were taken. Otherwise throughout this research, quotations of recorded conversations are literally reproduced, and in some cases, translations are included.

Subsequently, we assessed the quality of the discussions implemented in the various countries surveyed. Often, the beginning of the interview or conversation could emerge as relevant, but then the participants tended to digress to other topics. Getting off-topic sometimes allowed for relevant and interesting information; otherwise such digressions were disregarded. Having varied respondents within social networks meant that some respondents held differing opinions about the involvement of Nigerians in the international cocaine trafficking.

This primary data is based on empirical observations and is complemented with secondary data in related fields: academic work, media publications on cocaine and immigrant enterprises, reports from various international institutions and organizations on the Nigerian international cocaine traffickers. It used qualitative methods and ethnographic research that can enlighten the reasons and motives for Nigerian involvement in the illicit international cocaine trafficking. This work will help understand this development from the insider viewpoint.

Whereas participant observations and interviews were more exciting to implement than the gathering of secondary data, it also had its challenges.

Boasting is a form of cultural capital for cocaine hoppers. That someone spent USD2,000 per night buying drinks for friends or made millions of naira in one cocaine deal gives them clout. For instance, Saka told me, "Aspirant courier must hear success stories, see money spent, and enjoy it, too" (personal communication, January 12, 2013). Some boast because they are successful, others exaggerate their successes, and some lie because they want to appear successful to lure potential couriers.

Given that I was interested in facts and wide-ranging trends, I strived to observe a lot, to inquire face-to-face with others (cross-checking whenever possible) and to contrast the stories with information I gathered from close recluses. Information could be inconsistent if respondents provide a socially desirable response to the researcher, declaring what they thought I wanted or needed to hear (Bailey 1994; Grix 2001). In addition, participants might have opted to keep secrets for opportunist motives, such as not disclosing certain modus operandi or involvement in the illicit cocaine trafficking to keep out of the sight of the CJS.

Another common practical limitation was Nigerian informants and interviewees hardly came to appointments on time. Nonetheless, inherent in the qualitative approaches of this work are matters, including trust, socially pleasing information and the unrealistic presentation of self, secretiveness, and unwillingness to participate. Each of these topics could influence the validity of the information. I explained to the respondents that I was interested in interviewing and chatting with direct and indirect participants of the Nigerian cocaine traffickers. At a cursory glance, introducing myself in this manner could be seen as a case of academic self-destruction because I had to mingle with Nigerian cocaine traffickers, people who sometimes feel they are scapegoats and who might become more distrustful in response to such an introduction (Babbie 2001). However, elucidating my research equally as one wanting to dig into the root causes of the phenomenon that continues to claim many lives and its implications to Nigerians were good points that opened conversation. Conveying this and accepting invitations to socializing with respondents necessitate a certain level of adaptation to the social environment (Decorte and Zaitch 2016).

During fieldwork, the issue of distrust manifested itself in diverse ways. Distrust arose when the Nigerian traffickers did not know the researcher well—meaning that concerns about gaining trust remain central in acquiring information from interviewees. Moreover, trust shows its importance in the absence of observation as an option. Trust makes a difference between having a respondent or no valuable information at all. Various methods exist for researchers to win trust. These include patience, networking, showing honest interest, and giving something in return (Noaks and Wincup 2004). Over the years, I built positive contacts with people from diverse backgrounds.

For example, having helpful contacts provided me access to participate in a closed-door meeting of an important organization that worked for convicted Nigerian traffickers and to conferences in Brazil. Such was also the case in Hong Kong where I met with a group of asylum seekers. These contacts contributed to other respondents gaining trust and opening up to me.

Impediments to validity were dealt with in many ways by the researcher. First and foremost, by not regarding the respondents' reports at face value. Meaning it is essential to remain critical over their testimonials through contrasting acquired information from objective facts from similar research and by evaluating attitudes with actual behavior. Besides, holding extensive and repeated conversations assisted in exploring deeper to actual opinions. This author's years of experience made contradictions evident between behavior and words. Recognizing this dissonance entails using the three methods deployed in this fieldwork to shrink restrictions each posed singularly.

The rejection of generalizations outside the research population is imperative; as such, the results merely allow for conclusions regarding the role of Nigerians in the global cocaine trafficking. Analyzing the situations in Nigeria, Brazil, China, and other destination countries gives a well-rounded understanding of Nigerians' involvement in the whole chain. Findings in this work are relevant to other possible research cases. Indeed, some cases here could be transferable to other communities, "Transferability of the conclusion could also follow from theoretical generalizations" (LeCompte and Goetz 1982, 37–40).

Nigeria's negative image abroad evokes ideas of deviancy, insecurity, and violence for many criminological researchers. Qualitative researchers are of course subject to human factors and subconscious bias. Personality and background could affect the researchers' perception of the world, thereby influencing their ways of interpreting data and affecting the reliability of acquired information (Oberhuber and Krzyzanowski 2008, 197). This demands the researcher be able to distinguish and confront one's own biased tendencies such as prejudices and emotions and the ability to handle the bias and emotions of respondents. It also recalls the researchers' nonaligned position between the insider and the outsider perspectives, and in matters that concern dealing with personal relations and the expectations of respondents.

As a Nigerian native researching the new trend of illicit cocaine trafficking, I needed to be aware of my position toward the subject matter I was studying. I was both an outsider in regard to the world of illicit trafficking but an insider as a fellow Nigerian. Outsiders face the risk that they may fail to understand the insider perspective, either because they hold a conscious or unconscious bias against the reality of the insiders or because they lack a shared language and shared symbols that renders them incapable of understanding. On the other hand, the position of insiders can threaten the reliability of findings because it could constitute the researcher's submersion in the dangers of criminality. Consequently, a researcher may refrain from reporting certain findings, for example, out of fear of retaliation or because of conflicting interests (Ferrell 2005; Geelhoed 2012).

We refrained from participating in core activities related to drug trafficking, in other words, refusing to get involved in drug trafficking and drug money despite solicitations. Instead, "I assumed peripheral roles" (Adler and Adler 1987, 36) that only permitted mingling and talking with Nigerian cocaine traffickers to avoid direct contact with operational illicit plans. Experts have highlighted the personal risks involved in dangerous fieldwork (Williams et al. 1992; Ferrell et al. 1998).

While I took basic security measures, I did not feel threatened in any way during observations and interviews with Nigerian traffickers and indirect actors in the whole trafficking chain. Also, I had to confront ethical challenges. Protecting my informants and contacts was a priority. The researcher's personal opinion was not expressed, even if there was concern about lies or overstatements. Neither did I consider drug trafficking offenses nor unverified gossip as ample reason to breach the neutrality pledged to the informant. I have tried to restrict potential negative consequences for my informants in several ways by (1) discussing the topic with them to know and to inform them about limitations and problems; (2) avoiding leaking information, and respecting all security regulations put forward by informants during this work; and (3) altering real names in my fieldwork write-ups, and for the published version too. I changed names in most places to make it unrecognizable by using pseudonyms, withholding the interviewee's identity.

I did not do undercover research. I told people that I was doing research. I explained that this study is not intended to stigmatize Nigerian communities. On the contrary, I believe that some problems exist in it. These problems are a result of some institutional and political problems; however, I want to show the limitation of these problems.

It is not our intent nor should this work be used to blame traffickers for their involvement in international cocaine trade. Rather, it is my intent to contribute to initiating discussions on a society in search of respect, good governance, and development. This work is meant to show that political and institutional problems exist in Nigeria that have produced the phenomenon. The traffickers say it themselves that Nigeria has failed its people. There is lack of opportunities in the country. Many Nigerians are serving lengthy years of imprisonment, and several face executions for drug trafficking in foreign countries.

Nigerian drug traffickers keep fewer secrets than they pretend to in their activities that involve manipulation, public relations, and impression management, particularly when they did not feel threatened by the presence of law enforcement agents. Interestingly, the cocaine business is not discussed or carried out only in a secluded, murky underworld. It is talked about in private homes and flats, hotel rooms, warehouses, shops, and private offices. It is even discussed in some social gatherings (e.g., restaurants, bars, private parties, and nightclubs), marketplaces, on public transport, or even on church premises. The prolific discussion on the subject by direct and indirect actors feeds the demand in a growing market, as is reflected in this work.

Growing cocaine demand may be explained by the role played by intermediaries in drugs and tourism (e.g., expatriates) who want a cut of the financial reward. In 2014, the West Africa Commission on Drugs (WACD) published a report entitled, "Not Just in Transit: Drugs the State and Society in West Africa." In hotels and nightclubs in Nigeria, Cameroon, and Senegal that the author of this article visited, cocaine and synthetic drugs were regularly available (Cohen 2019, 37).

Cocaine mules sit next to other voyagers; cocaine cargos are loaded, transported, and stored by legal agents and businesses; bank and remittance bureaus handle its financial proceedings; and pastors pray for cocaine traffickers' deals to work out well and for couriers prior to departure. Participants talked about every aspect of trade, from buying, packaging, transportation, clearing, and distributing narcotics, depending on the environment and their personal experiences.

Nigerian traffickers had many reasons for sharing their knowledge about their activities with the researcher. Some talked because they were angry about deals that did not work. Others talked because they were disappointed that they had been sent to prison and about dreams that were not realized. Many talked about their bitterness following maltreatments or being cheated by copartners as well as their mistrust of friends. Yet, some talked to the writer because they considered him a friend. Even though most did not attend university, their desire was for their children to have good education.

They admired that writer had lived in several countries in Africa, SEA, and Europe and could speak foreign languages, including Italian, Dutch, Portuguese/Creole, and French. These are languages the writer acquired during international engagement as an Agricultural Engineer with Food and Agriculture Organization of the United Nations (FAO). They talked because they could speak the writer's vernacular (Igbo), Pidgin, English, and many other languages, because Nigerians are found everywhere. Surprisingly, a number of them talked because they want to attract new contacts by claiming that they know a lot about cocaine trafficking, and many talked and even boasted of their success in the illegal business.

Using both justification and neutralization techniques, most Nigerians in deviant activities, such as cocaine trafficking, human trafficking, and advanced financial fraud, see themselves as pushed into it due to crimes committed by the powerful elite. They pointed to the activities of the Nigerian elite who were embezzling the nation's wealth alongside foreign (often Western) associates. In these situations, the researcher's knowledge of and experience in foreign countries helped open up conversation among traffickers.

Fieldwork had its challenges as well. In a number of circumstances, the writer's official request for permission to enter fieldwork was refused. For instance, access to interview some Nigerian inmates incarcerated in Chinese prisons was refused. Securing an interview with a Nigerian Embassy official was problematic in Malaysia or Hong Kong because they were apprehensive about negative publicity should the research results be made public. Nevertheless, these experiences were outliers. Additionally, information from various brokers, or "strikers," and couriers was cross-checked where possible.

Finally, not all the stories collected during the fieldwork have been presented here. Some accounts were incomplete, and, therefore, they have served only as verifying background data. Instead, this study has featured a few key informants accounts only because their in-depth stories exemplify the experiences and influencing factors of so many of the Nigerian traffickers. Analysis of these observations, interviews, and experiences is the basis of this text.

STRUCTURE

The theoretical framework of this text is founded on the classic supply and demand model, though it has been distorted by the illicit nature of cocaine trafficking and the impact of globalization. There is a vicious cycle wherein the demand glamorizes the sale and use of cocaine, and the supply increases the demand in Nigeria. The circularity of the illegal business lies in the fact that Nigerians go abroad to supply the cocaine markets, and the Nigerian market is growing because of Nigerians going abroad. We choose this subject because of the growing risk for Nigerian society.

This book has been divided into nine chapters. The first chapter provides the framework for the text, including a general overview of the topic. Chapter 1 discusses the emergence of cocaine in Nigeria, presenting the historical origins and the development of Nigeria into a transit station for international drug trafficking. It analyzes the call to decriminalize and regulate cannabis. Following this, the Nigerian "State Crisis" in chapter 2 explores the role played by poverty, limited educational opportunities, and high unemployment rates as contributing factors in enhancing the illicit trade. Chapter 3 examines cultural factors motivating Nigerian cocaine trafficking. In chapter 4, we have the structure and modus operandi of Nigerian cocaine trafficking. It will provide insight into the social organization of Nigerian cocaine trafficking, network, and actors. It focuses on Nigeria's pioneer traffickers, cocaine consumption, types of traffickers, and the drive for both cultural and financial capital.

In chapter 5, we look at Nigeria's connection to Brazil. This chapter highlights cocaine traffickers' links with São Paulo (SP), Brazil. It seeks to answer questions frequently posed by scholars such as why Brazil? What is the relationship between Brazil and Nigeria? We will discuss the Brazilian reaction to drug mania, providing insight into the criminal justice response to the phenomenon.

We will see how the cocaine market is expanding, particularly into China, in chapter 6. We will also examine how the culture of cocaine trade and consumption in China differs from other countries, such as Brazil, and the nature of the Nigerian involvement in the drug business in the second world's largest economy. Following the goods in Nigerian trafficker's environment, we will provide insight into the influx of Nigerian traffickers into Guangzhou, China.

Chapter 7 focuses on Nigerian drug traffickers in Thailand, Malaysia, and Indonesia in spite of capital punishment for drug offenders. Cocaine hoppers' activities in the United States (US), United Kingdom (UK), and the Netherlands, which functions as European Union's distribution center for cocaine, will conclude chapter 7.

The unique nature of Nigerian international cocaine traffickers poses considerable problems for law enforcement agents in many countries. Therefore, chapter 8 discusses challenges for law enforcement agents seeking and handling Nigerian traffickers in Nigeria, Brazil, China, and Indonesia. Cocaine hoppers' operations persist in most countries because of the absence of effective control and corruption.

Chapter 9 will conclude this work by attempting to weave together the various threads of this study, emphasizing the multifaceted nature of the Nigerian cocaine business—its ideologies, business, and the larger consequences. The text delineates the short- and long-term challenges that Nigeria and the world face in illegal drug trafficking. Finally, it offers suggestions and possibilities for a new mindset in narcotics drug control mechanisms.

Chapter 1

The Emergence of Cocaine in Nigeria

This chapter looks at the emergence of the cocaine business in Nigeria to understand Nigeria's role as a transit and transaction hub and a consumer nation in the making. We will trace the origin of narcotics in Nigeria, including the influences of colonization, slavery, and the Roman Catholic Church (RCC). British colonialists, in their quest to ensure the expropriation of African natural resources, experimented with coca plantation in Nigeria. They pioneered import and export smuggling and trafficking activities in a country where the coca plant did not grow naturally. Nigeria, as other African nations, was pulled into the international drugs economy by the binary process of Western drugs demand and the failures of drug control measures, the "war on drugs."

We will examine the ways Nigerian antidrug agents, namely the NDLEA, have expanded their capacity, often with the assistance of external donors (Klantschnig 2016; Obot 2004; Allen and Burgess 1999).

This section will end by providing insight on the growing call for decriminalization and regulation of drugs to invest in harm reduction processes for drug users so that cannabis production can benefit poor farmers now labeled criminals and generate tax revenues, denying drug barons their lucrative monopoly on a resource that grows naturally in the country.

1.1 ORIGINS

According to recent UNODC reports, illicit drugs include cannabis, cocaine, opiates, amphetamine-type stimulants, and new psychoactive substances and trafficking are a worldwide phenomenon (2016). Cocaine was not a phenomenon of West African countries until the 1970s, when military regimes

17

controlled most countries in the region. However, the presence of illegal drugs in Nigeria was documented much earlier than cocaine's emergence in the 1970s. Lambo (1965), Asuni (1964), and Alemika (2013) noted that drugs made news headlines in Nigeria in the 1960s with the discovery of cannabis farms, arrests of Nigerian cannabis traffickers overseas, and incidents in Nigeria of psychological problems caused by cannabis use.

During informal discussions with Nigerian cocaine traffickers and their friends in small "underground" bars or joints, often located behind someone's residence or in drinking establishments in the slums, small towns, or villages, many smoked cannabis or "goof, wee-wee, monkey-head, or Indian hemp" (slang words for cannabis among smokers).

Different narratives exist on the genealogy of cannabis in West Africa and Nigeria. Nwannennaya and Abiodun (2017) traced the origin of Nigeria's trafficking problem to the period after the Second World War. Nigerian war veterans in Burma, India, and North Africa returned with seeds of the cannabis sativa plant. Introduced, cannabis (or Indian hemp, as it is known in Nigeria) found a very habitable home (Asuni 1964).

Minteh (2013) wrote that the drug trade in West Africa has existed since the 1930s. He posited that some Sierra Leoneans began to explore a market for cannabis in British West Africa, capitalizing on Freetown's importance as a major drug port. Yet the historian Emmanuel Akyeampong (2005) noted that little trade in cannabis products from West Africa existed in the first half of the twentieth century.

However, claims regarding the introduction of cannabis into West Africa and Nigeria remain contentious since first, cannabis smoking by returnee war veterans in various places enhanced its popularity, and second, the claims did not consider the fact that ex-slaves from the Americas and Europe were resettled in the nineteenth century in West African coastal countries such as Liberia, Sierra Leone, and Nigeria as we shall discuss in chapter 5. For example, Joseph Cinque and 53 others were abducted from their homes in Sierra Leone by Portuguese slave traders aboard schooner Amistad. Cinque led a successful revolt against the crew. In 1814, the U.S. Supreme Court freed the 35 Africans who survived the ordeal and cleared their passage ban to their home on the West African coast. This event helped inspire the beginnings of the abolition movement (Smith 2016). These returnees brought back acquired cultures that influenced those they returned on into. In the Americas, slaves grew *maconha* (marijuana) between the rows of cane and smoked during the periods of inactivity between harvests (Courtwright 2001). Many planters felt that allowing their slaves to smoke marijuana encouraged them to work hard (Bewley-Taylor et al. 2014). The returnees from the Americas and Europe who were resettled in the nineteenth century in Nigeria controvert the claim that cannabis smoking was only introduced by the Second World

War veterans half a century later. In addition, such claims overlook the influence of Europeans and Arabs during slavery and colonialism.

Researchers have emphasized that cannabis was introduced to eastern Africa from southern Asia around A.D. 1500, and Arab traders disseminated cannabis across the continent (Du Toit 1975). African tribes used cannabis in folk traditional medicinal practice: as a remedy for snake bite (Hottentots), to facilitate childbirth (Sotho), and in Rhodesia as a remedy for malaria, blood poisoning, and dysentery; it was also famous in curing asthma (Aldrich 1997). Underlined is Africa's history of managing cannabis like other herbal products to improve health and serve society.

Cannabis only became a policy issue when Nigerian lawmakers exploited the opportunity to focus on it, as we shall discuss later. But the international slave trade created an African diaspora and the presence of blacks in the Americas.

1.2 HISTORICAL FEATURES UNDERLINING EMERGENCE: SLAVERY AND COLONIALISM

The Portuguese, Spanish, French, British, Dutch, and Americans forced and brutalized African slaves to work in mines and on plantations in the Americas and beyond. To this list of countries, we must add the RCC headquartered in Rome. The brutality during Trans-Atlantic Slave Trade (TAST), its atrocities, and exploitation carried forward under colonialism have been exhaustively addressed by experts.

An estimated 10–11.2 million Africans survived the dreadful Middle Passage, between 1502 and 1866, in about 35,000 voyages of slave ships, and disembarked as slaves in the New World (Gates 2011). Of these 11.2 million people, Brazil got 4.8 million slaves; approximately 700,000 Africans arrived at Mexico and Peru; while 450,000 were brought to the United States. Others were taken to locations in the Caribbean, Central America, and South America, including Jamaica, Cuba, the Dominican Republic, and Haiti where they were brutalized and exploited on plantations (ibid., 2). In addition to the unspeakable horrors of slavery, this resulted in a drain of able men, women, and their offspring who could have contributed to the development of Africa.

1.2.1 Crime in "His" Name

Ignatius of Loyola (1491–1556), former Spanish soldier, and his six companions from Spain, France, and Portugal founded the Society of Jesus (also known as Jesuits, a religious order of the Catholic Church headquartered in Rome) with the approval of Pope Paul III in 1540 (Spiteri 2016). They conducted campaigns against "heretics and infidels" (De Luca 2012). While spreading knowledge of military architecture, their fortifications and construction had an explicit target (Murray 2007). The Elmina Castle, the first of several slave castles, was built by the Portuguese in 1482 and was taken over by the Dutch West India Company in 1642 (Teeuwen 2009). Like the castles in Ghana, Nigeria's slave cells in Badagry and Calabar existed to house slaves prior to the forced journey (Okoh 2018).

The first extensive shipment of black Africans was initiated at the request of Bishop Las Casas and authorized by Charles V in 1517 (Global Black History 2020). Having possessed about 15 slaves in 1717, Jesuits owned as many as 400–500 slaves by 1826. To contextualize this figure, Finn (1974) found that there were in 1850 only 56 slaveholders in the United States who owned between 300 and 499 slaves and only 11 others who had 500 or more. The Jesuit fathers of Maryland were collectively one of the largest slaveholders of the southern slaveholding system (Finn 1974; Beckett 1996).

1.2.2 Money Regardless

In his article, "The Reckoning is Real," Devitt James (2020) reported that in the 1830s the Maryland Society of Jesuits and Georgetown University sold more than 272 enslaved people from four Jesuit-owned tobacco plantations in southern Maryland to Henry Johnson and Jesse Batey, both Louisiana plantation owners. Of the 272 slaves, 206 were transported from Maryland to Louisiana; others avoided transportation to Louisiana, were left behind in Maryland, or sold to parts unknown (ibid. 2018). Jesuit clergy "called" to serve God sold men, women, and children for a total price of USD115,000 that today would be worth about USD3.3 million (Svrluga 2016). They broke families apart for horrendous exploitation under dreadful conditions on cotton and sugar plantations to serve the financial interest of the religious institution.

In his address to intellectuals in Cameroon on their role in society, Pope John Paul II apologized to black Africa for the involvement of white Christians in the slave trade. However, the challenge remains to address the injustices caused by the church that once ridiculed the idea of equality of men before the law. Scholars argue that if the RCC had exercised their power against slavery, the Atlantic slave trade could have been prevented. By the same logic, others argue that the church and its missionaries could have helped prevent colonization and the ensuing brutality of colonialism in Africa (Rodney 1973; Beckett 1996; Global Black History 2020).

First, the RCC did not oppose the institution of slavery until the seventeenth century when the practice had already become infamous in most parts of the world. Suffice it to say "that slavery was considered acceptable by Catholic moral doctrine until the early twentieth century" (Beckett 1996, 9).

For example, drawing from his predecessors, Pope Pius IX declared in 1866, "It is not contrary to the natural and divine law for a slave to be sold, bought, exchanged or given" (Global Black History 2020). The American legal system, under the Supreme Court's *Dred Scott* decision of 1857, defined black slaves as property (Reiman and Leighton 2017).

Second, Jomo Kenyatta, Kenya's first president, stated, "When the missionaries arrived, the Africans had the land and the missionaries had the Bible. They taught us how to pray with our eyes closed. When we opened them, they had the land and we had the Bible" (Brown 2018). Put simply, the church was the pillar of the slave trade. Sir John Hawkins, for example, the first slave ship captain to bring African slaves to the Americas, was a deeply religious man who insisted that his crew "serve God daily" and "love one another." Queen Elizabeth I became a partner in the trade and agreed to let Hawkins use the ship ironically called "The Good Ship Jesus" that left England for Africa in 1562 (Strom 2014).

Third, during slavery and colonialism, Africans were labeled black, primitive, heretics, subjects, inferior races, and niggers. Racist connotations were prevalent among British and French officials who practiced those ideas as a matter of course while ruling colonies in India or Africa. Such negative stereotypes were widely accepted and helped fuel the imperial acquisition of territories in Africa (Said 1993). They were used as justifications for the victimization of colonized, innocent people embedded in institutionalized racism, sexism, and classism (Agozino 2003).

Frantz Fanon's works, *The Wretched of the Earth* (1963) and *A Dying Colonialism* (1965), elucidated that slavery is a criminological issue of vast proportions and traced the structural penology through which the offended society go about redressing the crimes of imperialism.

In *State Crime Around the World*, Ebbe (2016) showed that the intertwining of states' interests and mafia interests is nothing new. Crimes of slavery, colonialism, and neocolonialism in Africa and Nigeria are no exception. Many states and state actors decried the immorality of slavery while actively creating and engaging in it. For instance, Portugal, thinking itself morally superior to Africa, justified its colonial rule in terms of the need to cast *"illumismo"* (enlightenment) over the dark continent; whereas genocidists like King Leopold of Belgium used antislavery rhetoric but massacred millions of Africans to improve forced labor, calling it a civilizing process. In Nigeria, the dishonesty of British colonialists became apparent when they started deposing African leaders as King Jaja and Nana, who had stopped trading slaves and were instead concentrating on legitimate production of rubber and palm oil. Agozino (2003) noted that none of the criminals who acted on behalf of imperialism were ever punished, even in extreme cases such as the 1905 shooting of Guyanese workers who were striking for minimum wages of 16 cents a day, when two senior police officers were prosecuted to appease popular anger but later acquitted (Rodney 1981).

Africa fell within the international capitalist economy from which surplus was drawn to enrich the Western economy as labor was cheap and the amount of surplus extracted from Africa was enormous. Wages paid to workers in Europe and North America were much higher than wages paid to Africans in comparable categories. For instance, a Nigerian coal miner at Enugu earned one shilling per day for working underground and nine pence per day for jobs on the surface. Such miserable wages would be beyond comprehension of Scottish or German coal miners who would earn in an hour what the Enugu miner was paid for a six-day workweek (Rodney 1973).

Today, in areas where the Afro-Colombian population has been historically excluded and marginalized, primarily due to the legacy of slavery, contemporary social and economic structures perpetuate this deeply embedded exclusion and exploitation (Herrera 2012). Ironically industrial exploitation of the coca leaf in Latin American and the Caribbean fostered the international illicit drug trade enhanced by the global "war on drugs," as we shall see later.

Cyril James (1989), the West Indian-born cultural historian, examined Haiti and the splendor of its revolution, unveiling how race was constructed and how race and class intersect. He emphasized that the race question is subsidiary to the class question in politics, and to think of imperialism in terms of race is disastrous. But to neglect the racial factor as merely incidental is an error only less grave than to make it fundamental.

The TAST transpired more than four centuries ago, but its spillover effects on the lives of Africans and Afro descendants are still felt—their world is embedded in discrimination, marginalization, criminalization, and victimization. The struggle for liberty and justice continues. Agozino described "democracy, law and order as organized crime" and emphasized the need for decolonization (2003, 121–130). The legacy of TAST has led to the "construction of criminal categories and victimization as policing" (ibid. 1997, 62–86). Furthermore, it points to the notion of "internal colonialism" (ibid., 51–60), the process of imperial domination that links black people abroad with those at home through policies like immigration control and the war on drugs funded by imperial powers and waged by the nominal independent neocolonial states (Black Lives Matter 2020).

1.3 NIGERIA AS A TRANSIT-TRANSACTION COUNTRY

In the past decades, Nigeria has become a transit and transaction nation and a consumer country of hard drugs, including cocaine and heroin. Nigerians have become more involved in international trade than ever. They are distributing cocaine to markets in Nigeria and internationally. Put simply, Nigeria and West Africa are accredited as a new edge of the international drug trade and the global war on drugs.

Media and officials report escalating drug issues in Africa, arrests of Nigerian drug traffickers, large-scale seizures—especially hard drugs like cocaine and heroin—and issues relating to narco-states in the subregion (*BBC* 2020; *The Guardian* 2021; UNODC 2021). For example, in 2020, Operation Navara led to the seizure of 1.8 tons of cocaine hidden in sacks of rice in a warehouse and USD3 million stashed in bank accounts. Twelve men, from Bissau-Guinea, Colombia, Mexico, and Portugal, were sentenced to between four and 16 years in prison (*BBC,* May 28, 2020). NDLEA at Lagos Airport seized 3,413,463 kilograms of illicit drugs in 2020 and apprehended 60 suspects (*The Guardian,* January 13, 2021).

Whereas the coca plant and cocaine have been attributed to colonial powers in Nigeria (Ellis 2009), the diffusion of heroin in the country has been attributed to the involvement of foreign associates of colonialist powers. In the period from 1911 to 1937, the expanding agricultural business in palm oil, cocoa, rubber, and groundnuts in Nigeria attracted thousands of Levantine migrants, mainly Lebanese, who competed with European colonial trading firms (Forrest 1982; Hopkins 1973). What's more has been the arrival in Nigeria and Africa at large of expatriates involved in the illicit trade of cocaine and heroin, including, according to international reports, Indians and Pakistanis, Dutch, Italians and other Europeans, and Malaysians (Allen and Burgess 1999).

The late British historian and professor at the Department of Social and Cultural Anthropology of VU Amsterdam, Stephen Ellis, told me while we were in Chicago together for the "Looking Beyond Terrorism: Middle Eastern and African Criminal Enterprises Conference"—and where I presented on "Criminal Networks" in July 2009—that Africa's real contribution to the international drug trade began in the early 1980s when a group of Nigerian naval officers undergoing training in India organized a trafficking ring to smuggle Southwest Asian heroin to Europe and the United States. He makes the case that, organized around a virtual army of couriers, this initial effort was boosted by the collapse of the Nigerian economy in the mid-1980s, allowing traffickers to be recruited more cheaply and in greater numbers (Ellis, personal communication, 2009). Some of the thousands of young Nigerians who went to the United States for higher education in the 1970s and early 1980s engaged in drug trafficking (Obot 2004). For instance, when pursuing my undergraduate studies in Italy, some of my fellow students supplied highly demanded Nigerian cannabis to their Italian contacts and were convicted for international trafficking. One of the persons convicted stated that his reason for engaging in drug trafficking was to raise money to pay for his studies because foreign students were not allowed to work (Jamba, personal communication, 1987).

The collapse in oil prices in the early 1980s pressured many Nigerian students in the diaspora into drug trafficking as an alternative means to survive and afford their education when family support could no longer be counted on (Cockayne and Williams 2009). A decade later, susceptible Nigerians in the diaspora engaged fully in the international drug trafficking "with highly adaptive organizations that varied in structure hierarchies, networks, and self-contained independent" and were reported to be active in countries, including Cambodia, the Czech Republic, the Philippines, Singapore, Turkey, the United States, and Australia (Uzuegbu-Wilson 2019, 2).

The major factor in Nigeria's rise as a transit-transaction country is the influence of colonial powers and foreign business. Ellis (2009) noted that in 1934, colonial authorities were experimenting with the cultivation of the coca plant in the botanical gardens in Calabar and other stations in southern Nigeria. Although Nigeria is referred to as a narcotics nation or a hub of drug cocaine trafficking by some antidrug enforcement institutions, it might be more accurate to suggest that the country was actually made a covert hub by the colonial occupiers even before Nigerians were at all involved with narco-trafficking.

In fact, the first documented case of West Africa, and Nigeria in particular, as a transit area for drugs destined for overseas markets dates back to 1952, when U.S. officials uncovered a Lebanese syndicate trafficking parcels of heroin from Beirut to New York via Kano in North Nigeria and in Accra, Ghana (Ellis 2009). The group made use of couriers on commercial airlines. In a memorandum for Mr. Ross of the U.S. Department of State, the U.S. Consul-General in Lagos was told by a Lebanese source that "heavy dope traffic" from the Near East to the United States via Europe was being diverted to Nigeria to avoid the attention of law enforcement officers on the European route. Furthermore, the UNODC (2007) points out that the Lebanese are among the leading traffickers of South American cocaine via West Africa and Nigeria to the United States.

Most of the traffickers interviewed commented that Lebanese, Pakistanis, and Indians hire Nigerians as apprentices and business partners. One informant, Chia, a 32-year-old Nigerian woman who spent four years in jail in France for trafficking about 1.6 kilograms of cocaine in 1998 for Lebanese smugglers, explained the role of foreigners in the trafficking process:

> I worked as salesgirl in 1997 for the Lebanese businessman who imports general goods in Lagos. After about six months, I started dating another Lebanese guy, who is also rich just like my boss. I will not mention names. He bought nice

clothes for me and took me [on] holidays. He gave me money that I used to help my mother and [to feed my] two brothers. You see, my father died when I was fifteen years old, and my mother managed to pay my school fees till I completed secondary school education. He took me to France on holidays. Prior to the trips, he asked to bring two passport photos and arranged a foreign passport for me. Before our third trip, he said I could make money and achieve my financial dreams if I could do work for him. All I had to do was to carry something in my private parts to France or swallow it. I was naïve. I accepted because he meant everything to me. I was afraid of disappointing him but at same time I dreamt of solving my financial problems. Above all he assured me that everything should work out well. So that is how swallowed about one kilo of cocaine on three trips to France and two to Italy. For each trip, I got about EUR3,000 on return to Nigeria. On the fourth trip to France I was caught on the airport with about 1.6 kilos and spent four years in jail on conviction. (Chia, personal communication, December 12, 2015)

Early cohorts of heroin and cocaine traders were presumably unaware of the fact that a Lebanese syndicate had been doing something similar a generation previous. "Prior to 1982," the U.S. embassy in Lagos stated, "Nigerians played an insignificant role in the marketing of narcotics and dangerous drugs in the United States" (*Daily Times* 1984, p. 3). Nigerian smugglers were sending heroin by air courier from Pakistan to Nigeria, where it was repackaged and reexported to the United States. A Nigerian newspaper in 1983 reported the existence of what it called "a tiny cocaine world" in fashionable Lagos society, and in May and June 1983 the *Guardian* (Lagos) carried a series of reports on this matter (Klein 1994). Nigerian drug trafficking raised eyebrows. Drug issues became a regular feature of discussions between U.S. and Nigerian officials. The U.S. Ambassador in Nigeria at the time warned that "narcotics trafficking has become a serious issue in Nigeria's relations with the U.S., as it has with a number of other countries, detracting from our ability to address other high priority concerns" (*Newswatch* 1987).

1.3.1 Myth of Elite Involvement

Early publications made claims implicating Nigerian military elites in international drug trafficking (Olusegun 2011; Ellis 2009; Labrousse 2001). The allegations were largely accepted by the public in Nigeria where crimes by the powerful are common and arrests rare. One would argue that these role models laid the foundations for the new trend traffickers. Consideration of this history may stimulate a debate that will illuminate the nature of involvement in the drug trade itself and the inability to control the phenomenon in Nigeria.

Gernot Klantschnig (2015) posited that evidence for high-level political involvement in the drug trade, as assumed in portrayals of West African "narco-states," is not available in Nigeria where state officials derive much larger sums from the diversion of petroleum funds. One well-known instance was that of Brigadier Benjamin Adekunle, known as "the Black Scorpion" and hero of the Nigerian army during the Biafra war. He was one of those named by a 33-year-old Nigerian woman, Iyabo Olorunkoya, jailed in Britain in 1974 for importing 78 kilograms of marijuana. Adekunle was suspended from duty thereafter (Ellis 2009). Since the Brigadier was not arrested, convicted, or jailed for drug offense, that claim remains unproven.

By the time of the first letter bomb assassination that killed the investigative journalist, editor, and founder of the *Newswatch* magazine, Dele Giwa, on October 19, 1986, the Nigerian public was already hinting about some drug cartels having links close to the summit of power. Uzuegbu-Wilson (2019) wrote that most of the country's newspapers at the time were full of insinuations surrounding the death. The Babangida military regime and high ranked intelligence chiefs were implicated in the letter bomb incident but also the drug courier, Gloria Okon. Ellis stated on the matter:

"Among the many scandals of the Babangida years was the murder by parcel-bomb of the newspaper editor Dele Giwa. It is widely believed in Nigeria that Giwa's death was connected to his investigations into elite drug trading. Specifically, he is said to have been targeted as a result of an interview he had conducted with a former drug courier, one Gloria Okon, who had worked for principals in very senior positions of the state bureaucracy or for their families"(Ellis 2009, 179).

Allegations persist from the Dublin Group—consisting mainly of the European countries—that General Babangida and his wife have engaged in cocaine trafficking, along with numerous other military officers (Labrousse 2001). However, the allegations remain mere speculation. The case was tossed from one investigative team to the other, which naturally bore no results.

The Iran-Contra scandal is a well-known blot on Ronald Reagan's regime. Colonel Oliver North sold weapons to the Iranian government to boost funding for the Contras: The CIA supported the Contras' trafficking of cocaine into the United States. "Contras would take delivery of planeloads of military apparel that had been sent to El Salvador by Nicaraguans living in the United States. For the return flight north, they would load the planes with cocaine" (Feiling 2009, 40).

Differing from Labrousse's allegations, poor street dealers or couriers or suspects would have been apprehended and were presumed guilty until proven innocent. Nigerian trader, Rafi, told me during an interview in Rotterdam that he was arrested because he happened to be at a friend's flat in Amsterdam during a police raid in 2009, "One nonsense courier police arrested at Schiphol airport mentioned my friend's name as the person who send him go carry 'market' [drugs]. That is how I spent three days in cell before they left me because I was not involved" (Rafi, personal communication, 2012).

These controversies and others like them exposed the real underpinnings of illicit cocaine trafficking, the repressive-centered approach that has failed to eradicate or reduce the phenomenon, and the enthusiasm of cocaine strikers in Nigeria.

1.4 NIGERIA'S WAR ON DRUGS

The modern drug war draws from the former U.S. president Nixon's war on crime in the 1960s and subsequent war on drugs. Persistent economic decline and the end of the Cold War have marginalized Nigeria within the international system. From being an actor during the oil boom in the 1970s—that, for instance, supported Nelson Mandela's ANC with an annual subvention of USD5 million to help in the struggle against the racist apartheid regime (Ana-Caj 2017)—into being a "problem" nation dependent on foreign aid for its security. The pressure on African states to take on more responsibilities compounds this. In the early 1990s, western states accepted some degree of responsibility for peacekeeping (or peace enforcement) and for humanitarian intervention. Recent U.S. policies have seen their role as limited to financial and logistic support, whereas the field responsibility (and the related risks) can be left to African troops (Allen and Burgess 1999). However, scholars note how embedded political and institutional interests shape drug problems and related policies. These interests are often the driving force behind drug policy and influence the framing of drug problems, which are not seen as given but socially and historically constructed (Akyeampong 1996; Klantschnig, Carrier and Ambler 2014).

The adverse consequences of the U.S. government's war on drugs do not stop at the borders. By combating illicit drugs abroad, the U.S. government hopes to curtail the war on drugs and subsequent sale and use of drugs at home. Also, by assisting foreign governments with drug interdiction, the U.S. government aims to maintain regional balances, disrupt international criminal syndicates that threaten domestic and international security, and push foreign entities to undertake policies that align with U.S. interests (Coyne and Hall 2017).

The pharmaceutical industry influences and often defines the parameters of the drug control regime, both through direct collaboration with government officials and indirect collaboration through the production and marketing of products, such as cocaine, which in turn ultimately became entangled with public outcry and calls for prohibitions (Reiss 2014). It is a trade in which the United States became the dominant global supplier of pharmaceuticals, the major power determining international coca commodity flows, and the driving force behind an ideological regulatory apparatus of the international drug control. But they could not control the international drug trafficking that resulted from the criminalization and prohibition of drugs (Gootenberg 1999). There is too much money in drugs trade because of high demand by both the rich and poor.

Nigerian drug policy remains obscured by three key narratives that date back to the 1980s and 1990s and are still in place to date, namely: a highly exclusive policy-making process, repression as the sole means of implementation, and a strong bond with international drug agencies (Klantschnig 2015).

Firstly, exclusion remains one of the hallmarks of Nigerian politics dating back to 1960s, particularly under the Abacha dictatorship that concentrated powers in a clique of political supporters, "experts," and military officers (Mustapha 2002; Othman 1989). NDLEA, for example, monopolizes drug control and policy decision-making and is the sole agency dealing with drug investigations, prosecution, and demand reduction. NDLEA stakeholders sidelined other agencies such as the Ministry of Health and police to consolidate responsibility for the control of drugs in the country under their own auspices. In this, NDLEA is unique in the world. It differs from the Netherlands where the police do not handle rehabilitation issues, or the U.S. Drug Enforcement Agency (DEA) that handles neither drug prosecution nor demand reduction. The Ghanaian Narcotics Control Board (NACOB) is mainly responsible for drug policy-making, whereas the Ghanaian Police and Ministry of Health implement those policies (Bernstein 1999). Exclusion allows the NDLEA chairman to concentrate decision-making in his hands. One NDLEA insider told me, "Here it is just like in any other government agency where for everything the signature of the chairman is needed." Exclusion means that new recruits to the agency maintain the practices of their predecessors. "NDLEA today is a house of indiscipline as irregular promotion exercise coupled with the questionable special promotion has made junior officers senior to their superiors," according to the petitioned signed by the deputy superintendent for Narcotics Musa Ahmed Yusuf, as cited in the article, "Is NDLEA Winning the War against Illicit Drugs?" (*This Day*, December 8, 2017).

Secondly, repression or reactive and coercive supply control is a key activity of NDLEA experts. Apprehension of small-scale drug traffickers and destruction of illicit cannabis farms prioritized by NDLEA officers have come at the cost of alternative medical and socioeconomic approaches. But the health dimension of drug control in the subregion should be an important part of the NDLEA's drug control mandate, as emphasized by the WACD (2014).

The former spokesman of NDLEA, Ofoyeju Mitchell, told me during an interview in his Lagos office in 2011 that drug traffickers are criminals, and greed motivated the people who are damaging Nigeria's image. That is why amplified control is required. Several other NDLEA officials view their work and the organization's mission statement as combatting the image crises symbolized by drugs and greedy criminal traffickers driven by fast money-making. Drug demand reduction and treatment were not a priority. "For those addicted to drugs, *na them wahala*" (it is their problem), several officers told me.

Thirdly, concerns over bureaucratic power are another major issue. Most drug officials interviewed, police and customs officers, said that the lack of funding from the Nigerian government is the major challenge hindering their work, and NDLEA is no exception. They found supportive allies in international drug control agencies. The U.S. DEA has opened offices in Lagos, Accra, Nairobi, and Pretoria and actively seeks to collaborate with local authorities (Klantschnig 2016).

Positive reporting on the Nigerian drug agency has continued and intensified since the end of military rule in 1999. The national media has published repeated stories praising the efforts of the NDLEA with titles such as "We Are Winning the Drug War" and "International Community Woos NDLEA" (cited in Klantschnig 2015, 34–35). Media reports more critical of the NDLEA and its leadership have been rare.

Nigerian drug control institutions, policies, and related narratives are holdovers of the military state. From General Abacha to General Bamaiyi—an infantry general with a reputation for strong-arm tactics and first chairman of NDLEA who tasked with improving the antidrug organization (Obot 2004)—and now Buhari's regime and General Marwa who Buhari appointed in January 2021—the NDLEA cannot escape the continuity of institutions, policies, and drug related narratives like "retribution for evil men and women who have set out to endanger the young and smear the name of the nation" (Allen and Burgess 1999, 52).

One unexpected upshot of the war on drugs is Nigerian traffickers were able to insert themselves between the points of production and consumption, reroute their "market" or cargo via Lagos, Abidjan, Casablanca, Dakar, or other stopovers, and still make substantial profit. In the illicit drugs trade, where profits are not proportionate to factor costs—that is, land, labor, and capital—but to risk and monopoly (Klein 1999). For comparison, there is about a 400% markup from farm gate to consumer on the price of a legal drug, coffee, whereas the percentage price markup for illegal drugs can run into multiple thousands (Fritter and Kaplinsky 2001). Cocaine hoppers can recoup the cost of risks through extreme profit margins.

1.5 *NA THEM WAHALA* (IT'S THEIR PROBLEM)

Nigeria's role as a major transit point in the heroin trail between Southwest Asia and the United States was one reason the country was subjected to narcotics certification (Central Intelligence Agency 1984). Because of insufficient progress in counter-narcotics, Nigeria was denied certification by President Clinton in 1994. "A major drug-transit country is one: (A) that is a significant direct source of illicit narcotic or psychotropic drugs or other controlled substances significantly affecting the United States; or (B) through which are transported such drugs or substances" [FAA § 481(e)(5)] (INCSR 2019, 5).

Nigeria has been identified as one of the major sources of precursor or essential chemicals used in the production of illicit narcotics and major money laundering. Afghanistan, Brazil, China, Indonesia, Peru, Mexico, UK, and the Netherlands are also identified in this capacity by U.S. authorities (INCSR 2018). Due to this status, failure to fulfill the obligations of the UN conventions, and refusal to cooperate with the U.S. government in the war against illicit drugs, Nigeria was subjected to narcotics certification from 1993 to 1998.

Countries listed as major drug-transit countries often think that the United States unfairly targets them for other reasons than drug control. Nigeria is no exception. Government officials seemed to believe that Nigeria was being given a bad name to hang it. This brought about an initially dismissive reaction by Nigerian officials that evoked Sykes and Matza's (1957) neutralization technique of responsibility and victimization denial. The first strategy was veiled denial or minimization of the role of Nigerians. In a conference on drug policy in May 1990, the first head of the NDLEA said that Nigerians transported minimal amounts—body packing only a few hundred grams of heroin or cocaine. Other officials asserted that Nigeria does not produce cocaine or heroin; it is only a transit country. Also, government functionaries blamed the United States, suggesting that if Americans stopped demanding drugs, then supply would disappear (Obot 2004). Military stakeholders often harped on the hypocrisy of their American position while responding to American decertification decisions as they affected the country, ignoring the fact that the certification process was instituted to demand tougher counter-narcotics measures by other governments. Operators in Nigeria were less concerned about the serious economic and political consequences suffered by the masses.

Drug control officials asserted that the contribution of Nigerians to the world drug problem was too insignificant to merit decertification. This is the line of thinking maintained by "cocaine hoppers," as we shall see in the chapters to follow. They argued that many of the people arrested were not Nigerians but other West African nationals traveling with forged Nigerian passports; if there was no demand, there would be no supply. They maintained that Nigeria was labeled based on considerations other than drug trafficking by its citizens. This was, according to General Bamaiyi, because "we have a military administration" (Agbo 1996, 10).

Involvement in drug trafficking by those who are meant to control it persists. In addition to the absence of rule of law, it is among the primary issues which have dominated U.S.-Nigerian relations for decades (Dagne 2005). President Clinton provided a waiver in March 2000, a Vital National Interests Certification, for Nigeria to allow support for the democratic transition program (U.S. Senate Committee on Foreign Relations 2000). The Bush Administration certified that Nigeria was fully cooperating with U.S. officials the following year (U.S. Senate Committee on Foreign Relations 2001); yet, in January 2003, in a report to Congress, President Bush identified Nigeria as one of 23 "major drug-transit or major illicit drug producing countries" (U.S. Department of State 2003). The measures the United States took against Nigeria were severely felt.

1.5.1 Consequences

When a country is denied certification, there is an austere price to pay. Decertification was meant to deter Nigerians involved in the illicit drug trade. Decertification means the United States will vote against that country receiving loans from international lending institutions. NDLEA (2010) acknowledged that the following remained challenging: (i) dismantling drug trafficking networks in Nigeria, (ii) extradition to the United States of suspected drug traffickers, (iii) increased capacity for interdiction at air and seaports, (iv) control of money laundering, (v) enactment of legislation to make it easier to effect property forfeiture, and (vi) enhancing the capacity to control corruption (Obot 2004, 21).

The stringent challenges faced by Nigeria were aggravated by the fact that support from international organizations, including the United Nations International Drug Control Programme and the European Union (EU), were cut back or eliminated. Military training and sale of arms to Nigeria were suspended, and Nigeria could not borrow from the World Bank or the Paris Club to maintain basic necessities. Decertification made life for Nigerians miserable, as innocent citizens far removed from drug trafficking saw their standard of life deteriorate. Nigerians had difficulty getting visas to travel abroad and were subjected to demeaning searches at airports globally. They suffered more because notices were placed at international airports cautioning travelers to Nigeria to be careful. Nigerians were portrayed as notorious drug traffickers and as culpable of various crimes, including the advance fee fraud (Department of Justice U.S. Attorney's Office Northern District of Georgia 2020; Almasy 2019; Oboh and Schoenmakers 2010).

Nigeria's narcotics policy, despite its strategic importance to national development, has been left to elitist high-security and policy-making bodies. The challenge is now for NDLEA and its new management to subject Nigerian drug policy to open, public, and rational debate in response to the advent of narcotic drug challenges and the need to fulfill international drug control obligations of the myth of a drug-free world.

For the country as for individual Nigerians, this state of affairs had serious economic and psychological consequences that were becoming unbearable. In the general atmosphere of corruption and insecurity that characterized developments in Nigeria's administrations since the 1980s, the country's role in the global narcotics trade grew. Frequent visitors to Nigeria were aware that corruption made the country immune to most regulations and well suited to illegal activities, but that immunity did not apply to traffickers caught abroad. When the head of the Ghanaian drug police visited Bangkok in 1986, he found many Ghanaians and Nigerians in prison for drug offenses (Quantson 2002). By 1988, there were few thousand Nigerians reported to be serving sentences for drug offenses abroad. By 1991, that number jumped to about 15,000, as acknowledged by Nigeria's own Ministry of Justice. Nigerians were the leading nationality arrested for drug offenses in India, Pakistan, Saudi Arabia, and Thailand (Nwannennaya and Abiodun 2017). During this authors' visit to Brazil, Nigerians topped the list of foreign inmates in Itai prison, with 361 in 2013. The director of Sungai Buloh Prison in Malaysia told me Nigerians ranked number one with 400 Nigerians inmates there in 2016. And if the numbers are to be believed, that trend has increased enormously following Nigeria's war on drugs, as a repressive militaristic focus is no solution for a social and economic issue such as drugs.

1.5.2 Effects on Subregions

The executive director of UNODC, Antonio Maria Costa, indicated that the entire West African ruling elite was complicit in narco-trafficking (UNODC 2008a). He warned that there was a growing risk of collapse for some West African states whose senior officials colluded with foreign and local criminal networks. In other words, the war on drugs has failed to eradicate drug trafficking or powerful drug barons.

However, this is not the case in Nigeria. Although Nigerians are key players in drug trafficking, the country has a legitimate extractive economy large enough to make proceeds from drug trafficking rather marginal, presenting no serious threat to the foundations of the state. Drug trafficking has, in this context, been seen largely as a law enforcement issue, rather than a political/state security issue. Should cannabis be decriminalized, many youths in Nigeria could find employment in the lucrative new sector rather than involvement in Niger Delta militant groups or in Boko Haram terrorist groups.

According to the UNODC, the worst affected state is Guinea-Bissau, where since mid-2000s, military warlords have turned the country into a narco-state after ousting interim president Raimundo Pereira and other officials. Drug trafficking has reportedly become the key economic activity of Guinea-Bissau's leading military elite who control the state. For instance, on March 9, 2019, Guinea Bissau authorities seized 789 kilograms of cocaine (UNODC 2019a). Dubbed "Operation Navara" recovered USD3 million stashed in bank accounts and apprehended 12 men of Bissau-Guinean, Colombian, Mexican, and Portuguese nationalities who were sentenced to between four and 16 years in prison. Former navy chief, Bubo Na Tchuto, pleaded guilty to conspiring to import drugs to the United States but was sentenced to only four years in prison because of good behavior and for cooperating with investigators (*BBC* 2020). In Cape Verde, on January 31, 2019, authorities at the Port of Praia made a record bust of 9.570 kilograms of cocaine inside 260 bales in a vessel. The interception in both countries of as much as 10.4 metric tons of cocaine is more than the total amount seized on the entire continent between 2013 and 2016 (UNODC 2019b). The arrest of 11 citizens of Russian nationality involved shows the importance of the West Africa as transit hub to destinations in Europe through North Africa.

It is a continuous top down and borderless activity in which law enforcement sometimes succeeds in intercepting drugs. The Algerian coastguard confiscated more than 700-kilogram cocaine concealed aboard a container ship carrying frozen meat from Brazil in May 2018. Since the emergence of West Africa as the new front in the drug trade (Andrés de 2008), about 50 tons of cocaine from Latin America enters West Africa every year en route to Europe, the sale of which garners roughly two billion dollars on the streets.

In narco-states, long-standing links between politics, crime, corruption, and drug money continue to function as structurally complementary elements. This logic makes crime the source of capital accumulation and the solution to difficulties inherent to the states and the rule of law—be it today in Nigeria or Guinea-Bissau or Ghana among other states. Nigeria has fostered complementarity between elites, politics, and the war on drug; Nigeria's links with the drug trafficking trade have not yet turned the state into a full-blown narco-state, which can destabilize entire countries whose still-fragile institutions are caught in the storm of globalization. In this context, the legacy left by elite operators of the country has given rise to organized crime from which the Nigerian global cocaine trafficking draws. Allen and Burgess (1999) noted that one major concern of organized crime is to ensure regular payoffs to key officials in the area, and competition is dealt with in two ways: incorporation or betrayal, depending largely upon the candidates standing in the locality.

It's worth noting I did not meet any Nigerian who openly claim to be Mafia. There are organized criminals, there are local groups or "area boys," toughs, and there is a crime scene, but there are no large-scale *Maffiosi*, well organized and sophisticated as indicated by Ikoh (2013), camouflaged by a formal exterior and in league with the state. Instead small groups operate under various names to protect the interests of its members. For example, in one of the main cannabis-growing regions in Delta State (often referred to by informants as "Jamaica"), cannabis growers attend monthly meetings.

1.6 DECRIMINALIZE AND REGULATE DRUGS

Africa has a long history of drug production, use, trade, and control. Several historians have explored this history and the ambiguous relationship that different African societies have had with substances as diverse as alcohol, khat, cannabis, and heroin (Akyeampong 2005; Anderson and Carrier 2009). In Nigeria, the local markets and concerns about some of these substances date back to before the contemporary prohibitive conventions.

In Nigeria, cannabis was initially legal under colonial governments (Asuni 1964). Cannabis was outlawed in 1925 when it became subject to international control under the Geneva Opium Convention and the first drug control law in Nigeria termed the "Dangerous Drugs Ordinance" of 1935 (Otu 2013). Attempts to prohibit it bore no results. Before long, cannabis was being exported to Western nations by Nigerians as local production increased. Within Nigeria, in 1961 and 1962, 823 and 7,152 kilograms of cannabis were seized, respectively.

Researchers show that Nigeria's traditional reliance on extreme punitive measures to curb supply and discourage demand, in response to U.S. certification demands, has not produced the expected results. Cannabis use is rampant in some social circles, and illicit production and trade continue. Recent examples include NDLEA's destruction of a 3,900-hectare cannabis farm in Ondo State, the arrest of many dealers in Adamawa State, and the arrest of several farmer offenders (*The Cable* 2019). The total value of cocaine seized at MMI airport Lagos in March 2021 was valued over N30 billion (*Vanguard* 2021).

Authorities acknowledge that cannabis consumption remains high in the state because of availability and affordability. During an interview, the spokesman of the NDLEA, Jonah Achema, expressed the dissatisfaction of his staff who feel neglected by the management that does not pay them well nor promote junior staff (*This Day* 2017). Achema suggested that "there is evidence of a vibrant cannabis cultivation business which appears to be fueling a youthful domestic market and a possible export market" (ibid.). Misrepresenting the positive effect a change of policy would have for the current and would-be farmers, the write-up asserted that the "drug barons" are producing and selling drugs with profit being assimilated unnoticed into the Nigerian economy, to the detriment to the country. To start with, decriminalizing drugs will revoke the label "drug barons" for farmers. Also, their contribution to personal financial needs and in boosting Nigeria's economy will be officially recognized.

In addition, NDLEA staff acknowledged the failure of the war on drug when they said that statistics of arrests and seizure drastically gone down, stating: "This nonchalant attitude towards bringing drug barons to book is gradually affecting the cordial working relationship between the agency and international collaborators like the United States government and UNODC. Unlike in the past, these collaborators were conspicuously missing at the 2017 World Drug Day commemoration in Abuja" (*This Day* 2017).

Country Representative, Mr. Oliver Stolpe, stated during a courtesy visit to General Marwa, "We appreciate the fact that the Agency is operating under a very difficult situation, but the future of international collaboration is bright. There is a whole lot of resources that will be invested in international cooperation and Nigeria is one of the beneficiaries" (NDLEA 2021). The U.S. government has also promised to increase its technical support for Nigeria in its effort to tackle the menace of drug abuse and illicit drug trafficking, according to U.S. ambassador to Nigeria, Mary Beth Leonard, during a courtesy call to NDLEA general Marwa (ibid.).

A key consequence of the war on drugs is growth in prison population, which stood at about 72,194 prisoners, with 98% being male inmate, as of April 2018 (Australian Government DFAT 2018). In 1989, NDLEA was founded in response to the United Nations Convention Against Illicit Traffic in Narcotics Drugs and Psychotropic Substances, 1988 (Otu 2013). The decree provides harsh punishment for drug offenses, including the forfeiture of assets of arrested offenders. Trafficking in cocaine, LSD, heroin, or similar drugs is punishable by life imprisonment, whereas possession or use attracts a sentence of 15–25 years. The assets forfeiture provision of the decree also empowers the NDLEA to "immediately trace and attach all the assets and properties" of an arrested person (Federal Military Government 1989, A730). Misuses of the decree were aggravated by the Money Laundering Decree of

1995 (Federal Military Government 1995) that gave greater powers to the NDLEA to mount surveillance on the bank accounts of suspects (Otu 2013; Obot 2004).

The drug prohibition policy was neither based on local priorities nor need driven, neither people oriented nor people guided (Klantschnig 2015). In fact, little is known in Nigeria about any inclusive, harm-reducing, human-rights-respecting, and sustainable approach to narcotics control.

1.6.1 Chat with Inmates

During fieldwork in Nigeria in 2013, this author hired three male inmates from Ubiaja Prison in Edo State to work for three days at the farm of Food for All International (FFAI), a nongovernmental organization for farmers and other small-scale agriculture based in Port Harcourt, which operates in Niger Delta States. Parole allowed them temporary release for this special purpose. The author paid N1,200 (about USD3) for each inmate for working about 6 hours before returning to jail. Two inmates were serving five and six years, respectively, convicted for growing cannabis or marijuana and trafficking. The other was sentenced to seven years for car theft. This temporary exit gave the inmates an opportunity to earn money to buy food inside. Aty, who was sentenced for trafficking about 19 kilograms of marijuana stated to me at Ubiaja, "They beat me too much. They take my motorbike and my money. We happy if each person get 200 naria from that money you pay them. Because they will take it, even if we need it to buy food, cigarette or even 'ganja' from them" (personal communication). Ironically, Aty was jailed for a marijuana offense, but he could buy marijuana from warders, part of the system that keeps him inside.

Aty and others were appreciative of the opportunity, however temporary, to work, eat comfortably, and earn some extra pocket money. Overcrowding is a thorn in the side of prisons in Nigeria. Prison cells are not suitable for human inhabitance as 20 or more people squeeze themselves onto the floor to sleep. Hygienic situations are pitiable. Occupational, skill acquisition, or educational opportunities and reformation exist on paper only. The NDLEA's 1992 Drug Data Collection Unit reported that 85% of the 243 drug traffickers arrested were unskilled, impoverished, and had minimum or if any education (Otu 2013, 128). Drugs are available in prison against payment, supplied by unscrupulous warders. Aty and the rest are in bad condition compared to Nigerian inmates I interviewed in the Netherlands, who could work in jail, get paid, and were better fed and accommodated.

Funds used by the NDLEA could be reallocated to programs like paid work or education programs for inmates, rehabilitation, drug treatment as a health issue. The cost unarguably eats deep into the treasury of Nigeria's meager resources. For instance, the NDLEA attracted a capital expenditure of about N37.4 billion (Otu 2013, 130). That is around N5.3 billion per year. Recent data show that the trend continues.

1.6.2 Call for Change

Counter-narcotic policies need to aim at sanitizing the system in order to ensure its effectiveness. Reinvest billions of naira wasted in combating a war on drugs that has no enemy, in diversifying Nigeria's economy by legalizing and regulating the cannabis market, as many other countries are doing.

The Netherlands is exemplary. The legal rules concerning narcotic drugs are set out in the Dutch Opium Act which differentiates between "hard drugs" and "soft drugs." Ed Leuw (1991) characterized Dutch drug policy as normalizing, pragmatic, and non-moralistic:

> "It accepts the existence of the use of illegal drugs as inevitable in modern society. Official reactions are directed at a reduction of social and personal harm.... It focuses law enforcement efforts on the higher levels of the supply system. Retail trade is tolerated in numerous 'coffee shops.' The use of hard drugs is primarily considered a public health problem" (229).

Further, Leuw observed that drug policy was based on the central notion that the drug problem is primarily a public health and welfare issue and that risk reduction is its core concept (248, 258).

The Dutch (Normalization) tolerance policy in drug cases means that even though drugs are technically illegal, the offender will not be prosecuted if certain conditions are met. Courts have the option to suspend the detention of an addict with a history of crime on the condition that he or she undergoes treatment in a special institution for intensive treatment (Gesley 2016). In "Drug Policy: The 'Dutch Model'," van Ooyen-Houben and Kleemans outlined the restrictions and specifications which include the maximum transaction per customer per day is 5 grams, access was restricted to persons over age 18, the maximum amount of cannabis in stock was limited to 500 grams, coffee shops are required to be alcohol-free premises, no advertising, and no coffee shop could be located within 350 meters from schools for secondary education and secondary vocational education (2015, 196).

Coffee shops function as reliable and safe places for the sale of cannabis to adults. The system contributes to the separation of consumer markets for cannabis and hard drugs and therefore to the achievement of the health and harm-reduction goals of drug policy. The Dutch win-win situation implies that adult users do not have to turn to illegal markets (van Ooyen-Houben and Kleemans 2015). Dutch coffee shops pay about EUR315 million in tax annually and turn an estimated profit of EUR1.6 billion annually (Waterfeld 2011).

1.6.3 Damage Persists

The collateral damage of the war on drugs includes economic cost, human rights violations, insecurity, health, and dependency on foreign repressive aid, which causes more crime and violence. Otu framed it this way, "The only benefit accruing from the war on drugs in Nigeria is that no one benefits; everyone in the war is a loser" (2013, 130).

Klantschnig (2015) reasoned that the continued propagation of the war on drugs utterly disregards and excludes more liberal and less intrusive alternative approaches to drug control. Nigeria's policies are deliberately geared toward satisfying the expectations and pandering to the wishes of friendly foreign government sponsors of Nigeria's military approach to drug control, even when and where they have proven largely ineffectual.

So, why is the failing CJS—that neither protects society nor achieves justice—allowed to continue? The CJS has failed in three ways. It fails to implement policies that stand a good chance of reducing crime, to treat as crime the harmful acts of the rich and powerful, and to eliminate political/economic bias in criminal justice itself. According to Reiman and Leighton (2017), this is because the current system's failure produces benefits for the wealthy in America, as in Nigeria. This is achieved not through a conspiracy theory but through "historical inertia" or the persistence of a criminal justice model that dates from the preindustrial era and which does not recognize many of the harmful acts of the well-off. They emphasize the Pyrrhic defeat theory that aims to explain the *persistence* of this failing criminal justice policy instead of its origin. The focus on one-on-one crime reflects the main ways in which people harmed each other in the days before large-scale industrialization; the refusal to implement policies that might reduce crime (like legalization of drugs or amelioration of poverty) reflects a defensive and punitive response to crime that is natural and understandable, even though neither noble nor farsighted (Reiman and Leighton 2017, 167).

Those with wealth and power profit from the triple failure of the CJS policy because it diverts attention from the harmful, if noncriminal, acts of the elites and redirects it toward the poor, as reflected in the "Carnival Mirror." Petty thieves or cannabis farmers such as Aty are more likely to end up among the 179,000 prisoners in Nigeria than elites who commit crimes with a much wide impact zone. The system weeds out the crime of the powerful, and the effect of this message is to create (or reinforce) fear of, and hostility toward, the poor. It leads people to ignore the ways they are injured and robbed by the acts of the well-off and to demand a tougher dose of "law and order" directed mainly to the lower classes. More importantly, in Nigeria, as in the United States, it nudges people to defend the conservative views of Nigerian society with large disparities of wealth, power, and opportunity, and nudges them away from the progressive demand for equality and a more equitable distribution of wealth and power. On the other side, those who are mainly victimized by the failure to reduce our high rate of street crime are generally the poor themselves.

Those hurt the most by the failure of the CJS are those with the least power to change it. In Nigeria, the rural poverty was about 73.2% in 2010 (NBS 2017), and 40% of the total population, or almost 83 million people, live below the country's poverty line of N137,430 (USD381.75) per year (World Bank 2020). They do not have life insurance nor property insurance against theft. They do not receive social security from the Nigerian government. They live on the minimum income and those without income at all depend on handouts and extended family for survival.

Change is needed. The drug trade in Nigeria rapidly expanded as the U.S. and EU's demand for cannabis and other drugs increased dramatically. This resulted in the expansion of a distinct trade route, which exported cannabis from Nigeria and the subregion. Nigerian drug traffickers took advantage of trading networks created by Malian and Berber traders in colonial times to move drugs through vulnerable neighboring countries to consumption hubs in destination countries (Bybee 2012).

Through militarized assistance and aid, Nigerian stakeholders maintain the status quo and crush any effort to change. "Just Stop Killing Us" demanded Nigerian youths who protested against a police unit plagued by a history of extra-judicial killings, torture, and extortion (Akinwotu 2020). The cries for change in Nigeria recall the Black Lives Matter movement in the United States, mostly from a younger generation in a country where youth are the largest demographic. The same youth are confronted with increasing unemployment, insecurity, and poverty and met with a lack of urgency, bemusement, and threats of force by a generation of elderly governing officials. The youth uprising was brutally crushed and "left 69 people dead including 51 civilians, 11 police officers and seven soldiers," President Buhari told the *BBC* (October 23, 2020).

Cannabis could boost exports and provide employment if there is an overhaul of the repressive drug policy in Nigeria. It could even kick-start sustainable agriculture not based on rhetoric prohibitive but centered on business-like attitudes driven by the private sector.

1.6.4 Cannabis: Green Gold Alternative

Intercropping is a common agricultural technique in Nigeria and in underdeveloped countries. With the exception of palm, groundnut, and cocoa that are quite labor and water intensive, small plots can be intercropped for food cultivation and will yield a far higher income than do rival crops. For example, research by OGD (1999) reported ratios of 50:1 in favor of cannabis production against groundnuts in Senegal; 10:1 for the Gambia, and 300:1 against cocoa in the Ivory Coast. While these figures are rough estimates, they do suggest strong reasons why peasants may be turning to cannabis and khat, either of their own accord, or triggered by offers of guaranteed prices by buyers who may also supply seed (Allen and Burgess 1999, 8).

The growth of the informal sector makes the sale and transit of drugs easier for unemployed youths and famers, especially the internal and cross-border trade in cannabis. During fieldwork in Djibouti, and Hargeisa in Somaliland in 2013 and 2014, this author observed that khat or *qaf* consumed in the Horn of Africa is widely imported from Ethiopia or Kenya. "Khat is good business, help my family survive!" said one petty seller, Abdulahi in Hargeisa. It helps people deal with life. For instance, it neutralizes jet lag after a 10-hour flight from Amsterdam to Djibouti. Roekija does not like khat, "Qaf is good, tried it but it keeps me sleepless. If I don't sleep good, I cannot function well next day." Their differing opinions imply that controlled and regulated use is normal as with alcohol, for example.

Production and use of such mass drugs as cannabis and khat is ubiquitous in Africa, and the continent is becoming ever more drawn into the international trade estimated by the UN to have been worth USD400 billion in 1995, some 8% of world exports; only the arms trade was larger, at USD800 billion. UNODC (2018b, 40) noted that while most of the cannabis produced in Africa is for consumption within the region, a number of African countries (Nigeria, Ghana, SA, and Zambia) have identified European countries as the final destination, notably the United Kingdom and the Netherlands.

The European Industrial Hemp Association noted "reasonable regulation of Cannabidiol" in food, cosmetics, and medicinal products. In 2016, 30,000 hectares of cannabis were cultivated in the EU (see EIHA 2018). Cannabis or hemp extracts containing Cannabidiol (CBD) can be utilized along with hemp fibers and shives, providing extra income to farmers. For instance, CBD is increasingly used as a food supplement and as an ingredient in cosmetics, thereby generating new investments and creating employment (van Klingeren and Ham 1976, 10). More than EUR500 million has been invested in the cannabis industry, as Europe blooms into the world's largest legal cannabis market. New legislation regarding the growth, sale, or consumption of cannabis is on the way in the EU. Cannabis investments in the United States and Canada quadrupled in 2018, catching the eyes of European policymakers, and EU countries' investments in the sector are primed and ready to harvest EUR123 billion by 2028 (*Consultancy.eu*, February 4, 2019).

Countries invest in novel green gold cannabis while aiding NDLEA and police in the failed war on drug to eradicate cannabis—intentionally or unintentionally eroding civil liberties, jailing the poor, and labeling farmers as criminals. "We can't incarcerate ourselves out of the drug crisis," stated former U.S. president Barack Obama (Sullum 2011).

In the late 1960s, an estimated USD4 billion was being spent annually at the national, state, and local levels to pay for police, courts, and correctional facilities in the fight against crime (Katzenbach 1967, 35). The yearly cost to the public of this brand of domestic tranquility was more than USD265 billion by 2012, with 2.4 million persons employed by the CJS (Reiman and Leighton 2017, 28).

Nigeria cannot afford the billions of dollars the United States spends on the enormous number of prisons and prisoners it is warehousing. For example, Nigeria approved a record N10.59 trillion (about USD34.6 billion) to run the country in 2020 (Rueters 2019). Despite increasing the budgetary allocation of N613.5 billion to the Nigerian Prison Correctional Service, the prisons remain in squalor (Akpede 2019). In many ways, the ongoing war on drugs appears to be a tool for domination over poor countries lured into receiving huge foreign aid intended to wage war on citizens in the guise of the war on drugs.

There is greater evidence to suggest that drug use should be treated as a public health issue. The NDLEA acknowledged about 40% of high-risk drug users in Nigeria wanted treatment but were unable to get it for various reasons, including cost of treatment, no treatment available, fear of stigma, and lack of information. The "Development of the National Drug Control Master Plan 2021 to 2025" has been challenged to "ensure healthy lives and promote well-being for all at all ages" and "strengthen prevention and treatment of substance abuse, including narcotic drug abuse and harmful use of alcohol" (UNODC 2021).

Tobacco use and secondhand smoke is a major risk factor for cardiovascular disease, including coronary heart disease, stroke, and peripheral vascular disease, contributing to about 12% of deaths from heart disease. Nigeria is Africa's leading tobacco market, with over 18 billion cigarettes sold annually, costing Nigerians over USD931 million (Ake 2018). Alcohol is the sixth leading risk factor contributing to most death and disability. Alcohol-attributable deaths in both sexes for liver cirrhosis, road traffic accidents, and cancer in 2016 were 42,120, 15,365, and 4,687, respectively (ibid.). Abiona et al. (2019) found that "one out of ten Nigerians still smokes daily." These excesses represent more deadly problems facing Nigeria. Spending billions on a foreign imposed war on drugs only benefits the drug czars and warlords themselves, with devastating consequences for society, drug users, and struggling farmers.

Reiman and Leighton (2017, Chapter 4) contend that the CJS does not actually fight crime—or does only enough to keep it from becoming impossible to control and to keep the struggle against crime vividly and drastically in the public view, but never enough to substantially reduce or eliminate crime. They call this way of looking at criminal justice policy the Pyrrhic defeat theory. "A Pyrrhic victory" is a military victory purchased at such a cost in troops and treasure that it amounts to a defeat. Pyrrhic defeat theory argues that the failure of the CJS yields such benefits to those in positions of power that it amounts to a victory (Reiman and Leighton 2017).

Kamala Harris (U.S. vice president at the time of writing) and Joan Hamilton's (2009) *Smart on Crime* points out in the introduction that "in California State, we spend more than USD25 billion annually on crime, more than twice what we spent on higher education, but 70 percent of the 125,000 individuals released from our prison each year are back behind bars within a couple of years." They emphasized the need to reject the myths and outmoded approaches of the status quo that have led to the situation where we are today.

Leadership is crucial; education and awareness are paramount. Commitment to creating an informed society should be the focus of policies and interventions for harm reduction of drug, tobacco, and alcohol use. Nigeria has excise tax on beer, wine, and spirits but lacks written national policy (adopted/revised) and other measures including legally binding regulations on alcohol advertising, legally required health warning labels on alcohol advertisements, and national monitoring system(s) (World Health Organization [WHO] 2018, 175). Calls for change are growing, and the time is ripe. Decriminalization and regulation of drug use are already a reality across the world.

Decolonization calls attention to the relative autonomy of victimization as an institutional practice that is linked to classical colonialism, neocolonialism, and internal colonialism and, consequently, emphasizes the need to resist recolonization, as well as to de-marginalize and empower the poor in the neocolonies and internal colonies globally. Victimization is not always something that a person or group does to another person or group but is also something that the state does to categories of people in civil society (Agozino 1977). The decolonization process cannot afford to turn a blind eye to cultural, political, and economic problems underpinning the war on drugs in Nigeria and beyond—nor to the problems like Africa's debt burden and African's demand for remuneration for the crimes of slavery, colonialism, and imperialism.

As Nigerian authorities continue to live in denial about the booming local cannabis industry, other countries of the world have started to see the economic potential of cannabis. By 2024, the total global forecast of the legal cannabis market size is estimated at about USD103.9 billion and approximately USD2.6 billion for Africa (Prohibition Partners 2019). This billion-dollar business could exist if drugs are decriminalized and regulated.

1.7 NIGERIANS ABROAD

Throughout the interviews conducted for this study, the possibility of traveling abroad was often cited as a reason for becoming a cocaine courier. The alternative for many individuals is to borrow money to pay smugglers, risking their lives through the Sahara Desert and the Atlantic Ocean in an attempt to enter Europe. The dream of entering a multicultural society fades quickly as newcomers are faced with legal status issues, complicated integration processes, and financial problems. Due to the negative effects of some specific governmental policies that put significant restrictions on immigrants, many become marginalized and are passively pushed into illegal activities as a means of survival (Bovenkerk and Yesilgoz 2004; Oboh 2016). Faced with survival issues in a new country and pushed into debt in Nigeria, for some, cocaine trafficking becomes an attractive option that delivers quick monetary rewards. They maintain networks of family, friends, and acquaintances who can assist them in making fast cash to pay off debt and get rich. "Reverse social capital," whereby wealth by any means necessary is the accepted rule, has become the basis for much of Nigerian society, especially those who are well connected. While there is no way to track how many Nigerians live abroad, and how many are actually trafficking drugs, the UNODC Individual Drug Seizures records have cited arrests of Nigerian nationals in at least 45 countries since 2000 (UNODC 2008b, 24).

As Nigerians are becoming more and more active internationally, they illuminate contemporary processes of globalization of the drug trade and the concept that crime results equally from direct or indirect dependency and exploitation by core, rich countries or poor, peripheral countries. According to Bovin (2010), the world economic systems regarding cocaine trafficking highlight an organized trade that inextricably links the developed and underdeveloped countries. There is enormous demand for cocaine in Nigeria. This demand for drugs is impossible without the supply, mainly from Brazil, which I will discuss ahead in chapters five and eight.

However, the new trend in trafficking reaches far beyond Brazil. Globalization enabled the spread of trafficking to other countries, be it the United States, United Kingdom, Saudi Arabia, UAE, China, Malaysia, Indonesia, or Australia. We will see how this market is expanding—meaning that to increase the supply, Nigerians exploited new horizons and possibilities. African cocaine traffickers persist despite the fact that some destination countries of Asia and Central America have the death penalty and life sentences without parole for cocaine trafficking. Prior to discussing this in the chapters ahead, let us look next at how features such as endemic poverty, population growth, limited educational opportunities, and a high degree of unemployment have bolstered the making of cocaine hoppers.

Chapter 2

"State Crisis" and Fostering Cocaine Culture

This chapter focuses on the Nigerian "state crisis," contextualizing historical and contemporary developments in Nigeria, which has allowed for the contemporary criminogenic environment that fosters deviancy—from which the new trend in international illicit cocaine trafficking emerged. Despite its vast natural resources, including oil and gas, the Nigerian government has failed to remedy the crushing poverty that affects a majority of its citizens.

The country is a democracy in transition and has been besieged by a number of political and socioeconomic problems that Aziaki (2003) points to as a major cause of crime. Ruggiero (1996) averred that geopolitical factors are crucial for a group or region to succeed in illicit activities, less as social problems (backwardness, poverty, wars) than in terms of social advantages (good natural resources, modern economic infrastructures, know-how, good connections, etc.). Demographically the large population (most of whom live in poverty), as well as the various ethnic groups and their distrust of one another, also contributes to creating a criminogenic environment. Historically, critics point to Nigeria's history, such as the impact of colonization in fostering distrust and fragmentation, as well as political instability and failed leadership. In particular, they reference the impact of the Nigerian civil war (1966–1970) and the mismanaged oil boom in the 1970s.

Seen through another lens, criminogenic experts identify organized crime in Nigeria as a root cause of illicit cocaine trafficking emerged. The government of Nigeria could be defined as a "predatory state" (see Lupsha 1996; Hirschfield 2015; Ebbe 2016), where the head of state rules and decrees like the head of an organized crime family, using criminal cronies to engage in the despicable and condemnable acts of looting his nation's wealth.

The predatory state nourishes international cocaine trafficking and renders drug control virtually impossible in Nigeria. Nigerian organized crime has come to symbolize the "soft state" or "weak state," endemic corruption, and celebration of criminality.

Each of these principal features will be explored in this chapter to better understand the internal causes of Nigeria's role in international cocaine trafficking. Finally, each of these factors will be discussed in the context of reverse social capital, wherein the theory of beneficial connections between social networks and communities is driven not by a code of conduct that positively benefits a community and society through education, democracy, and social responsibility, but rather through a system which elevates those who perform illegal acts to positions of authority and power in Nigeria.

In all, this chapter will discuss permeable and ineffectual borders control, historical influences, understanding crime in the soft state or weak state Nigeria, lack of good governance, the effects of poverty, population growth, limited educational opportunities, undiversified economy, unemployment and youths' nightmare, stumpy law observation, "the Nigerian Dream," and "Chop money" syndrome. These conditions have boosted the involvement of Nigerians in the illicit cocaine trade and proliferation.

2.1 PERMEABLE AND INEFFECTIVE BORDER CONTROL

Nigeria has exhibited an ineffectiveness in managing its extensive border areas. Spanning 923,768 square kilometers total, 13,000 kilometers of border areas are water and 910,768 square kilometers are land (see Central Intelligence Agency [CIA] accessed April 23, 2020). These massive swaths of ungovernable space have led to internal lawlessness, as demonstrated by Boko Haram in the north and Niger Delta insurgences in the south of the country. Membership in the Economic Community of West African States offers free movement of people and goods. Widespread border crossing arising from ethnic and religious proximity with neighboring nations is typical. Traditional trading practices, as well as weak border control systems, have led to permeable borders in West.

Such vast and porous borders provide an ideal environment for drug trafficking. Nigeria has 22 commercial airports, and about seven million passengers travel through Lagos's MMIA annually (MMIA 2013). On average, around 6,000 passengers travel through MMIA airport daily, and over 90% of drug suspects arrested at the airports were found to have ingested illicit drugs (Fatokun 2016). Nigeria boasts hundreds of miles of unpatrolled coastal lines from the high sea to delta communities, featuring 3,000 riverine waterways of the country. There are bays, islands, and peaty swamps too numerous to reach and awkward to patrol. In all, Nigeria's porous borders are linked to its state crisis because budget funds for acquiring equipment and training personnel are embezzled by unscrupulous public officers. Coupled with the geographical locations of the country, Nigeria offers a comparative advantage for West African and South American drug traffickers.

In addition to porous borders, several other factors have fostered the upsurge of illicit cocaine trafficking in Nigeria's past.

2.2 HISTORICAL INFLUENCES

The Nigerian state crisis from which illegal economies and the new trend drug trade flourished is rooted in European colonialism. Though credited with the introduction of Western-style education, religion, and governance, colonialism laid the foundation for a weak state resulting in the present criminogenic environment.

First, it actively supported *comprador classes*, natives of a colonized country who act as the agents of the colonizing actors to impose systems of control for covert economic exploitation in Africa (Agozino 2003). Colonialism reduced many African rulers to the status of middlemen for European trade as; it raised ordinary Africans to that same middleman commercial role; and it created a new trading group of "mixed blood-the children of European or Arab fathers" (see Rodney 1973, 169). *Compradors* served as economic, political, and cultural agents extending European activity from the coast into the hinterland. Kwame Arhin's "Rank and Class" characterized compradors, "The assumed superiority of the educated, qua educated, over the non-educated; the adoption of European life styles by the educated as some kind of status symbol; and aversion to manual labor as the supreme index of the attainment of 'European status'" (1983, 17).

Britain deployed direct and indirect rule; the French, Belgians, and Germans tried assimilation; and the Dutch embraced rule by apartheid. By definition, colonial rule was unaccountable to Africans and reliant on the military to suppress dissent, noted the World Bank (Ali et al. 2000). Colonized countries were systematically stripped of their natural resources, with few benefits accruing to the local population. In this regard, colonialism espoused a system of organizational deviance where the goal, means, and control were inseparable. I explain that states and corporations act together in a criminal manner on interactional, organizational, and institutional levels. In Kauzlarich and Kramer's (1998, 148) organizational theories on political economy and organizational crime, criminal behavior at the organizational level results from a coincidence of pressure of goal attainment, availability and perceived attractiveness of illegitimate means, and an absence of or weakness of social control mechanisms.

Second, British indirect rule grouped together more than 250 different ethno-linguistic tribes in Nigeria without considering long-standing, deeply entrenched cultural differences. Metz (1992) averred that in the north, the system benefited the colonists due to the preexisting, centralized Islamic system of governance and Sharia Law; in the southeast it was inadequate because of the absence of a centralized system and governance by elders. Afigbo (1972) pointed out that disrupting the existing, coherent system caused widespread social and political disorder, fostering erosion of informal social control system, because Nigerians saw the colonialists as illegal occupiers and exploiters.

Third, it instituted weak governance as aftermath that cemented the divisions underpinning the Nigerian state crisis. Wole Soyinka expressed in his 2006 memoir, *You Must Set Forth at Dawn*, that the signs of independence were hopeless from the beginning: The 1959 elections that led to the First Republic of Nigeria were rigged—by the British! Even the Nigerian census was falsified, giving an artificial majority to the North that was largely feudalist by tradition and conservative in political outlook. The final results of the election were manipulated in favor of the political conservatives (Soyinka 2006, 54).

In a society besieged by neocolonial divides, clientelism and patrimonialism became preeminent. *Patronage* or, more broadly, *clientelism* in anthropology and political science is a political exchange: a politician (i.e., a "patron") gives patronage in exchange for the vote or support of a "client" (Robinson and Verdier 2013, 262). "Patronage refers to the way in which party politicians distribute public jobs or special favors in exchange for electoral support" (Weingrod 1968, 379). Patronage and clientelism are often used interchangeably (Kitschelt and Wilkinson 2007). Clientelism is a much broader phenomenon than patronage, with patronage being simply one specific type of clientelistic exchange, perhaps restricted to "the use of resources and benefits that flow from public office" (Hicken 2011, 295).

Patrimonialism and its derivative neopatrimonialism, particularly in the political science literature, are commonly understood (with reference to Weber) to denote systems in which political relationships are mediated through, and maintained by, personal connections between leaders and subjects, or patrons and clients. In other words, "Authority and the social linkages through which it is exercised are vested almost as personal property in an individual, rather than in impersonal institutions or in a mandate conferred and withdrawn by citizens" (Pitcher et al. 2009, 129–130). Neopatrimonialism could be viewed as a synonym for corruption, patronage, clientelism, the "big man" syndrome, godfatherism, warlordism, predation, kleptocracy, or perhaps as a range of practices that are highly characteristic of politics in Africa, namely nepotism, tribalism, regionalism, factionalism, and so on (Medard 1991).

Weber (1978) asserted that patrimonial authority is exercised through personal ties between rulers and their subordinates. Official duties are defined not by rules but by personal loyalties. Clientelism can thrive in conjunction with modern, bureaucratic government. Law and bureaucracy provide the framework within which patrons can offer to advance their clients' interest by exercising discretion (or influencing its exercise or "bending" the rules).

The result has been a culture of election manipulations in Nigeria, riven by deep internal cleavages centered upon ethnic, religious, linguistic, or regional division, overlaid by extremes of wealth and poverty. Under such conditions, it is difficult for an overall consensus—in the sense of basic agreements on rules of the political game—to emerge. An atmosphere of acute distrust prevails; politics becomes a ruthless zero-sum contest in which contending parties strive not simply to stay on top but to eliminate their opponent altogether. Under such circumstances, it is easy to appreciate the immense significance attached to building up and maintaining clientele networks (Theobald 1990). The historical, sociopolitical, and economic features linking Britain and its allies' indirect control over Nigeria contributed to the Nigerian state crisis. In a situation where crude oil was first exported in 1956 (Simpson 2000), well before the country's independence, imperialism continues because members of the capitalist class constituted a "ruling class," and through their political representatives, controlled the state—its dangerous effects notwithstanding.

Furthermore, the contemporary criminogenic situation arising from the Nigerian state crisis is also linked to the negative effects of wars. During the Cold War, Africa became an ideological and strategic battleground where "trusted allies" received foreign assistance regardless of their record on governance and development (Ali et al. 2000). For instance, Nigeria aligned with the West, yet state power was effectively personalized, and nascent ethnic conflict emerged from the failure of governments in the subregion to manage quarrels and conflicts effectively and to distribute national resources equitably. Conflicts impose enormous costs, including crime. The Biafra Civil War (1967–1970) resulted in between one and three million casualties, economic disaster, the marginalization of Igbo people, and alienation from the institutions of governance (Achebe 2012).

Many Nigerian cocaine traffickers point to the negative effects of the war as what drove them into the illicit trade. Explaining the principal causes of quarrel and war, Thomas Hobbes in *The Leviathan* (1968), Ch. XIII para. 6–7, noted that war primarily arises not because material resources are scarce, nor because humans ruthlessly seek survival before all else, nor because we are selfish, competitive, or aggressive brutes, but because we are fragile, fearful, impressionable, and psychologically prickly creatures susceptible to ideological manipulations, whose anger can become irrationally inflamed by even trivial slights to our glory. The primary source of war, he argues, is

disagreement because we read into it the most inflammatory signs of contempt (Hobbes 1968; Abizadeh 211).

Contrary to popular belief, Africa's conflicts do not stem from ethnic
diversity. Rather, conflicts are driven by poverty, underdevelopment, and
lack of economic diversification, as well as by political systems that mar-
ginalize large parts of the population. Civil war lowers per capita gross
domestic product (GDP) by 2.2 percentage points a year; above all, dynamic
sectors that use or supply capital and transact—manufacturing, construction,
transport, distribution, finance—suffer disproportionate losses (Collier et al.
2001). Countries recuperating from civil war could experience high levels of
crime as its aftereffects, as the Nigerian state crisis evidenced. Because civil
wars are directed largely at the civilian population, they rupture the fabric of
society and its institutions.

Research points to civil war's intergenerational impact on crimes, including drug abuse and the use by ex-combatants of the skills of war in criminal
activity. The relationship between Boko Haram's campaign of terrorism and
drug trafficking is further evidence of this correlation. The 2013 report from
Inter-University Centre for Terrorism Studies in the United States confirms
that Boko Haram and Ansaru are funded by drug cartels in Latin America
through their activities as illicit drug trafficking, kidnapping, and piracy
(Onuoha and Ezirim 2013).

In all, the undermining of the Nigerian state's foundation and the effects of
war have enhanced the contemporary criminogenic environment in Nigeria.

2.3 UNDERSTANDING CRIME:
"SOFT STATE/WEAK STATE"

Postindependence Nigeria typifies a *soft state* and *weak state*, as it was
besieged by military rule, dictatorships, corruption, and mismanagement
from the mid-1970s to 1990s. A soft state is characterized by "deficiencies or
willful neglect of rules and directives by public officials and civil servants,
and the collusion of government officials and top civil servants with powerful
individuals and groups whose conduct they are supposed to regulate" (Gould
and Amaro-Reyes 1983, 18). Where the patrimonial state is based on patron-
client ties, in the soft state Nigeria, national interests were subordinated to the
interest of politicians and their supporters who viewed public office as private
property. Furthermore, the soft state relies on an overcentralized government
that undermines local initiatives. Nigeria has a long history of economic
mismanagement that costs the nation enormously. As Maynard (1992) stated,
"African governments have often exhibited a perplexing tendency to disregard basic economic principles" (6–7). In all, Nigeria shows resemblance to

a 'soft state' with its highly dependent economy, endemic corruption that hinders innovation, perpetuates corrupt attitudes, and prevents change.

Other trends in Nigeria reveal its links to a weak state. Nigeria is convulsed by internal violence and can no longer deliver positive political (public) goods to its citizenry. The government risks losing legitimacy, as the nature of the nation-state itself could become illegitimate in the eyes and minds of increasing number of disenchanted Nigerians. Rotberg (2003) noted that modern states focus and answer the concerns and demands of citizenries: They channel the interests of their people, often in furtherance of national goals and values. They buffer or manipulate external forces and influences, champion particular concerns of their adherents, and mediate between the constraints and challenges of the international arena and the dynamism of their own internal economic, political, and social realities (2).

Soft and weak states slide toward failure. It is a wake-up call for stakeholders in Nigeria to design methods to prevent failure, to revive the economy, and help in the rebuilding process. Newman (2007) noted that such states "should be primary focus for the prevention of instability, to avoid the emergence of 'black holes' within which fanatics can operate with impunity. Failed states can be seen as a strategic—and not only as a humanitarian—challenge" (464).

If a soft and weak state could be seen as one in which formal rules, laws, and procedures properly stated are applied arbitrarily and unscrupulously, rather than in a coherent and fair way, then Nigeria should be included. This has proved disastrous from an economic and institution-building point of view, as evidenced in the country between the 1980s and 1990s. Such institutional decay helped make way for criminal networks to find safe haven and to develop an illicit economy in the country that became a transit-transaction hub for drug trafficking. There is barely punitive justice for offenders amid elites and their cronies regardless of the gravity of the offense; only the powerless in the society suffers.

Institutional flaws and cultural facets of its citizenry have contributed to soft and weak state Nigeria and illegal drug trafficking. Myrdal's (1968) work, "Asia Drama," described the developing world as one where breaking rules and flouting laws are part of the cultural norm rather than the exception. People are confronted with soft and weak Nigeria that lack the capacity and/or will to perform core functions of statehood effectively. Government does not control its territories, borders, and institutions effectively. This work attributes the ongoing exploitation of West Africa by foreign drug cartels, as in Guinea Bissau, in collaboration with established local networks to a large extent as a result of relatively weak state capacity, weak drug control, low law enforcement capacity, and the ubiquity of corruption in the country which made it a soft target for drug trafficking organizations from many countries, including Columbia, Mexico, and Portugal.

While the activities of Nigerian international cocaine trafficking will be detailed in the chapters ahead, the root causes underscoring the criminogenic environment are what this chapter seeks to divulge. Nigeria is a soft and weak state because its operators have refused to implement underlined characteristics of a well-functioning state which includes the capacity to maintain nationwide peace, law, and order; secure individual equality before the law; and control on the arbitrary exercise of power; public sector financing of and provisions for key social, infrastructure, legal, and administrative services; sanctions against criminals regardless of their social and political status; and reinforce transparency and effective service delivery. All these peculiarities of Nigeria as a soft and weak state create an environment for deviant activities through the inability to implement transformative and inclusive governance.

2.3.1 Poverty

Poverty is a multidimensional phenomenon, both in cause and definition. It is complex and multifaceted with manifestations in the economic, political, social, environmental—indeed in all aspects of life. In recognition of this complexity, researchers have moved from a targeted focus on income indicators in the 1960s to the inclusion of nonmonetary indicators of poverty in the 1990s and beyond. Poverty, rising inequality, and exclusion threaten global well-being (UN 2020). Poverty is linked to the concept of social exclusion as an emerging phenomenon in both developed and developing contexts. Researchers showed how the well-being of children is affected by indices of poverty (Main and Bradshaw 2016). The existence of new poverty in even the most developed societies, as in the European community, was discussed by Room (2016). In Africa and Nigeria in particular, poverty remains a key topic of discourse. Poverty has been related to social gender issues (Onwuameze 2013), protection (Barrientos and Hulme 2008), climate vulnerability, and health challenges (Danaan 2018).

During the World Summit on Social Development in Copenhagen in 1995, 117 countries adopted a declaration defining absolute poverty as a condition "characterized by severe deprivation of basic human needs including food, safe drinking water, sanitation facilities, health, shelter, education, and information" (UN 1996). It depends on income, access to services, and participation in decision-making as well as in civil, social, and cultural life. It occurs in all countries: as mass poverty in many developing countries, pockets of poverty amid wealth in developed countries, sudden poverty as a result of disaster or conflict, the poverty of low-wage workers, and the utter destitution of people who fall outside family support systems, social institutions and safety nets (UN 1996, 38; UNDP 1977).

In Nigeria, widespread poverty is a reality. Nigeria has become the poverty capital of the world (World Bank 2019a, 33). The National Bureau of Statistics report, "2019 Poverty and Inequality in Nigeria," highlights that 40% of the total population, roughly 83 million people, live below the country's poverty line of N137,430 (USD381.75) per year (World Bank 2020).

It is a phenomenon that includes a lack of basic amenities experienced all over the country. Underpinning Nigeria's abject poverty is the disgraceful performance of poverty alleviation initiatives—rife with poor design and implementation, policy inconsistencies and discontinuity, and poor funding. High population growth, unemployment, an undiversified economy, income inequality, and laziness exacerbate the problem further. Poverty in Nigeria is perpetuated by environmental calamities, marginalization of women, as well as contemporary international process.

Poverty is also embedded in Nigeria because widespread corruption became entrenched as a normal social practice, as we shall see later. Destabilizations and social tensions stemming from cultural and internal political fragmentation, religious and ethnic conflicts, as well as racial divisions have contributed to the perpetuation of poverty. The lack of employment opportunities constitutes a principal factor of poverty because if jobs become scarce, poverty rates increase as people cannot make ends meet. This is aggravated by a low level of education, as higher education often correlates to higher income.

Moreover, the importance of family planning as a means of reducing poverty is often neglected. In effect, if one has too many children, it becomes harder to afford education, feed, and provide for all. According to the NBS Demographic Statistic Bulletin (2018, 8), Nigeria's current population is about 193.3 million. The United Nations Economic Commission for Africa (UNECA 2017) highlighted that Nigeria had an estimated 182.2 million inhabitants in 2015 with almost 70% of the populace aged below 30. The population was young and urbanizing fast, and was expected to reach about 392 million in 2050, becoming the world's fourth most populous country.

Yet, enormous obstacles exist to lowering Nigerian birth rates. Fertility surveys suggest that the average Nigerian woman would like to have about five to six children during her reproductive lifetime (NBS 2015). This is because the preference for large families runs deep in the culture, to the extent that the celebration of fertility is ingrained even in daily greetings. Nigerian parents enjoy being surrounded by an admiring crowd of family and children. They are their happiness, wealth, and power. Furthermore, Nigerians admire everything big: individuals, families, villages, towns, political groups, and even religions all want to be numerous. In addition, more than half of Nigeria's people adhere to orthodox Islam, and a substantial portion of the rest are Christians, meaning that the majority of Nigerians also reject Western birth control methods on moral grounds.

In popular discussions, opposition to Western birth control programs spanned the religious spectrum. In general, family planning programs have been viewed suspiciously by Nigerians. Population programs are stigmatized as a form of foreign intervention, an imperialist plot to keep Africa down, and are reasons why politicians, civil servants, and religion activists all feel that the programs may run counter to the basic spiritual beliefs and emotions of the African society.

However, notwithstanding the fact that population control would offend the "spiritual beliefs and emotions" of the Nigerian people, regardless of the obvious conflict with the personal wishes of the country's women, and despite widespread political and moral objections that hinder Western-dictated population policy, new norms of gender relations are key to promoting contraceptive use and smaller families. Nigeria has very high rates of fertility and low use of modern contraceptive methods. Izugbara et al. (2010) found in researching "Poor Spousal Contraceptive Communication" that the total fertility or the number of children each woman has on average and contraceptive use rates or the percentage of respondents who use it in northern Nigeria stand at 6.5 and 6.4, respectively, contrasting sharply with rates of 4.3 and 23.7 in southern Nigeria (219). They concluded that more awareness of spousal contraceptive communication and support for women's access to contraception will improve the uptake of family planning in Nigeria.

In Nigeria, severe poverty is an actuality. Poor people in Nigeria face health issues due to the lack of basic health amenities and competent medical practitioners. Most children do not have the opportunity to be immunized, and this leads to certain physical defects in some children. Because all that could go wrong has gone wrong in Nigeria, the distinction between the causes and effects of poverty is fuzzy. Child malnourishment is widespread, with one-quarter of children under five classified as malnourished in 2014 (UNECA 2017). The masses lack opportunities, empowerment, and security. The window of opportunity remains closed to the poor, and this makes them practically "inactive" in the society. As the population increases, the consequences of overall poverty limit their empowerment and choice in almost everything. People's lack of security makes them vulnerable to diseases, violence, and deviant activities, including drug trafficking.

High poverty rates intertwine with high population growth, inadequate availability of basic public goods, and unsuccessfully implemented family planning programs. There is a need to harness Nigeria's burgeoning youth population to boost economic development and reduce widespread poverty. Improvements in health care remain a necessity to encourage and to better enable parents to plan for smaller families. There is a need for increased educational attainment, especially among women, who are the managers of families.

2.3.2 Limited Educational Opportunities

From a global perspective, economic and social development is increasingly driven by the advancement and application of knowledge. Education in general and higher education in particular are fundamental to the construction of a knowledge economy and society. However, accomplishing this responsibility is frequently thwarted by long-standing problems of finance, efficiency, quality, and governance in Nigeria. The Nigerian government's education philosophy aims at using education as a tool to build a democratic and self-reliant nation full of opportunities for all citizens (National Policy on Education [NPE] 2013).

Notwithstanding that development of universal primary education dates back to the final decade of the colonial era, the practice of indirect rule then resulted in a regional imbalance in education that persisted after independence in Nigeria. While the Yorubas and the Igbos, who are largely Christians, accepted education during the missionary movement of the middle and late nineteenth century, the Hausa/Fulani in the northern region, who are mostly Muslim, have resisted Western education since the Sokoto caliphate fell under British rule in 1903 (Marchal 2012, 3). The mentality of resistance to Western education is borne out in enrollment numbers; for example, of 944 students enrolled at University College in Ibadan in 1959, Yoruba students numbered 408, Ibo 333, Fulani six, and Hausa only three (Bevan et al. 1999, 21). The mentality against Western education has been carried forward now by Boko Haram that forced children—girls in particular—to abandon school in northern Nigeria.

This made reforms in education a necessity and desirable for the advancement of the country. Government implementation of universal primary education sparked an educational revolution. For instance, enrollment of pupils in primary education increased from about three million in 1970 to approximately 20 million in 2010 (Onwuameze 2013). Notwithstanding, the progress in the quantity of enrollment has not significantly curtailed disadvantages.

Education was made 'free,' but the quality of education provided was not guaranteed. Lapses in management, educational demand/supply gaps, gender discrimination, and quota systems of admission degraded educational standards. As a result, nearly 75% of college applicants in Nigeria fail to get in every year. For instance, between 2010 and 2015, of the 10 million applicants that sought entry into Nigerian tertiary institutions that had the capacity to carry about 600,000 students, only 26% gained admission (Kazeem 2017). Access to university education has become vital in Nigeria as a result of the role university education plays in the development of the individual and the nation. But the high rate of demand for university education has overstretched the limited resources available, thereby affecting the quality of programs in the universities.

Nigeria's pattern of low education funding is one critical challenge to achieving a knowledge society. According to World Bank's (2013) analysis, total public spending on education by all levels was 1.7% of GDP. As a share of total public spending, it increased marginally from 10.2 to 12.5% over 2009–2013. Nigeria's spending on education is thus lower than the Sub-Saharan Africa (SSA) average of 4.6% of GDP and 16% of total public spending (World Bank 2019a, 19). Smaller African countries are far ahead of Nigeria in the funding of education, "Budgetary allocation of countries like Uganda, 4th (27.0%), Botswana, 10th (20.0%), Lesotho, 14th (17.0%) and Burkina Faso, 15th (16.8%) respectively, are higher than Nigeria's 20th (8.4%) position in world ranking of education funding" (Asiyai 2015, 62). In its 2016 budget, education received N369.6 billion, representing about 6.01% of the budget (Obia 2016). Nigerian educational institutions would be inadequately funded from such paltry budgets. Quality education is an asset, and this has been overlooked due to poor funding. As a result, there is poor human capital in the country. A 2013 Service Delivery Indicator survey in four Nigerian states found that only one-third of grade four pupils had acquired minimum numeracy and literacy skills. Inadequate learning has contributed to Nigeria's low rank on the Human Capital Index (HCI) of 0.34, placing the country at 152 out of 157. Nigeria's HCI places the country lower than the average for SSA, its region, and for lower-middle-income countries, its peers (World Bank 2019a). Nigeria should realize that educational institutions are not just institutions; they are the foundation of the modern society. They are the pillars of innovations, creativity, inventions, highest level of training and knowledge acquisition, strategies, and control.

Another critical challenge to achieving a knowledge society is the Quota System of Admission (QSA) that the government implemented to curtail the widening gap between north and south in education development of tertiary institutions (Anyanwu 2010; Folarin et al. 2014). QSA would enhance national unity by enabling students to interact and learn together in federally funded tertiary institutions. In practice, it has been applied to discriminate against prospective university candidates based on their state of origin. Lower scoring students from particular states of origins are offered university admission to the detriment of other candidates with higher scores just because they happen to come from different states. In this view, the QSA consciously enthrones irrationality and injustice. Above all, it perpetuates mediocrity in Nigeria since well-deserving candidates are robbed of opportunity and the country is robbed of a real chance for development.

Deficient quality education is reflected in the low ranking of Nigerian universities. In 2018, only one of Nigeria's universities was listed among the top 1,000 in *The World University Rankings*: The University of Ibadan (UI) ranked 801. Universities from other African nations such as Uganda, Ghana, and SA are ranked higher. Universities were judged based on performance indicators across all of their core missions: teaching, research, citations, international outlook, and knowledge transfer. Within Africa, five of Nigeria's top universities were among Africa's lowest ranked, including 41st and 43rd (Abubakar 2017).

Low performance by Nigerian universities can be attributed in part to mismanagement by university authorities and course content that does not reflect marketable trends in society. Because research and the appointment of lecturers and professionals are politicized, inadequacies undermine the goals set out in the NPE. The result is lapses in admission, recurrent strikes, failing academic programs, deficient development of intellectual independence and sustained high-quality standards needed to create a competitive academic, and entrepreneurial environment. Quality education would sharpen the minds of the individual and help transform the Nigerian society economically, socially, and politically.

Nigerians are disenchanted as they see knowledge and its institutions in the country deteriorate at all levels. For one university vice chancellor in Nigeria, the low level of internet availability in the Nigerian university system caused their poor ranking among institutions of higher learning in the world (Abubakar 2017). However, that interpretation is too simplistic. Nigerian universities do not lack the required facilities; the lack is grounded in a culture of non-transparency, non-accountability, corruption, and mismanagement. This resulted in the deterioration of facilities that has had a negative impact on the quality of teaching, learning, and carrying capacity.

Connectedly many students are excluded from the benefits of the digital world. Nigeria lacks digital skills, ranking 121st out of 139 countries in the Global Competitiveness Report's assessment. The World Bank (2019a) noted Nigeria does not participate in international or regional student assessments, after completing grade four only 66% of public school students can read at least one of three words and only 78% can add single digits; Nigeria trails Ghana, Kenya, and Senegal in the quality of its math and science education. Such shortages of foundational skills will make it difficult for Nigeria to heighten digital literacy and will lower the chances it can take advantage of the opportunities the digital economy offers (30).

Nigeria's history of corruption affects its tertiary institutions of learning. The University System Study 2013 report identified corruption and fraud as a major jeopardizing feature. Bribe payers in Nigeria spend an eighth of their salary on bribes. This data stems from the Nigerian Corruption Survey 2017 published by the National Bureau for Statistics. The survey revealed an overwhelming percentage of Nigerians will accept a bribe when offered or pay a bribe when demanded. Nine out of every ten bribes paid to public officials in Nigeria are paid in cash, "estimated in the 12 months at about N400 billion, the equivalent of $4.6 billion in purchasing power parity," a sum equivalent to 39% of the combined federal and state education budgets in 2016 (UNODC 2017b, 5; Uncova 2017). Corruption manifests in cases of misappropriation and misapplication of money meant for buildings, libraries, and laboratories. Embezzlement of annual funds results in eyesores of unfinished projects in universities: talents are underdeveloped or killed, and values of young people distorted. Blurred lines exist between right and wrong, legal and illicit, good and evil. Nigerians are made to tolerate the theft of billions of naira by authorities in universities across Nigeria (see Tyessi 2017; Lawal 2018).

There is a relationship between corruption and the poor state of academic standards. Corruption is a crisis of ethical standards that has permeated every aspect of academia—students, lecturers, nonteaching staff, and the administration of the institutions (see Adebayo 2018; Amini-Philips and Ogbuagwu 2017). Syndicated plagiarism by students and staff entails admission racketeering, examination malpractice, falsification of academic records, certificate scandals, and lack of commitment to work by lecturers. What is more, allegations of corruption are neither thoroughly investigated nor are the culprits often punished. In one incident, a Nigerian university dismissed a professor who was caught on tape allegedly demanding sex from a female student in exchange for upgrading her marks (Busari and Adebayo 2018). In all, there was no criminal prosecution. He only lost his job. Unfair allocation of grades, contract inflation, or employment of unqualified staff is stripping educational facilities and destroying the future of Nigeria (see Amini-Philips and Ogbuagwu 2017).

Inadequate educational opportunities intertwined with other aggravating push and pull features to perpetuate directly and indirectly crimes including drug trafficking. In spite of the progress made so far, educational outcomes remain meager in Nigeria. It is a crisis of maladjustment between educational systems and their Nigerian context.

2.3.3 "Sorting" It Out: "Half-Baked" Graduates

Researchers published that many Nigerians, as students of tertiary institutions, are convinced that poverty, endemic corruption, and indiscipline have led to the proliferation of cultism and exacerbated other crimes in most Nigerian institutions of higher learning (Chukwu and Lato 2016; Adedeji et al. 2016).

These features contribute to lower lecture attendance among students because they could bribe professors for passing grades. Popularly known as "sorting," dishonest students bribe their way to unmerited scores and "obtain good grades" in examinations (see Chukwu and Lato 2016). Most of the time, such students either would have failed the courses involved or may not have written the examination in the first place. Sorting threatens the standard of education in Nigerian universities and demoralizes hardworking students who are compelled to also "sort" despite their personal efforts. In addition to monetary sorting, some lecturers take advantage to exploit students with demands for sex in return for high grades (see Adedeji et al. 2016). Inadequate learning maintains examination malpractices and bribery of dishonest lecturers. Inadequate learning also has serious human capital implications as it often leads to the production of "half-baked or unbaked" graduates. Such graduates have low self-esteem as they lack the intellectual proficiency required to thrive in the twenty-first century job market and workplace.

Inadequate learning also stems from the high cost of education in Nigeria that leads many who cannot afford it to drop out. Nigeria now has the highest number of out-of-school children globally. A recent survey conducted by United Nations International Children's Emergency Fund estimated that the population of out-of-school children in Nigeria has risen from 10.5 million to 13.2 million, the highest in the world, due to instability in the country (*Voice of America* 2018). Research found that school dropouts are one of the most serious problems for Nigeria's educational system since independence (see Adesina et al. 1983).

In his research, Ajaja (2012, 148) noted that the high rate of insecurity in the country is linked to youths who dropped out of school. They were found to have perpetuated over 85% of the criminal activities in Nigeria. This claim raises eyebrows as crime is not limited to only school dropouts. For instance, two young students of Olabisi Onabanjo University were kidnapped and murdered in a bush on May 28, 2018. The murderers were two university dropouts and members of the cult group Black Axe Confraternity (Also known as, aka, "AIYE"). After their arrest, 29-year-old Murtala Babatunde and his 18-year-old friend, Taiwo Razaq, confessed to committing the crime (Omonobi 2018).

These crimes are symptoms of a wider cancer eating up Nigeria. Grinding poverty, rapid population growth, inadequate investment in education, and mismanagement are exacerbated by corruption. It has been estimated that close to USD400 billion was misappropriated from Nigeria's public accounts from 1960 to 1999, as stated by UNODC's Antonio Maria Costa (*PM News* 2015). Illicit financial flows from the country between 2005 and 2014 are estimated to have totaled some USD182 billion (Hoffmann and Patel 2017). This stolen wealth represents the investment gap in vital infrastructure and alleviation of poverty in Nigeria, including upgrades to the education system.

When education was made free in Nigeria, it was meant to train students into the needed professionals in a fast-changing world. Instead, disappointments frustrate many into "shock troops" of deviant activities who easily connect with cultism, committing heinous crimes and bolstering international cocaine hoppers. Many interviewees claimed that Nigeria had failed them because Nigerian elites' self-centeredness has deprived others the opportunity to pursue quality education, legitimate job markets, and a respectable way for achieving self-actualization.

2.3.4 Insufficient Governance

As mentioned previously, the legacy of a soft or weak state includes insufficient governance, low law observation, and futile crime control. Achebe (2012) writes that the Nigerian people argued that the problem with Nigeria is the lack of good governance—namely, a failure of leadership. Since Nigeria won its independence, democracy and leadership have not fared well in terms of governance.

Agozino (2003) used the phrase "executive lawlessness" to describe the widespread practice of habitual lawbreaking by people in office. He emphasized that politics of law and order are mainly rhetorical given the widespread disregard for the law by those who are empowered to uphold it in many countries. The democratic crisis in Africa is mainly the crisis of hegemony where the ruling ethnic-gender classes have consistently ruled by force and fear rather than consent—contrary to the "authoritarian populism" that Hall (1988) identified as a model of the law and order state in Britain under Margret Thatcher or the similar American model of the administration under President Trump. Nigeria in particular exalts law and order without an equal emphasis on social justice, which has inevitably resulted in great injustice and abject poverty. The African experience is embedded in colonial and neocolonial authoritarianism that shuns the populism of Thatcherism by executives breaking the law itself. In other words, because executive lawlessness went largely unchecked, allowing corruption to continue, "hegemonic groups will continue to be authoritarian rather than democratic in their exercise of power" (see Agozino 2003, 113–114).

Consequently, myriads of socioeconomic and political issues are the order of the day. There has been an avalanche of problems surrounding ethnicity, power struggles, and citizenship issues. In addition, these were exacerbated by weak and dysfunctional institutions, sectarian violence, entrenched corruption, Boko Haram terrorism, drug trafficking, and chronic poverty. This is due to the country's legacy of weak governance and economic mismanagement. The government is rich, but the majority of people are poor, living under the poverty level, and crime is high because of failure in governance, causing the Nigerian state crisis. How much the country has earned from the production and exportation of crude oil remains unknown. Unofficial figures from the Standard Bank estimate that Nigeria made six trillion USD in oil revenue over the last 50 years (see Greenwood 2010). The World Bank averred that political and economic liberalization in the late 1980s and 1990s led to the adoption of structural adjustment policies opening up markets, encouraging deregulation and private initiative, and reducing state economic intervention (Ali et al. 2000).

Cooper pointed out in his article, "The new liberal imperialism" (2002), that postmodern imperialism could take the form of voluntary imperialism of the global economy, usually operated by international, multilateral conglomerates through financial institutions such as the International Monetary Fund (IMF) and the World Bank. These organizations offer help to governments longing to reintegrate back into the global economy with the promise of investment and prosperity. Financial institutions make policy demands that in their view address the political and economic failures that have contributed to the original need for assistance. If states wish to benefit, they must open themselves up to the interference of international organizations and foreign states just as, for different reasons, the Western world has opened itself up. Often because of mismanagement, the negative effects of such interference in underdeveloped nations lead to further exploitation and economic impoverishment of the less connected.

In all, economic mismanagement, a failed structural adjustment program, and continuous political contestation marked the decline of the Nigerian state. For instance, in the period from 1970 to 1997, while countries like Benin, Burkina Faso, Gabon, the Gambia, and Mali recorded increases in their GDP, Nigeria, Senegal, Togo, Ivory Coast, Ghana, and Sierra Leone experienced negative economic growth (Ali et al. 2000). Nigeria plunged in a low-level equilibrium of poor institutional capability and ineffective economic transformation that led to an economy of plunder or of captured state, as shall be discussed ahead. Weak institutions and poor governance resulted in an undiversified economy, the exclusion of a majority of Nigerians, and paucity, as wealth was distributed quickly and unevenly among political, military, and economic elites.

2.3.5 Undiversified Economy

The soft state and lack of good governance are reflected in the undiversified economy defined by high poverty rates and underdevelopment and crimes through heightened rates of unemployment, urbanization, and inequality. A principal reason for the undiversified economy is Nigeria's heavy dependence on oil for export receipts and fiscal revenue. The Nigerian economy was hit hard by the decline in oil prices that began in 2014. Now oil price collapse and ongoing coronavirus pandemic have exacerbated threats of poverty and instability in the country. Reliant on oil sales for her economic survival implies that Nigeria could lose billions of U.S. dollars as a result of the oil prices drop. This could plunge the country into another recession within six years. In 2015, oil accounted for over 90% of exports, 70% of government revenues, and less than 13% of overall GDP (IMF 2017, 5). The revenue it generates when prices are high could cause "Dutch-Diseases" that Brahmbhatt et al. defined as a phenomenon reflecting changes in the structure of production in the wake of a favorable shock (such as a large natural resource discovery or a rise in the international price of an exportable commodity). "Where the natural resources discovered are oil or minerals, a contraction or stagnation of manufacturing and agriculture could accompany the positive effects of the shock, according to the theory" (Brahmbhatt et al. 2010, 1).

As one of its major effects, the extensive influxes of money generated from oil proceeds encourage reckless spending. Soaring oil revenue raises exchange rates that in turn promote an adverse balance of payment as the cost of imports rises in Nigeria. Government restrictions on access to dollars for importers had the opposite effect by threatening food supplies and driving up prices. Nigeria relies on imports to meet its national requirements for grains, especially wheat, corn, and rice. Bloomberg (2020), in the article "Nigerian Inflation Rate Rises," noted that consumer prices surged 13.7% in September from a year earlier; food costs rose 16.7% from a year earlier, 1.9% in the previous month. Goldman Sachs expects Nigeria's inflation to accelerate in coming months, peaking close to 18% year-on-year in the second quarter of 2021, and the IMF expects Nigeria's economy to shrink 4.3% (Olurounbi 2020). Among the causes of this dire situation are the coronavirus crisis and currency devaluations. Boko Haram insurgencies have also disrupted domestic supply chains. Rising food inflation and growing unemployment increase pressure on food security in Nigeria, according to the United States Department of Agriculture (Nzeka 2020).

In all, Nigeria's dependence on oil has fostered unemployment, inequality, and underdevelopment in Nigeria by destroying incentives to invest in nonoil sectors, and it has disrupted competitiveness of important sectors like agriculture, research, and manufacturing. Indeed, resource-poor countries have outperformed the resource-rich countries compared by a considerable margin. Ross (2001, 2012) explains that countries rich in natural resources, especially oil, grew slower than those without. This could be the case looking at countries like Congo, Colombia, Venezuela, Iraq, Yemen, and Libya, for instance, where there is lack of rule of law and good governance. In contrast, oil is a blessing to states with rule of law such as the United States, Norway, Canada, England, and Dubai.

Oil export dependency for development does not work for Nigeria. The economic effects of this dependency evoke the concept of oil states being "rentier states" (Ross 2001, 329). Ross asserts that states reliant on external rent, like oil, develop a different bond between government and their citizenry from those that rely primarily on taxation. Such states are less likely to be democratic than those that are tax reliant. In the oil-rich rentier Nigeria, the society is not compact. Adversarial and primordial sentiments reign. Government uses low tax rates and patronage to relieve pressures for greater accountability. Lack of multiple and active economic actors leads to social and political stagnation that hinders sustainable development (Ross 2012).

All too often, the economic benefits accrue to a small business or government elite and agents of multinational companies, while an array of burdens such as expropriation of land, disruption of traditional ways of life, and environmental devastation are imposed on local communities. Self-interested political elites collaborate with some multinational companies to construct weak environmental regulations, inefficient implementation of those regulations, control mechanism and sanctions against offenders, as experienced in Niger Delta of Nigeria. These conditions allow companies to operate with disregard for the affected communities and to use destructive processes, toxic substance, and pollutants that are banned or severely restricted in developed countries. Nigeria is an example. All these negative variables that accompanied the exploitation of crude oil cumulatively represent 'Dutch Disease,' implying as outlined in the literature of development economics, the impediments of oil revenue to economic growth and development of oil-dependent Nigeria. The huge financial proceeds resulting from oil tend to foster overzealous and irresponsible spending as evidence in the country.

In Nigeria, the undiversified economy has been a source of conflict, war, and international drug trafficking, as evidenced by Niger Delta or Boko Haram terrorist insurgences, and the dearth of vital sectors that could generate jobs and development.

2.3.6 Frustrated Unemployed

Another risk factor fostering deviant activity is the high rate of unemployment in Nigeria where in 2018 an estimated 21 million were unemployed but actively looking for a job (World Bank Group 2019, 8). Most affected are the youth and women. In the same period, about 37% of 15- to 24-year-olds were unemployed. About 19.3 million youths were either unemployed or underemployed in the fourth quarter of 2016 (National Bureau of Statistics [NBS] 2018b). Despite high and sustained rates of growth in the past decade, unemployment in Nigeria rose. This consisted of also newly qualified graduates, new entrants into the economically active population actively seeking work.

One reason for this is the failure to develop the agricultural sector, which engages about 60% of Nigeria's labor force and generated in 2016 about 26%

of GDP (NBS 2017). Prior to the discovery of oil in Nigeria, the agricultural sector was the mainstay of Nigeria's economy, contributing about 95% to the foreign exchange earnings and approximately 56% to GDP (World Bank 2013). Neglecting Nigeria's promising, primarily agrarian economy, displaced in favor of the oil industry, had its repercussions. Most affected are people under 30 who constitute the majority of the population. As discussed in chapter 1, reinvesting the billions spent on a futile, foreign-imposed war on cannabis could boost employment, provide sustainable income, and improve the general standard of living, and generate revenue for government.

A youthful population is a vital asset for innovation and creativity in society. However, these characteristics become a social risk factor when not properly harnessed.

For instance, it propels migration of youths to cities in search of better jobs and greener pasture, given rural poverty was about 73.2% in 2010 (NBS 2017). Unplanned urbanization resulted in congestion, overcrowding, poor living conditions, and lack of basic amenities. Desperate young males were drawn into criminal activities beyond drug distribution. There are many examples in Nigerian media, including the 69 suspected kidnappers and armed robbers of a local criminal gang called "Shila boys" whom police arrested in Adamawa State. Members confessed to kidnapping two businessmen and collecting N1 million as ransom (*Premium Times* 2020).

Accelerated urbanization has the potential to disrupt traditional customs and regulations of behavior that oversee justice, regulate people's conduct, and preside over social relations in former communities. It could disperse the bonds amid people and weakens social organizations, unveiling conditions for deviancy. The withdrawal of the Nigerian state and informal forms of authority from urban areas result inevitably in alternative forms of power and control. This lowers the barriers to deviancy and leaves hopeless youth seeking fellowship, community, and identity through gang behavior and through connection with Nigerian international cocaine traffickers.

In Nigeria, there is no viable private sector and that undermines youth employment. The frustration with city life is heightened because the industrial and service sectors in the country could absorb only a small fraction of the labor force. On the one hand, the Nigerian economy is described as vibrant because its economy has grown recently at about 6–7.5% per annum, but unemployed youths do not enjoy the benefits of that growth. Likewise, Nigeria lacks an empowered entrepreneurial middle class with the knowledge and skill to establish small- and medium-scale companies that would create more jobs and foster growth. Now Nigeria's non-inclusive growth has not served to substantially reduce poverty or inequality, but it has served to produce the Nigerian state crisis, instability, crime, and the inability to attract investors. The ability to attract investors could be enhanced by improving factors like national power supply, infrastructure, legislative reforms, property registration systems, trade policies, regulatory environments, the judicial system, security, and corruption.

An international survey indicated that major factors hindering doing business in Nigeria include access to financing, corruption, inadequate infrastructure, policy instability, and crimes (World Bank 2013). It is in the very nature of the capitalist mode of production to overwork some workers while keeping the rest as a reserve army of unemployed paupers, as averred by Marx (1848) A reserve army of surplus labor (underemployed and unemployed) that creates downward pressure on wages because workers fight among themselves for scarce jobs at lower and lower wages. On the one hand, a quick glimpse portrays unemployment as futile because the jobless do not increase profits. On the other hand, it remains profitable within the global capitalist system through lowing of wages and costs.

The few available jobs for the battalion of youth job seekers are politicized. Unless the job seeker is connected to a political godfather, he may not get a job in Nigeria. This evokes that capitalism has given rise to and perpetuated segmented labor markets, "Dual Labor Market." Reich, Gordon, and Edwards (1973) defined it as the historical process whereby political economic forces encourage the division of the labor market into separate submarkets, or segments, distinguished by different labor market characteristics and behavioral rules (359). For example, research by University of Chicago and Notre Dame economists found the number of Americans living in poverty rose by about six million, and the poverty rate jumped from 9.3% in June to 11.1% in September 2020. Those most affected are black people and people without a college education. Meanwhile, "Wall Street Profits Surge as Poverty Rises" reported the *New Yorker* in October 2020. Morgan Stanley announced it reaped USD2.7 billion in profits from July to September, a rise of 25% compared to the year before. Goldman Sachs reported quarterly profits of USD3.62 billion, virtually double what the firm earned in the same quarter in 2019 (Cassidy 2020).

On the one hand, there is a primary sector in which employment was stable, where pay was good, and where there were strong unions. On the other, a secondary sector exists in which employment was unstable, where pay tended to be low, prospects of promotion poor, and unions of small importance (Bosanquet and Doeringer 1973; ILO 2016). Among the most affected are the young people in the country.

2.3.7 Youths, Poverty, and Crime

High poverty rates in Nigeria have caused many hopeless and chanceless individuals to commit crimes, including kidnapping, oil theft, terrorism, stealing, human trafficking, and illicit drug trafficking in their struggle against exploitation, marginalization, and uprisings in Nigeria's Niger Delta. The huge wealth that is generated in the Delta contrasts sharply with the ingrained poverty of most of its people. Extreme wealth of the elite contrasted with desperate poverty of the majority is one key reason fueling the grievances of the Movement for the Emancipation of the Niger Delta (MEND).

Despite the overbearing religious camouflage of Boko Haram's mission, there is an almost ignored underlying causal factor—poverty. It is certainly not a coincidence that the regions of the country where militant Islam has been most prominent are also the poorest. It is a direct response to insecurities about their spiritual and socioeconomic future (Forest 2012). Former U.S. secretary of state, John Kerry, pointed out that the challenge in confronting Boko Haram lies in fighting poverty (Goodenough 2014).

Nigeria is a nation of superlatives: richest country in Africa, the biggest oil producer, fastest growing economy, and yet it has failed to lift majority of its citizenry out of crushing poverty. However, poverty in terms of basic human needs only as discussed previously does not necessarily cause criminal behavior. Most people who become poor, even quite suddenly or have recurrent experiences of living in poverty, never engage in criminal activity. A minority of people who are known to them and surround them in their everyday lives nevertheless often commit crime. Diaspora Nigerians are no exception. For example, when I was pursuing my undergraduate studies in Italy, some of my fellow students supplied highly demanded Nigerian cannabis to their Italian contacts and were convicted for international trafficking of cannabis from Nigeria to Italy. One of the persons convicted stated that his reason for engaging in drug trafficking was to raise money to pay for his studies in Italy because foreign students were not allowed to work, as in Malaysia currently, which will be discussed in chapter 7. But for others, deviant activities were a bridge too far. Crime is connected to their lives because they are more likely to be victimized by it and in these circumstances.

Establishing whether poverty has an impact on crime remains controversial, as links between poverty and crime can be elusive in the criminological literature. Some attribute it to a defective family structure or arrested personality adjustment. Others recall factors such as poor socialization process, economic conditions and inequality, environmental influence, or unforeseen life events, noted in "Poverty and Crime Review. Anti-Poverty Strategies for the UK" (see Webster and Kingston 2014, 5–7).

Poverty might be a factor, but it is not a sufficient reason or condition why an individual engages in criminal activity. Living in poverty on its own is unlikely to lead to engagement in criminality (Webster and Kingston 2014). Indeed, it must be noted that poverty as a factor in crime is not a cultural universal. Some religions regard poverty as given by God and "that which

God has given to you should not be dropped, but rather should be cherished" (Nigerian Islamic Society). Invariably among Muslim societies, crime is low not because of the draconian punishment, but on account of members persuaded to believing that with poverty on earth, their kingdom is in heaven. As Ebbe (2013) pointed out, northern Nigerian Muslims (over 49 million) alter poverty and begging as honor of grace. There poverty became a culture of the people. This implies that poverty as an elucidation of crime is relative to place and religious connection.

Crimes could result as a fault of the social system whose institutions do not work equally for all its members, noted Taylor (2009) and Webster and Kingston (2014). Several researchers have found a weak or nonexistent relationship between socioeconomic status and crime, for example, between parents' income and children's onset of offending (Wikström and Butterworth 2006). Some posited that little direct influence of poverty on crime could be true when more reliable self-report data is used (Dunaway et al. 2000). Nevertheless, other scholars have found a strong and direct relationship between socioeconomic status and offending, particularly in respect of the impact of childhood poverty and the effects of growing up poor on persistent youth offending (Braithwaite 1981; Hay and Forrest 2009). Webster and Kingston (2014) noted that a resurgence of recent studies has found the relationship between social class and offending to be strong. Studies on rising poverty in the 1980s and early 1990s highlighted that violent and property crime were associated with absolute and relative deprivation and economic inequality (Kawachi et al. 1999).

Mostly, crime is common in societies where large disparities exist between the standards of living of its members, as in Nigeria or in the United States. Reiman and Leighton (2017) emphasized known sources of crime to include poverty and inequality, prison and guns, and drug prohibition. With respect to crime and inequality, "the idea that structural inequality contributes to community-level variations in crime is uncontroversial" (Ousey and Lee 2013, 363). Researching the mechanism, scholars examined the economic policies on employment, public benefits, education, and taxes, showing that factors like distribution of income, wealth, and economic power shape these policies and the context within which individuals make choices.

A research review covering 214 studies on street crimes concluded that relatively strong indicators of "resources/economic deprivation theory" on crime were well supported, according to Pratt and Cullen (2005).

Yet, high levels of crime committed by the powerful—white collar and corporate crime—cannot be explained by poverty, wrote Reiman and Leighton (2017). This is exacerbated by systems of inequality because criminology largely ignores class. In analyzing poverty and white-collar crime links, John Briathwait (1992) posited that inequality worsens both crimes of poverty motivated by need and crimes of wealth motivated by greed. "Need" applies in an absolute sense to people lacking basic needs to survive. It also leads to crime based on expectations for a decent standard of living that includes fancy houses, cars, and holidaying. Financially disadvantaged people may not have the means to acquire such things legally, and still they are led to believe they should have access to them because of advertising and dramatization of bourgeois lifestyles. Violence can be generated by resource deprivation and the humiliation of the poor who are bombarded by images of the "American Dream" and messages highlighting that success is attainable for all (Briathwaits 1992; Reiman and Leighton 2017).

Increasing inequality implies that wealth is concentrated in the hands of those who can create "new forms of illegitimate opportunity" fraud included, and "the more capital the more the opportunities" (Briathwaits 1992, 85, 87).

The relationship between class, poverty, and offending is established through intervening events or experiences that are contingent on opportunity and motivation on the one hand, and structural factors such as family parenting, supervision, and organization, on the other. Developments in Nigeria show that these factors interacting together with high levels of poverty represent a risk for committing crime. Connectedly the country is ranked among lowest in the category of low human development nations: 152 out of 187 countries in 2015 (UNECA 2016). Hardly anything had changed for the masses over the preceding decade. Instead, things got worse as Nigeria's non-inclusive growth path frustrated many impoverished people. Most affected are the young people. Due to mismanagement, strong population growth, and migration from rural to urban areas, and despite high and sustained economic growth, unemployment persists in Nigeria. This is a situation that poses great danger to the Nigerian society in terms of crimes and social vices, as young people face insecurity crisis in all senses. Such a large population of unemployed, unengaged, angry, and unproductive youths in any society will constitute a menace and security risk because their lives appear hopeless and, yet, they are full of energy. Criminality and terrorism, which have further crippled the economic development of the country, are perpetrated by young people (Uwa et al. 2016).

These are social problems resulting from the disproportionate distribution of social resources, reflected by the persistent high-income inequality rate in the country; for instance, 38.7% in 1985, 46.5% in 1996, 58% in 2007, and now a prevalence of about 45% (Alabi 2014). Endemic poverty, deteriorated educational standards, and inequality in Nigeria are due to ill-use, misallocation, and misappropriation of resources. Inequality is said to affect social relationships especially in a situation in which while the income of the rich rises, the poor feel relatively more deprived. Such deprivation can lead to alienation and, subsequently, crime. Research shows that, on the one hand, an increase in income inequality has a significant effect of raising crime rates, while on the other hand, that GDP growth rate has a significant crime-reducing impact, indicating that the rate of growth and distribution of income jointly could determine the rate of poverty reduction (Fajnzylber et al. 2002; Bharadwaj 2014). Notwithstanding the BBC's media report (2014) of Nigeria's GDP for 2013 of USD509.9 billion, most Nigerians would not be better off tomorrow because of that announcement. It does not put more money in the bank or more food in their stomachs. It changes nothing.

While this matters for the World Bank and multinational companies, it does less for the ordinary Nigerians. It has failed to diversify the economy, and its snowballing effect is low productivity in the mainly subsistence agricultural sector and manufacturing. It has made Nigeria an import-dependent economy nation, with 63% of consumption expenditure directed to food, out of which more than 43% is imported. Furthermore, about 80% of government expenditures are recycled into foreign exchange, coupled with the excessively high domestic production costs partly resulting from erratic electricity and fuel supply, which have reduced industrial capacity utilization to less than 30% (Oduh 2012). Consequently, Nigeria's ineffectiveness in addressing the Nigerian state crisis has fostered instability, insecurity, and underdevelopment while perpetuating unemployment and inequality.

Unemployment could lead to crime as a result of the feeling of deprivation, rejection, and personal failure, which in turn could lead to mental stress, apathy, and illness factors that could pave way for criminal behavior. In other words, during economic recessions, crime tends to grow rapidly. Economic recessions result in greater unemployment, and this could drive people into criminal behavior. In their work, Masih and Masih (1996) summarized most of the literature on the relationship between unemployment and crime and stated that 33 studies found this relationship positive, and 19 negative or no relationship. Fajnzylber et al. (2002) found while applying panel data for 45 developed and developing countries from 1965 to 1995 that violent crime rates decline when economic growth improves.

Countless unemployed young people exist in several cities across Nigeria, participating in visible idleness. They congregate at bars and restaurants to drink, watch football matches, converse, and/or smoke marijuana for substantial parts of the day. Interviews with some members of Nigerian international cocaine traffickers revealed that such atmospheres are good places for recruiting drug mules, as we shall discuss in chapters ahead. Devoid of a legitimate means of livelihood, they grow up in a culture that fosters deviant activity. They survive by engaging in various activities such as petty trading, casual work, petty gambling, stealing, pickpocketing, prostitution, and touting. Some have become drunkards; others are on drugs such as marijuana and crack cocaine.

With a very weak economy and a high rate of unemployment, the poverty scourge has continued unabated. Youth poverty is a result of the high unemployment rate that is a consequence of the exclusion from viable economic activities. Nigeria has underdeveloped the youth population, and this abject neglect has led to hawking vandalized and adulterated petroleum products, "area boys" syndrome in Lagos, rabbles of militants in the Niger Delta, Boko Haram in Maiduguri, while the female youths resort to sex work and call girl activities. Some unemployed youths have upgraded to armed robbery, kidnapping for ransom, drug trafficking, internet fraud, and other forms of fraudulent activities. For Ucha (2010), the reservation wage they get from these activities is typically barely enough to take care of their basic necessities. On the contrary, crime is big business in Nigeria. Many have realized that it is an open enterprise, attractive to whoever has the means to join the chain. Being involved in the illicit drug business can be an alternative to the lack of formal employment.

In the Niger Delta, drugs are one of multiple interchangeable currencies along with stolen oil, weapons, and cash. This links a variety of criminal activities to the drug trade, ranging from kidnapping expatriate oil company employees for ransom to oil bunkering. Oil thefts—a long-time problem in the Niger Delta—persist despite government officials and international companies offering dire warnings about the effect on Nigeria's crude production. Just like most international cocaine traffickers did, several condemned armed robbers interviewed in varied prison facilities in Nigeria claimed poverty and unemployment as major factors. For instance, research by Odekunle at the Abeokuta, Agodi, and Kirikiri prisons in Nigeria highlighted that "the typical criminal is illiterate, unskilled and unemployed," underlining that between 86% and 89% of inmates were unemployed at the time of their criminal offense (Dambazau 2009). This remains an exaggeration because a crime is not limited to unskilled and unemployed, as Nigerians expressed it "Crimes committed by the elites are worse than those committed by armed robbers."

In all, poverty in terms of basic human needs only as discussed previously does not necessarily cause criminal behavior as various criminological perspectives such as positivists, sociological, psychological radical, and critical schools portray crime and its causes. Yet, in Nigeria, affluence represents a risk factor motivating deviant activates. First, many people place a high premium on economic affluence for everybody, regardless of the fact that a majority of people lack the basic educational and financial stand to succeed through legitimate means; second is the cultural influence that places emphasis on the extended family system in which the family pressure on the males of a community to succeed financially is very high and aggravates this situation.

The widespread mentality in Nigeria is the more successful someone becomes, the more recognition he gets by way of traditional and societal titles, while *how* the person made his or her wealth is not subject to inquiry. Government officials loot the public treasury without the slightest pricking of conscience and in many instances, such looters are hailed as successful and honored with tittles of dubious value. Wealth is not only glorified; it is worshiped. In a country such as Nigeria, this is inflamed by the lack of control.

2.4 LAW AND "THE NIGERIAN DREAM"

The failure to apply the rule of law and satisfactorily punish criminals is a further distinction of a soft state. In Nigeria, the rule of law is deficient, and a breakdown in law and order is widespread. Transgression rarely attracts punishment, particularly when it involves the powerful. There has been excessive use of force by security agencies whereby they extort money and indulge in extrajudicial killing with impunity. Within the society itself, assassinations, ritual killings, and kidnapping are commonplace, and the government has not been able to resolve or react to most of these incidents (Oboh 2011; Udama 2013).

The judiciary functions as the third arm of government and is important in the fight against crimes, including illicit drug activities; however, the CJS in Nigeria has functioned far below the expectations of most Nigerians and beyond—in most instances delivering highly dubious rulings. In one case, James Ibori, a former governor of an oil-rich state in the country, accused of corruption was set free in court. He misappropriated millions of dollars from a state where civil servants were not paid adequately and where good infrastructure did not exist. However, the very same evidence that was discounted by the Nigerian judiciary was used to convict him in the United Kingdom. Having admitted to 10 counts of conspiracy to defraud and money laundering in early 2012, he was jailed for 13 years for fraud totaling nearly GBP50 million or USD77 million, reported the BBC (2012).

Similarly, offenders implicated in the Halliburton bribe scandal of at least USD436 million were punished in the United States, whereas the Nigerian state continues to protect its citizens who were involved (Nigeria Curiosity 2009). It typifies a classical state of affairs that perpetuates the criminogenic environment for crimes. Corruption sucks money out of the economy, which affects the building of roads, provision of power, and the provision of other social amenities. The Nigerian judiciary has been overwhelmed by the shortage of competent personnel, shortage of funds to remunerate prosecutors and judges adequately in spite of large caseloads, and decent working conditions. These shortcomings foster judicial personnel's vulnerability to corrupt practices, lured by drug traffickers among others. In terms of their capacity to enforce the rule of law in their territories, weak states are typically under-resourced and subject to corruption. Due to the lack of basic resources, many West African states lack a functioning CJS to respond to either the drug trafficking problem or official corruption (UNODC 2008b).

Willful neglect of rules is an endemic feature underscoring the Nigerian state crisis and a unifying feature of life in Nigeria. In Nigeria, where leaders are not accountable to those they serve, it inhibits development as they help themselves to money that would otherwise be used for development projects.

Nigeria has become a society that adores criminals and money. It is of no concern how one makes money; rather, all that matter is whether one is rich. It is the end not the means that matters. As Daniel Smith (2008) adequately noted, condemnation and acceptance of criminal behavior can coexist in the same society or even within the same person in Nigeria. This destructive practice is openly acknowledged in Nigeria, and the consequences of corruption for the country and its people are indisputable.

It is the collective actions or inactions of the people in relationship with one another in Nigeria that determines the economic outcome of such a society. In a context in which corruption is the expected behavior (as evidenced in Nigeria), there would basically be no actors, by and large, willing to take on the role of controlling corruption. This imbued logic among the citizenry becomes what the Swedish Nobel laureate, Gunnar Myrdal, emphasized as, "Well, if everybody seems corrupt, why shouldn't I be corrupt?" as it makes no sense to be the only honest player in a "rotten game" (see Persson et al. 2010, 6). When one lives in a society where everybody steals, thievery becomes common because the probability that you would be caught is low, and even if you are caught, the chances of you being punished for a crime so common are even lower. By contrast, if one lives in a society where theft is uncommon, the chances of being caught and punished remain high, which deters stealing. In this context, the *collective action theory* rings true for Nigeria. It recalls the paradox that when almost everyone is corrupt, honesty is the deviant behavior.

Nigeria is now a country where individualism dominates. This evokes Durkheim's (1964) explanation of deviance as a product of cultural definition. "The sickness of infinity," which Durkheim observed during France's rapid industrialization, caused a massive transformation in the social structure and the social ethos—especially the rise of a culture of individualism and decline in more solidaristic, traditional values. He averred that a society whose core cultural values exalted individual competition and offered incessant and ever-retreating goals was one which would be inevitably unstable and conflict-ridden. Since this is an outcome of the cultural creation of capitalism rather than a natural state, a society with less crime and conflict could occur if a unifying culture were developed out of trust, meritorious reward, and finite achievement. Furthermore, Durkheim (1964) writes that in a "society of saints," some would come to be defined as criminal (68–9) and that deviance arises not from the act, but from the rules that forbid (1965, 43).

McLaughlin and Muncie (2005) defined *anomie* as a state of ethical normlessness or deregulation, pertaining either to an individual or a society. Drawing on Durkheim's work, Merton in "Social Structure and Anomie" (1938) emphasized that crime and deviance, rather than being a matter of individual pathology, are in fact a "normal" response to particular cultural and structural circumstances. In this view, the nuance of "poverty causes crime" does not hold. Instead, the stress on "the American Dream," the notion that success and social mobility is open to all, grinds against the actual structural limitations on success. This American value causes deviance and disorder as "anti-social behavior is in a sense 'called forth' by certain conventional values and by a class structure involving differential access to the approached opportunities" (Merton 1938, 24). In addition, the overemphasis on success goals, in place of the means of achieving them, represents a criminogenic feature that could cause deviant activity. As Merton suggests, this jointly—the cultural emphasis on success at any cost and limited opportunities—created a terrible strain. One way to adapt to this strain is to commit crime through the innovative creation of new means to achieve the cultural goals of success. In this subcultural perspective, crime and deviance are viewed as cultural and material solutions to contradictions in wider society.

As Merton pointed out regarding the influence of monetary accumulation in the American Dream, as mentioned afore, the same can be seen in "the Nigerian Dream." In effect, society is not worried about how one makes money—what matters is whether one is affluent. The Nigerian Dream recalls a culture hooked on materialism and showing off with designer clothes and shoes, latest car models, ownership of mansions, private jets, luxury yacht, super vacation homes, watching television the whole day, sharing the mainstream culture's obsession with violence, as well as worshipping success, wealth, and status. All of this is reminiscent of Merton but where, in a late modern context, the implosion of the wider culture on the local is increased dramatically (Young 2007).

This delusion generates frustration among people in Nigeria, especially the educated youth and the "middle class." I wonder if the term middle class is still suitable in that society. What is appropriate are concepts of the few "haves" and the masses of "have-nots." Most Nigerians are deprived of the legal means of acquiring a decent life. This relative deprivation combined with inequality is one of the driving forces toward deviant activities, including the international cocaine trafficking.

A good number of cocaine traffickers and aspirant ones have asserted that "norms of the game" have changed into the "game of the normless," underlining that most Nigerians have become impatient people who want everything and who want it immediately. They want it because most are frustrated by the illusions of the get rich fast syndrome, deprivation and poverty, and vulnerability. Vulnerability remains connected to assert ownership, and the more assets someone has the less vulnerable they are, and the greater the erosion of people's assets, the greater their insecurity (Moser 1998). The means of resistance are the assets and entitlements that individuals, households, or communities can mobilize and manage in the face of hardship. The cocaine trafficker, Kodo, had this to say: Life in Nigeria is like in a ghetto. CNN shows life in the ghettos many times. But it's even better in the ghettos of America, because they have the basics like water, electricity, roads, and all that. Here these amenities are dreams because they embezzled the money. Please don't be fooled. Here illegality is legal. Look, the foreigners rob this country as much as they can. Nigerians do it as well regardless of tribe or ethnicity. The northerners have defrauded the nation as much as they can, likewise the westerners or easterners and the southerners. The government deserted the country long ago. Nigeria is a ghetto! (Kodo, personal communication, June 10, 2011)

But Kodo's comparison with American ghettos is an interesting one. Many in Nigeria would dream to be in American ghettos, just because there are basic amenities that are affordable only to the wealthy in Nigeria. In addition, Kodo takes on the marginalization of poor, black Americans who have often been ostracized to the fringes of civil society. Wacquant (2004, 2009) points to two fundamental, interconnected processes in the making of the black American ghetto, namely the concept of decivilizing at the social-relational level and demonizing at a symbolic level. Similarly, Nigeria's slums have cultivated pools of frustrated, unemployed youth who are pushed into survival activities based upon informal (or illegal) economies. In this regard, the process that gave rise to slums and its crimes in Nigeria is related to the fact that in the de-civilizing process, slums are created and maintained by ineffective governance, the disintegration of local institutions and public services, and social relations. The masses in Nigeria express the fact that the government has abandoned them at all levels. In its place, it has created a criminogenic environment and a serious lack of adequate infrastructure and efficient public institutions. The process of demonization occurs when the government plays down a segment of its citizens as despicable drug traffickers associated with evil, greed, and violence.

Many people point out that the Nigerian government has succeeded in portraying the country and its citizens to the world as poor, fearsome, evil, and even criminal. They are disappointed with the elite stakeholders who, in many people's minds, siphon the nation's wealth. From this perspective, an interaction between fear, violence, and the state leads to de-pacification of everyday life, informalization of the economy, and crimes (through such activities as international cocaine trafficking, minor prostitution abroad, and advance-fee fraud). Nigerians themselves refer to their country as a risky place, a "jungle," or even a "ghetto." Equally, Nigerian elites consider the slums of Lagos and other cities as unsafe areas and hot spots for crimes and criminality, thereby shifting the failure of their governance to that of the society.

In this view, it is not difficult to see how the concepts of de-civilization and demonization caused by the Nigerian state crisis contribute to the new trend cocaine trafficking and stigmatizing Nigerians globally as "criminals," while traffickers point to the operators of the nation and their foreign partners who enhance and celebrate criminality.

2.5 "CHOP MONEY" SYNDROME AND GLOBALIZATION

"Chop money" in Nigeria is common slang for misappropriation of public funds. For example, one often hears things like, "Aaa! Bros you hear say them chop N20 billion naira?" (Hey friend, have you heard that N20 billion was embezzled?). There have been numerous accusations or formal corruption charges brought against officials in connection with embezzling public funds that end with little or no sanction against the offenders. Endemic corruption fosters Nigerian international cocaine trafficking through its mutual relationship with a lack of accountability, integrity, and transparency granted by the state to its agents.

Independence in Nigeria or administration in government agencies resulted in the struggle by various ethnic groups for its share of the "national cake." Politicians, with interest in representing his own local governments and state governments in the federal administration, embezzled with impunity the funds entrusted to his care. People had hoped that embezzled funds would be returned for the betterment of their own hometown or region to provide public goods like potable water, goods roads, schools, and rural electrification. However, Nigeria's politicians saw an opportunity to benefit themselves. In effect, despite the laws against bribery and stealing from the government, there was no sense of culpability in graft and wanton malfeasance among politicians and high government officials in Nigeria. Public mismanagement of resources contributes to reproducing inequality, compromises opportunities for inclusive growth, and pushes many into cocaine trafficking. As indicated by the Economic and Financial Crimes Commission (EFCC), between 1960 and 2005, approximately USD20 trillion was stolen from the treasury

by public officeholders in Nigeria. This sum is bigger than the GDP of the
United States in 2012 (about USD18 trillion), noted Ajayi and Ifegbayi
(2015).

Such practices have fostered the contemporary criminogenic environment
that underpins drug trafficking and all sorts of organized crime that in relation to the state develops as follows: first is a predatory stage in which gangs
employing violence attempt to gain territorial control and a monopoly over
the use of force and bring subjects to the forces of law and order; second is a
parasitical stage in which state prohibitions, war, conflict, UN sanctions, and
so on, create the condition for criminal organizations to flourish and connect
with the corrupt sections of the political elite; and third is a symbolic stage
in which "organized crime has become a part of the state, a state within a
state" (Lupsha 1996, 30–32). At the extreme of *predatory states* are *captured
states*, such as Nigeria under Sani Abacha, Zaire under Mobutu, and Liberia
under Charles Taylor. Nigeria became more than ever a literal *kleptocratic
gangster state*, a system of government by theft and bribery. Unlike in stable
democratic states, they use security forces not to defend or protect the rights
of individual Nigerians but as tools of monopoly enforcements and wealth
accumulation for elites. In *kleptocratic* states "economic predation, territorial expansion and wealth extraction are the organizing principles of their
existence. Governance in the interest of citizens is an afterthought, if it is
considered at all" (Hirschfield 2015, 14–16).

According to Geneva's public prosecutor, Switzerland will return to
Nigeria about USD380 million linked to the former military leader, late
General Sani Abacha. Whereas some USD500 million had already been
returned to Nigeria, the Abacha affair began in 1999 when Nigeria asked the
Swiss judicial authorities to help it recover USD2.2 billion (Smith 2015).

The government of Nigeria could be defined as a predatory state: A predatory state is a government that resorts to wholesale abuse of government
power, using criminal cronies to engage in the despicable and condemnable
acts of looting his nation's wealth (Ebbe 2016; Lupsha 1996). To this end, he
places desired loyalists in charge of government agencies, cabinet ministers,
and directors of statutory corporations as bribe collection agents. In Nigeria,
high government officials become integral players in organized crimes. And
"the national interest and the interest of organized crime are now inextricably
intertwined" (Naím 2012, 101–102).

Devoid of relatively strong and efficient civil administrations, the pursuit
of political power and authority is integral to private gain. The political environment and the way socioeconomic groups interact with state officials affect
the prevalence as well as the perception of corruption. This aspect relates to
the relative prominence and powers of the public sector vis-à-vis the private
sector in the economy.

As the Nigerian case demonstrates, the public sector wields enormous influence on the pattern of resource allocation, which is why it constitutes the key arena of corruption. Ironically, the public sector has effectively become a reliable tool in the hands of the private sector's self-enrichment process. Through the phenomenon of state capture, which depends on the relative power of interest groups, the private sector players are helped to accomplish their goals in a reciprocally beneficial way at the cost of society. Thus, the ruling elite enriches and empowers itself, and accumulation via theft of resources is transformed into political power (Green and Ward 2004).

This recalls Marx's ([1867] 1976) notion of primitive accumulation that highlights the historical processes that lead to uninterrupted capitalist production, which is linked to the subordination of the underdeveloped to the developed world economy. In the context of Nigeria, this view could shed light on the paradox of a country that is simultaneously extremely wealthy and extremely poor. In the first place, it points to an accumulation of capital amassed primarily for speculative reasons. Second, accumulation in the hands of this class is incapable of ultimately transforming this hoarded wealth into an actual means of production. This call to mind the widespread irritation amid Nigerians who are aware that although their national wealth is desperately needed for development at home, instead it is siphoned to countries where it enhances the means of production or is borrowed back as a loan to Nigeria or the like.

Relevant here is Amin's (1974) intrinsic to continuous primitive accumulation seen as transfer of value in the world economy. As the rich in Nigeria fail to invest the stolen money in the country, they forget that relations between the formations of the developed world and that of the underdeveloped world are affected by the transfer of value. Whenever the capitalist mode of production enters into relations with precapitalist modes of production, transfers of value take place as a result of the mechanisms of primitive accumulation. These mechanisms belong to the prehistory of capitalism; they apply in the contemporary context as well. It is these forms of primitive accumulation, modified but persistent, to the advantage of the center that forms the domain of the theory of accumulation on a world scale (Amin 1974).

Nigeria is Africa's largest oil exporting country and is the world's ninth-largest crude oil exporter in 2018 (Workman 2020). Notwithstanding the estimated six trillion USD in oil revenue made over the last 50 years; yet, poverty reigns in the country. Oil became of interest to the colonialists in Nigeria in the first half of the 1900s and was first drilled commercially in the Niger Delta in 1956 by the Anglo-Dutch oil giant, Shell Oil. Having gripped Nigeria since the 1930s, Shell claimed it had inserted staff into all the main ministries of the Nigerian government, giving it access to politicians' every move in the oil-rich Niger Delta, according to a leaked U.S. diplomatic cable

(Smith 2010). It is nonstop embedded corporate crime in Nigeria as Shell, Italian oil firm, Eni, and JPMorgan Chase were sued regarding a USD1.3 billion plus bribery payment made to secure an exploration license in Nigeria (Walt 2019). Corrupt deals cost Nigeria billions in oil revenue.

Some aspects of the *world systems theory* (Wallerstein 1979, 2004) could be instrumental in elucidating the mechanism behind Nigerian cocaine trafficking. From the macro-sociological viewpoint, the world systems theory attempts to explain the forces of the capitalist world economy as a total social system. More recently, Chase-Dunn and Grimes (1995), and Pomeranz and Topik (2006), have argued for its use as well. In this view, crime in the "third world" could be caused by inequality and uneven economic development. Crime could result as a product of direct or indirect dependency and exploitation between core rich Western countries and poor peripheral countries. The main mechanisms involved are the exercise of arbitrary political or economic power and uneven expansion of capitalism. Furthermore, crime surges as a result of restrictions and demands from developed countries such as policies aimed at drug prohibition, migrants, arms embargos, human trafficking, prostitution, precious metals, and the oil trade. As evidenced in Nigeria, the imbalance results in crimes of resistance and rebellion such as terrorism, drug trafficking, destruction of lives and properties. In addition, the network and trade structure of the world economy between core countries and peripheral nations also relates to the world systems theory. Bovin (2010) suggested applying the concept to international trafficking of drugs such as cannabis, cocaine, heroin, and synthetic drugs. The world systems, with respect to cocaine trafficking, highlight an organized trade that inextricably link developed and underdeveloped countries. International drug trafficking is comparable in its trading outline to that of luxury goods and leisure: affordable only by a select few at very high prices in a world where the local has a global impact.

While globalization boosted international network of flows of material, resources, and human social capital, it is also the case that this new dynamic process involves illegal trade, as demonstrated by net new trend illicit cocaine trade. Processes parallel to those which made globalization good for the interdependent world economy have also enabled criminal organizations to emerge and thrive. Similarly, globalization with multinational corporations may cause local events within countries that could have negative or devastating effects, such as the vast environmental damage that has occurred in the Niger Delta in Nigeria, one of the world's largest wetlands but also home to Africa's biggest oil industry. Indeed, while oil companies have reached record profits year after year, in Africa the per capita income that had grown by 34.3% from 1960 to 1980 fell by about 20% from 1980 to 1997 during the era of globalization (Brecher et al. 2000). Instead of economic development and financial benefits, it has pushed the majority into poverty and directly or indirectly pushed many into deviant activities, including cocaine trafficking.

In the past, the Nigerian state has given extensive protection to oil companies by violently repressing local Nigerians who express dissent because they have never felt the impact of the revenue generated. The violent suppression of these protests is committed either by state security forces or by private security forces trained by the Nigerian state and which remain closely connected with state security forces (Alemika and Chukwuma 2000). Protests and resistance are brutally crushed, as was embodied in the 1995 hanging of Nigerian writer and environmental activist, Ken Saro-Wiwa, by the government under Abacha. In an attempt to compensate Nigeria for decades of devastating effects from its activities, in June 2009, Shell paid a sum of USD15.5 million in restitution for the murder, torture, and other human rights abuses of Saro-Wiwa and other members of the Ogoni tribe of southern Nigeria (Zambito 2009). There have also been charges of major environmental pollution, and despite the United Nation's exoneration of Shell, international environmental and human rights groups are calling for further legal action to ensure proper compensation and adequate compliance and regulation (Vidal 2010). Additionally, as mentioned previously, U.S. oilfield services giant, Halliburton, came under fire for its corruption practices in Nigeria. Former U.S. vice president Dick Cheney, who led the energy company Halliburton as CEO and chairman of the Board from 1995 to 2000, was charged by the Nigerian anti-corruption agency EFCC for corruption in Nigeria. The government considered a settlement (in lieu of prosecution) of USD250 million with Halliburton, which stemmed from approximately USD180 million paid in bribes to Nigerian officials (Byrne 2010).

2.6 STRUCTURAL UNDERPINNINGS

Abacha's kleptocratic authoritarian regime is long gone, yet there remains a strong overlap between the political elites and those who hold economic power. Loosely enforced campaign finance laws often result in situations where policy-making processes and the functioning of institutions are hijacked and skewed to work in favor of the economic and political elite. The Oxford Committee for Famine Relief (Oxfam) report on exclusive economies aptly sums up these dynamics: "Wealth has the potential to capture government policymaking and bend the rules in favor of the rich, often to the detriment of everyone else. The consequences of this include the erosion of democratic governance, the diminishing of social cohesion, and the vanishing of equal opportunities for all" (Oxfam 2017, 27).

Organized crime such as illicit drug trafficking has become central to building political authority. For instance, there is the example of a Nigerian senator-elect, Buruji Kashamu, wanted and arrested for conspiracy to import 6.6 kilograms of heroin in the United States in 1994 (*PM News* 2019); there was also a cocaine-trafficking aspiring politician, Eme Zuru Ayortor, who was arrested for attempting to smuggle 2.12-kilogram cocaine in his stomach (Akpan 2010).

Critics point to the structure that facilitates embezzlement, and in some cases, it is possible to trace the flow of money through the testimony of whistleblowers, like the ex-governor of the Central Bank of Nigeria, Mallam Lamido Sanusi. He revealed the Nigeria National Assembly consumes 25% of the country's overhead expenses. Nigeria's lawmakers have since been found to earn the highest salaries worldwide for their position, earning up to USD2 million a year (or N397.9 million). More than 70% of the federal budget is spent on the salaries and benefits of about one million government officials that leaves little revenue to help Nigerians living in poverty (Winsor 2015). Federal lawmakers constitute 0.0002% of Nigeria's population, yet an overwhelming amount of state funds are expended for their upkeep. A Nigerian lawmaker receives an annual salary of about USD118,000 (N37 million), which is 63 times the country's GDP per capita (2013). Nigerian legislators' entitlements are more than that of their counterparts in the UK (whose average equivalent is USD105,400), the United States (USD174,000), France (USD85,900), SA (USD104,000), Kenya (USD74,500), Saudi Arabia (USD64,000) and Brazil (USD157,600) according to Modern Ghana (2013).

Documents from the Revenue Mobilization Allocation and Fiscal Commission show a senator receives N19.66 million, while a House of Representatives member gets N18.26 million in the first year of each legislative session; they receive allowances that are payable once every four years. They receive much more than this amount through hidden allowances (Oxfam 2017, 32–33). The earning of a Nigerian senator per day is more than the yearly income of a doctor; it is more than the salary of 48 university professors or 70 commissioners of police, despite the fact that the minimum monthly salary is less than USD100, and the average earning of 80% of the populace is below N300 per day (Kalama et al. 2012).

In a country such as Nigeria where drug traffickers and fraudsters (or "419'ers") become lawmakers, ministers, or governors, it's no wonder why so many choose this path. Imo State governor, Rochas Okorocha, said it was preferable for people to become armed robbers than to smoke marijuana. Explaining the gravity of the punishment that will be meted out to anyone found selling it, Okorocha stated in an article on the *Daily Post* of January 26, 2018, that "weed has killed my children in Imo state. Anybody selling weed or consuming it, that person's house will be demolished. Where we are now, it is better for someone to be an armed robber than to smoke weed" (Opejobi 2018). Okorocha will be remembered for his eight-year regime during which he has failed to pay salaries and pension to civil servants and used public funds to erect statues of his role models, including that of disgraced ex-president of SA, Jacob Zuma. Okorocha promised probity, openness, and accountability but instead corruption and scams have become pandemic in the running of government affairs. One of the many scandals during Okorocha's tenure was the case of the Lebanese company, Hommiprese, that absconded with a N3.5 billion payment by the Imo government, and the company and its leaders have faced zero repercussions (Uzorma 2018). Should this allegation be true, it means Hommiprese has taken advantage of a corrupt leader to defraud Imo State.

Social capital as discussed by Putnam (1993) and Bourdieu (1993) implies that some people are better connected to exchange certain goods or favors. In other words, social capital could be seen as an expression of advantage (Bourdieu and Wacquant 1992), which can be exploited by criminals. The unscrupulous ex-governor has used his social capital, cronies who benefited from widespread criminality in the country, to siphon funds out of state coffers. This is certainly true in the links between drug traffickers and politicians or political hopefuls in Nigeria. Other theorists have examined social capital in structural and cognitive forms (Uphoff and Wijayaratna 2000). The former is characterized by relatively external and visible components such as roles, rules, procedure, precedents, and social networks that establish ongoing patterns of social interaction. In contrast, cognitive forms of social capital are more internal and subjective. Its characteristics include norms, values, attitudes, and beliefs that incline individuals to cooperate in achieving reciprocal communal goals. It is believed that all cultures have the basic elements of social capital within them, but social structures and shared values can be disinvested in by neglect or misuse (ibid. 2000). In addition, social capital can exist as: (1) family and kinship connections or bonding social capital that is a very strong bond often found among family members or ethnic groups; (2) (wider) social networks or bridging social capital that is a weaker bond that exists, for instance, among business partners, for instance, between friends from various ethnic origins in common activities; (3) linking social capital, which is the type that exists, for example, between people from different social classes; and (4) political social capital that is related to informal institutional arrangements that may result in clientelism (Pantoja 2000, 26)

Akçomak and ter Weel (2008) indicated that if social capital is an asset that paves the way to community governance (cf. Bowles and Gintis 2002) or to achieve goals that could not be achieved or could be achieved only at a higher cost (Coleman 2000), then any factor that would lead to disorganization and detachment in the community would eventually reduce social capital.

Social capital helps the well-connected garner profitable opportunities and be flexible in anticipating and adapting to unforeseen problems along the line, as observed with drug traffickers' networks. However, the disadvantages of social capital include the fact that it can enhance conduct that deteriorates rather than improves economic performance. It can obstruct social inclusion and social mobility; act as pervasive factor that divides instead of uniting people, communities, or societies; cause education underachievement, health and environmental damage; and in particular cases, it may encourage deviant activities and crime more willingly than decreasing it (Aldridge et al. 2002).

Furthermore, underscored in this work is the notion of *reverse social capital*, which may help to understand the prevalence of cocaine trafficking as a "legitimate" means of financial success in Nigeria. In other words, the financial and social gain from illegal behavior has become the motivating factor for individuals involved in the trade. In contrast to the traditional social capital theory, reverse social capital encourages illegal and criminal behavior as a way to advance in society, resulting in networks that allow drug traffickers, police, and politicians to perpetuate and even encourage Nigerian international cocaine trafficking.

2.7 NONSTOP LOOTING

In Nigeria, reverse social capital and structurally underpinned economies of plunder resulted to a lack of confidence in government and contributed to the rise in international Nigerian cocaine trafficking. Russian anti-corruption activist Roman Borisovich's "Kleptocracy Tour" in London unveils properties purchased with laundered funds by corrupt foreign politicians. Among the "operators of Nigeria" exposed was Bukola Saraki, a prominent Nigerian politician who earns around £30,000 a year, but according to the Panama papers, he also owns £30 million in property purchased through an offshore vehicle (Barker 2017). Saraki purchased most of the multimillion-pound properties by among others looting the Saraki family-owned Société Generale Bank of Nigeria (SGBN) that eventually collapsed. The allegations of fraud which led to the collapse of the bank were one of many corruption allegations against Saraki. Saraki, director of the defunct bank, was indicted over N1 billion alleged to have been looted from the bank's treasury. A *Pulse.ng* article of 2018 published that Saraki and others physically looted the bank vaults to aid the advancement of his siblings in state and national elections. The EFCC officials concluded plans to arrest and prosecute the Sarakis for destroying the SGBN. They prepared 30 charges but before they could file their cases in court, the EFCC's chairman, Nuhu Ribadu, was suddenly sent on compulsory study leave. His predecessor, Ibrahim Lamorde, who attempted to file the charges, was thwarted and replaced with Mrs. Farida Waziri, who had tried through unofficial channel to have the charges against the Sarakis dropped (*Pulse.ng* 2018).

Saraki was no exception. Diezani Alison-Madueke, the former Nigerian petroleum minister, purchased properties around London valued around £11 million with funds illegally acquired with oil monies laundered from Nigeria. Similarly, General Abdulsalami Abubakar, the former military head of state, and other prominent Nigerians have been featured on "kleptocracy tours" of London (Barker 2017). Looting of Nigeria's wealth by the powerful has gone unchecked for years. Indeed, as Gaffey noted, "Several high-profile officials are facing trial for corruption, but no major convictions have been achieved since Buhari came to power in May 2015" (2017).

Whistleblowers citing World Bank data alleged that military 'hijackers' of Nigeria looted billions of U.S. dollars that were discovered in overseas banks in Switzerland, United Kingdom, United States, and Germany. Though the World Bank denies revealing the list containing 21 names of the looters, the Nigerian government reported cash recoveries in various currencies totaling billions in Nigeria naira and U.S. dollars, millions of British pounds, and thousands of euros (Urevich 2010; Ogundipe 2016).

The issue is whether the recovered money and assets will be effectively used to provide much needed basic infrastructure, such as water supply, schools, hospitals, and above all electricity power supply. About 80 million Nigerians have no access to electricity, and despite recent privatization measures, the power supply is still inadequate and unreliable because weak governance and erratic contract enforcement combine to undermine operational efficiency and financial viability (World Bank 2019). The government of Nigeria awarded a USD5.8 billion contract to revive the construction of the 3,050-megawatt Mambilla hydroelectric power project in the state of Taraba. The Chinese Export-Import Bank would finance 85% of the development, with the Nigerian government contributing 15%. The project has been under development for over 30 years and billions of U.S. dollars spent, but little progress made (Monks 2017). In an attempt to redeem these shortages—as Nigeria's trade with China grows 700%—the Nigerian government moved to secure a USD3 billion loan for infrastructure projects, including the electricity power supply (Nordstrom 2013). This is because the financial minister estimates that the Nigerian needs about as USD10 billion yearly to improve the infrastructure, such as roads and electricity to improve standard of living and sustainable economic growth. Among the major projects is a USD1.3 billion loan for the construction of four airport terminals and a 700-megawatt hydropower station that will be signed with the export-import bank of China. Critics point out that China brings its own workers for the projects; investors said this is essential because of human resource shortage in Nigeria.

In all, these excesses recall the negative effects of reverse social capital, eating deep to the heart of the country's development. It represents a structurally underpinned phenomenon that encourages deviant activities and crime. Seen from this angle, social networks could enhance corruption and opportunism. Informal networks can be "anti-modern," in so far as they are utilized to corrupt formal organization. Like the role of mafia in southern Italy or Russia, so it in Nigeria, where cocaine traffickers brag about how easy it is to corrupt law enforcement agents because of the dysfunctional states. In such circumstances, social networks are associated with the development of "delinquent communities" and "bandit capitalism," rather than economic efficiency; and whereas the state has ceased to function, the profusion of social networks is viewed as a source of "stateless order" (Little 2003). Put another way, Nigeria has fallen prey to a kind of governance devoid of government that fuels pervasive corruption and the activities of Nigerian international cocaine traffickers.

Chapter 3

Cultural Factors Motivating Nigerian Cocaine Trafficking

Several cultural peculiarities underpin the new trend in illicit cocaine trafficking. This work underlines the immense role played by the traditional belief in witchcraft in boosting the morale of Nigerian drug traffickers. Whereas this will be discussed later, this chapter will zoom in on how customary features such as the informal economy mentality, disappointed apprentices in enterprising Nigeria, patrilineal culture of inheritance, extended family liabilities, and "Foo-Foo" swallowing culture interact to enhance the Nigerian involvement in international drug trafficking. Individually and in combination, these cultural factors represent a push factor into the illicit cocaine trade for many frustrated helpless young Nigerians, who claim that the formal economy is "effectively occupied" and blurred.

3.1 INFORMAL ECONOMY

There is no standard definition of *informal economy* in the literature, though terms such as *shadow economy*, *black economy*, and *unreported economy* have been used to define it (Medina et al. 2017; Benjamin et al. 2014; Fox and Sohnesen 2013). As applied in this work, the informal economy comprises economic activities that circumvent costs and are excluded from the benefits and rights incorporated in laws and administrative rules covering property relationships, commercial licensing, labor contracts, financial credit, and social systems. The characteristics of the informal labor workforce include mostly unskilled workers operating in low productivity jobs, in marginal, and often family-based activities. They are self-employed or salaried workers in small, precarious firms without a signed contract in compliance with labor regulations.

Estimates on the number of people involved in the informal sector vary as greatly its definition. Measuring the informal economy is a challenge to researchers, mainly due to its nature: by definition the informal economy is covert and, therefore, it is nearly impossible to measure its volume directly. Scholars have identified high tax burdens, corruption, administrative barriers, and nonexistent or deficient rule of law as the main causes of the existence and development of the informal economy (Jamalmanesh et al. 2014; Hashimzade and Hedy 2016).

Recent research by the IMF (2017) indicates significant heterogeneity exists in the size of informality in SSA, ranging from a low of 20–25% of informal sector output in Mauritius, SA, and Namibia to a high of 50–65% in Benin, Tanzania, and Nigeria. They point out that the share of informal economic activity in SSA remains among the largest in the world. The SSA unweighted average share of informality reached almost 38% of GDP over 2010–2014. This is surpassed only by Latin America, at 40% of GDP and compares with 34% of GDP in South Asia, and 23% of GDP in Europe (Medina et al. 2017, 5, 13).

Informal household enterprises are the most common resort for nonagricultural employment for those who lack education or who are geographically disadvantaged (Fox and Sohnesen 2013), and the urban informal sector plays an important role in absorbing rural migrants (Benjamin et al. 2014). Over 65% of people employed in SSA are engaged in farming, but nearly 70% of employment outside farming is in the informal sector. Furthermore, illustrating the sector's importance to employment, World Bank's analysts estimate Nigeria's informal workers at 54.6 million people, representing 53% of the labor force, which is among the highest on the continent. About 75% of all new jobs are informal (World Bank 2019, 10).

Nigerian entrepreneurs involved in illicit trade also form a kind of informal economy. They see it in terms of covert supply and demand, drawing from others in existing transnational black markets in Africa. Due to the Nigerian state crisis, as discussed previously, along with the procedures of deregulation, globalization, and weakening states, informal forms of economic organization have become pervasive—perhaps the most pervasive form of labor in Nigeria.

Falling oil prices in the early 1980s, rising debt, deteriorating economic management, and political instability then combined to throw Nigeria into a debt crisis. The IMF offered financial assistance and debt rescheduling if the government underwent the process of economic liberalization known as Structural Adjustment Program (SAP). Among the strings attached to IMF/World Bank loans were deep cuts in public expenditure, sacking of public employees, economic deregulation, and devaluing the naira (Africa Research Institute 2016). The military dictatorship of IBB quickly opened talks with the IMF and World Bank, and adopted a "comprehensive and radical" program of structural adjustment (Biersteker 1993), plunging about 70% of Nigerians who live under poverty line into acute financial difficulty. This was undoubtedly an incentive to some to make money regardless of means.

During my fieldwork, many Nigerians told me they hold their so-called leaders, as well as the West, responsible for the degradation of their country. Several publications exist on the informal economy in Africa and in Nigeria (Meagher 2010; Hart 2006; Portes and Haller 2005; Castells and Portes 1989). The dominant view is informal African economies are impenetrable to social scientific investigations, and informality has been conceptualized as an alternative terrain of regulation operating outside the framework of the state.

In response, this work aims to provide insight into one of the important new trends of the informal economy in Nigeria. In 2009, Africa's drug trafficking market was worth approximately USD3.2 billion, most of which went to Nigerian organized crime groups (UNODC 2011).

Drawing from works of other researchers, Meagher (2010) expressed that the meaning of informality has settled on the notion of "extra-legality," diffusing the accepted definition of the informal economy as "income generating activities that take place outside the regulatory framework of the state" (Castells and Portes 1989, 12). However, from the global drug trafficking that attracted the attention of Nigerians or Africans in the past decades and commodity chains to conflict diamonds, dumping of contraband goods in underdeveloped countries, research illustrates how goods from unregulated or illegal underdeveloped nations are integrated into main stream economic systems, signifying the emergence of an economy in which interrelationships rather than distinct sectors are the norm. "As a paired negotiation each marker depends on the integrity of the opposing term. But with criminalisation, the key referent of formality has defected across the binary divide, and become absorbed by informality. The rest is simple: no formal sector, no informal sector" (Klein 1999b, 568).

Among the 162 countries studied by Schneider et al. (2010) during the period 1999–2007, 107 had an estimated informal share greater than or equal to 30% of total GDP, including 18 with a share over 50% (Cantens et al. 2015, 2). Keith Hart, the pioneer of the concept, suggested that the entire economy could become "informal," because of which we are entitled to ask whether the term has outgrown its usefulness (Hart 2001, 2006).

In this regard, researchers questioned the relevance of the concept of informality to the contracting states. Highlighting that deregulation has erased the division between formality and informality, Portes and Haller (2005) emphasize that "where the state does not regulate anything because it is at the mercy of the market forces, there is no formal economy" (409). On the contrary, the realities of government failure in Nigeria and in other underdeveloped countries turn the state and the informal economy into increasingly "fuzzy concepts" (Peattie 1987). The concept of the informal economy is now more substantial in most countries.

As highlighted by Young (2007), effort, delayed gratification, and meritorious progress toward a goal have given way to immediacy, instant gratification, and short-term hedonism, and they are interlaced with formal economic structures such that the old concept of an informal sector or informal economy has been called into question.

3.2 INFORMAL APPRENTICES

Apprenticeship and entrepreneurship are long-standing and much-studied traditions in Nigeria (Uwameiye and Iyamu 2002; Olutayo 1999; Ottenberg 1959). Like in other African nations, two modes of apprenticeship training exist in Nigeria: apprenticeship training in a formal institutional setting and informal sector apprenticeship training. Both have disappointed those they were meant to serve and deprived them of reliable employment.

Apprenticeship training in formal, institutional settings entails vocational education sponsored by government departments or private businesses concerned with meeting technical needs of the industry. In most cases, the number of these apprenticeships available is small. Although some craftsmen who were trained under this model are self-employed, the general outcome is wage employment. In a country with a high rate of youth joblessness, as discussed previously, this mode of apprenticeship, therefore, offers limited employment and training opportunities for young school leavers.

The informal sector apprenticeship system is by far the most popular. It is an age-old method used in training young people in trades and crafts, agriculture, business, and catering. In 1981, the Federal Republic of Nigeria envisaged that the widespread roadside apprenticeship, which provides opportunities for training adolescent school dropouts, would be accredited for training by the National Board for Technical Education, but that policy has never seen the light of day (see Uwameiye and Iyamu 2002). By 1990, this indigenous system included more than 50% of the school-age population and operated almost entirely in the private sector; there was virtually no regulation by the government unless training included the need for a license (see Olutayo 1999). If the "unemployed school leaver" is viewed as one who completes at least primary education and cannot find a job even after seeking employment for months or even years, then, it would be right to say that the problems in Nigeria have reached a critical stage which requires the urgent attention of government and parent alike.

3.2.1 Untapped Potential

At the economic level, the informal sector of the economy has failed to improve economic potential for the majority of workers that is necessary for the fundamental transformation of the Nigerian economy. Then the question is whether informality is a blessing or a curse. Informal sector activities are the main training ground for entrepreneurial initiative, as they are the most accessible and competitive part of African economies. The informal sector is crucial and has become a link for creating jobs at lower cost. Maximizing potential depends on chances available to the would-be entrepreneurs, their responsiveness, motivation, and ability to engage in the sector.

3.2.2 Enterprising Nigeria

In popular discourse, the dominant view remains that Nigerians acquired better trade skills through intense, protracted interaction with colonialists. Even prior to the current period of tremendous migration, Nigerians were renowned for their receptivity to change (Ottenberg 1959). Nigerians are found almost in every country, like the Italians or the Dutch, Chinese, or Indians. The beginning of the business learning culture was the trade apprenticeship system. Success meant building economic skills and strategies through progressive business models, business management, and personal entrepreneurial skills.

Agriculture was the economic mainstay. The agricultural revolution that occurred earlier in some parts of Nigeria enhanced important cultural changes and innovations. For instance, production of cash crops like oil palm, groundnut, and cocoa is traditional, and cannabis is now produced in many states including Edo, Kano, Ondo, Oyo, Kogi, Osun, and Delta State (NDLEA 2016).

In Nigeria, people "placed a premium on occupational skill, enterprise and initiative," upon which status mobility is dependent (Olutayo 1999, 152). Varied features can be used to elucidate the entrepreneurial ability of individuals. Entrepreneurship requires some fundamental characteristics to foster success. These include confidence in personal abilities, the desire for immediate results, willingness to assume responsibilities and preference for a moderate risk, high energy and vision, organizing skills and the desire to achieve above moneymaking, high level of commitment, and flexibility, as Burduş noted in "Fundamentals of Entrepreneurship" (Burduş 2010).

Nigeria is from the outset capitalistic but people live in communion with other members of society. They did not acquire entrepreneurial skills from the Europeans, as some scholars asserted. For example, the Benin kingdom was famous prior to arrival of Europeans. Benin boasted booming trade, and archeologists have found well-preserved ivory, terracotta, and bronze sculptures (Rodney 1973). The Hausas have engaged in long-distance trading for many centuries. Traders exchanged gold from the Middle East for leather, crafts, and food. Hausa communities can also be found in other West African nations, according to Sabiu et al. (2018). Among the Igbos, the institution of kingship, *Eze Nri*, maintained law and order in the area of better land use and equity. People attained giant strides in agricultural development, iron casting, and administration of long distance trade (Ezeudu et al. 2013, 119).

Rather it is colonialism that eroded Nigerian traditional and economic values regarding their communalistic development, and strengthened individualistic ways of living that also deepened entrepreneurship, and the formal or informal trade.

Thus, *Enterprising Nigeria* dates back centuries. All ethnic groups in Nigeria are involved in the illicit cocaine trade, as interviews and research in this book show. The reality is that the illegal drug trade follows the legal trade, and Nigeria and Nigerians are no exceptions.

Notwithstanding the entrepreneurial capacity amid Nigerians, the reality is that a majority remained predominately informal, petty, and small-scale traders, for whom "survival regardless of means" became the motto. Medina et al. (2017) averred that tax and social security burdens were among the main causes of the informal economy. The larger the difference between the total cost of labor in the official economy and after-tax earnings, the greater the incentive to avoid this by joining the informal economy. In Nigeria, like many places, paying tax is unpopular—a holdover mentality from colonial rule. A French adage stated that the colonies were created for the metropole by the metropole. The colonized did not enter into any social contract with "European robber statesmen" at the Berlin conference (Rodney 1973, 160, 187), for expropriation of Nigerian natural resources, which was done through the exploitation of surplus values of African labor (Agizino 2003). While coal miners at Enugu were underpaid for their labor, as discussed under chapter 1.2.2, the price of goods and resources derived from their land rose well beyond their means. For example, in 1924 in Nigeria, a yard of khaki which was three shillings in prewar days went up to 16 shillings; a bundle of iron sheets formerly costing 30 shillings went up to 100 shillings in 1945 (Rodney 1973). Colonial UAC trading company reduced the price of palm oil from 14 shillings per gallon to seven in 1928 and to slightly over one shilling in the following year.

Heavy taxation imposed on people whose resources were being depleted led to widespread militancy that shook the colonial edifice. Processing and marketing palm oil, the primary source of income for many women, led to the "Women's War" against colonialism in Nigeria, often mislabeled "Aba Women Riots" though the uprising spread beyond Aba. Men usually went into hiding to avoid tax collectors or colonial police (Afigbo 1972; Agozino 1997).

Notwithstanding the economic depression then, the UAC made a handsome profit of about £6.3 million and a dividend of 15% was paid on ordinary shares (Rodney 1973). The "maintenance of law and order" simply meant "maintenance of condition most favorable to the expansion of capitalism and the plunder of Africa" (ibid., 196).

Instrumental to this plundering was colonial taxation which was imposed to finance the repressive apparatus of imperialism and, above all, to force the indigenous labor force into wage slavery. For instance, despite that women were not directly taxed, the imposition of "hut" taxes by the colonial administration made women very vulnerable since most African polygamous husbands housed their wives in different huts. To lessen this burden, Africa men who married several wives built larger huts and housed all their wives in one hut, at the risk of increasing tension among the competing co-wives. The colonialists reacted by taxing each man for each wife in a system of poll tax, noted by Shivji as "wife tax" (1982, 43; Agozino 1997, 34).

Walter Edward Guinness, or Lord Moyne, former financial secretary to the Treasury in Britain, was mandated to investigate the general budgetary position of the colony. He examined taxation as it affected the compliance of the African people and recommended various means of drawing more Africans into the tax net. A fundamental conclusion of Lord Moyne's report, germane to Issa Tarus's (2004) "A History of the Direct Taxation of the African People of Kenya," is that by 1932 Africans were responsible for 37.5% of the colony's total revenue. Africans paid 29% through direct taxation in the form of the hut tax and poll tax (ibid.). The fact of the matter was that marginalization and colonial taxation policies never allowed the African people an opportunity to participate fully in the accumulation process. Wunyabari Maloba (1993) linked the Mau Mau "Peasant Revolt" with the loss of land and economic independence exacerbated by high taxation. These factors created the conditions for a revolt as taxation in all its forms was a vicious and punitive means of extraction. Exploitation continues as imperial "police" disguised under neocolonial policies forcibly extract taxes from those who cannot pay due to poverty or infirmity.

In all, distrust for the exploitative colonial administration that forced tax on locals resulted in a strong distaste for tax burdens and love of fiscal freedom. All things being equal, a larger tax burden is likely to encourage more economic activity to remain in the informal economy.

Next, as development in Nigeria has demonstrated, institutional quality has a strong bearing on competitiveness and inclusive economic growth. A weak judiciary system, excessive bureaucracy, lack of transparency, and strategic enterprises exacerbate the incentives for informality. Medina et al.

(2017) noted in informal economies in SSA that the stronger the enforcement capability and quality of government are, the lower the expected size of the informal economy. The emphasis remains that lack of respect for the law and control of corruption, as well as government instability, encourage informal activity. In addition, unemployment and lack of work in the formal sector will force some to seek work in informal economic activity (ibid. 2017).

During and after the colonial period, many Nigerian traders and farmers had little or no access to loans because they lacked securities or collateral. Consequently, the difference between the prices of raw materials like palm oil and the import of manufactured textiles like khaki constituted a form of unequal exchange, preventing indigenous traders from accumulating capital in an export business monopolized by colonialists. Banks and financial houses dealt only with other capitalists who could guarantee the bankers that the bank would recover its money and make a profit (see Rodney 1973). Nigerian traders and farmers relied on cash and goods advances from expatriate trading firms, which had capital resources and shipping facilities, and banks discriminated against Nigerian businessmen but favored foreign ones (Forrest 1995).

In Nigeria, interest rates are high. The Central Bank of Nigeria's current interest rate is 14%; in comparison, Brazil's is 7%; China, 4.35%; Indonesia, 4.25%; United States, 1.5%; and 0% in the Netherlands. What is more is the rates are much higher from commercial banks. For example, for the Standard Chartered Bank Nigeria, the home loan rate starts at 19% and the personal loan rate is 22% (Trading Economics 2020; Standard Chartered Bank Nigeria 2020). Due to a lack of coevolutionary networks of supporting institutions, many enterprises are supported in their innovative activities by less visible or less commonly known, informal institutional links.

Furthermore, because informal economic activity dominates, people engaged in it usually conduct their activities in cash. This is particularly true for people who do not want a paper trail of illicit transactions. Cocaine hoppers are no exception, as they recycle their money through frontline businesses or simply carried cash. For example, monetary exhibits seized from drug traffickers included about N4.4 million, EUR326,000, and around USD90,000 (NDLEA 2016, 33).

The shadow economy outgrew agriculture and manufacturing as the civil service and business professions became more attractive; these job fields were an opportunity for desired contacts with Europeans and foreign firms that monopolized import/export business. Hence, the distorted mentality in Nigeria that all that is Western is best.

In addition, the informal economy mentality became embedded because indigenous elites' urge for independence and economic control (particularly in the eastern and western regions), the colonial administration shifted to overprotection of foreign firms, syphoning resources which impeded the formation of private Nigerian capital needed for development (see Federal Government of Nigeria 1958). And above all, politics became the most attractive avenue for making profit; yet, the businessmen were not well accepted by the political class.

3.2.3 Apprenticeship as Communal Spirit

Nigeria has well-developed institutions of apprenticeship that gave entrepreneurs a comparative edge. They have been able to build upon these institutions by generating and maintaining a communal civic spirit. The communal spirit is the lifeblood of the entrepreneurial ability of Nigerians, and it manifests itself in the apprenticeship network founded to achieve economic progress, be it at Idumota market in Lagos, Dawano market in Kano, or Ariaria market in Aba.

It is a necessity, considering their background of Nigeria's sociopolitical structure (see Eusebius and Chigbo 2014). As retail traders, the apprenticeship network increased their population in the diaspora. People formed mutually beneficial associations, credit societies, and improvement or progressive unions which had ties with villages, towns, and among diasporas, be it in Lagos, Amsterdam, Kuala Lumpur (KL), Guangzhou, SP, or Atlanta.

Remarkable is the courage, perseverance, and determination with which Nigerian entrepreneurs have advanced—notwithstanding traumatic experiences following the civil in the 1960s, economic mismanagement and depression during the oil crisis, or insecurities from Boko Haram terrorists and the Nigerian Delta insurgency. An example of this is Innoson Vehicle Manufacturing in Anambra State: Africa's first indigenous car manufacturer is producing durable and affordable automobiles for Africans.

However, these advantages face challenges in the contemporary globalized world economy and disintegrating values. The long-existing illicit trade mentality in Nigeria has demonstrated its potential to attract informal traders to cocaine trafficking. Due to lack of credit facilities, many Nigerian cocaine traffickers told me they have been motivated to go into the illicit trade to raise capital for starting a private, licit business, as we shall discuss further on.

3.2.4 Disappointed Apprenticeship

Indenture (agreement) and the system of master-apprentice relationships have long been practiced in England, European countries, and the United States. Traditional apprenticeship developed as a system of technical training in English towns around the thirteenth century and continued in the same vein for many centuries afterward (Dolan 2017). Today most apprentices begin training between the ages of 18 and 24. Many businessmen and women told me they became an apprentice as alternative after financial impediments forced them to abandon academic or other dreams. Others decided at a young age to become a trader, so that begins with apprenticeship. Traditionally, to engage the youth in apprenticeship involves parents handing over their youths who they could not train beyond the elementary education level to master a trade.

In this agreement, sometimes without a formal agreement and tutelage, the master craftsperson commits to training the apprentice in all the skills relevant to his or her trade over a significant period of time, usually between three and seven years, while the apprentice is assigned a variety of responsibilities including promoting sales, store management, and contributing productively to the work of the business.

Whereas this concept was envisaged to help young people acquire a trade, fieldwork information indicates that the quality and duration of apprenticeships have been eroded. Similarly, Meagher (2010) found in her research that among shoe and garment traders in Aba market in eastern Nigeria, masters had settled less than 10% of the apprentices in 2000, whereas the hope is to apprentice under relatives and townspeople and be settled at the end of stipulated period. There are several contributing factors. The relationship between the master and apprentice is a complex one, and conflicts often arise because of age difference, subordination, and the domestic nature of apprenticeship. In Idumota market in Lagos and the main market in Fegge, Onitsha, I found that many masters considered some male apprentices to be immature and reckless in their behaviors. Others claim their apprentices syphoned money off the business or wasted company money. And quite a number told me disobedience or the death of the master could lead to unfinished apprenticeships. Furthermore, masters attempt to maximize the use of cheap apprentice labor while increasingly breaking their obligations. In contrast, apprentices attempt to minimize the time spent under the control of the master, in an effort to maximize their own income-generating potential. In other words, the needs of the master and apprentice are often at odds.

Most apprenticeship contract terms are legally unenforceable because they contravene the provision of Nigerian Labour Act (1971, sect. 49–53, 59–60), which states that every contract of apprenticeship shall be written and authorized by a labor officer (ibid., sec.50), and which prohibits young apprentices from working more than eight hours per day and at night time (ibid., sec 59, 60). These regulations are ignored by the prevailing norms of service in small businesses be it in Port Harcourt, Aba, Onitsha, or Lagos. This is why Kodo risked becoming a drug courier in hopes of raising USD12,000 to start a business. Kodo stated:

> It is a horrible feeling that makes most young men go drug trafficking. Igbo must stop this widespread problem. My boss gave me equivalent of about USD400

only after eight good years of apprenticeship under him. He also owned a good cosmetic distribution business in Idumota, and two buildings in Lagos. They will exploit you and dump you at the end. The reason he gave me was that his containers of goods were stolen from the Apapa port and that business is bad. They always come up with one reason or another. When you do not have any one to help what do you do? (Kodo, personal communication, December 29, 2012).

This view was shared by many interviewees. In its ideal form, apprenticeship provides start-up capital at the end of the training period and socializes the trainee to value denial, hardship, and discipline, seen as crucial in business success. The end result is that most apprentices, like Kodo, become victims of exploitation by the very system that was meant to set them free.

For most Nigerians, the primary means of survival is trading. But small time trade has not adequately supported development. Instead of improving investments in education (including evening adult business education for traders) to support trade development, governments maintain ideologies that undermine strong collective efforts toward social development, favoring individualism instead. Efforts should be directed toward consolidating the private sector and modern entrepreneurship, similar to those in Guangzhou where Nigerians excel amid African traders as we shall discuss later, as well as disengaging from other traditional practices that hinder development and foster deviant behavior.

3.3 PATRILINEAL CULTURE OF INHERITANCE

Another mechanism characterizing the enthusiasm around cocaine trafficking is embedded in a traditional inheritance system that concentrated resources in the hand of the oldest son in some parts of Nigeria. Intergenerational transitions include assets and, in some cases, liabilities which are handed down to succeeding generations. Nigeria and other African communities have their own cultural mores and customs governing their affairs, including inheritance and legal succession.

Reflected in Nigeria's plural legal system, the indigenous customary law developed rules of inheritance for intestacy through the traditional canon of descent, adapted over the years to changes in the society and the rule of natural justice as applied by the courts (Oni 2014). Succession, the transfer of property on death, under Intestate Customary Law dominates in Nigeria. Customary Law embodies customs as practiced by the people which they regard as binding on them. Each of the many ethnic groups has its own peculiar characteristics. The general principle of Nigerian law is that a person carries his customary law with him; hence, regardless of the customary law of the place of his residence or abode, his personal law shall prevail (Bello 2017). Therefore, succession does not occur in accordance with common law or statute but in accordance with the traditions, beliefs, customs, and practices of the local people and are enforceable and binding between the parties which are subject to it.

Customary laws differ amid Nigerian ethnic groups and indeed within single groups. For example, customary succession among the Igbos, including Anambra, Imo, Enugu, Ebonyi, and some parts of Rivers and Delta, is predominantly patrilineal; therefore, inheritance is governed by the principle of primogeniture in the sense that the eldest son of the deceased, known as *Okpala* or *Diokpa*, inherits the estate and automatically becomes the head of the family. In a situation where the deceased had more than one wife, the eldest sons of each of the wives share the deceased's estate. However, few communities exist where succession is matrilineal. For instance, in Ohafia division, according to the customary law manual, a man's intestate estate is inherited by his maternal relatives, their sons and daughters. Having succeeded the deceased father, the eldest son is entitled to special property by virtue of his status in the family. He enjoys *ala Iasi Obi* (his father's compound) and the property during his lifetime to the exclusion of his brothers. The exception to this rule exists in Afikpo and Bende areas of Ebonyi and Abia States which are bi-lineal, where women have full legal capacity to own land and to transmit their rights and interests to others either among the living or death. Daughters, like wives, do not inherit under Igbo customary law. However, a daughter can inherit if she remains unmarried in her father's house with a view of raising sons in her father's name (Obilade 1979).

Among the Markis group of the Verbe of northern Nigeria, the rule of ultimogeniture applies, whereby inheritance is by the youngest son (Oluyede 1989). It is a rule of Yoruba customary law that an intestate estate may be distributed among the children by the *Idi Igi* mode that is per stripe or the *Ori Ojori* mode that is per capital. In the per stripe mode, the property of the deceased is divided according to the number of mothers (wives of the deceased) of the children of the intestate—the share attributable to each mother being then subdivided equally among her own children. Whereas, in the per capita mode of distribution, each child enjoys an equal share, it has been found a relatively modern method adopted as an expedient to avoid litigation (Nwogugu 2014, 413–414).

In all, the law of inheritance and succession under customary law is often a source of conflict. Some beneficiaries are accorded rights of inheritance and others are not. This customary law contravenes the repugnancy doctrine test that was introduced into Africa during the colonial era. "By virtue of the test an indigenous law, tradition, or custom is not to be enforced if it is distasteful, offensive to equity and good conscience, and is opposed to natural justice" (Kiye 2015, 89).

This customary law more importantly breaches international conventions against discrimination. It contradicts Section 42(1) and Section 42(2) of the Constitution of the Federal Republic of Nigeria 1999 and violates Article 1 of the UN Convention on the Elimination of All Forms of Discrimination Against Women that defines discrimination as "any distinction, exclusion or restriction made on the basis of sex in the political, economic, social, cultural civic or any other field."

The rule of primogeniture is unfair to the younger children of the family; hence, it is repugnant to natural justice, equity, and good conscience. However, primogeniture and ultimogeniture have also been identified as possible solutions to the problem of fragmentation in land tenure that has hindered large-scale agriculture and economic development insofar as it creates an effective base for capital formation, though only for a single person. The result is subsequent sons are forced to seek their living in crafts or trade. It is one of the push factors underpinning the drive toward international cocaine trafficking. For example, Mipo, whom I met several times in SP, was deprived of promised starting capital after apprenticeship, and with no help from elsewhere, he was lured into radical experiments in self-actualization through deviancy that in the contemporary globalized world sometimes means entrée into cocaine trafficking. The ex-drug courier, Mipo, stated to me: "I am the last of four boys of my father who is a famer. I inherited nothing. Master, Saraf, was a thief! He gave me nothing after seven years. I turned a street area boy in Lagos. I risked cocaine trafficking and succeeded because I used the money to start my business. I had to survive!" (Mipo, personal communication, December 30, 2012).

In line with Agnew's Strain theory (1985), poor treatment made affected Nigerians feel angry, frustrated, depressed, and anxious. One way to respond to these emotions is to engage in international cocaine trafficking, especially in the Nigerian context where the cost of crime is low and the reward is high. Involvement in cocaine trafficking or production is a survival strategy for Kodo, Mipo, and others like them. The underprivileged and uneducated are without a direct way into legitimate opportunities. Often, it is only through illicit trade that people generate the means to enter licit forms of business, "Even for the line workers in deviant industries, the money accumulated over a few years can often form a nest egg of capital to start more legitimate businesses" (Gilman et al. 2011, 7). But for most Nigerian traffickers, several other factors constrain their move into less hazardous areas of business once they have accumulated a start-up stake.

3.4 EXTENDED FAMILY LIABILITIES

It is a dominant view that demands from family members form serious extra-financial burdens on many Nigerians and Africans at large. Intertwined with other push and pull factors discussed earlier on, the need to support one's family can drive some helpless and chanceless individuals into deviant activities for the promise of profit. Unlike the Western contextual terminology where the family is described primarily in its relationship to the individual, the Nigerian family draws on ancestral ties, and this trend cuts across the more than 250 Nigerian ethnic groups. Once a common ancestry is established, the degrees of separation become irrelevant. In practical terms, it is a multiplicity of primary familial relationships usually determined by kinship ties, implying in reality not an extended family but an extensive primary family (Obayan 1995). It refers to that patrilineal social structure or unit, which has a man, his brothers, sisters, and their immediate families who can trace their origin by blood to a common ancestor or progenitor. It is a group of people closely related by blood, for example, children and their parents, their cousins, aunts, and uncles (Ekeopara 2012). It is a social system lacking a fixed number of specifiable positions (e.g., husband/father, wife/mother), but consisting of two or more familiar positions of which one or more resulting dyads is not a nuclear dyad (Uchendu 1995).

The family has the power and authority to exert influence in the attitudes, behaviors, and conduct of individual members of its unit. Its influence covers the area of social relationships, interaction, and morality. Using certain integrative mechanisms such as norms and values, the extended family serves as a vehicle for the maintenance of socio-ethical order in society, including personal freedom, group support, social security, exclusiveness of the family, dependency, and psychological imperatives.

Socialization begins in the extended family circles, wherein the basic cultural norms and values are inculcated in the lives of its members. These include respect for elders and one's seniors, hard work, loyalty, and discipline, depending on one's family background among the various ethnic groups in Nigeria. However, individual freedom could be determined along boundaries set by the extended family unit. One is free but accountable to the collective goal and norms of the family that influence choices, actions, and decision of the individual. Furthermore, socialization practices in Nigeria encourage dependency, as closely affiliated families incline toward the exclusion of "outsiders" from certain forms of interaction, especially, those involving trust, and a tendency toward keeping secrets. This is what Imouokhome (1989) refers to as the undisclosing nature of the Nigerian client. Close-knit family ties are the reference point in the determination of psychological status and self-esteem. It makes explicit the role of kinship networks in informal exchange and public good provision. It offers support and risk sharing in the face of deficit state caring.

3.4.1 Social Security Pillar

Most Nigerian drug traffickers told me that the need to meet extended family responsibilities was a push factor for engaging in the illicit drug business. They carry culturally imposed, shared obligations. Economic literature on extended family and kinship networks (Cox and Fafchamps 2006) noted that a majority of transfers between households take place between close relatives. Rosenzweig (1988) rejected the concept of full risk sharing in favor of partial risk sharing. And Fafchamps and Lund (2003) demonstrated that risk is often shared via gifts, transfers, and informal loans. They showed that risk sharing takes place within networks made primarily of relatives and kin members. While close relatives provide gifts, more distant relatives make informal loans. These loans are hybrid debt contracts whereby money is lent at zero interest in exchange for the promise of future repayment. Further repayment of such loans is contingent on shocks affecting both parties, and contingent repayment takes place by letting borrowers in difficulty delay repayment and pay off part of the debt in labor (Cox and Fafchamps 2006).

Funeral societies are another illustration of informal insurance institutions in Africa. In times of death, extended family members and kin participate in raising funds and materials required for the burial of the deceased. Extended families incorporate contributions and the enforcement of contractual obligations to protect productive assets, such as the building of village roads, bore whole water and town halls, or the preservation of communal resources such as schools and churches.

Thus, an African adage states the family is like a cobweb which no matter at which angle or spot it is touched, vibrates to the center. The extended family and kinship networks provide many forms of insurance and protection against external events. "Kinship ties defined the status and roles of every person in the society and determined the behaviors of members towards themselves and the outside world" (Ifemesia 1979, 40). Those who are in trouble seek shelter among relatives and kin whenever possible. The extended family unit serves as a shock absorber to the emotional, financial, physical, and social needs of family members. Affluence or poverty, honor or shame or gain or loss reflects on the entire image of the extended family. This is why the people say, "When the eye cries, the nose also cry," because they are inseparable and intricately united by blood.

However, the extended family social system has been metamorphosing. Change, they say, is the only constant factor in human endeavors. Culture is not static, rather one of its fundamental properties is change. Noticing this change, Onunwa (1990) affirmed, "A new social order is emerging partly out of the old and partly as a response to the new contact with powerful external change agents" (31). The spirit of solidarity that characterized life in the extended family system is gradually giving way to individual life and living.

As discussed in previous chapters, state crisis and the criminogenic environment in Nigeria have affected the status and mode of operation of the family. The individual is disengaging from his/her extended primary family. Thus, the influence of the family in the light of its ability to provide support, inculcate and transmit values, encourage mutual and reciprocal sharing is reduced. Due to globalization, the influx of the Western mass media, and the adoption of Western values and beliefs, the right of the individual has shifted from traditional values toward Western ideals. Because the social mechanisms for enforcing traditional values have been displaced, communal morality has been replaced by individual morality, leading to indiscipline and moral anarchy. Globalization can be said to be a factor in moral decay for reasons that include speedy cultural exchanges, growing capitalist and middle classes, and overpopulation.

Urban-rural migrations have brought about gaps in family interaction. In its stead, there has been a tendency for Nigerians to create surrogate family units linked more by social interaction than by kinship ties. This interaction may be a result of a common ethnic origin, area of residence, professional ties, and so on. This has through time resulted in new relationships which tend to modify traditional relationships and develop the sense of community within urban settings, be it in Lagos, Amsterdam, London, KL, Texas, Guangzhou, or SP. It is a trend derived from a "cultural osmosis" shaping an individual's set of values. It is to this extent that it is possible to talk about a Nigerian mode of behavioral response, disposition, and values.

3.4.2 Filling in the Gaps

Though the structural tradition of patriarchy has been somewhat eroded in the developed world during the twentieth century, traditional institutions of extended family have survived in Nigeria and Africa because they fulfill security and social gaps left by the soft state. Extended families are important just about everywhere, but especially so in poor countries, where social safety nets are incomplete or nonexistent, and households must cope with an unforgiving environment of severe poverty and shocks to economic and physical well-being. Immigrants send money to family members for food and housing, personal maintenance, education fees, hospital costs, and other basic needs. Cox and Fafchamps (2006) showed the interplay between kinship ties and public sector efforts to alleviate poverty and mitigate risk. They found that public safety net interventions can dilute incentives to maintain a private, informal coping network. This is happing but not in Nigeria. Writers have emphasized the relevance of networks of blood and kin that provide shelter and help to freshly arrived migrants, creating tightly knit migration networks linking village of origin and place of destination. They serve to relay important information for job or business opportunities, matching workers and employers (Granovetter 1995), and experienced workers identify suitable recruits (Montgomery 1991). These are often relatives and kin members that make information about business opportunities circulate in family and ethnic networks.

However, cooperation transcends the exchange of useful information, as when individuals pool resources to create a new business. At the heart of many businesses a partnership could be found, and many partnerships are grounded in family and kin ties. For example, in rural areas, relatives pool their efforts into cultivating larger agricultural farms. Likewise, individual traders join their savings by creating rotating savings and credit associations. These associations often transcend family relationships. Youths put efforts into surviving, improving their lives, gaining social capital, and recognition.

But for many frustrated and helpless youths who have seen these social and family networks eroded or collapsed, deviant activities become an alternative. Ethnographic literature has shown that people are considered "young" because of their age and regarding their position within generational categories (Christiansen et al. 2006; Durham 2004). In Nigeria, many young men are frustrated by not being perceived as a *Oga* (Chief or "man of respect, an adult") because of their inability to meet social expectations, like being economically independent or having enough resources to starting a family. The cocaine trade could represent an alternative for some desperate individuals. As cocaine hoppers in search of respect and social mobility, they borrow or contribute money to form a working capital for ad hoc transaction. In this context of searching for social mobility, youth takes on the meaning of unfulfilled progression, and becoming an adult becomes closely related to achieving financial independence and social recognition.

Therefore, Nigerian youths' aspirations toward independent adulthood might render them more prone to taking risks and being involved in drug dealing activities because of the high premium placed on economic affluence regardless of means.

The widespread mentality in Nigeria is the more successful someone becomes, the more recognition he gets by way of traditional and societal titles, while how the person gained recognition or wealth is not subject to inquiry. Nigerians who are prominent in the drug trade, be it professional warlords, or drug lords, or couriers, do not choose this career to become professional criminals in the Western sense, but primarily as an avenue to wealth and social esteem. During fieldwork, several individuals who have nothing to do with drug trafficking nevertheless indicated that they might carry cocaine to make quick money if they have a good chance of succeeding. Their intention was doing it on a short-term basis for financial gain and not becoming a professional courier. This is the same thinking expressed by many couriers interviewed. Some of them had jobs or private businesses before becoming part-time traffickers.

Some part-time traffickers have gone as far as using their children for trafficking. For instance, NDLEA arrested a couple, Mr. Jimoh Oladega Bashir and Mrs. Mulikat Adebukola, who used their six-year-old twins in smuggling cocaine at MMIA Lagos. They were arrested with 4.05 kilograms of cocaine prior to boarding a flight to London Heathrow; during screening, 350 grams of cocaine were found on each on the children, while 3.35 kilograms was found on their mother (Ehigiator 2010). Many part-time traffickers indicated that they were introduced to it through a relative, friend, or acquaintance. Primarily, they were asked to link with either a family member or a friend of a friend to purchase cocaine in exchange for money or sometimes cocaine. For instance, Dimpa, 42, is a part-time trafficker who grew up in South America since the age of 10 and has citizenship in an undisclosed South American country. He has been running a successful business in Lagos for four years. Dimpa explained that he has a regular job but that he has no problem making connections between actors who move *ahia ocha* (white market, as cocaine is referred to by Nigerian traffickers). Dimpa travels regularly to Nigeria and other South American countries such as Peru or Venezuela for work. During one interview in Eko, he explained that it was a night to celebrate because one of his friends *Ogburu ozu* (made a big catch). They reserved an exclusive corner in a private club away from the dancing spots and proceeded to boast about *ahia ocha*: "I started as a middleman for some guys who wanted me to connect them to good sources for buying pure cocaine. I have good documents, and I can find my way. I have good local friend who get regular supply of pure cocaine. So, all I did was to make the connection and assist them with getting the right guys to packaging the shit. After my Naija guys paid some cash and the South American guys paid me with about five kilos of pure cocaine. I got to sell to my guys, and that's how I started making some cash" (Dimpa, personal communication, June 8, 2013).

Just like Dimpa, most couriers confirmed that several friends and acquaintances with regular jobs in many countries do part-time trafficking. Similarly, Taduk had a good job in a factory in Germany where he worked on the production line. His friends lured him into cocaine trafficking during his holiday period: "My friends who were swallowing cocaine introduced me to it, and I travelled with my South American friends to Jamaica and other places. I succeeded in bringing in about 900 grams on each trip. But I was caught on my fifth trip and jailed for four years in Germany. That is how I lost my job and was deported to Nigeria thereafter" (Taduk, personal communication, June 8, 2013).

Ultimately, no matter which type of trafficker, from *Ogas* (big bosses) to part-time traffickers, the common thread is the view that cocaine trafficking is an open market. As Dimpa noted:

It is a business done by individuals from various parts of Nigeria irrespective of tribe. It is a trade, and the most capable succeeds because they have the right means. Anybody can do this business in Nigeria, but some are better in it. Furthermore, the damage done by the powerful in this country is worse than that of cocaine trafficking. Those who are pointing hands actually belong to the worst embezzlers of the nation's wealth. They should realize that when one of their fingers points to the drug traffickers, the other four fingers points back to them as the cause of the problem (Dimpa, personal communication, June 8, 2013).

While Dimpa and many other traffickers note that any and all ethnic groups in Nigeria participate in the cocaine trade.

3.5 EXCELLING AS TRADERS

In Nigeria, raw capitalism prevails. Wealth is a means of gaining social prestige and acquiring position. The general belief is that wealth is more valuable when it is acquired through personal effort and hard work. This is a key reason why many no longer look to the government for salvation but work toward self-reliance. For instance, most people depend on water from private boreholes at home or light from fossil-fuel combusting electricity generators, risking lung cancer and miscarriages in pregnant women among other health issues from inhaled dangerous gases (Oguntoke and Adeyemi 2016).

They believe in purposeful hard work and communal efforts to improve the standard of living, reduce unemployment, and ensure financial security. And yet, a survey covering five commercial cities in southeast Nigeria revealed that "close to 26% of entrepreneurs are above 60 years; majority don't know when they would retire, or not even thinking of retiring and 94.2% have no succession plans" (Onuoha 2013, 103). Nigeria falls short of developing new skills through well-funded technical education and vocational training programs for those millions of Nigerians outside the formal school system or those with only elementary education. Neither has Nigeria realized that unlatching private sector partnerships through incentives and boosting entrepreneurship via apprenticeships remain vital ways the authorities can spur on growth and Small and Medium Enterprises (SMEs).

A write-up in *The Nation* (October 8, 2017) claimed that SMEs contribute approximately 48% to Nigeria's GDP. Researchers found that nearly 96% of Nigerian businesses are SMEs, compared to 53% in the United States and

65% in Europe. They contribute around 1% of GDP, compared to 40% in Asian countries and 50% in the United States or Europe (Igwe et al. 2018, 187). SMEs are key drivers in emerging economies in various areas like entrepreneurship development, job creation, innovation and technology development, stimulation and attainment of more equitable economic growth, redistribution of wealth, and social infrastructure development at local levels. In Malaysia, for instance, SMEs contributed almost 36% to the total GDP in 2015 (Chin and Lim 2018). In Brazil, they account for 98.5% of all legally constituted companies, 27% of GDP, and 41% of the total payroll (OECD 2018).

Nigeria's inability to unlatching private sector partnerships and boosting entrepreneurship via well-funded apprenticeships has pushed many chance-less youths into deviant activities including drug trafficking, which most traffickers emphasize is a cross-ethnic business in the country.

3.6 "FOO-FOO" SWALLOWING CULTURE

Nigerian cocaine traffickers have developed particular methods that make it easier for them to ingest wrapped cocaine for air travel. These include what Nigerians popularly refer to as the swallowing practice, which prepares them for the ingestion of wrapped cocaine, or "suicide balls," as they are popularly referred to amid Nigerian traffickers. Frequently, interviewed traffickers pointed out that an important factor encouraging Nigerian cocaine traffickers is the culture of swallowing certain staple foods, such as *foo-foo (or fufu)*, a thick dough-like food made from boiled, pounded-up starchy edible root such as yam and cassava and served with soups. *Foo-foo* is a staple food in West Africa. The traditional way of eating it is to pinch off a small-sized ball of *foo-foo* in the right hand, making an indentation in the ball with the thumb to use as a scoop for the soup. Among several ethnic groups in Nigeria, the ball is often not chewed but swallowed whole since chewing foo-foo is considered impolite. This practice is acquired even at a young age: swallowing *foo-foo* starts at about two years old. For Nigerian traffickers, it was a big factor in the move to ingest balls of cocaine.

Ingesting anabolics such as ketamine, typically given as a sedative to cows and horses, enhances couriers' performance by making them feel physically strong and emotionally ready. They compare themselves to cows that walk unimaginable distances without resting; the courage, attitude, and emotions exhibited by many couriers of the Nigerian international cocaine trade constitute one of the factors of their success. In this subcultural strain context, the combination of hard physical work, consumption of pain relieving and strength enhancing medicine, coupled with the attractive financial reward from cocaine when successful, turned some individuals into dare-heart couriers ready to extend the limits of edge work, swallowing more cocaine. The larger the quantity risked, the more they were compensated, either in money or in cocaine.

Nigerian traffickers refer to cocaine pellets as *suicide balls* due to the chance of cocaine balls bursting in the stomach. One kilogram of cocaine costs about USD500 to wrap. For a good wrap, the procedure is as follows: inspect the condom for visible openings. Then, weigh about 10–20 grams of cocaine with a small spoon and put it at the end part of a condom. Press down the content and twist the condom a couple of times while holding the edge. Double fold the condom, and then close and seal the top by heating with a lighter. In some cases, the condom is wrapped in aluminum foil to throw off any machine that might be able to detect it. The final step is to seal the pellet with black solo-tape, about three or four times round. A well-sealed pellet should remain sunk at the bottom of the basin. If it floats to the surface, it means that it is not air sealed. If there is an opening on it somewhere, there is a high risk of it bursting in the stomach. In this case, it has a defect and should be unpacked and redone. If it is well sealed, it can be swallowed with the help of slippery sauces. Likewise, it is encouraged for couriers to slightly cover the surface of the wrapped ball with some *foo-foo* before swallowing so that the digestive acids in the stomach only attack the *foo-foo* and not the cocaine ball. Swallowing the cocaine can take hours. Couriers tend to eat lightly during trip to avoid needing to use the toilet. Finally, upon arrival at the destination, couriers excrete the swallowed balls. Drinking milk assists excretion, and the process can last for several hours, if not days.

In addition to swallowing, also prominent amid Nigerian cocaine traffickers is the *kele* trafficking method, which consists of anal or vaginal insertion of the cocaine, initially more common with women but later used by both male and female couriers. In the *kele* system, the quantity trafficked is less, fluctuating from a few grams to about one kilogram. The average is about one kilogram; otherwise, it becomes difficult to walk, according to most couriers.

Chapter 4

The Structure and Modus Operandi
of Nigerian Cocaine Traffickers

Nigerian international cocaine trafficking is influenced by individual choices, decisions, and the conduct of others involved and society at large. As some traffickers have noted, unbalanced social capital could have contributed to this. Given the opportunity and chance, vulnerable populations may be less attracted to cocaine trafficking if friends, family, and society discouraged it; however, if a society is neutral to or even rewards deviant behavior, this shifts the social capital in favor of criminal activity such as Nigerian international drug trafficking.

Who are the actors, the Nigerian cocaine traffickers, and smugglers? What is the basis of their trade networks? What kinds of traffickers are they? What are their social backgrounds? What are the connections between them? What can we say about their culture? This part provides a clear profile of the hub of the cocaine market in Nigeria, the networks that exist, and the various kinds of Nigerian traffickers, from the *Ogas* (big bosses) to the part-time traffickers who only occasionally involve themselves in trafficking.

Lagos is the largest city in Nigeria, home to the country's largest seaport and the gateway of Nigeria's economic activity. It is also the hub of criminality and cocaine trafficking. Lagos Island is the commercial heart of the city, where most of the corporate businesses are located. While there is criminality in most parts of Lagos, Ajegunle and Lagos Island areas are of special interest to cocaine trafficking. This is due to the fact that the slums of Ajegunle guarantee a steady pool of potential traffickers, while the Lagos Island hosts the Idumota market, which is the big wholesale for imported goods covertly exploited by traffickers. In Nigeria, "white market" is the term for the cocaine trafficking business. "*Bros you don make am!*" is the traditional phrase for "'Brother or friend,' you have made it!" While it is still a common expression, it is now used to express success and achievements among businesspeople. Likewise, cocaine traffickers use it to mean a successful deal. When used in trafficking, *Bros you don make am* can indicate that the shipment has been received in good condition, that the courier has arrived safely, or that expected payment has been collected. Finally, it is used as a term for making a "big catch" or big sale.

Identifying the six groups of Nigerian traffickers and the Nigerian participation in each of them will assist to illustrate the complexity of such an involvement (avoiding simple pictures that hardly distinguish among the people engaged) in terms of background, chances, skills, commitments, expectations, social and labor relations, power and gender differences, and so on. What follows categorizes and explains the roles of each of the types of brokers and distributors, having created market at wholesale, small quantity, and retail levels.

4.1 EARLY ORIGINS FOR MODERN NETWORK

Drawing from the historical trade routes, Nigerian drug traffickers took advantage of trading networks created by colonialists, Malian and Berber traders (Bybee 2012), to move drugs to through the subregion to consumption hubs including Europe and the Middle East. Current involvement in international cocaine trafficking has underscored Nigeria both as transit and transaction nation. Nigeria's geographical location fostered easy transportation of Latin American cocaine into the country. Its historical connection with Brazil, through the slave trade, helped consolidate Nigerians' participation in the international cocaine trade. In effect, Nigeria became a consumer country because of the involvement of Nigerians in the international trade, and international trade facilitates the illicit cocaine trade. Hard drug trafficking through Nigeria to overseas markets dates back to 1952, as discussed in chapter 1.2, with the involvement of Lebanese trafficking syndicates. The involvement of an Italian intelligence officer in the deal underscores how intertwined illicit drug trafficking has been with the work of secret intelligence agencies and elite participation from an early period. The colonialists sanctioned the entry of a group of middlemen that linked European companies in the capitals with producers in the hinterland. In West Africa, the middlemen were mainly Lebanese nationals who became a market-dominant minority that owned most of the productive sectors of the economy. However, the Lebanese are among the leading traffickers of South American cocaine via West Africa and Nigeria to the United States (see UNODC 2007). What started with the coca plant cultivation trials by the British colonialists later expanded to include actors of varied ethnicity and race.

The global structure of narcotics drug consumption, trade, and primary destinations indicates that the new trend of illicit cocaine trade through SSA is a convergence of interests by Nigerian traffickers and various drug trafficking groups. These include members of Lebanese, Pakistani, Mexican, Colombian, Venezuelan, Surinamese, and European organizations operating in the same territory and plugging into the same pipeline, who Douglas Farah (2012) described in the "Fixers, Super Fixers and Shadow Facilitators." And as has been the case in Brazil and Mexico, transit countries, including Nigeria, often become user countries because of the availability and affordability of cocaine. Seizures and arrests in several places in Nigeria and West African countries have revealed trafficking networks facilitated by a range of individuals, including business professionals, politicians, members of the security forces and the judiciary, and youths. The arrest of offenders from Igbo, Yoruba, Hausa, Edo, and Nigerian Muslim pilgrims to Saudi Arabia for the Hajj shows that the phenomenon stretches across ethnic groups and religions.

Nigerians and Lebanese traffickers congregate in several countries across Latin America, particularly in the Tri-Border Area (TBA), where Argentina, Brazil, and Paraguay meet. Experts outlined the convergence of transnational organized crime groups in the TBA, a general clearinghouse for shipments from South America. Native criminal syndicates helped to create a criminogenic environment that in turn fostered organized crime groups from other nations, including Colombia, Italy, Russia, Taiwan, Ghana, Lebanon, Japan, and Nigeria (see Roth 2017, 454). The TBA was a meeting point for Nigerian traffickers forwarding cocaine to Nigeria and beyond. This coincides with the fact that prior to 2003, only 10% of the cocaine destined for the European market first transited through West Africa, but by 2007, the estimate had risen to nearly 60%, representing 180–240 metric tons, about 18% of the total world cocaine production, noted William Wechsler (2009) in "Confronting Drug Trafficking in West Africa."

4.2 FOREIGN PARTNERS

Nigerian traffickers claim that their foreign partners are important in the trafficking chain. Nigeria's centrality in this the mule economy is nothing new. In the 1950s, heroin trafficking networks between Lagos, Abidjan, and Beirut were identified in the United States while in the 1960s Nigerians and Ghanaians exported cannabis to Europe and heroin trafficking soared, sometimes with the help of the CIA (McCoy 1991).

In popular discussions, these foreign traffickers are popularly referred to as "Oyibo JJC" ("White Johnny Just Come"), who are either on a short visit to Nigeria for a deal or who are entrepreneurs or residents of Nigeria or neighboring countries. *Oyibo* can be of European origin, Arab, Asian, or people of mixed ethnic backgrounds. Most traffickers who were interviewed commented that Lebanese, Pakistanis, and Indians often employ Nigerians as apprentices and business partners. Good apprentices and business partners learn every aspect of the business from the boss, including sharing important strategic contacts and establishing front companies and safe houses, and money laundering.

The creativity and entrepreneurial skills of Nigerian drug traffickers attracted the attention of smugglers wanting their services in South America and in several destination markets in Asia. Additionally, most Nigerian cocaine traffickers indicated that their toughness, described as "shock absorbers," is an ulterior motive for why their counterparts overseas look to them. A successful cocaine trafficker, Tambu, stated: "These guys want to do business with us no matter what. They said it's because of our ability to handle cocaine and that we are serious. They recognize Nigerians for being *"shock absorbers"* of risks. Nigerians know how to absorb shock. This is the difference between [Nigerians and] other Africans" (Tambu, personal communication, August 8, 2013).

Tambu's comments are not the exception. Most Nigerian traffickers shared the same view that Nigerians are hardened individuals, or shock absorbers, because of their experiences with colonial rule, civil wars, dictators, poverty, and corruption. Their entrepreneurial skills and their hardened perspective on life formed by Nigeria's chaotic environment have helped them establish a worldwide network.

Many Nigerian traffickers have settled in other countries involved in cocaine production, transit, and consumption. In collaboration with their local counterparts, Nigerian traffickers, such as Tambu, have exploited the interconnectedness between legal and illegal commercial activities in supplying South American cocaine through Nigeria and other countries in SSA to meet demands in Europe and beyond. Nigerian traffickers have exploited several macro- and micro-competitive advantages and shipping methods to reach destination markets. They steadily move small and medium quantities of South American cocaine to contacts in destination countries, sometimes never even touching down in Nigeria. The cocaine may go directly to contacts worldwide, implying that the match between Nigerian "shock absorbers" and their foreign associate *Oyibo* underlines this shift in international cocaine trafficking through West Africa.

4.3 CROWNING

Intensified interdictions have made it harder for Colombian and Mexican cartels to move cocaine directly to the U.S. or European markets. The changing global cocaine markets and declining value of the U.S. dollar comparative to the Euro have encouraged Latin American traffickers to look for alternative routes. The successful disruption of the FARC cartel by the Columbian government resulted in an upsurge of smaller groups, including Negras and Aguilas, seeking to fill the power vacuum and find partners elsewhere. Nigerian international traffickers ended up being their best match, resulting in at least 50 tons of cocaine being shipped annually to Europe via West Africa (see UNODC 2013).

To understand Nigerians' vast network in international cocaine trafficking, take a pioneer country such as Peru for instance: law enforcement authorities affirmed that international drug traffickers operating in the country included Europeans, Asians, and Africans. In the past decade, officials seized about 42,000 kilograms (arround 42 tons) of cocaine at Peru's main port, El Callao, where more than 30 workers have been killed by rival gangs fighting for exit routes for drug shipments (Al Jazeera 2018). Colonel Luis Gonzalez of Peru's national police made public in Al Jazeera's (2018) *Peru: The New Cocaine Kingdom* that only 203 drug traffickers were arrested in the last seven years. Due to endemic corruption, everything is fixed—production, transport, and shipment to global destinations from El Callao Port. Despite efforts made by authorities, about 300 tons of cocaine gets through every year, in a trade which generates roughly USD10 billion laundered yearly from the country. From December 2014 to March 2016, about 22 tons of cocaine were seized en route from South America via West Africa to Europe (UNODC 2016).

The new trend of illicit cocaine trade has succeeded in part because traffickers have taken advantage of Africa's proximity to cocaine-producing nations across the Atlantic Ocean, permeable borders, volatility, poverty, corruption, and weak law enforcement. Due to poorly equipped police, military, and intelligence institutions and infrastructure, West Africa's borders of more than 2,600 miles of coastline remain mostly unguarded and porous, and several governments have feeble legal and judicial structures and inefficient customs authorities (Braun 2009). Traveling by sea from to the Port of Santos in Brazil to Apapa Port in Lagos-Nigeria takes about 19 days, and traveling straight from SA to the Gulf of Guinea takes only two days by boat or six hours by plane (Carson 2012).

Nigerian traffickers claim that smuggling cocaine through Nigeria's—or neighboring—seaports is successful due to ineffective policing and corruption. Nigerian international cocaine traffickers deploy various shipping methods such as containerized concealments in different packages and goods, postage using conventional mail services, and the drug courier approach in supplying markets overseas and Nigeria.

4.4 COCAINE CONSUMPTION IN NIGERIA

Drug abuse is prevalent in Nigeria, and cocaine is no exception. Drug abuse refers to an unusual, wrong, and excessive use of substances; the excessive and persistent self-administration of a drug without recourse to the medically or culturally accepted pattern (National Agency for Food and Drug Administration and Control [NAFDAC] 2000); or use of a substance that alter mood.

UNODC World Drug recent reports asserted that overall drug trafficking increased, and the cocaine and synthetic drug markets are thriving. Coca bush cultivation increased by 30% during the period of 2013–2015, mainly as a result of increased cultivation in Colombia (UNODC 2017a). Total global manufacture of cocaine reached 1,976 tons in 2017, representing an overall increase of 25% on the previous year (UNODC 2019c, 8). Cocaine use is increasing in emerging markets in Oceania (namely Australia and New Zealand), and in the traditional large markets in North America, Western and Central Europe, and South America (UNODC 2019e, 13). Self-reported consumption among the general population and testing in the workforce have shown there is an increase in cocaine use in the United States. And in Europe, analysis of wastewater in selected cities has found an increase in cocaine consumption of 30% or more during the period of 2011–2016 (UNODC 2017a).

Drug trafficking in West Africa has led to increased abuse of heroin and amphetamine-type stimulants in addition to cocaine in the subregion. This implies that illicit cocaine trade is rising with a new consumer base. Drawing from the NDLEA's rough estimates, an estimated 16 million Nigerians use Indian hemp or cannabis while another seven million are on cocaine and heroin. These figures come from Ahmadu Giade, former NDLEA chairman, who disclosed this at the official presentation of an antidrug abuse campaign tagged, "Be Smart, Don't Start." The campaign that includes a television commercial is jointly promoted by the agency in collaboration with the Celebrity Drug-Free Club.

These figures serve to highlight a serious new trend illicit drug trade and its spillover effect. These figures show, as the NDLEA chairman noted: "We must continue to work very hard in reducing the number of persons who use drugs and support the agency in preventing casualties in the war against drug cartels. Every contribution towards drug control is a worthy investment towards a peaceful and secure society. Let me appeal to donor agencies to see this as a viable investment opportunity" (Ezeamalu 2015).

The figures raise eyebrows; however, it should be understood at the outset that when describing any facet of the cocaine economy, supposition can all too easily take the place of fact. Writing objectively about an illicit activity is difficult at the best of times and most observers seem happy to err on the side of wild exaggerations (Feiling 2009).

There is lack of data on the estimated number of drug users in Nigeria for several reasons. First, there is no efficient national central data coordination unit set up for this purpose, with the exception of figures derived mainly from hospitals. As NDCMP acknowledged, such data is deficient as it excludes street users who do not have access to and are unable to afford paying for hospital care (NDCMP 2015). Second, individual researchers and academics with limited resources conduct most of the drug abuse studies in the country. These have been mainly hospital based and retrospective, making prediction of the trend rather difficult. And third, epidemiological studies done in Nigeria have been localized and covered mainly easily accessible populations such as students. Lastly, national drug use and abuse surveys are few and far between, with all but one being funded by international organizations (Onifade et al. 2011).

Drug abuse is a worrying issue as many Nigerian adolescents and youth ignorantly depend on one form of drug or the other. They experiment and use drugs for reasons that include curiosity and desire to explore the effectiveness of a specific drug, to reduce stress, or to feel grown up. Such drugs include soft drugs like cannabis (most consumed) and hard drugs such as heroin, pharmaceutical opioids (tramadol, codeine, morphine), cocaine, amphetamines, and ecstasy. This is reflected in the result of UNODC's recent report on prevalence of drug use by gender in Nigeria in 2017—the first large-scale nationwide survey that examined the extent and patterns of drug use in Nigeria (see UNODC 2018a, 13).

Drawing from the above, contrary to popular belief, hard drugs such as cocaine and heroin are no longer out of the reach of the common man in Nigeria. Cocaine is sold and used in Nigerian cities such as Lagos, Abuja, Aba, and beyond. In addition, cocaine has a euphoric effect, which helps people to deal with life in a world dominated by stress, uneasiness, information overload, and how costly everything has become.

The consumption trend appears to have stabilized in North America and Western and Central European markets that account for roughly one-half of cocaine users worldwide, but it is increasing in Africa.

According to UNODC (2016), about 2.9% of youth between 13 and 25 had consumed cocaine in the previous year in Ghana. In a recent qualitative study of 45 female sex workers in Kenya, 32 reported heroin addicted. Researchers unexpectedly found widespread cocaine use, too, and 76% of the individuals surveyed injected heroin. Users were pooling to buy cocaine from Nairobi, even if it was seen as a powerful and expensive drug, and trafficking the drugs further to Uganda and Tanzania (Syvertsen et al. 2016, 2019).

Studies found that most drug addicts started smoking in their youths; as they grow older, they seek new thrills and gradually enter into hard drug abuse. A nationwide survey of high school students in Nigeria reported that 65% used drugs to have good time with their friends, 54% wanted to experiment to see what it is like, and 20–40% used it to alter their moods, feel good, relax, relive tension, and overcome boredom and problems (Igwe et al. 2009; Madaki and Dukku 2017). Ajayi and Somefun (2020) researched the prevalence and frequency of drug use among 784 male and female students between 16 and 39 years old, from two Nigerian universities. Results revealed that 24.5% of students had used drugs for recreational purposes, and 17.5% were current users of mind-altering substances like codeine, marijuana, and tramadol.

As I observed during fieldwork, drugs are rampant in Nigerian towns, motor parks, street corners, university campuses, uncompleted buildings, and under flyovers in most cities. Drugs are used in varied settings of Ring Road outlets in Benin City, Ajegunle in Lagos, Mabushi in Abuja, and under flyover in Onitsha, which are areas of rife drug consumption, particularly young consumers.

As we shall see later, some Nigerian drug couriers take painkillers, like ephedrine, to foster their activities. The UNODC (2018a) world drug report noted that in 2017, the prevalence of any drug use in Nigeria is estimated at 14.4% or 14.3 million people aged between 15 and 64 years. The extent of drug use in Nigeria is high when compared with the 2016 global annual prevalence of any drug use of 5.6% among the adult population. More men (10.8 million) than women (3.4 million women) used drugs in Nigeria. The highest levels of drug use were among those aged 25–39 years (ibid., 12). One in four drug users in Nigeria is a woman. One in five high-risk drug users injects drugs, roughly 80,000 users (ibid., 9).

In Nigeria, as in Ghana or Kenya, drug use amid youth is reality. There is a compelling need to address recreational drug use on Nigerian campuses by educating students about its adverse impacts.

4.4.1 Street Dealing: Price and Cutting

In Lagos, crack is available for N300 (less than USD1) from a young retailer of about 22 years old. My contact, Owo, will not buy that. *Na ye ye* (it's useless), he said. Owo had sold a gram of what he called "better quality cocaine" for N10,000. Owo and his friends' lives revolve around crack cocaine dealing, one fix after another in search of the ultimate high. They seem unconcerned about arrest. Owo had this to say, "Dicey! Do not worry because the police collect their share of the 'cake' [money] and some even buy it too. My guys are capable of anything. They will deal with anyone suspect of menacing their interest" (Owo, personal communication, August 10, 2013).

Over the past decades, Nigeria has become a major importer of cocaine, including by-products of the refinement process, notably crack. In Lagos, "joints or bunks" refer to places where drug users hang out. Many are located in grimy environments in Lagos Island (around Mandela's Square, the Central Mosque) and near hectic streets in Ajegunle, Agege, Ikeja, Mushin, and Alakija. Cocaine is becoming more available for use within the hinterland, places without any direct air link where it may be easy to access illicit drugs on transit. The NDLEA (2016/2017, 25–27) annual report revealed that contrary to the previous practice where cocaine was only being seized in Lagos, Port Harcourt, and Abuja, the agency recorded cocaine seizures in 20 states and the Federal Capital Territory.

The states included in the seizures were Akwa Ibom, Abia, Bayelsa, Cross River, Delta, Edo and Enugu, Imo, Kaduna, Niger, Ogun, Rivers, and Kano. Drug use is also affecting Nigerian families.

Cocaine is expensive in the Nigerian market when compared to production and transit countries in South America. However, it is not as costly as in most consumption hubs in Europe or Asia. Using the UN World Drug Report and user-submitted data, the Havocscope's Global Black Market (2017) compiled a list of how much cocaine costs around the world. Kuwait tops the price charts at USD330 a gram, while in Peru it is sold for USD4.50 per gram, and in Bolivia and Colombia, USD3.50 per gram. The farther you are from its source countries of Colombia, Peru, and Bolivia, the more expensive cocaine becomes.

During my research, I found that at wholesale, a kilogram of quality cocaine attracts a price of conservatively N7–7.3 million (about USD19,700–20,500) in Lagos. Dealers test for purity using at-home testing methods. The higher the quality, the higher the price. One reason dealers test for quality is due to the risk and difficulty drug traffickers face in smuggling the drugs in and out of the country. Once the cocaine crosses the Atlantic, the price skyrockets because a gram of the street priced cocaine fetches between EUR25 and EUR30 in the Netherlands, EUR50 in Britain, and as much as EUR80 in Norway. The price also rises because transporting cocaine is a risky job—the hardest in the cocaine trade because deceiving customs and police agents is a constant challenge. For a good financial return for the risk taken, Nigerian cocaine traffickers often mix pure cocaine with other readily available chemicals, a practice called "cutting." Part of the value of pure cocaine is the ability to make incredible amounts of profit by cutting it with cheaper substances or freebasing the raw material, turning it into crack.

Quality cocaine is in high demand in Nigeria because it is adulterated prior to re-exportation to markets overseas, be it Holland, Italy, Sweden, United

Kingdom, United States, Canada, Australia, or China. A 55-year-old Nigerian prince, a member of a Nigerian royal family, famously packed his luggage with shrimp and malodourous, dried fish in an attempt to throw customs officials off the scent, but he was nevertheless intercepted by a sniffer dog at London's Heathrow airport. A black hold was found inside his suitcase containing 23 apparently ordinary onions and the fish. A closer inspection revealed 17 of the onions had been carefully cut open and packed with small carbon paper wraps. The wraps contained a total of 3.21 kilograms of 67% pure cocaine. Convicted Prince Adegbenie Olateru-Olagbegi was sentenced to 12 years in prison for smuggling cocaine worth £163,000 (News 24 Archives 2005).

Researchers in England have found that cocaine is heavily cut with other substances, including anesthetics and animal worming agents. Police seizures of cocaine in 2009 averaged 27% purity, with some as low as 2–5% according to recent cocaine trade reports in Britain and the Psychiatrist and Addiction Medicine Specialist of recent *Global Drug Survey* (Winstock et al. 2017). Adulterants imitate some of the biological effects of cocaine to increase its perceived quality, and diluents act as simple fillers to enhance the bulk, and consequently the profits of the drug dealer. Distinctive adulterants include caffeine and anesthetics such as procaine, lidocaine, levamisole, and benzocaine. For good returns on investment, local dealers adulterate cocaine further.

Adaki stated to me, "I cut my 'ahia ocha' [white market or cocaine] with talc, plaster, starch. Or better, with procaine that I buy here in Lagos and cut pure cocaine to 60%. I must double the gain" (Adaki, personal communication, November 27, 2013). People can buy cheap cocaine at hidden corners in any city, fueling a market that the UNODC (2017a) estimated at about USD85 billion annually.

4.5 "WHITE MARKET" AND THE "BIG CATCH" ACTORS: CATEGORIES OF NIGERIAN TRAFFICKERS

4.5.1 "Big Man" Smugglers

In popular discussions among Nigerian traffickers, "big man" smugglers include elite of all sorts in public and private sectors, both indigenous and foreign, amid established entrepreneurs of general import and export companies, hotels, and manufacturing businesses. As smugglers, they have money or reverse social capital to be able to import large quantities of cocaine or other drugs that small traffickers cannot. Nigerian "big man," large-scale cocaine smugglers include foreigners—likely hundreds of thousands of them—popularly referred to as *Oyibo JJC*, as mentioned earlier. Several small-scale traffickers told me their dream was to become a successful *Oga* (or graduate, as they express it). The parlance *Oga* or *Oga pata pata* or *Oga madam* could mean boss, senior, or person in charge, but it is also used to indicate the status of a wealthy person. In Nigeria, status and titles are important. *Oga*, *Alhaji*, and *Chief* are examples. When inadequately addressed by subordinates, it is a sign of disrespect. In the cocaine trade, you have to please Oga if you want to have access to the cocaine imported by Oga because Oga would not assist someone who disrespects him.

Several Nigerian traffickers told me that they strive to succeed as brokers for a Latin American cocaine boss because it is a once in a lifetime opportunity. One major reason for this is Nigerian traffickers receive large amounts of cash, typically at least 10% of the cocaine shipment, as payment for services. Minimum wages in Nigeria averaged N24,000/month from 2018 until 2019, reaching an all-time high of N30,000/month in 2019 (about USD83.00) and a record low of N18,000/month in 2018 (Trading Economics 2020). Recall that, at wholesale, a kilogram of quality cocaine could attract a price of conservatively N7–7.3 million (about USD19,700–20,500) in Lagos. If a trafficker crowns a deal of 100 kilograms of cocaine with Latin American associates and receives 10 kilograms of cocaine as payment, that is, in the whole market in Lagos at least N70 million. That is big dream come through for Nigerian cocaine trafficker and a much greater payoff than average wages earned.

One way that South American and Asian cartels have nurtured their operations is by residing in transit countries and partnering with local associates in establishing front companies and illegal networks to facilitate drug trafficking, storage space, safe houses, banking, among others—in Nigeria and in African countries such as Guinea-Bissau, Ghana, and SA. Members of Mexican, Colombian, Venezuelan, Surinamese, and European organizations are operating in the same territory, protecting shipments and making deals. Already in 2007, Africa was the operational base for about nine top-tier South American and Mexican drug trafficking groups, and several such groups own residences and businesses in West Africa (see Farah 2012). A clear indication of this is the seizures of methamphetamine manufacturing facilities near Lagos in July 2011 and February 2012, which led to the arrest of Nigerian and Bolivian traffickers. Since then, the NDLEA has detected 11 methamphetamine manufacturing laboratories, concentrated in Lagos and various south states of Nigeria. In March 2016, an industrial-scale crystal methamphetamine laboratory was dismantled in Asaba Delta State. Four Nigerians and four Mexicans were arrested for establishing a factory which had the capacity to produce four tons of crystal meth per week and were aiming to sell its product in Asia (*Vanguard* 2016).

Interviews I conducted with experienced, wealthy, big man smugglers revealed that Nigerian traffickers have deployed containerized smuggling of cocaine and heroin since the late 1980s sometimes taking two or three months to arrive in Nigeria. Some successful Nigerian big man smugglers told me that big deliveries are made by cargo ships, including crude oil vessels. Oga Dede stated, "Route and plan change as the 'law' moves in. Have you heard of *Shark couriers*?" he asked. "Sharks" work on the ships, and they move tons of cocaine, not in containers but in various specially made cavities in the ships. Sharks move cocaine into Nigeria from various Latin American countries such as Brazil and from there to destinations abroad, including the Netherlands and China. Corruption in Tin Can Port Lagos makes it easier to commit trade crimes that involve concealment of true goods and quantity, under-declaration, and under-invoicing by importers to short pay government. Trade crimes cause losses in government revenue every year, but battling against these shortcomings remains difficult due to the activities of Nigerian organized crime.

For instance, there have been major seizures involving Nigerians and other nationals. On July 22, 2010, NDLEA uncovered 450.4 kilograms of cocaine from Chile. The drug was neatly concealed in customized wood flooring inside a shipping container, which was cleared by customs and taken to a private warehouse in Lagos. A Taiwanese, a Chinese, and three Nigerians were apprehended in connection with the shipment. This underscores the strong collaboration between direct and indirect "big men" Nigerian traffickers—because the 20-foot container was opened, thoroughly examined, and confirmed to contain only processed wood and other furniture materials. Employees of numerous agencies would have examined the cargo and released it at the Tin Can Island Port, and yet, only the Taiwanese trafficker and his Chinese coconspirator were found guilty of crimes. The Taiwanese trafficker was sentenced to 30-year imprisonment by a federal high court in Lagos, and the coconspirator received 18 years. The three Nigerian clearing agents alleged to be their accomplices were discharged and acquitted due to lack of evidence (Street Journal 2011a).

The achievements of the "big man" draw on well-structured organized crime. For over a century, its etiology has been based on categories such as tradition and absence of the state (Lombroso); "cancer," pathology, and lack of control (Durkheim); the lower classes' adaptation (Merton); disorganization and cultural deviance or learning processes involving selected individuals (Sutherland); and delinquent subculture (Cohen). Emphasized in all these categorizations is a paradigm of deficit, whereby the causes reside where a dearth exists, be it one of control, socialization, opportunities, rationality, and so on.

The concept of deficit—social and material deprivation, traditional and absence of state and social control deficit among others—is used to explain organized crime, as Ruggiero (1993) wrote, but they fail to uncover why certain deviances become organized and why certain deficits do not lead to deviance or clearly block the chances to succeed as a criminal. For instance, geopolitical factors are crucial for a group or region to succeed in illicit activities, less as social problems than in terms of social advantages. Ruggiero (1996) argued, "Organized crime can only reproduce itself if it develops external relationship with street crime, collective clienteles, power structures, and the legal economy and society at large" (33). This implies that organized crime and society are linked symbolically and exchanged materially in Nigeria. Furthermore, he contended: "Organized crime thus could be interpreted as an outcome of unfettered production, generated less by a deficit than a hypertrophy of opportunities. It could be seen as the effect of the gigantic and uncontrolled proliferation of ways in which status can be achieved; as an outcome of development rather than the consequences of underdevelopment" (Ruggiero 1993, 135).

This might explain why some of the wealthiest drug dealers in the world are ethnic Dutchmen (Siegel and Bovenkerk 2001). The illegal world has a meaningful relationship with the legal world—as between organized crime and the legitimate societal context—and the relationships between legality and illegality are by no means necessarily antagonistic or aimed at avoiding one another. Instead of operating in a social vacuum, organized crime has a habit of interacting with its social environment (Van de Bunt et al. 2014).

Nigerians are open about the fact that heads of states have a propensity to run the country like crime bosses. Nigerian organized crime is structured at various levels of the society. A fundamental flaw in Nigerian politics, economy, and society comprising from heads of state to business leaders as mentioned afore. Elected officials, heads of state, government workers, and members of the ethnic and religious groups who feel they have a right to a share of government revenues among themselves. Organized crime is evident in the endemic culture of civil servants or intermediaries who secure at least 10% of the contract money involved in bribes for fast tracking deals, operating top down from Nigeria's three tiers of government: federal, state, and local departments (Ebbe 2016). Leaders at the local level send part of the illegal money to their supervisors at state departments, and these send some to their directors at the federal level, subsequently to the permanent secretary or to the minister of the department to secure their positions. Joseph (1987, 2013) used the term "prebendalism" to describe how Nigerian public officials view their position as a personal financial right, much as local officials (a.k.a. prebends) in medieval Europe did. Perhaps Nigerians may not recognize the term prebendalism, but they are aware of the practices and standpoint it represents.

In reality, bribery and corruption are the modus operandi in public offices, including the Customs and Excise Office, Judiciary, the law enforcement agents, and society at large. This is why measures and laws meant to fight Nigerian international cocaine trafficking and corruption remain mostly meaningless due to lack of political will and capacity to implement them, resulting often in confiscated cocaine "vanishing" instead of being destroyed, antidrug control agents aiding smugglers, and some Nigerian cocaine traffickers remaining "untouchable" due to their privilege and connections (see Udama 2013). The de facto immunity enjoyed by large-scale Nigerian cocaine traffickers is due to their ability to undermine the work of antidrug agents through systematic corruption driven by persistent organized crime. To combat this kind of impunity, the U.S. DEA extradites arrested traffickers to face justice in the United States rather than in Africa, where the chance of avoiding prosecution is high.

In all, the Nigerian "big man" smugglers import and export large quantities of cocaine. Their success is powered by Nigerian organized crime and endemic corruption, a mentality embraced at all levels of government. The "big men" represent a role model, fueling the activities of the Nigerian cocaine small traffickers who assist large-scale importers and participate in the international illicit cocaine trade for their own benefit.

4.5.2 Small-Scale Traffickers

Traffickers who import about three to 20 kilograms of cocaine are included in the category of small-scale traffickers. My findings revealed that small-scale traffickers come from a range of backgrounds and may be educated and uneducated, male or female (though most are male), and most employ the use of strikers (middlemen) and couriers, or, in the case of imports under two kilograms, "suicide birds." Their success is bolstered by several factors. First, they employ close, trustworthy individuals to perform the risky task of smuggling because recruits remain accountable to small-scale traders if apprehended and will not implicate them, or in the case of dirty play, small-scale traders could threaten or target a courier's relatives for retribution or reimbursement. Second, the courier sees their participation as a favor to the small-scale trader or as a means of achieving societal values—keep in mind the Nigerian Dream discussed in chapter 2.4. All of this is reminiscent of Merton but where, in a late modern context, the implosion of the wider culture on the local is increased dramatically (Young 2007). Third, there is a pool of frustrated individuals willing to take short-term risks for what are seen as long-term gains; these individuals are pushed not only by negative personal circumstances such as deprivation, unemployment, debts, social exclusion, or specific calamities but also by a more positive mechanism—the pressure for upward mobility in the context of violent competition and overnight turnovers in which successful role models have "made it" by illegal means. Lastly, as entrepreneurs, they have the ability to plan, coordinate, and execute multifaceted responsibilities involved in business transactions. These tasks often entail human and material resources: skilled and unskilled labor forces, communication devices, entrance to restricted areas, vehicles, houses, hotel rooms, warehouses, local contacts with wholesalers, and resources to move and deal with large cash amounts.

Small-scale traffickers are mostly found in markets in Nigeria, including Lagos, Kano, Onitsha, Benin, Aba, and Port Harcourt. In Lagos, for instance, they are found among entrepreneurs in shoe, jewelry, and textile imports in Idumota market, as well as amid the importers of electronics, furniture, building materials, car dealers, and suppliers of items as varied as cosmetics and pharmaceutical manufacturers in other markets. For instance, Teku has his legal business located in the Idumota market, one of the busiest wholesale markets in Lagos Island frequented by traders from all over West Africa. In one setting, we agreed to meet in a restaurant that many businessmen and women frequent for lunch. As we were eating, mobile telephones rang at random in the restaurant. Some people discuss openly in locale languages or broken English issues related to cargo goods, shipment in containers, or clearing their containers at ports worldwide. While at first it seemed like legitimate business, from time to time, they jokingly called each other names like "Alhaji Escobar" and "Mr. Peru," subtly indicating the connection their business likely had to illicit cocaine trafficking. During the phone conversations, some discussed their business transactions, including white market (or cocaine) and black market (or heroin). I also heard names of cities such as Guangzhou, SP, Amsterdam, and Napoli.

This highlights the relevance of cell phones as an important tool of the new trend illicit cocaine trade. Paradoxically, a will to restrict its use for security reasons clashes with more objective needs: personal meetings could be even more dangerous; transactions lack the channels available to legal trade; and imperfect or false information forces Nigerian traffickers to stay in touch regularly. Moreover, unexpected changes and improvisation are such common features in the business that they have to be online to check, confirm, or repeat instructions. After all, deals involving millions of dollars are closed by pure verbal communication (Zaitch 2002). The 43-year-old Teku, a successful *Oga*, imports shoes from Italy, Spain, China, and Brazil and owns three trading companies in Lagos. However, he is also a successful cocaine trafficker. Teku stated: "Business is business. I really do not feel bad doing cocaine. It's a commodity in demand. *So wey tin you de talk?* (So, what are you talking about?) Things spoiled right from the top. We are in Nigeria, money talks! It's whom you know" (Teku, personal communication, October 7, 2013).

Teku, like many others, is aware that cocaine is an illegal trade. He told me that the cocaine trafficking business is like time because no one can stop it—scanning all goods or even big ships moving in and out of Nigerian ports is an impossible task. Applying Syke and Matza's (1957) neutralization technique, Teku sees his illicit cocaine trading not intrinsically as crime. He and his friends contribute money to make substantial orders of desirable goods that meet a demand. After all, if NDLEA did not apprehend Okolo Emenike Kingsley for smuggling 9.15 kilograms of cocaine hidden in the soles of shoes and luggage, the small-scale trafficker could have made it (Odita 2017).

Many small-scale traffickers pointed to the Nigerian state crisis and what they see as the villainous IMF's SAPs that led to a series of macro-economic policy changes that rigorously bankrupted Nigerians, strangled businesses, and stymied industrialization. Another factor was the Nigerian government's attempt in 1988 to regularize the pharmaceutical sector through establishment of the NAFDAC; Promulgation of Decree number 21 was aimed at eradicating the sale and distribution of fake medicines in open markets and streets by unlicensed dealers. This move displaced many people who were previously self-employed in the sector who could not employ the services of pharmacists, as required by the new regulation of the NAFDAC. Before this, Teku and friends were petty pharmaceutical traders who sold medicine such as tranquilizers, anabolic steroids, and analgesics. With his trade knowledge and economic frustration combined, Teku couriered for some big man traffickers for a few years and moved up to well-established "businessmen." This supports the idea that through experience, individuals internalize external structures (fields and its rules), providing them with a sense of how to act in everyday life. This may actually facilitate the spread of deviant behaviors in severely disadvantaged communities. Many Nigerian traffickers confirm these arguments. Another successful cocaine trader, Ekete explained to me:

> The West is like a crocodile. They cry while they are swallowing you up. These days it's all about Nigerians. Common man! Did you say you're living in Holland? Many Dutch people in Brazil do that shit! Also, Germans, Italians, Spanish, Lebanese and the rest are involved. They are worried that Africans discovered it and making it. Well, let them know that we are fighting poverty through this. They used everything at their disposal to make money and are still doing it covertly. What is happening to Nigeria has much to do with some western countries hunger for money and hypocrisy (Ekete, personal communication, November 8, 2012).

These justifications are often heard from traffickers. They see their activities as just one part of a larger culture of corruption that exists in Nigeria. In effect, given the historical, economic, and social fraud, Nigeria has become a *shadow state*, in which Nigerian rulers draw authority from their abilities to personalize national resources and their material rewards. Small-scale traffikers see cocaine trafficking not as an illicit activity in a world characterized by oppression, poverty, inequalities, and relative deprivation but as a means of obtaining their own share, wealth, and power in that society. Despite its illegality, traffickers frequently view the illicit cocaine trade as the only way to redistribute wealth from the north to the south, arguing that mainstream commercial channels are effectively occupied. In her research on drug couriers in Britain, Green (1996) puts all the emphasis on the relative poverty and economic hardship impelling couriers into trafficking. Though recognizable, these factors alone do not explain why they are pushed to deviate from mainstream survival strategies.

Decades of studies carried out on both crime and causalities by institutions and experts indicate that small percentage of people exist in all societies who deliberately choose to commit deviant activities or to live as career criminals (Wolfgang et al. 1972; Greenwood and Abrahamse 1982). But in Nigeria that percentage is much higher. Year on year, corrupt government officials commit outright fraud and theft of public funds.

Nigeria's foreign debt jumped from approximately USD28.5 billion in 2001 (Shaw 2003) to USD85 billion as of 2020, attracting a whopping sum of USD4.45 billion in service payments in early 2020. External debt rose by 616% in 14 years, according to Nairametrics (Adeso 2020).

In "State Collapse and Criminal Expansion," Shaw (2003) noted that economic mismanagement, a failed structural adjustment program, continuous political contestation, and harsh periods of military rule marked the decline of the Nigerian state. From 1985, the unprecedented diversion of revenue depleted resources and aggravated the debt burden. Overtly illegal activities became a major portion of Nigeria's shadow economy with more than a billion dollars annually (about 15% of government revenues) flowing through criminal networks, often with the collusion of the country's elite. For example, about USD6 billion of so-called trade debts in England alone was siphoned away, tied up in a certain bank which is very nearly bankrupt, without equivalent material imports to Nigeria (Executive Intelligence Review [EIR] 1986, 53).

In this sense, Nigeria has the largest shadow economy in the world, looking at size, cause, and consequences (Schneider and Enste 2000).

The Shagari regime (1979–1983), one of the most corrupt in Nigeria, presided over the oil boom era but still accumulated external debt of about USD8 billion (Shaw 2003). Multinational corporations, foreign entrepreneurs, and organized crime networks engaged in all kinds of fraud: over-invoicing, falsification of import and foreign exchange transactions, and assisting public officials in laundering ill-gotten money into foreign bank accounts. It is in the context of this discussion on the persistence of these organized criminal networks that many Nigerians hold the West responsible for the deterioration of the country (ibid. 18, 19). That, for many, has provided justification for their involvement in criminal activities and was often mentioned in interviews with Nigerian traffickers.

4.5.3 Strikers

Strikers are a kind of middleman in cocaine trafficking. Owo is one of my main contacts in Lagos during fieldwork and is regarded by many as the "Number One" striker. His experience in trafficking has allowed him to move up the ranks since he began trafficking cocaine in 1982. He has served time in jail four times in both Europe and the United States. Owo explained: "Actually, I went in there good and came out totally bad. Worst, because I made a lot of friends in the prison from Latin America, the United States, Europe, Asia and Africa. Then, I learnt a lot about cocaine, heroin, crack, and speed. As courier, I made my contacts, traveled and packaged my 'thing' myself, swallowed and brought it back myself" (Owo, personal communication, December 16, 2012).

He dropped out of secondary school after his second year in Lagos because no one could pay his school fees following his father's death, and after an eight-year apprenticeship in a pharmaceutical distribution company in Lagos, his boss settled him in 1980 with a starting capital of just N600 (then the equivalent of about USD200). Lured by a friend, Owo became a drug courier. While this underlines the role of vulnerability and the importance of education, a supportive family and discipline, it's important to note that he also became successful and powerful in his business dealings.

One of the striker's most important tasks is the recruitment of couriers or birds. An important feature of the Nigerian system that makes effective police detection difficult is the use of independent specialists who bridge the gap between the "job owners" and the courier. Full-time strikers are highly valued and well respected among cocaine traffickers because they possess detailed information about many, if not all, details concerned with cocaine trafficking, from recruitment and counseling of new couriers to procurement of cocaine, travel documents and routes, prison experience, and global contacts.

In Lagos, traffickers do not look for couriers because lots exist. It is a "soldier go, soldier come" mentality. It is comparable to a battlefield because there will be causalities. This is why successful Nigerian cocaine traffickers sponsor as many couriers as possible so that some *crown* or succeed in evading authorities. The problem is not finding couriers but finding ones who can carry more than one kilogram of cocaine. Potential couriers advertise themselves according to the quantity swallowed. In Lagos, Owo has several agents for recruiting couriers. They play their role as middleman and earn commission from the owner of the cocaine and from the courier.

4.5.4 Entering the "Birds" (Couriers) Nest

The use of couriers on commercial air flights is a favored technique of Nigerian cocaine traffickers worldwide. How often a courier works depends on ability to secure travel documents, like passports and visas, in Nigeria or other countries in sub-Sahara nations. Interviews with law enforcement officers in Nigeria, Brazil, and Netherlands revealed that other common profiles are foreigners, frequent travelers, or even diplomatic passport holders. This affirms the view that depending on levels of risk, Nigerian traffickers draw on multiple networks within the context of the courier markets—having a low versus high profile affects how much a courier is paid.

Strikers recruit couriers or secure travel documents against payment among other functions. Nigerian drug traffickers claim that an EU visa can cost as much N450,000 (about USD1,250). In other cases, high-profile frequent flyers do not need an exit visa. For instance, many couriers combine their trafficking with legitimate business trips and holidays, or they are overseas-based residents of other countries. A cheap courier could earn about USD2,000–3,000 for delivering about one to two kilograms of cocaine. Low-profile courier, Fida, stated to me in Lagos, "Bros, I work five year before I made money to begin my clothing business" (Fida, personal communication, October 28, 2016).

Through this they control their business as important partners in the distribution of small quantities of cocaine in consumer markets. The wholesale cocaine trade with Europe is subjugated largely by Latin American organizations that generally work with their European distribution networks, but Nigerians should not be underestimated. Many cocaine traffickers refer to Nigerian slums as the breeding ground for low-level drug couriers.

In such places, I found desperate individuals who said they would want to become drug couriers just to escape from Nigeria, underlining what is often heard from traffickers—that they do not look for low-level couriers because many readily available exist. Many aspiring traffickers expressed the fact that Nigeria is already difficult to live in for the pool of frustrated people and, consequently, it does not matter much if they risk their lives or migrate abroad to earn money. Nigeria's ineffectiveness in addressing poverty has encouraged some of the youth to go into illicit drug trafficking and other criminal enterprises. Most of them do not have the skills required for regular employment. This condition has resulted in a cheap price placed on labor and on their lives.

Additionally, whether through hearsay or through their own rationalization, many think that airports overseas are just as ill-equipped for detecting couriers as those in Nigeria. For example, high school dropout and aspiring courier, Ada, stated to me, "Life is already unbearable in this country. It's a country where you can lose your life any time and nobody cares. Didn't you see some dead body on the roads in Lagos? For me I better become a courier, gain some money or use it as way to migrate abroad" (Ada, personal communication, October 26, 2012). It is common to see the same disregard for human life Ada mentions. During my fieldwork in October 7, 2010, while

I was on my way to Lagos Island for interviews, a dead body was lying on the Eko Bridge that leads to Idumota. The body was half crushed by car, and nobody seemed to care. This shocking sight reveals the dismissiveness by many for human life (and death) in Nigeria. Similarly, Owo's observations about "suicide birds" or couriers also demonstrate this. Owo noted that Nigeria is a "battlefield" that will inevitably have "casualties." However, rather than considering the effects of this disregard for human life, he dismisses these casualties only as an element of the business. Many complain about the hopelessness of life in Nigeria, and Ada's observations reflect the destitution and poverty that most Nigerians face.

4.5.5 Part-Time Couriers and Freelance Traffickers

No one talks about being a full-time trafficker; most noted that it sounds too negative, even in Nigeria. No one wants to be known as a smuggler of cocaine alone because of its illicit nature. It is something that goes hand in hand with a conventional business. Thus, even for those who are fully involved as career traffickers and dealers, they still prefer not to carry the heavyweight of being called a full-time cocaine trafficker. Instead, being a "part-time" trafficker is more common.

The title "drug courier" primarily evokes an image of exploited persons. However, it is not limited to only poor individuals from the slums. I found that all sorts of individuals have been involved as part-time drug couriers and range from despairing young men and women of urban areas to well-established migrants in cocaine-consuming nations, from friends, or family members of drug traffickers to middle-class adults hoping to move upward, but also stranded students deprived of study grants and work possibilities. Part-time or freelance traffickers invest their savings or pool money with friends, family, or business partners to purchase cocaine, usually less than a kilogram but sometimes more. Trafficking freelance, Ekete established his business in Lagos and travels often to other countries for work. He invests also in other part-timers. Samke stated: "First you start by thinking to do it only once. Then you make the first money and you discover that it is possible. Then you do it again and again. It is like this, once you start it's hard to go back so you combine it with your normal activity" (Ekete, personal communication, October 5, 2011).

Drug couriers normally involve persons with residence permits, individuals who owe debts, who have good contacts in Nigerian and a taste for conspicuous consumption, or even VIP high-profile couriers with local connections and a strong sense of invulnerability. This was the case with Ali Bala Adamu, an employee of the NDLEA; Ijeoma Ojukwu, niece of a late politician; and three other business men who were arrested in early 2016 for alleged conspiracy to import 2.5 kilograms of cocaine from SP at MMIA Lagos (Eteghe 2016). High-profile couriers are considered a diversification tactic of cocaine hoppers. They carry more drugs and are accordingly remunerated more than the low-profile mules, earning up to USD5,000 per kilogram or more.

However, I could hardly find any stable Nigerian professional living in the Netherlands, Brazil, China, Germany, or the United States as a legal alien who would work as a drug courier. The risk is not worth the payoff at that level. On the other hand, since it is difficult to get a visa for a simple courier, the new trend traffickers and strikers look for citizens of developed nations, someone with a second nationality or a permit to stay in developed nations, a relative to visit, a course or study to follow, and so on. As table 4.2 demonstrates, eight of the nine couriers arrested at Schiphol airport Amsterdam in 2011 were residing overseas. Police data show that in the first half of 2015, 75 people were arrested arriving or departing from Lagos airport on drug charges. Of these, 15 were documented Nigerians with an address in SP (Cohen 2019).

In his work on Colombian traffickers, Zaitch (2002) averred that on many occasions, they have improved their educational levels; however, their expectations are truncated either by being denied access to the labor market or by unsatisfactory jobs in terms of personal aims and achievements. Similarly, I found amid Nigerian international cocaine traffickers, individuals of both sexes, but mostly male from lower or middle class, usually adults in charge of a household, that several had specific, acute financial problems, whereas others were facing few opportunities for the future. Underscoring the risk for middle-class families involved in trafficking, the Nigerian couple arrested for having used their six-year-old twins in smuggling about four kilograms of cocaine at MMIA Lagos in 2010, owned a grocery store in an elite part of Lagos, had assets valued at roughly N50 million, and had traveled to London 17 times since 2006 on visitor visas. Their stated reason for carrying drugs was they had been swindled of N2.2 million and needed to smuggle the drugs to pay the school fees of their children (Ehigiator 2010).

I noticed that on average Nigerian traffickers are aware of the dangerous nature of the job, but their discernment is often diminished by a number of conditions. Risk is often talked down by the suffering of a misfortune, a too fatalistic or too positive attitude toward adversity, the excitement of potential rewards, a strong identification with surrounding successful couriers, or the trust endowed to friends and relatives who often mediate in the recruitment. Zaitch (2002) affirms that cocaine exporters with an active policy of misinformation promote these mechanisms further. They do that by denying controls, sweet-talking couriers, lying about the freight, trivializing the risks around the delivery, and even hiding the fact that they will be denounced to the police.

4.6 HOW ACTORS EVADE CONTROL

Deployment of couriers who swallow cocaine balls is rampant and involves all sorts of individuals from various social, professional, and economic backgrounds. This is why any person can be suspected and taken for a drug scan test, but also why Nigerian traffickers succeed. Several Nigerian cocaine traffickers claim that despite increased control at major Nigerian airports, assisting couriers to avoid control is no big deal. They claim NDLEA's efforts mostly succeed in arresting novice traffickers who either take unnecessary risks, do not want to pay and/or pay the wrong contact person or agent, or pay agents who then do not share the bribes appropriately with other corrupt colleagues involved.

Whereas this claim lingers, the destination of 86 drug couriers arrested at MMIA, Lagos, in 2016 shows that the inflow of drugs into Nigeria is about 48.84% whereas the outflow of couriers is about 51.16%. Of the 24 destination countries of the arrestees, China topped the list with seven couriers. Others include SA, six; Greece, five; Turkey, three; UK, two; and even Australia with one courier (NDLEA 2016/2017, 31). The fact that some are apprehended underlines the importance of Nigeria as a transit nation.

On a return trip to the Netherlands in October 2010 during fieldwork, departing from Lagos international airport, I was subjected to a drug control scan by an NDLEA officer. This offered me a chance for observation. At the customs check and police control, I was among eight men randomly selected for a scanning test that lasted about 20 minutes. I was dismissed when the scan came back negative and was shown the stomach X-ray on computer screen. Two out of the eight men had positive results to which they admitted. But it also demonstrated the chance that several other couriers were not picked up and escaped control. This is the chance exploited by Nigerian cocaine traffickers. Given the availability of an army of potential couriers, the chance of evading arrest at entry and departure points encourages traffickers (see table 4.1).

This table shows that the influx of drug into Nigeria when compared to outward movement of couriers is about 21.21%, which indicates the fact that Nigeria is still being used mostly as a transit nation. The United States tops the list of outward destinations of the couriers from Nigeria, followed by Malaysia and United Kingdom. Whereas no courier was reported apprehended by NDLEA to the Netherlands in 2011, records on cocaine couriers

Table 4.1   Destination of Drug Couriers Arrested by NDLEA in 2011 at MMI Airport in Lagos

SN	Destination	Frequency	%
1	Nigeria	28	21.21
2	USA	25	18.93
3	Malaysia	23	17.42
4	UK	14	10.60
5	Italy	6	4.54
6	Japan	5	3.78
7	India	5	3.78
8	Spain	4	3.03
9	Hong Kong	3	2.27
10	Greece	2	1.52
11	Thailand	2	1.52
12	China	2	1.52
13	Turkey	2	1.52
14	UAE	2	1.52
15	Germany	1	0.76
16	France	1	0.76
17	Mozambique	1	0.76
18	South Korea	1	0.76
19	Czech Republic	1	0.76
20	Australia	1	0.76
21	Gambia	1	0.76
22	DP Congo	1	0.76
23	Vietnam	1	0.76
	Total	132	100

Source: NDLEA 2011 Annual Report.

arrested by Royal Netherlands Marechaussee—The Duct Military Police Schiphol Airport Amsterdam in the same year—show that eight couriers were apprehended from flights that departed Nigeria: five from Lagos and three from Abuja (see table 4.2).

This means that Nigerian cocaine traffickers are able to evade control for several reasons. First, the flow of a huge number of people through Lagos airport makes detection difficult because good border management seeks to balance the competing goals of facilitating and expediting access for people and goods and secondarily interdicting and stopping "bad" persons and "bad" things. Traffickers succeed due to the difficulty of accurately and efficiently identifying high-risk passengers and cargo, target them for inspection, and prevent the entry of dangerous goods and people without impeding the legitimate flows cross-borders. Second, many Nigerian cocaine traffickers buy their safety through bribes when crossing couriers at control points.

"Pushing the courier," as popularly expressed by cocaine hoppers, or paying kickbacks to corrupt law enforcement agents, is traditional. Most traffickers claim they pay between USD500 and USD1,000 to antidrug

Table 4.2 Schiphol Airport Amsterdam: Data Drugs Couriers, Nigeria 2011

2011	Positive Arrest	Innocent Suspects Couriers	Methods of Smuggling
Abuja	3	1	Swallow 1 Hand Luggage 1 Body-Parker 1
Lagos	5	9	Swallow 3 Luggage 2
Total	8	10	

Country of Departure	Country of Birth	Country of Residence	Nationality
Abuja	Nigeria 2 Brazil 1	Nigeria 1 Brazil 1 Italy 1	Nigeria 2 Brazil 1
Lagos	Nigeria 1 Suriname 1 Ghana 1 Curaçao 1 Mexico 1	Netherlands 1 Spain 1 Brazil 1 Mexico 1 Unknown 1	Nigeria 1 Ghana 1 Mexico 1 Netherlands 2

Source: Royal Netherlands Marechaussee, 2011.

agents or other security for a courier to evade control at the airport in Lagos. Distinctive is their air courier tactic called the "shotgun method" or the "battlefield approach" as many express it. This method involves placing as many as 24 couriers on a single flight, as we shall discuss in chapter 5, knowing that some may be apprehended. Several interviewee ex-convict couriers claim the owner of the cocaine betrayed them by purposely informing antidrug control agents to arrest them to let other couriers proceed, "sacrificed" as expressed by Nigerian cocaine traffickers. They have established in many countries in SSA that offer excellent transport and criminogenic environment for imported cocaine to be repacked and re-exported to markets abroad.

4.7 UNIQUE NATURE OF NIGERIAN INTERNATIONAL COCAINE TRAFFICKERS

4.7.1 Widespread Contacts

Relations between cocaine hoppers are based on maintaining and making further contacts that could help them in their business. This consists of talking about business connections and inquiring about earlier encounters, friends, acquaintances, and friends of friends. Among the people I interviewed, their focus was on establishing effective, reliable, and trustworthy links among players in the business. In certain circles, some talked about *white market* and how to use each other's social capital; in other contexts they discussed relationships, such as powerful people in key positions—"long leg" or "Ibrahim" (a godfather or godmother) as they say in Nigeria. In these situations, it was also common to hear stories about someone's relative, friend, or acquaintances who "got into problems" (e.g., was arrested or jailed for drug trafficking conviction). Likewise, there were also discussions, arguments, and speculations about the reason why the person got into problems. It is clear that Nigerians talk openly about cocaine business and issues when in the right environments.

As has been shown throughout the interviews, cocaine traffickers and many potential traffickers stressed that the cocaine business in the country is succeeding thanks to the good social relations the trade has developed within the larger Nigerian society. They argue that it has become part and parcel of doing business in Nigeria and with Nigerians everywhere for many people. Moreover, it has provided work opportunities and financial reward directly or indirectly for people connected with the business such as transporters, clearing agents, warehousing facilities, customs officers, police, and many others. Some businessmen and women have invested the financial proceeds to create further employment opportunities and provide financial means to unemployed, elderly, and young family members.

4.7.2 Chain of Command

In contrast to the dominant notion of big cocaine gangs, barons, and syndicates, I observed that Nigerian international cocaine traffickers are a network with no specific corporate structure or chain of command. Nigerian traffickers are dissimilar to criminal organizations that follow the "godfather," mafia-type corporate model, with obvious hierarchies and divisions of labor that seek to monopolize criminal enterprises nationally and internationally and have a symbiotic relationship with the government with the intent to gradually infiltrate or influence political and administrative functions (Nikiforov 1993).

The new trend traffickers tend to use the enterprise model instead. In part, this is also a reflection of the activities they are engaged in—multiple, interconnected, and overlapping with each other. Many Nigerian traffickers form loose and often temporary alliances or associations formed around specific projects. Individuals or small groups of people are best described as nodal points in a larger web of criminal activity. They adhere to flexible and adaptive networks that expand and contract to deal with the uncertainties of the illicit enterprise. Nigerian cocaine traffickers are organized only to the extent that they can effectively carry out their activities. Their methods are reminiscent of other research on the entrepreneurial character of organized crime in Nigeria that underscores the transitory alliances of risk takers who seize opportunities to make large profits on investments akin to drug trafficking. Furthermore, apart from a rather small core group, most are brought in as needed to provide special services. This is one of the reasons why Nigerians from varied backgrounds are involved in the cocaine trade be it in Nigeria, Brazil, China, England, France, the Netherlands, United States, Indonesia, Malaysia, or Australia. The responsibility, ability, and risks vary. Likewise, the actors involved in "white market" and their chances of "big catch" are also variable in their roles.

Within Nigeria, they frequently form groups based upon regional, ethnic, or friend groups. Above all, due to the secret nature of the transactions, trustworthy or reliable partners and contacts are essential instruments. One important way to build trust is through the intervention of a trusted third party who can introduce or recommend a newcomer. Cocaine hoppers operate in networks of people who know each other very well and work together on the basis of faith and friendship. To start with, trust is established, making use of relatives and close friends. In addition, reciprocal trust between criminals is more important than between businesspeople, likely because of the severe consequences such as jail or even death. For instance, among some traffickers and their friends during a traditional marriage ceremony in Lagos, I observed people arguing about disappointments from trusted contacts and friends. Maike, a small-scale trafficker and spare parts businessman, who I met severally in Lagos noted: "I trusted Lomo but he embezzled my money. He ran away with my 1.8 kilos of pure cocaine. To this day, I have not seen him, and I heard that he is living illegally in London. I complained to his father. He promised to settle the case and asked me to cool down" (Maike, personal communication, March 14, 2010).

Because of the nature of cocaine trafficking, traitors are not brought to the police. To avoid violence following burned bridges of trust, family members of those held responsible often reimburse traffickers financially or with property. Otherwise, kidnapping and violence can result.

A *Vanguard* write-up of 2018 published that Aloysius Ikegwuonu (a.k.a. "Bishop") and his friend Ginika Nwoko (or "Giniyee"), a university drop-out, moved in 2000 to SA where they became successful drug traffickers. Almost two decades later, a drug deal dispute between them led to several deaths in SA and Nigeria. Bishop claimed that drugs, worth millions, which he handed over to Giniyee to deliver to a buyer ended up with some falsified stories and loss of the drugs and money. An intentional fraudulent plot and betray, Bishop asserted. Mediation proved abortive, even with intervention of the king of Ozubulu in their hometown. Cocaine hoppers took the law into their hand. Following Giniyee's assassination in September 2015 in SA, violence between the drug gang left more than six Nigerians dead. Ozubulu, a small town in Anambra State, was unknown to many until August 6, 2017, when a gang of gunmen busted into St. Philips Catholic Church during morning mass. When they finished, 13 people were killed including Bishop's father, and 18 others were seriously injured. This happened because Nigerian drug traffickers often dupe themselves. Drug money disputes turned deadly as members of Nigerian cocaine strikers failed to adequately account for the money realized from consignment of drugs from foreign counterparts. Enraged associates vented their anger on the innocent extended family and friends of those involved in the breach of trust. Bishop himself escaped the attack, having traveled to Lagos the night before. Four men aged between 30 and 57 years old were arraigned for the crime.

Viewed from the Nigerian context, successful drug traffickers are liked by many and disliked by few. On the one hand, Bishop is described as audacious and mean; on the other hand, he was philanthropic and gave back much to his community. Ironically, he renovated most of the churches at Ozubulu (including where the carnage took place), the Igwe's (king) palace, and established a charity foundation. He also made donations to the state government, state police, and local vigilante groups (Ujumadu 2018; Ugwummadu 2017).

Whereas most traffickers said they are conscious about who to trust, the illicit nature of the cocaine trade adds to already established trust. Many stressed the importance of working with close relatives, friends, and acquaintances with good recommendations. Most traffickers work with between two and five individuals who collaborate in a flexible manner. At the same time, they make use of services from others based on strong recommendations within their reverse social capital networks. In this way, transactions with the various actors involved are based on trustworthy oral agreements and financial reward. In this sense, trust, confidence, and flexibility are what cements all deals between individuals that can trace themselves back to their villages and even families in Nigeria.

4.7.3 Ritual Priests and Pastors

Important are the non-trafficking actors who, while not actively participating in the trafficking process themselves, condone and assist the Nigerian cocaine business. One group in particular is the ritual priests and pastors, who are frequently involved in "absolving" traffickers and couriers of their sins or bless their journeys to their final locations. Priests have an incredible influence on society and play an important role in SSA societies. Consequently, traffickers frequently use religious rituals such as blessings or prayers or juju/voodoo ceremonies, which they believe will enhance their mental and emotional mindset needed for overcoming the fears that arise during trafficking. For instance, this may involve the consultation of ritual priests or fortune-tellers in invoking ancestral magical powers or the use of artifacts and symbols as protective mechanisms to boost their "luck" in avoiding detection by law enforcement agents at entry or exit points or to prevent swallowed cocaine balls from bursting in the stomach.

However, religious rituals may also be used as a fear mechanism. For instance, the big man trafficker or *Oga* forced courier Owo to swear oaths of allegiance to him that if broken would result in harm coming to them or their families through the ceremonial ritual. Research points to the misuse of religious practices by trafficking rings in Africa (Siegel 2011; Bovenkerk 2001) and Latin America to seek out supernatural protection and guidance. In the United States, for example, federal authorities have discovered indigenous practices of Nigerian juju, West African voodoo, and Latin folk magic being used to maintain control of organizations and keep victims of trafficking in silence (Kail 2008).

In popular discussions in Nigeria, people explained that witchcraft and magic are an integral part of the culture, even among Nigerian prison inmates, as in Brazil. Sorcery, witchcraft, medicine men, and priests still play an important role in the life of many Africans. Indeed, ritual priests or witch doctors often amass fortunes and earn official designations, enjoying the direct exercise of power. Nigerians are open about the role voodoo or juju plays in the daily lives of people, and some traffickers interviewed indicated that there is frequent consultation of traditional religious priests. According to the U.S. Attorney's Office in the Eastern District of Texas, Christopher Omigie, a Nigerian and naturalized U.S. citizen, was sentenced to 168 months in federal prison for his role as spiritual adviser to two Texas cocaine-trafficking operations (Lomax 2015). "Tricky" Omigie claimed to be a witch doctor who possessed natural mystic powers or juju and could safeguard their product and operations through the supernatural protection services he rendered. Omigie was paid hundreds of thousands of dollars to provide supernatural protection against apprehension by antidrug control agents. Now, many are coming to terms with the fact that many so-called witch doctors, voodoo priests, fortune-tellers, and pastors are disguised conmen; they are self-centered "419" as Nigerians say—exploiting vulnerable people for personal gain. Omigie's lies crumbled when he was not able to protect himself from being jailed.

It is normal, upon request from some pastors, to say prayers and fast to be successful. Pastors often give examples from the Bible, for example, Sam 7:35 or 7:51 in which God ordered fasting from 6:00 a.m. to 12:00 p.m. and prayer at midnight for 21 days. Be it in Nigeria, the Netherlands, Brazil, China, or Malaysia, many cocaine hoppers including couriers indicated the importance of receiving a blessing from pastors or preachers prior to their undertaking cocaine deals and trips. For example, the adamant and successful courier, Toli stated:

> I always consult my pastor to do a special prayer for me so that deals and travels go well. The pastor of my church has special powers, and things do move well for me with his prayers and blessing. So, I am open with the pastor about my cocaine trafficking. He prays hard for me anytime I swallow and travel. Above all, through prayers he receives special power from Jehovah. He sees a lot through dreams and advices me when or when not to travel. I know that friends also relay on the prayers of their priests as an additional means of protection. It's God who gives good luck and money. So that's why I need prayers from a powerful priest (Toli, personal communication, March 12, 2010).

But some who are wary of these services exist, as Owo demonstrated:

Yes, prayers and pastors are part of the business. But I have seen it all! For me one thing is clear, "Not all that glitters is gold." I have my doubts about the so-called powers of the pastors and their dubious ways of performing miracles. Prior to my trips to the U.S. and to Holland, I consulted my pastor. He prayed, and downloaded all those spiritual emotions and mental preparation in Jesus' name. He cited all sorts of quotations from the bible and gave me lots more prayers to say before going to bed and as first thing each morning (Owo, personal communication, March 12, 2010).

Yet, Owo was caught and jailed for cocaine trafficking several times. Nonetheless, the practice persists because some traffickers call up wives, girlfriends, or relatives to say midnight prayers together. In some churches in Lagos, Amsterdam, SP, and Melaka, pastors persuade "flamboyant guys" to give ample donations and 10% tithe from financial proceeds to "provoke" God to provide more substantial returns. Nigerian pastors have realized the spiritual game, "In God we Trust: All Others Pay Cash" (Shepherd 1991). But Nigerian cocaine traffickers, like Owo, are catching on. Many pastors have been educated in the United States or have come to understand the psychology of the drug traffickers through experience. Traffickers want hope and courage to undertake the risky job. And what is that hope? The hope for them is God. The request is to pray more. In this way, they are lured into believing that by praying more, they will be successful.

4.8 RESILIENT NIGERIAN TRAFFICKERS

The persistence of Nigerians in the illicit trade is a frequent subject of
local media that cover arrests at domestic and international airports, police
raids, and stops and search operations. For instance, the apprehension of 24
Nigerian couriers at SP airport in early August 2011 and another 23 less than
a month later (Stone 2011) calls to mind the distinctive battlefield or shotgun approach. Mass trafficking approaches sometimes lead to mass arrests.
According to SP airport officials, on any given day 250,000–300,000 people
pass through their terminals, and SP international airport averages approximately 830 flights per day (Alves 2014). The combination of a major flight
hub with the widespread availability of cocaine in São Paolo has made it easier for Nigerian traffickers in SP to export cocaine by commercial air because
drug mules are easy to find but difficult to catch given the sheer volume of
people transiting through the airport. The UNODC (2013) points out that
mules couriering cocaine are found on flights from Brazil to Luanda, Lagos,
Doha, SA, and Europe and that 90% of those arrested at the SP international
airport claim they got their cocaine from Nigerian groups. On two flights
from SP to Luanda in 2011, Angolan authorities screened every passenger
and found more than 20 cocaine couriers on each flight. After providing for
consumption in southern Africa, the remainder is couriered from these countries to West Africa or directly to Europe (UNODC 2013).

   Not only is it common in media reports to encounter stories of drug arrests
but also in conversation and daily life. During fieldwork, I heard many such
reports. One interviewee, Chuba, was apprehended in SA in June 2012 with
about 1.2 kilograms of cocaine. In another instance in September 2012,
another contact received a call that his friend, who ingested about two kilograms of cocaine pellets, was arrested in Morocco while on transit to Lagos.
One courier, Sharpi, jokingly asserted, "Ah! What does that mean to Chuba?
He has gone to relax again because he had previously served years in different countries Portugal, South Africa, Nigeria, and Mali" (Sharpi, personal
communication, September 29, 2012).

   What is notable is the resilience of Nigerians traffickers who attempt to
reach markets in Africa, Asia, America, and Europe. Among the several reasons for this includes the possibility of drug couriers evading control at the
busy SP airport. Nigerian cocaine traffickers persist in SP because interdiction is problematic due to a huge amount of people and cargo to be screened.
They want to export "cocaine currency" using the preferred courier method
to send cocaine to contacts in destination markets directly from SP. Nigerian
traffickers have become fully global by creating demand at the small-scale
trafficking level. They have established their presence in retail in various
consumption hubs and, as a result, are now torchbearers for other Africans

in the European market. The largest European markets for cocaine remain the UK, Spain, Italy, France, Germany, and the Netherlands, and Nigerian involvement is prominent throughout. This explains why most of the African couriers arrested in European airports come from Guinea, Nigeria, Mali, and Senegal. More than half of the airborne drug traffickers are of Nigerian origin, even on flights that do not originate in Nigeria (UNODC 2008b). Nigerians have found balance between norms of group solidarity and more instrumental links across social cleavages, "getting the social relations right" to enhance their achievements.

Chapter 5

The Brazil Connection

This section focuses on the activities of Nigerian cocaine traffickers in SP, Brazil. The two countries are trade partners, dating back centuries, brought together by the illicit trade in human beings, as discussed previously, to the present-day business in natural resources and manufactured goods.

The statue of Christ the Redeemer glorifies the history of Western Christian philosophers, theologians, colonists, and racist anthropologists and neglects the estimated 4.8 million Africans forced to and brutalized in Brazil during the slave trade. Pius Adiele called it a "Requiem" for black Africa composed by the Catholic Church and her Catholic kings, "Four hundred years of European, Christian cruelty, of papally and theologically sanctioned inhumanity that afflicted on Africa a loss in men, in happiness, freedom and dignity" (2017, 1).

What later became the slave trade was originally genuine trade by barter between Africans and enterprising Europeans who were interested in natural and crafted goods such as gold, ivory, and cowries in exchange for manufactured goods such as clothes, trinkets, and alcohol. Young men and women were tricked into bringing purchased goods to their boats on the seashore and were forced into slavery. European deceit and war subdued resistance by African chiefs and elders and forced millions of Africans into slavery (Ogbaa 2003, 112–113).

After the abolition of the slave trade in 1888 in Brazil (Khapoya 2010; Shareef 1998), the historic resettlement in Nigeria of freed slaves or returnees from Latin America and other countries had a great impact on the country, as well as on the one they left behind. Brazil shifted its diplomacy from subservience to Portuguese colonial interests, formalized in the 1953 Luso-Brazilian Treaty of Friendship and Consultation, to support for African nationalist aspirations, underlining Brazil's connection among others in terms of its strong cultural and linguistic ties with Africa (Forrest 1982).

The international slave trade created an African diaspora in the world, and the presence of blacks in South America has meant that now West African travelers to South America are not racially out of place. I observed amid Nigerians in Amsterdam during the 2014 World Cup in Brazil that some people were making mobile phone calls to relatives, friends, or business partners in Brazil during exciting moments of the match. Likewise, it was remarkable to hear some cocaine traffickers who take advantage of the moment making mobile telephone calls to gain some information from business partners in SP. For instance, Kman, a Netherlands-based trafficker, inquired, "Brother, how much is 'market' now? Oh! 5.2, is ok. We talk later" (Kman, personal communication, July 12, 2014).

Zooming in on the excitement of Kman and others will provide insight into the nature of Nigerian cocaine traffickers in Brazil further on. Through fieldwork findings, their role within the pressing questions on smuggling of cocaine globally from SP will be emphasized by the traffickers themselves, since they have the ability to both corroborate as well as contradict published information by researchers and law enforcement agents. Explained next are accounts of the historical background that links both nations and how the resettlement of the returnees from Brazil and other places in Nigeria was affected by their sociocultural, educational, and economic contributions in the country they returned to, as well as its impact on the one they left behind.

5.1 HISTORICAL CONTEXT

Brazil's relations with Africa date from the beginning of the slave trade following the colonization of the new world by Christopher Columbus on behalf of Spain in 1492. The Portuguese landed in Lagos around 1444, and the city derived its name from the Portuguese. This is redolent of the odor of bloodshed that greeted the New World "discovered" by Cristobal Colon, "with its redolent self-congratulation, its unconcealed triumphalism, its grave proclamations of responsibility" (Agozino 1997, 21).

The atrocities of the slave trade, the resilience and perseverance of Africans, and the revolutions and uprisings in Latin America and the Caribbean until its abolition in 1888 in Brazil are well documented (Sansone et al. 2008; Afigbo 2006; Brown and Lovejoy 2010). These works emphasize the repatriation movement to Africa that took place between the 1840s and 1860s and the harsh, discriminative post-slavery environment after the abolition of slavery forced many slaves from different parts of the world to seek prosperity and security elsewhere, especially in West African countries such as Nigeria, Sierra Leone, Liberia, Ghana, or Togo.

The returnees that engaged in slave trade became neocolonial entrepreneurs. However, their wealth did not translate into development because of the nature of the trade. In a trade controlled by the colonial mentality, most of the money went abroad due to the fact that slavery was substituted with colonization, and Nigeria's inability to shake off the neocolonial mentality keeps the Nigerian state crisis in place. This implies that colonialism-directed trade and travel from Nigeria to the Western metropolis creates different patterns of movement.

5.1.1 The Returnees' Influence in Nigeria

In their journeys to and from Nigeria, the returnees or freed slaves created new African societies in both regions, and they also affected cultural, economic, and political factors. On the other side of the Atlantic, slaves made an enormous cultural impact on the Brazilian society. Their impact includes their economic contribution to the Brazilian economy through centuries of unpaid hard labor, trade with African continent, a more multicultural society, and folklore typified in Samba music and carnival festivals. To this day, there is widespread use of Yoruba language or its hybrid, and the Nigerian religious practices such as *Candonble* are observed in the Brazilian social life in Bahia, as I observed during fieldwork. During the worship, practitioners make sacrifices, beat drums, and sing Yoruba folklores. *Abada* (a long robe of Yoruba origin) dress is common in these rituals.

Since most of the returnees were of Yoruba descent, they chose to resettle in Yoruba-populated areas in West Africa, including Togo, Benin Republic, Ghana, and Nigeria. By the middle of the nineteenth century, there was a regular flow of thousands of Bahian ex-slaves, especially into Lagos and Abeokuta and the hinterland of Nigeria, including Benin City, Onitsha, Port Harcourt, and Calabar (Araujo 2011; Olinto 1985). They resettled in the central part of Lagos Island called Popo Aguda; hence, they were known as *Agudas* and their counterpart in Sierra Leone, *Saros*.

5.1.1.1 Sociocultural Influences

Sociocultural influences are seen in architectural design. Roofing made of bricks and facades remains in Lagos on the few historical buildings that still exist. David Aradeon pointed out in *The Unmaking of Tradition* that the style created a new building type in Nigeria. The Shitta-Bey Mosque was derived and developed from Brazilian religious architecture (Aradeon 1996). Portuguese and English surnames are common in Nigeria, including Da Rocha, Da Silva, Candida, Fernandez, Pears, Ranson, Kuti, Macaulay, and so on. The 84-year-old granddaughter of Da Rocha said to me in Lagos, "I appreciate that you are digging into the past connection between Nigeria and Brazil" (Madam Oyediran, personal communication, August 30, 2011). She explained that Brazilian returnees popularized the agricultural produce, cassava, which is an important staple food in Nigeria. They equally fostered the spread of Christianity, Islam, and local African religions.

5.1.1.2 Knowledge and Political Influences

The returnees contributed immensely to the advancement of knowledge and politics in Nigeria. Whereas those from Sierra Leone (*Saros*) deeply influenced the fields of education and politics, their counterparts from Brazil or Latin America (*Agudas*) contributed mostly in the areas of business and craftsmanship. Access to education allowed most returnees to enter into professional careers as lawyers, doctors, and politicians. For instance, Sir Adeyemo Alakija, the son of freedman Marcolino Assunção, became one of the founding fathers of the first Nigerian political party, the Action Group. The famous Nigerian musician, Fela Kuti's families were renowned medical doctors, and his mother was the first woman to own and drive a car in Nigeria. Through their activities, the returnees contributed to the development of knowledge and politics in Nigeria.

5.1.1.3 Economic Influences

The returnees also made a significant economic contribution to the societies where they resettled. As the commercial heart of Nigeria, Lagos had already transformed in the late eighteenth century from a subsistence economy into a complex commercial system, where the slave trade brought abundant wealth to the ruler of Lagos—from the tolls and customs duties levied on European slave traders—and to the well-connected elite.

Kosoko, the ruler of Lagos, adopted a freed slave Oshodi Landuji and made him the chief customs collector and interpreter. The rich entrepreneur/ freed slave, Muhammad Shitta-Bey, financed the building of the Central Mosque in Lagos (Aradeon 1996) by himself in 1892.

The returnees enjoyed privileged status from the British colonists that led to wealth. Before 1914, England ruled Nigeria through councils and chartered companies such as the Royal Niger Company and by deploying indirect rule in their forceful pursuit for conquest of Yorubaland and the hinterland areas of "Nigeria." To help this agenda, the British exploited the returnees as intermediaries. To secure their cooperation, they were rewarded for their expedient relationship with land allocation in Lagos, the "desired" British education, and raised elite status in colonial Lagos.

Several returnees became wealthy entrepreneurs who engaged in the regular shipping lines and commerce that flourished from Bahia or established factories in Lagos. Captured in the book, *The Water House* (Olinto 1985), the Da Rocha family became successful in business by selling water in Lagos. Brazilians returnees were good entrepreneurs and artisans whose services were in demand and many were already in business in Brazil. Having brought money, they made more through investment.

All the economic contributions of the returnees presaged the fact that as of 2012, Brazil is Nigeria's fifth largest export trade partner, and in 2015, the fourth top export destination of Nigeria, according to the Observatory of Economic Complexity (2018).

5.1.2 Brazilian Returnees and Descendants

My contacts, Herbert and Uchenna, were participants in the interactive conversation with Brazilian descendants Antonio, Paulo, and Tunde. They condoned Nigerian involvement in illicit cocaine trafficking, asserting that it is an effective means to fighting poverty. They argued that Nigerian drug peddlers are more concerned with making ends meet than the legality of their actions. The focus of our discussion became the moral/immoral question of some ex-slaves (or freedmen) in the same slave trade and contemporary Nigerian international cocaine trafficking. The reality is there is still slavery in Nigeria in one way or the other: Have you not heard about kidnapped children rescued from human traffickers in Nigeria? It's in the media in Nigeria and those involved do it for money. Though decadent, but will go on as long as they could get away with it. The point is that there is poverty in Nigeria, and it is getting worst every day. This country is in a big mess and there is unemployment, so some people must survive either through legal or illegal means, inclusive cocaine trafficking (Antonio, personal communication, August 30, 2011).

Whereas slavery persists indirectly in Nigeria, the new trend illicit cocaine trafficking continues because the Nigerian youth constitutes a pool of would-be, exploitable traffickers. The Nigerian diaspora, which can be found in countries around the world, is a legacy of the slave trade. The learned respondent Tunde added: "Cocaine business is about linking people and getting it'across. They will not tell you that it is a criminal thing. They see it as a business, and it's left for you to figure out the question of legality or illegality. Do you understand? Hunger and poverty can frustrate some to taking risks and doing all sorts of things for money. What matters is being able to survive. Europeans did it by all means. But cocaine trafficking should not be punished with death" (Tunde, personal communication, August 30, 2011).

In all, most returnees set their goal toward entrepreneurship because of the desire for financial independence. However, it remained a contribution at the micro level that did not transform Nigeria into a sustainable economy. Many returnees have done well, but the following generations have not been as successful. First, most of the descendants of the returnees were privileged people who did not experience poverty, which meant they are not as desperate for success as the natives. Second, they are still culturally different because most of them are Christians and Westernized. They were not close to the native traditions and ethnicity, which often causes them to feel displaced. In this area, despite being privileged and having access to public funds, where some returnees' offspring succeeded, most went astray, carried along by the Nigerian state crisis and illicit trade.

5.2 NIGERIAN COCAINE TRAFFICKING IN SP

This part focuses on Nigerian participation in the areas of brokerage and exportation of South American cocaine from Brazil. Many publications exist on drug trafficking in Brazil and Latin America and its socioeconomic and political impact on the society (Arias 2006; Mingardi 2001; Transnational Institute Drug and Democracy [TNI] 2015; Cohen 2019). Nevertheless, no substantial work has detailed the nature of Nigerian involvement in the international cocaine trafficking in this area. This work aims to fill in that gap through fieldwork, observation, and data reception close to the source to gain a more comprehensive understanding of Nigerian involvement in the international cocaine trade.

Nigerian cocaine traffickers refer to Brazil and other countries in the region with the mystic expression, *Spirit*'s home that underlines the risk involved: lengthy imprisonment, death due to bursting of ingested drugs, and attack or murder by criminal gangs. Nonetheless, it remains clear that Nigeria and Brazil are connected. Both countries found themselves as global hot spots for the export or transit of Latin American cocaine to its destination markets.

According to several Nigerian traffickers, their activities happen in SP more than in Rio. While SP lacks the natural charm of Rio, "it is precisely the Paulista economic dynamism that serves as the civic identity and pride of place" (Godfrey 1999, 117), but "São Paulo's rapid economic growth is unevenly spread among its population leading to deep-rooted social and economic disparities" (Wu 2012, 4; Caldeira 2001). Nonetheless, as interviews suggest, SP remains a burgeoning city for Nigerians (Ibo, Yoruba, Edo, Benin, etc.) and other Africans from Ghana, Angola, Cameroon, SA, or Congo. The actual number of Nigerians in SP or Brazil remains unknown. As an estimate, Nigerian community director Kingsley Ikechukwu told me that about 5,000 Nigerians are living in SP. According to Federal Police of Brazil (2014) the number of Africans living in Brazil increased 30 times, jumping from about 1,000 in 2000 to around 31,000 in 2012 .

However, due to the nature of the illicit trade and the media attention it attracts, their number appears larger than reality. Contrary to the dominant view, Nigerians do not form ethnic enclaves in SP because they still maintain a small minority group. They are neither predominantly proletarized in the mainstream economy like the Japanese nor do they have a fully developed ethnic enclave economy as with the Lebanese. This evokes some of the peculiarities of *middleman minorities*. Coined by Blalock (1967), the term refers to minority entrepreneurs who mediate between dominant and subordinate groups. Their customers are typically members of marginalized racial or ethnic groups that are segregated from the majority group (147). Also, middleman minorities tend (1) to be self-employed or to work for a coethnic, (2) are usually concentrated in small business, (3) tend to rely on the in-group for resources, and (4) fill a gap in the receiving society (Cobas 1987).

In all, as middleman minorities, Nigerians in SP are not part of the ruling elite, although few may become quite affluent. It is this lack of power which makes them vulnerable to violence. They have strong ties with their homeland, visible levels of ethnic solidarity, urban favorites, low political participation, travel experience, hostility from the surrendering societies, and in some instances, the concentration of trade and entrepreneurial activities held in contempt by the conventional economy. On the other hand, they lack other key aspects of middleman groups because they do not perform as real brokers between local elites and subordinated groups. In reality, Nigerians in SP are far from the "trading people with a history of traditional capitalism" (Bonacich 1973, 591–592). Nigerians in SP also lack the language skills attributed to middleman, and they push for assimilation through intermarriage or the education system with relative success. A heterogeneous class and ethnic composition within the group often limits solidarity to the level of kinship or locality of origin.

5.2.1 "New Generation" Nigerians in SP

The recent trend of immigration to Brazil started in the early 1970s and 1980s and has increased since then for many reasons. First, the Nigerian federal government scholarship scheme that sent students to Canada, Poland, the United States, Italy, and others in the late 1970s also brought some students to Brazil. Those who attended schools in Brazil often stayed in Brazil, working professionally as lecturers, doctors, engineers, lawyers, and so on. Among this first wave of Nigerians in SP, it is said that they look at themselves as elites who do not want to associate with others. The teacher, Ropa stated:

"These new guys in town have something else in mind. Apparently, they are here for a special reason, and that's totally different from our mind-set and behavior. So, I do not want to identify with them to stay away from troubles. They do not give a damn, very loud and fighting opening and doing all sorts of things in the name of business than doing normal work" (Ropa, personal communication, December 15, 2011).

To most Nigerian traffickers, the nostalgic world Ropa referred to has changed. It evokes Hutton's (1995) notion that the shift from Fordism to post-Fordism characterized by disentanglement of the world of work where the primary labor market of assured employment and safe careers decreases; the secondary labor market of short-term contracts, flexibility, and insecurity increases; as well as the development of a larger lower class. This shift resulted in a series of macro-economic policy changes that adversely affected the lives of the masses in Nigeria through currency devaluation, trade liberalization, downsizing of the public sector, and fiscal and governance reforms, as discussed earlier. The persistence of the state crisis, as an ulterior part of the experiences of late modernity, presents itself to Nigerian cocaine traffickers, not only in the form of a chaos, reward, and identity but also in the form of an incoherent sense of unfairness and ontological insecurity: a powerlessness to meet the heightened metanarratives of meritocracy and self-fulfillment, as emphasized by Young (2007). Because the world is not what it used to be is perhaps the reason why the trafficker, Monkey No Fine (MNF), does not understand other Nigerians such as Ropa. MNF expressed: "When we came here, I had plans for studying and seeking for a respectable life but not trafficking drugs. However, since it became too difficult to survive without job, a friend suggested trying cocaine trafficking. That is how I started" (MNF, personal communication, December 12, 2011).

Having discovered a way out, MNF called upon close associates subject to the same economic and social pressures to join the influx. Similarly, referring to the migration of Brazilians into Japan, Higuchi (2006) emphasized that migrants from a certain village are canalized to a certain district of the destination through chain migration, which brings "transplanted" social relations and foster daughter communities in receiving countries (Massey et al. 1987).

Furthermore, internal migration literature recognizes the important role played by close associates and families in chain migration (Mincer 1978; Vaughan 2017). In this way, the number of Nigerian traffickers increases in SP. Interviews with some Brazilian law enforcement agents confirm that in the past decade, the international cocaine traffickers in the country included nationals from Nigeria, Kenya, Lebanon, Mozambique, and Angola among others; however, on the whole, Nigerians were most notable. The illicit trade flows alongside conventional trade; therefore, Nigerians established trading networks that fill in the increasing gaps in the nations' informal economy through the development of local and global linkages.

5.2.2 Extensive Networks

People who excel at a particular aspect of cocaine trafficking are a hot topic in Nigerian circles in SP. It is performing their parts well despite uncertainty, distrust, and anxiety that characterize Nigerian cocaine trafficking. Some people are called wizards for concealing cocaine, others in wrapping cocaine pellets, quite a few have contacts for industrial packaging or with cocaine wholesalers. Knowing whom to meet for what is the key. Some Nigerian international cocaine traffickers have moved a step forward into specialized activities.

Successful traffickers are regarded as "witches," having mysterious powers assisting them to make contacts and money from trafficking cocaine. Witches are also believed to use power from Satan in their evil ability. Some believe the power lying witchcraft is none other than that of malevolent ancestral spirits. Nigerian traffickers deploy these beliefs in several ways, calling on the powers of God to achieve success or Satan to condemn competitors. I will return to this later.

Successful traffickers avoid attention by not frequenting the streets of SP like the novices. Instead, thriving Nigerian traffickers maintain good contacts with associates from Brazil, Venezuela, Argentina, Bolivians, or Colombia who deliver high-quality cocaine at the best price. Contrary to the dominant view that Nigerian traffickers operate in closed-circuit, opaque groups, it is actually the opposite: they use a network that transcends ethnicity, involving partners from various countries globally, as their activities in SP evidence. Their ability to antiparochialism fosters the expansion of their networks and success. It emphasizes that such networks are epitomized as informal organizational structures that curb opportunism through embeddedness in strong ties of communal solidarity, reciprocity, and social sanctions (Coleman 2000; Granovetter 1995) or as anti-structural properties of networks, viewed as weak ties that operate across social cleavages to promote agency and provide access to new sources of information and resources. However, effective network governance is increasingly seen as a balance between the norms of group solidarity and instrumental linkages across social cleavages, what Woolcock and Narayan (2000) refer to as getting the social relations right, "It's not what you know, it's *who* you know" (Woolcock and Narayan 2000, 225). Similarly, the concepts of bridging and bonding ties (Narayan 1999) or fragments and flows (Geschiere and Meyer 1998) accentuate the dependence of effective network governance on the appropriate combinations of ties. In this way, several Nigerian international cocaine traffickers represented in this work have focused on bottom-up cultural networks to weak ties with outsiders, connecting groups into new information sources and markets. It demonstrates that the aptitude to establish effective ties is perceived as a production of cultural competences for cooperation and intergroup relations, instead of hanging on the formal institutional environment in which those networks are embedded, as indicated by Schmitz and Nadvi (1999). This explains why several traffickers in SP are questioning the effectiveness of working within the Nigerian strong ties, an informal regulation based on personal relations such as kinship, friends, or co-ethnicity. The trafficker, MNF stated, "Working with fellow Nigerians mostly is not good. It does not work because it causes fighting among ourselves because of who we are. Then the 'python' (meaning police) will round us up easily" (MNF, personal communication, December 12, 2011).

Research explains that economic efficiency could be suffocated by too much embeddedness. Groups can become insular and introverted where bonding ties are strong, restricting access to new ideas from outside the community (Huggins and Thompson 2014). Portes and Landolt identified four negative consequences of social capital: exclusion of outsiders, excess claims on group members, restriction on individual freedoms, and downward leveling of norms. For example, "The same strong ties that enable group members to obtain privileged access to resources, bar others from securing the same assets" (Portes and Landolt 2000, 533). Interacting together, these peculiarities could stunt the growth of business initiatives. Nigerian traffickers working primarily with conationals have a lot of time at their disposal for arguing and quarrelling due to jealousy, cheating, debt settlement, or circumstances arising from business deals gone wrong. For these reasons, experienced traffickers like MNF would rather avoid them. He only has contact with one or two individuals, since the economic strength of social networks is disrupted by the inability of some social groups to form weak ties across cleavages, leading to the formation of closed parochial networks and a propensity to communal violence as demonstrated by the recent bloodshed in SA and Nigeria between two Nigerian drug gangs, as discussed in chapter 4.7.2.

Furthermore, a society's social capital "concerns not the internal cohesiveness of groups, but rather the way in which these relates to outsiders" (Fukuyama 2001, 14). I observed that some innovative thinkers within the Nigerian circles in SP succeeded by adhering increasingly to tactics and strategies such as living outside areas usual to other Nigerians, keeping to appointments with local partners, and expressing themselves in local accents; these strategies enhance partnerships outside their conationals because, where cultural norms restrict intercommunal ties, efficient networks require openness instead of enmeshment. Arrests of Nigerian nationals have occurred in most countries, including areas not normally associated with African migration, such as Afghanistan, Finland, Kyrgyzstan, Indonesia, and the Republic of Korea. Rather than contesting markets already well served by local trafficking groups, these networks are highly adaptive, addressing markets overlooked by others or working in cooperation with established organizations (UNODC 2008a).

The deployment of extensive network concepts has assisted Nigerian traffickers to strategically settle in cocaine production and transit hubs, delivering good quality and high quantities of cocaine shipped to transit countries in SSA where Nigerian traffickers dominate the market. Most are residents in the countries where they operate and make use of local partners who provide access to needed travel documents through corrupt means. Due to membership to the free movement of people and goods throughout the Economic Community of West African States region, cocaine concealed in goods entering any country could go to another without passing through border controls. For instance, in January 2013, Ghanaian NACOB officials apprehended two Nigerian international cocaine traffickers for importing about 200 kilograms of cocaine from Bolivia to Tema Harbor. The cocaine was concealed in a 40-foot container loaded with 1,946 boxes of shampoo. The arrested trafficker had in his possession four Nigerian passports with different names.

5.2.3 Buying Cocaine Cheap

Good entrepreneurs aim to get their goods from cheap sources. Nigerian cocaine traffickers accomplish this by basing themselves in cities across South America. Locally based traffickers could buy it at about USD1,300 per kilogram from their Latin American partners at a primary source in Peru and Bolivia. This is what experienced Nigerian traffickers target—exporting cocaine themselves and turning profits by selling to others in SP at wholesale prices between USD4,000 and USD4,400 (as of April 2020). That same kilogram, while in transit, has a wholesale price of between N7 and N7.3 million (about USD19,700–20,500) in Nigeria. A kilogram of relatively pure cocaine, later tailored with additives, has a street value of between EUR25,000–30,000 in Amsterdam and about EUR70,000–80,000 in Switzerland, depending on the purity.

In all, the success of Nigerians in the illicit trade is reflected in their ability to construct extensive networks in producing and consuming hubs globally. Proponents of the weak ties thesis (Granovetter 1983) uphold that strong ties are weighed down by parochialism, while weak ties facilitate the enlistment of new resources and information in response to changing circumstances as in international drug trafficking. While strong identity-based ties have been celebrated as an important source of popular entrepreneurship, their aptitude in advancing economic growth in fast changing conditions remains a concern.

Most Nigerian illicit cocaine traffickers in Brazil and Asia exemplify a shift from strong to weak ties.

5.3 EXPORT METHODS

Nigerian traffickers in SP are brokers forwarding illicit Latin American cocaine to transit and consuming nations globally. They connect their conationals and other buyers to counterpart sellers for payment in cash or cocaine. They export small and medium quantities to contacts in Nigeria or elsewhere using couriers, concealments in various goods forwarded by cargo and container shipments, and deployment of conventional post services. The first two methods, courier and cargo, will be discussed next, whereas the last, postage, will be discussed in chapter 6.

5.3.1 Cargo and Container Packaging

Concealment in travel baggage or in items sent by cargo or container is a method used by Nigerian traffickers to forward cocaine from Brazil to counterparts in destination countries, including Nigeria. Cargo and container packaging generally contains small quantities up to 10 kilograms and medium quantities up to 250 kilograms. Whereas small traffickers are busy with one or few kilograms of cocaine, financially buoyant ones focus on bigger deals while also sponsoring couriers trafficking small quantities.

SP is home to perhaps the largest Nigerian community in the region, and according to the Brazilian authorities, this group has been progressively taking control of cocaine exports from Brazil, leaving the domestic market to local gangs. They have been accredited with organizing up to 30% of the cocaine exports by ship or container from Santos, Brazil's largest port, up from negligible levels a few years earlier. In 2010–2011, about 2,093 kilograms of cocaine was seized from shipping containers related to West Africa (UNODC 2013).

Fieldwork reveals that Nigerian traffickers cannot control the export market of cocaine, but they do participate. Research points out that various groups perform such activities, (1), by local groups with access and control over those local resources, such as First Command of the Capital (Primeiro Comando da Capital [PCC]) criminal factions, Mafiosi, legal entrepreneurs, or officials; (2), by local, illegal entrepreneurs protected by them; (3), by ethnic minority groups from source, transit, or destination countries with their own local infrastructures; and (4), by partnerships between all three aforementioned groups. With such compelling weak tie connections, Nigerian traffickers' cultist groups like Aiye and the Neo Black Movement (NBM)—which we will discuss in chapter 6—participation is often "crowned" (successful) due to the difficulties in examining bulky goods at departure and entry points. In this regard, Brazil is no exception.

In addition, Nigerian traffickers like to export concealed cocaine from countries of origin with less risk of the cargo being found. A cargo from Colombia, Venezuela, or Ecuador would very likely be checked thoroughly. Most traffickers expressed that better choices are Argentina, Paraguay, or Uruguay, and transiting ports in Europe where it will not be checked prior to arriving at the desired seaport in SSA. Nigerian traffickers are aware of that without foreign intelligence. One successful trafficker stated to me, "They got my consignment by chance because someone speaks out. That is why I went to jail in Brazil. Caught because that motherfucker collaborator told the *Koti* [police]. If not, they are unaware. Deals will keep on moving!" (MNF, personal communication, December 20, 2012).

Nigerian traffickers rely on dependable partners, especially individuals working in manufacturing and wholesale companies licensed to export goods out of Brazil. For instance, they purchase goods worth thousands of U.S. dollars from a wholesaler, which are directly shipped or sent by cargo from the company after packaging. They are aware that companies treasure and maintain good business relationship with valuable customers. With such atmosphere, goods are bought and assembled in the warehouse of the company. This gives traffickers a chance to switch some goods bought through the company with identical others that have kilograms of cocaine concealed in them without anyone noticing. On the other hand, where they have insider contacts in a manufacturing company, industrial concealment of cocaine in various items becomes a "gentleman's agreement." Then, the whole goods are packed and transported directly from the company to the airport or seaport to the destination. Since it is coming directly from a company with a good reputation, export procedure is expedited and relaxed. This way, a small or medium—but steady—quantity of cocaine finds its way out of SP and Brazil generally to global markets. They evade constant harassment from the antidrug agents, fake police, and robbers in SP by deploying their Brazilian counterparts to pick up and deliver purchased cocaine. Against the payment of about BRL500–1,000, or roughly USD250–500, reliable Brazilian contacts pick up parcels of cocaine and deliver it to expert artisans who will work it into desired goods—be it spare parts, household goods, personal care, and other items for export. Such artisans could open up whatever component, construct a lookalike, and reassemble it after having loaded some small packages of cocaine in the cavities or object. The trafficker, Sharpi, added, "My local engineers can rework cocaine into any object. He becomes worried if I do not have job for him. It's big income because he could make USD$2000 in 10 days" (Sharpi, personal communication, January 12, 2013).

Without the collaboration of local artisans, transportation services, and manufacturing and retail sectors it would be difficult for Nigerian traffickers to excel in this regard. However, whereas the cargo and container packaging method remains prominent, Nigerian traffickers also capitalize on moving cocaine through individual mules with small quantities of cocaine.

5.3.2 Drug Courier Approach

The deployment of drug couriers plays a major role in the new trend in Nigerian-led illicit cocaine trafficking, as evidenced by arrested and convicted offenders serving time in various jails. Demographically, in Itai maximum-security prison near SP, most of the 500 Nigerian cocaine trafficking offenders currently imprisoned in Brazil are males. Interviewees stated that Nigerian male couriers are preferred because they can ingest pellets of cocaine that weigh about 20–22 grams, while women couriers swallow between 10- and 15-gram pellets.

I observed that some male couriers want to make money quickly by taking more risks and swallowing 2.5 kilograms of cocaine pellets or more. Sometimes the risk is ignored in hopes of greater profits, especially by Lagos street dealers. Couriers from such backgrounds view cocaine trafficking as a good opportunity for making money and ending suffering. For instance, Ehi, a courier, bragged about swallowing two kilograms (120 pellets of cocaine), and another courier, "Let Go," ingested 2.6 kilograms without incident. They would find it offensive, they said, if the net content of their cocaine pellets and total quantity were tampered with. In discussion with a man preparing the cocaine pellets for him, Let Go warned:

> Please make them complete. I do not want nothing less than 2.6 kilograms in total and 20 grams each pellet of cocaine. I am ready for it. I am warning you. Let it be complete and in case you are not aware, I am alias *Lama* [cow]. I have suffered enough as truck-pusher. Further as a physic hard worker, I am used to taking cows medicine in Nigeria. Please do not let me remember that I was a gravedigger in my village prior to working in Lagos as *area boy* [street boy] and a day paid laborer. So, I will succeed because Jehovah is King, in Jesus name (Let Go, personal communication, December 27, 2012).

Many exist who think like Let Go. Couriering is judged as an acceptable risk. They feel that if they are caught and imprisoned in Brazil, it is better than working with motor packs and spending the little earned buying painkiller tablets like ephedrine. Ehi avowed, "My brother you are right. It is a do or die thing. As a man, I have decided to swallow two kilograms this time because it is women that do one kilogram these days" (Ehi, personal communication, December 27, 2012).

The majority of Nigerian female inmates in Brazil are in the Women's Penitentiary of the Capital (Penitenciária Feminina da Capital [PFC]) located in SP city. I interviewed 14 Nigerian female inmates in December 2011 during the fieldwork, including 60-year-old Mrs. Chi, jailed for five years and 11 months, and 74-year-old Mrs. Hafsat Awosade (popularly called "mama" or Mrs. Balogun at PFC) and who died prior to being sentenced. The gray-haired grandmother told me of her struggles in prison and how she came to be involved in cocaine trafficking. The death of her son left her with his four children. Sometime afterward, a family friend residing in SA offered to take her to Brazil for medical treatment of her high blood pressure and acute back pain. After 12 days in SP, her friend asked her to assist carrying some load when traveling back to Nigeria. She added, "We went to the doctor, but he was not around, and they said I should come back next week. But I told them that I want to go back because nobody was looking after my grand-children" (Hafsat, personal communication, December, 2011). She did not know how many kilograms of cocaine were found in her luggage. "The judge has not yet sentenced me. I heard people saying that they should not judge someone over 70 years old. They should not let me die here. It is with God, I hope they consider my age," said Mrs. Awosade. As in this case, some individuals could be unaware of the risks involved when drawn to cocaine trafficking by relatives and friends. They are often misinformed about the risks. As a wage earner in such a difficult context as the Nigerian society, most are left to raise their children singlehandedly, under great pressure to feed, clothe, and educate them.

Research carried out in the United States found that indeed, drug mules may be sufficiently desperate that they do not even ask to be informed about the exact nature of what they are carrying (Bjerk and Mason 2014). Most Nigerian women told me they got involved in the drug business out of desperation, claiming that it had to do directly with poverty and hardship in Nigeria. The only alternative was prostitution, which came with the risk of AIDS. The Nigerian female inmates I interviewed claimed they had been tricked into trafficking cocaine and/or had given under financial pressure to save their families. They differ from other female couriers who were clearer on their reasons for involvement in the illicit trade, as we shall see later.

5.4 BRAZILIAN REACTION TO NIGERIAN COCAINE TRAFFICKERS

According to the TNI, drug crimes fall under "Heinous Crimes Law" (8.072 of 1990) that classify them as serious offenses in Brazil; therefore, several rights and benefits of the accused are suspended such as freedom pending trial. The Drug Law of August 23, 2006 (Law n.11.343/06) made considerable improvements, having decriminalized consumption, disallowed incarceration for drug users, and alternative consequences through Article 28. However, critics have averred that drug crimes are classified as severe crimes comparable to murder, rape, and kidnapping without taking into account the degree of participation. Additionally, preventive detention is not compulsory in Brazil. Courts apply it fairly frequently in the case of drug crimes—regardless of the gravity of the felony—making it among the principal causes of overcrowding in prisons. For instance, in 2012, almost 40% of the prison population had not been sentenced and 25% was imprisoned for drug charges (TNI 2015).

It has called into question the ongoing war on drugs. Colombian president, Juan Manuel Santos, asserted that the incessant drug war is stuck on a "stationary bike" as demand persists despite efforts to crack down on traffickers. He stated in a write-up on *The Fresh Toast* of 2017, "We're like a static bicycle—pedaling, pedaling and you're left in the same position—so something is wrong with this war on drugs: It's not working. We need a less punitive, more health[-based] approach" (Hacienda 2017). It is a situation that increasingly demands alternative solutions. For instance, Uruguay's president presented a bill to legalize and regulate marijuana sales and production, and Colombia's Constitutional Court ruled in favor of decriminalizing limited quantities of marijuana and cocaine because, despite high conviction rates for drug-related crimes, drug trafficking and the efforts to stop it have generated increased violence. The consequence of this rise in violence is that repressive policing policies are justified, and the poor are forced to rely on criminals and corrupt police for protection. It is also the result of highly organized, politically connected drug dealers feeding off the global cocaine market, as well as the rising crime rate prompting repressive police tactics and corruption running deep in state structures (Arias 2006). Commenting on the issue, the Brazilian ex-president Fernando Henrique Cardoso, a strong advocate of drug decriminalization, expressed that "treating drug use as a police case is useless and disastrous; and that mandatory internment [of addicts] has been internationally condemned as inefficient, stigmatizing and a violation of human rights" (*Agence France-Presse* 2012).

Contrary to the international trend toward drug decriminalization civil society has been expecting, the Brazilian House of Representatives passed a law on May 22, 2013, that amended several portions of Brazil's 2006 drug law. Among these were the mandatory treatment of problematic drug users, federal funding for "therapeutic" treatment centers, and the implementation of a minimum mandatory sentence for drug traffickers—five to eight years in prison (Bateman 2013). It is a move that called for finding new spaces to utilize as prisons. However, what is needed is a holistic approach that would change the dominant public opinion about imprisonment and lead to less people in prison.

5.4.1 "Label": Every African a Nigerian

The number of Nigerians in SP is uncertain; unofficial estimates suggest about 5,000, as previously mentioned. This would appear insignificant in a city of about 12 million people (World Population Review 2020), but their presence is noticeable. The United Nations reported that five out of every 10 Africans living in Brazil were Nigerian, and most Brazilians refer to every African as Nigerian. Nigerians are seen as a group having defective standards that contradict those of the "normal" majority. This perspective of othering, or essentializing the other, seeks to transfer the problem area "to purge impurities, to wall off the stranger" (Gitlin 1995, 233). Nigerian cocaine traffickers contribute to the conversation about crime in SP and everyday narratives, commentaries, and even jokes that have crime as their subject. The talk of crime provokes perpetual feelings of fear that in turn create stereotypes that exacerbate the divide between populations (Caldeira and Holston 1999).

The negative attention garnered by Nigerian cocaine traffickers echoes the disembeddedness of the late modem society, the upset of pluralism and insecurity. One solution to such a loss of firm identity is discrimination toward the constructed or invented other. As Hobsbawm and Ranger (1983) explain this concept, it is a fixed identity centered on the idea of cultural essence that is affirmed, rediscovered, and elaborated upon. This essentializing of the self, the allocation of oneself and friends and relatives, forming virtues entrenched in one's culture goes unavoidably associated with essentializing and denigration of the other, a black and white of moral photography (Young 2007).

Often due to the nature of their activities, some Nigerian cocaine traffickers opt to settle issues in their own way. When disputes get out of control, they fight among themselves, thereby attracting the attention of the public and law enforcement. A major contributor to their frustration is life in SP is expensive, and most of them encounter problems sooner rather than later due to unforeseen delays and circumstances. For example, the courier "Big Papa" planned to stay 10 days in SP, but ended up spending 20 days due to scarcity of quality cocaine. Doubts and frustrations about uncertainties of delivering the cocaine, paying the hotel bill, eating, and similar expenses led to aggressive disputes that attracted attention. Sharpi stated, "These Nigerians have no wisdom. Coming in, they realize that things are hard. Then they face it with annoyance and frustration. It leads to quarrelling, fighting, and violence. Then everything spoils because it brings in the police. That is how Big Papa and two others were arrested and jailed when police found five kilograms in their flat and they could not pay USD$5,000 each to 'settle' [bribe] the police" (Sharpi, personal communication, December 24, 2011).

Sharpi and I met Big Papa during temporary exit from prison. Reflecting back on what happened, Big Papa said, "I am already seven years inside, and

I must do another three years in Itai prison. It is almost finished. I regretted fighting on the street" (Sharpi, personal communication, December 24, 2011).

5.4.2 "Students" on Saidinha (Inmates on Temporary Outing)

My fieldwork in SP was planned to coincide with a period when eligible inmates on semi-open and open prison regimes are granted temporary outing or *saidinha*. I met many of them in the Galleria mall located close to Republic Square in SP. The mall is like the Canal market malls (nicknamed "Little Africa") in Guangzhou, China, or the Chunking Mansion, Hong Kong. Also, known as *Galeria Presidente or Galeria De Sotto* (named after Mr. Sunny Izomiwu, [A.K.A "Sotto"], the first Nigerian businessman to rent a shop in the mall in 1994). It is home to hundreds of Africans and Nigerian businesses where various articles such as African clothes, craftwork, food, and music are sold. This sprawling edifice of about six floors recalls SP's *Ajegunle* in Apapa or *Oluwole*, a suburb of Lagos Island notorious for crime. Yet, it is more than that. It is a melting pot for Africans—especially Nigerians—as it offers commerce, relaxation, and sometimes confrontations with the law. People go up and down floors making calls from their mobile phones and chatting up with associates regarding earlier transactions or expected ones. They speak in Nigerian languages such as Igbo, Yoruba, Edo, and Benin. Deals involving thousands or even millions of naira are closed by mere oral agreement. One shop owner stated to me, "That is the way it is here. At the end of the day, some will go into certain things they do not even know how they got into it, and consequently the prison is filled up with Nigerians" (Kona, personal communication, December 22, 2011).

The temporary outings permitted in SP remain unique in confirming the borderless collaboration between Nigerian traffickers and associates internationally. Standing beside the entrance of Butanta Female Prison in SP, I watched several hundreds of inmates come out during the temporary outing in December 2012. Most were Brazilians. In-depth conversation with some inmates revealed they were poor slum residents, jailed because of drug trafficking. It is an indication that the slums offer a pool of would-be couriers, as most Nigerian traffickers asserted. According to the 2010 *Instituto Brasileiro de Geografia e Estatística* Census, about two million people live in favelas or slums in SP. Rooted in Brazil's history of slavery and military dictatorship, the slums are ever-present symbols of poverty, social inequality, marginalization, and drug trafficking. In this regard, Jaguaribe (2009) expressed, "The mappings of social disarray tend to locate the favelas, the main terrain of the drug trade and a zone of scarcity, as crucial areas of violence" (220).

Most of Brazil's middle and upper classes view the slums as loci of violence and sources of criminality. State officials and law enforcement spread this view with repressive action, from constant police raids to destroying shanty homes that are often justified in the name of the fight against crime. From January through November 2018, police killed 1,444 people in Rio de Janeiro state alone, according to the Public Security Institute. That was 39% higher than the same period in 2017 (Human Rights Watch [HRW] 2018). From 2001 to 2011 alone, the Rio de Janeiro police officially recognized that it had killed more than 10,000 civilians, but as a justification, they identified the victims as "bandits" and "traffickers" (Misse 2017, 76).

Whereas othering and demonization persist, slum dwellers in SP, as in Lagos, assert that drug trafficking remains a potential alternative because of the withdrawal of the state.

Essentializing is common due to the dominant crisis of identity. As Jock Young emphasized, if the chaos of reward creates ready hostility toward the underclass, the chaos of identity rasps upon them as an aberration with all the opposite characteristics of the world of the honest hardworking citizens; yet, the more the poor resemble the wealthy, the more they are othered by them, and the more the poor become like the rest, the more they resent their exclusion (Young 2007). In other words, what the wealthy hold against the underclass in their midst is its dreams and the model of life it desires that are so uncannily similar to their own (Bauman 1998).

What is common with these concepts is their applicability everywhere, as the activities of the Nigerian international trafficker are borderless ones. Nigerian cocaine traffickers remain unaware that in the era of proactive policing, making illicit money and having a good standard of life while having no legal job leads to the inquiry, how did you make the money? The general feeling is those who work little or not at all are getting an easy ride on your back and your taxes. In this area, Young (2007) expressed that the middle class could feel sympathy toward the lower class because their relative satisfaction could translate into feelings of charity. But, whereas the larger constituency of dissatisfied is more likely to demand a stamp down on dole "cheats" but not punitive rationality, tied to such a quasi-rational response to a violation of meritocratic principles are those that seek to redress a perceived reluctance to work: punish, demean, and humiliate (Pratt 2000).

High levels of drug trafficking and violence in Brazilian favelas are caused by a combination of government shortsightedness, police unaccountability, and scarce opportunities for favela youth. With the escalation of the drug trade in the 1970s and 1980s, drug traffickers filled this vacuum left by the absence of the state. Despite the fact that social programs have attempted to restore rights to residents of the slums, rampant police and state corruption undermine these same rights. In this regard, Dowdney (2003) highlighted that power legitimized by community acceptance or neutrality, in which drug factions enforce social order in the community through a series of behavioral codes that serve both their needs and those of the community for law and order, has led to narcocracy or narco-dictatorship.

Furthermore, as in Nigeria, Brazil experienced a serious economic crisis, in which hyperinflation and then a collapse in economic growth impoverished millions of Brazilians (International Bar Association [IBA] 2010). Brazil experience growth with an inconsistency that left the society stratified into what is now considered among the most unequal countries globally. Also, Brazil had a dramatic social change that transformed it from a rural to a more urban society within a few decades. In addition, increased demand for labor and higher demographic growth rates promoted further migration and rapid urban growth. Available data shows that due to the intensification of rural–urban migration, Brazil now has more of its total population living in towns and cities than most European countries do. According to the 2010 Demographic Census, over 84% of its population resided in urban areas, with large segments of the population inhabiting poorly located and ill-served informal settlements (McGranahan and Martine 2014). In all, the realities in the slums, inequality, and poverty are features that could frustrate many chanceless slum dwellers into drug trafficking and collaboration with Nigerian traffickers.

5.5 CRIMINAL JUSTICE RESPONSE TO NIGERIAN COCAINE TRAFFICKING

5.5.1 Legislative Measures

For Nigerian cocaine traders, the punishment applied by the contemporary law requires extremely stringent criminal handling: "Article 33: to import, export, refer, prepare, produce, manufacture, obtain, sell, expose to sale, offer, store, transport, carry, keep, prescribe, administer, or deliver for the consumption or supply, narcotics—even if for free—without authorization or in violation of the legal or regulatory norms. Punishment: Imprisonment for 5 (five) to 15 (fifteen) years and payment of 500 (five hundred) to 1,500 (one thousand five hundred) days fine" (TNI 2015).

The idea was that harsh legislation should deter Nigerian international cocaine traffickers and prevent narcotics from reaching the booming Brazilian market—between one and two million cocaine users, the world's second largest market (UNODC 2013).

In this area, observers point to a number of positive initiatives, including the 2011 amendments to the Criminal Procedure Code: (1) "stipulating that preventive detention is to be considered a last resort and applicable to those who have committed crimes with less than four years imprisonment", (2) providing alternative measures to deprivation of liberty as the Law of Penal Execution provides "benefits such as reduction in prison sentences if the prisoner took the initiative to pursue education", and (3) implementation of the task force of the National Council of Judges, which visits prisons and assists in releasing many of those who were illegally detained (United Nations Human Rights Council [UNHRC] 2014, 10).

However, in spite of these recent improvements, drug trafficking is a crime that most express disapproval of in Brazil as demonstrated by the public campaign, "Drug Law: It's Time to Change" (César 2012). Recent data show an increased prison population of about 690,000 in Brazil (Walmsley 2018). Numbers of those incarcerated for drug trafficking increased fourfold between 2005 and 2013 and are estimated to represent about 25% of all Brazil's prisoners (Coyle et al. 2016). It is a consequence of "tough on crime" changes in national legislation and a weakening of civil liberties and protections that implies that Brazil has effectively implemented a mass incarceration policy.

According to Eliott Currie (2011) the amount of crime and violence in a society is strongly influenced by the social and political choices in a given country.

Reiman and Leighton applied the Pyrrhic defeat theory and Pyrrhic victory in the U.S. context, but its relevance in Nigeria and Brazil is evident. If the CJS does not actually fight crime sufficiently—or at least to some extent—what works to reduce crime? We know that education and creating good job opportunities for youths reduce crime. Poverty and inequality, warehouse prisons, drug policy emphasizing criminalization, and deficient gun control policies make crime more likely because of how these factors shape families, communities, and individual choices (Reiman and Leighton 2017). In *Crime and Punishment in America*, Currie (2013) concluded that the four priorities seem especially critical: preventing child abuse and neglect, enhancing intellectual and social development, providing support and guidance to vulnerable adolescents, and working extensively with juvenile offenders. Most importantly, Currie added that "the best of them work, and they work remarkably well given how limited and underfunded they are" (81, 89).

Punitive legislation and war-on-drug-style militant measures have failed to deter drug trafficking as globalized markets transform cocaine trafficking. Corentin Cohen (2019) points to the "development of the Brazilian drug market toward Africa." Brazil is the primary country for cocaine transshipment to Europe, Africa, and Asia; according to the 2018 UNODC's annual questionnaire to states, Brazil was the second most mentioned country of origin (16%) for cocaine seized in Europe, just after Colombia (20% of the mentions).

5.5.2 Combat: Paddling the Streets

Allegations of arbitrary arrest and extortion during stop-and-search opera-tions carried out by civil police, military police agents, or even fake undercover police are common among Nigerians in SP. They claim that preparation of the 2014 Football World Cup stepped up the control against drug trafficking in the cities and at the borders. Effective stop-and-search and following-the-money concepts are strategies for crime prevention, including drug trafficking. Money laundering is the lifeblood of transnational organized crime. However, though nations have prioritized following the money to identify criminals and deter citizens from turning to crime, Nigerian inter-national cocaine traffickers launder the proceeds of the cocaine trafficking mostly through purchasing of consumer goods exported to Nigerian and African markets. As averred by the Council on Foreign Relations (CFR), Global Regime for Transnational Crime, "Ultimately, anti-money laundering tools, which were designed to combat organized crime, have been ineffec-tive," according to a 10-year review of the Palermo Convention. The report emphasized that less than 1% of illicit financial flows globally are seized and frozen. This takes away much of a nation's necessary resources and allows criminals to profit illegally and remain at large (CFR 2013).

Likewise, while the stop-and-search strategy aims for proactive crime pre-vention including drug trafficking, it can and has been misused by dishonest police officers in extorting money from the arrested. Or in cases where brib-ery isn't the aim or an option, the person is apprehended and charged, thereby exacerbating the problem of prison population and overcapacity. For instance, in an in-depth conversation, Otiyo, a former courier, explained his encounter with the civil police agents in SP. Otiyo had previously been arrested at the international airport in SP with 1.5 kilograms of cocaine he ingested; he was convicted and spent three years and 10 months in jail. After his release, he was subject to a stop and search by four undercover police agents who yelled, Voce Africano! (You African). They assumed that as an ex-convict of traf-ficking, he must have drugs and forced him to take them to his residence. Searching his room without a warrant, they found about USD2,000 and EUR500 notes. Explaining that it was money from someone to buy goods and send to Nigeria, the police said it was drug money and threatened him with formal arrest and imprisonment. Despite taking the money, they demanded extra USD5,000 to let him go. Terrified, Otiyo agreed, stating, "I said ok even though I did not have the money. So, they let me go. That is how I did not get back to jail. But I am now in-debited" (Otiyo, personal communication, September 23, 2012).

It is up to the arresting police officers to make the distinction between trafficker and user. Being classified as a drug trafficker is largely dependent on race and social class rather than the quantity of drugs in possession or the existence of evidence of intent to sell (Bateman 2013). Nevertheless, in a demonstration of willful extortion, the involved police officers called back repeatedly demanding the USD5,000. Otiyo stated:

> I changed my telephone number and moved to another address in town. Yet they found my number, called and told me my new address. It was horrible for me because they threatened, they knew my new address, and that I should bring they money. I said I do not have such money. But they said I should borrow from friends. So, I believed they had a Nigerian informant. These police guys are robbers in a way. They use the arm and uniform to rob! So, I am afraid of them. I hope not to meet them again. I am sick of this kind of life. That is why I am looking for a normal work. Why are these police allowed to continue doing this? (Otiyo, personal communication, September 23, 2012).

His fear is reasonable because extrajudicial execution by police is rampant in Brazil. Dom Phillips (2014) writes that Rio police killed two teenage boys alleged of being involved in drug trafficking. The boys were picked up from the street and shot in a nearby forest. In SP, the police ombudsman examined hundreds of police killings in 2017, concluding that police used excessive force in three-quarters of them, sometimes against unarmed people (HRW 2019). In 2010, UN Special Reporter Philip Alston condemned Brazil, reporting that extrajudicial killings remain widespread and that few of the perpetrators are prosecuted or convicted, especially when they are police officers (UNHRC 2010). A 2017 law shields members of the armed forces from trial in civilian courts for unlawful killings of civilians. The law also moved trials of military police accused of torture and other crimes to military courts. This implies that Brazilian military police and armed forces investigate their own members who are accused of crimes. Yet under international norms such crimes and abuses by police and the military must be investigated by civilian authorities and tried in civilian courts (HRW 2019).

Critics point out the paradoxical situation—neoclassic notions of equality of citizens in the face of the law, but on the streets, policing remains indubitably biased in terms of race and class. Furthermore, Young (1999) expressed that the bulimic nature of late modern societies could shed more light on the nature and tone of the dissatisfaction of those on the underside of society or the system, rooted simply in the contradictions between the thoughts that legitimatize the system and the reality of the structure that makes it up. In the wake of this, Otiyo and others who have nothing to do with trafficking remain scared of being set up by corrupt police agents.

The decision to opt for repressive penal responses to drug trafficking contributes to the increase of the Brazilian prison population. The prisoners are mostly small-time drug dealers sentenced to long prison terms that serve to reinforce their marginality and the stigma to which Otiyo and others are subjected. Intimidation and threat of arrest as bargaining tools for extortion have serious consequences, since police make arrests and charges. A first offense in trafficking comes with a penalty of three to 15 years in prison. With such ample freedom and power, the police could determine someone's judicial outcome, especially since they could "provide" all evidence.

There is widespread collusion between corrupt police officers and organized crime drug traffickers and its related violence in Brazil. The connection constitutes an illegal network (Arias 2006), symbiosis (Mingardi 2007), or parallel power (Leeds 1996). It is a problem that stems from the traditional exchange-based politics and clientelism in the Brazilian political economy. Emphasized here is the powerful organized crime group, PCC, "controls the majority of illegal contraband and drugs coming into/out of the prisons in São Paulo, and remains an organization of great interest to the government of Brazil and the police" (OSAC 2019).

The DENARC (State Narcotics Division) noted that the Nigerian group was responsible for the annual shipment of approximately a ton of cocaine to Europe and the United States (Lozano 1997). A DENARC investigation led to the arrest of Peter Christopher Onwumere, a major Nigerian drug baron, and four others. He bought cocaine in Bolivia, where he lived seven years, and used Brazilian or Bolivian smugglers to transport cocaine to SP in batches of 10–15 kilograms. Like all criminal organizations, international trafficking cannot exist without links to the repressive apparatus of the countries where it operates. In the Brazilian case, this means maintaining contact with the federal and state police, concluded Mingardi (2001). Investigations undoubtedly show that African traffickers have continued unabated because the police are turning a blind eye to their activities.

The PCC and other organized crime groups, like the *Familia Do Norte* and *Commando Vermelho*, compete to control major ports and hubs used to send cocaine to Cabo Verde and Europe, either through sailboats or cargos (Cohen 2019).

The influence of PCC is diffused in space as it controls large parts of the urban periphery and exerts pressure upon a police system suffering from organizational weaknesses. This affects policing and society for several reasons.

First, "street-level police officers, both civil and military, are often residents of the same low-income communities controlled by criminal groups". Second, cutting "ties between police and the underground world is difficult as the symbiotic relationship could emerge at neighborhood levels or work places or at both. The divided organizational structure of the civil police, which firmly distinguishes between education levels and career advancement prospects for investigators, prison agents, registrars, and delegados (police chiefs), means that most police are not upwardly (or spatially) mobile. This situation, combined with dependence on a secondary source of income, leaves police susceptible to illegality" (Willis 2014, 15).

In this regard, military and civil police in Rio and SP are susceptible to corruption, in part, because they have very low salaries that do not reflect the challenging nature of their jobs. An entry level police officer earns an average yearly salary of about USD11,418 (equivalent). A senior level police officer earns an average salary of around USD19,575 (equivalent). That is average base salary of approximately USD15,752 per year (Salary Explorer 2020).

Brazilian authorities raised salaries for officers in the past decade, by more than double for some; however, police complain that with deductions the difference in take-home pay is negligible.

On the one hand, Klitgaard (2010) highlighted that an increase in the average wages—especially in the public sector—contributes to reduced corruption. Attractive wages in the public sector reduce the incentives to engage in corrupt transactions by reducing the corrupt agents' utility (Vieira 2013). On the other hand, the symbiotic relationship between corrupt police officers and organized crime drug traffickers persists. One reason for this is the existence of a criminal authority, the relative weakness and exposure of street-level police, and an asymmetric balance of power between the extralegal spaces occupied by coercive criminal groups and the formal legal space of law and state power. In "Antagonistic Authorities and the Civil Police in São Paulo," Graham Willis (2014) asserted the police are pragmatic and relatively autonomous actors who find ways to navigate this asymmetry. Off-duty police have also been implicated in death squad and militia activity in several parts of the country, and extortion groups or police forces commonly demand their share of the profits of extorted cash under threats of arrest, as most Nigerian traffickers stated.

5.5.3 Law Enforcement: Incursion, Shops, and Homes

Another repressive move meant to combat cocaine traffickers is the unexpected bust of those suspected of involvement in the illicit trade. Nigerian petty shop owners and businesses in SP are the victims of raids for extortion by police officers and their cronies. An example is Saka's case that happened in December 2011 and again in January 2013 during my fieldwork. It took place at the Centro Commercial 116, Galleria shopping mall. Unscrupulous police officers would go there, present some drug to the individuals and demand monetary settlement; otherwise, the subject would be threatened with arrest and jail. Saka explained to me:

It happened on a Friday when five armed police showed me their ID quickly and put it off. They blocked my shop, a business center for internet browsing and

making international calls. My Thai worker was here, also present were techni-
cian Simon that was repairing computers, and other customers. One police told
me to open my drawer. While opening it, another one dropped a small bag of
marijuana behind the step and called me to come and see something. I laughed at
them and said that it is not from here because marijuana is never sold or used here.
They searched all and found nothing. They took a mobile phone that belongs to a
customer because I could not give them receipt of the phone. They also took two
laptops computers and my iPad. Then they made a phone call to their informant,
a Nigerian I guess, who knows where I keep money. Because thereafter the police
went to the toilet and collected BRL20,000 [about USD$10,000] from that spe-
cific place (Saka, personal communication, January 12, 2013).

The police also attacked another Nigerian and got about BRL30,000.
Suspecting these were corrupt officers, Nigerian traders in the mall overwhelmed them and freed the handcuffed Saka. Whereas some Nigerians
offered to "settle" with money, the majority refused, demanding that the
Policia Militar (PM) must be called to intervene. On arrival, the PM seized
the gun from the officer and took him away. Saka did not report the case officially. He added: "My lawyer asked me to wait. But let me be plain, actually,
I do not want any problem because I suspected that those guys were police
friends. Police work together with some of our guys. Let them go! My life
is more important, and I pray that God takes control" (Saka, personal communication, January 12, 2013).

During the interview, a *Delegado de Policia* (police chiefs) told me to
persuade Saka to come and make an official report, but he refused. A cursory
glance at the issue shows that eventhough many Nigerians have spent years in
Brazil, it seems they are not fully integrated in society, as they frequently face
police harassment. Nigerian involvement in cocaine trafficking does affect
those not involved in the illicit trade, however. For instance, most Nigerians
recounted that two years ago nearly one hundred Nigerians' houses were
raided, and many residents are still being detained. These raids are not limited
to Nigerians; other foreigners such as Angolans or Chinese experience similar
exploitation. Many Nigerians choose to avoid reporting incidents like this due
to the fear of retribution. For instance, one shop owner remarked in response
to Saka's shop incursion: "The police can do anything they want. They will
detain, beat, and torture hell out of you or waste someone, and nothing will
happen. Do not forget that this is Brazil. Don't you see the rampant killings
shown on the TV? Yes, he could make the report and then? Who will save
him if they come after him? Even it is better to pay them and go your way"
(Nigerian shop owner, personal communication, January 12, 2013).

During fieldwork in early October 2012, undercover police allegedly busted
the flats of three Nigerians in connection with drug trafficking. Though a few

kilograms of cocaine were seized, the three men negotiated "settlement" and paid USD5,000 each to avoid arrest. Holloway (1993) wrote, "Beatings and arbitrary arrest were contemplated to be a basic part of the police's strategy of deterrence and punishment in Brazil. Their deployment continued even after the judicial authority to administer correctional detention and corporal punishment was removed from the police rights in 1871" (284).

Should this be true, it demonstrates that those engaged in drug trafficking could pay kickbacks to carry on with the illicit activity. Where some fail to make official reports, several said they would because they were not involved in drug trafficking. For instance, Pastor John told me that antidrug control agents busted his flat and held him and his family under gunpoint while they ransacked the rooms. Having no drugs or money, John made an official report to the police to prove his case. He stated, "I take the risk to bring the issue to the attention of the authorities" (Pastor John, personal communication, January 12, 2013). By making an official report, John would disprove rumors and prove that as a pastor he was not involved directly or indirectly in the illicit trade.

The military police have a reputation for being trigger-happy; they shoot first and ask questions afterward. The number of people killed by the police in Rio de Janeiro alone jumped in 2018 to a high of 1,538 (Londoño and Andreoni 2019). In the first five months of 2019, Rio police killed 731 people—nearly five a day—marking an almost 20% increase compared with the same period in 2018, noted Rio's Public Security Institute figures. Despite the issue of legitimate use of force in real threats of violence from gang members, police can usually get away with oppression, as the victims are afraid of the police and therefore do not report them. A study conducted by UNHRC (2010) outlines the impunity of rampant police killings conducted in Rio de Janeiro and SP, usually without any negative repercussions for the police involved.

Critics assert that conflict of interest and rivalry amid Brazilian civil and military police groups renders investigations generally perfunctory and ineffective, and hinders uniting the two forces. Policing has largely been aimed at controlling the poorest and most vulnerable sections of Brazilian society. Such practices were permitted to continue because the weakness of Brazilian democracy meant their victims were largely powerless, while the affluent Brazilians remained unaffected (IBA 2010; Willis 2014). While this contention continues, traffickers use the language of money to keep their businesses running smoothly (Huguet and de Carvalho 2008), and the police use suppression as a menace and take kickbacks, which allow Nigerian traffickers to maintain their activities.

5.5.4 Inside "School"

In the past 20 years, Brazil's population has grown by 30% while that of its prisons and police cells have almost quintupled to over half a million (TNI

2015). Brazil has the third-highest prison population in the world behind only the United States and China (Chowdhury 2019). According to the National Justice Council, it registers as many as 812,000 incarcerated people in state prisons, while there is officially space for fewer than 418,000 (Quirino et al. 2020).

Most of the Nigerian prisoners in Brazil are held in the SP prison system where about 131,000 people are. Every month, the number increases by roughly 1,000. The majority of prisoners are low- or medium-risk offenders who are forced to share cells with violent professional criminals. According to the official list from the Penitentiary Administration Secretary of São Paulo State Government, there were 272 Nigerians in Brazilian prisons as of December 2011. Of these, 247 were in SP (233 men and 14 women), most of them convicted for cocaine trafficking offenses. More recent reviews indicate the number has increased to about 457 Nigerians serving various jail terms over drug-related offenses as reported by *Premium Times* (2012). Nigerians topping the list of foreign inmates in Itai prison, with 361 in 2013, followed by Bolivia with 133 and Peru 122 inmates (Lissardy 2013). According to a prison census, the largest group of foreigners detained in SP is Nigerians (Mingardi 2001).

The number of people per room varies depending on the influx of prisoners. For instance, the Nigerian inmate OB stated, "I am in 'school' [jail] since 2008. I share room meant for six with ten inmates from various countries (Angola, Bolivia, Peru, Colombia, Yugoslavia, Spain, Italy, etc.), with four people sleeping on the floor. For the so-called bed, it is first come first serve" (OB, personal communication, December 28, 2012).

These shortcomings reflect the paucity of legal advice that would enable inmates to benefit from Brazil's theoretically world-class laws on parole and alternative sentences such as community service. With too many prisoners flowing in, and not enough flowing out, a cesspool festers in the middle. On paper, Brazil's prisons are a paragon of modernity. In practice, as in Nigeria, they are medieval leading to terrible conditions for inmates. Sluggish justice systems mean that many Nigerian prisoners remain on remand who might otherwise be free. This was the case for 73-year-old Hafsat Awosade who died in prison and was denied rights to progression and good medical attention.

5.5.5 Arbitrary Arrest and Denial of Rights to Progression

Crime in a straightforward sense is lawbreaking, or more conditionally, violation of the criminal law as agreed within a given jurisdiction at a particular time, although criminal law is usually enduring once established. Although some laws such as those against killing and the use of violence seem universally agreed as based on society's moral consensus, other laws may codify the interests of the influential, powerful, and rich, and therefore are biased against the interests and wishes of the poor, the powerless, and those without a voice.

Crime is conventionally described as the action or omission of an individual against the state (see Henry and Milovanovic 1994). Crimes of the state against society are called human rights violations. Agozino (2003) reconceptualizes crime to include the crimes of the state and criminality to include the criminal state. Invoking the legal principle of *nullum crime sine lege*, which simply says that crime cannot exist without being so defined by criminal law, Reid (1976) argues that a legal definition of crime is inevitable because "the system of criminal justice with which we are concerned is based on criminal justice."

Reiman and Leighton (2017, 64–100) noted the CJS acts as a "carnival mirror" that fails in the fight against crime while making it look as if crime is the work of the poor. It perpetuates a particular image of crime: that it is a threat from the poor. Labeling some acts "crimes" and by identifying those acts as so dangerous the law makes inevitable the use of extreme coercion to protect society against them. Thus, although the criminal law does not create crime, the CJS—from legislators to law enforcers—is just a mirror of the real dangers that lurk in our midst. Reiman and Leighton further noted: if police did not arrest, prosecutors charge, or juries convict, there would be no "criminals" (64).

It's no coincidence that the prison population contains disproportionate numbers of people who have lived in the most socially deprived areas.

Overrepresentation of blacks in Brazilian prison can be attributed in part to the biases of arresting officers and law enforcement culture generally. As summed up by the Conectas Human Right Group, in an article on *California Correctional Crisis* of 2014, "A light-skinned yuppie smoking pot on the beach is a user and left in peace, a dark-skinned slum-dweller lighting a spiff on the street is a peddler and thrown in jail" (Aviram 2014). The penal system is intrinsically elitist, which is one reason why pressure for prison reform has been scarce, as not all of Brazil's incarcerated population suffers equally. Those with a university diploma and social capital are often issued separate cells and better conditions. The poor are seldom afforded such treatment. Also, more than 80% of prisoners cannot afford to hire a lawyer, and no public defenders exist in more than 70% of all the judicial jurisdictions (Muggah and Szabo de Carvalho 2014; Quirino et al. 2020). These are all circumstances that also affect Nigerian inmates in Brazil.

Furthermore, several Nigerian inmates in both Itai and PFC prisons complained during interviews about lengthy sentences, as well as the denial of rights of progression in prison. For instance, Nigerians jailed for 34 or more years exist in Itai prison, according to the official list from Penitentiary Administration Secretary of São Paulo State. A recurrent complaint was the penalty applied to foreigners is higher than those of Brazilians for same drug trafficking offense. This could be attributed to differences in Brazil's state and federal laws. Drug trafficking falls under state laws, while international trafficking falls under federal laws. Federal laws are more severe, which affects Nigerians and other foreigners. International drug trafficking draws higher jail sentences because it has the offense of criminal association, which increases the sentence for an offender. At PFC prison in SP *all* 12 Nigerian female inmate interviewees were affected by the denial of rights of progression. For example: "I was told that I would be inside for three years and two months. I have been working for three years and two months now. It means I have remission. But I am already three years and two months inside. So why am I still here? Where is my remission, and why have I not been on semi-open regime outside?" (Rosa, personal communication, December, 2011).

This situation arises because an effective criminal justice lawyer needs to gain access to Nigerian offenders after arrest, offer advice during interrogation, and guarantee that their constitutional safeguards are not violated in detention. Whereas public defenders do not lack the necessary competency and qualification to carry out their responsibilities, the overwhelming workload they have to manage remains a major hindrance. As expressed by the UNHRC Working Group on Arbitration Detention (2014) the deficiency in obtaining effective legal assistance has constrained pro bono services, which are often unavailable to detainees, such as in the State of São Paulo. In some places, there are insufficient judges to deal with criminal cases. In addition, pro bono service is also aggravated by hindrances such as lawyers being only paid BRL500 per case, which is a small fee, given the amount of time usually involved in representing someone in a criminal lawsuit. It results in lawyers being less likely to devote sufficient time to conducting a professional job (IBA 2010).

For Nigerian inmates, this is compounded by difficulties in providing necessary documents required by law to grant permits for parole. SP's criminal justice agents, including public defenders, prosecutors, and judges, require that foreigners who leave the prison system provide documents and prove their financial means to rent a home or a room that most members of Nigerian cocaine trafficking outside prison are unwilling to assist with because Nigerian inmates must obtain the documentation needed to establish an identity, such as proof of residence, the name of a father or mother, or a birth certificate. Compared to their Brazilian counterparts in terms of accommodation and work contracts, Nigerians generally are unable to provide all these documents. Most Nigerians outside are afraid of involving themselves due to the fact that most are not innocent and do not want to risk guilt by association. In other words, they might also directly or indirectly involved in cocaine trafficking. While the intent may not be to make getting parole more difficult for Nigerians, that is certainly the effect of such administrative requirements. It is difficult for Nigerians outside to provide an address necessary for granting parole or partial freedom. Based on experience, they do not want to attract the police to their homes—most said that law enforcement agents have robbed them at some point in the past. They could also stand to lose their residence status if parole is broken. For this reason, most are afraid to give conational inmates their addresses.

5.5.6 Lack of Good Medical Attention

Another shortcoming affecting Nigerian inmates is the lack of quality medical attention. Brazil's national health system—*Sistema Único de Saúde*—has been an outstanding success. The 1988 constitution enshrined health as a citizens' right and requires the state to provide universal and equal access to health services (WHO 2008). Nevertheless, the first large-scale epidemiological study performed with the prison population in Brazil revealed high rates of psychiatric disorders among men and women (Quirino et al. 2020).

This remains a paradox in Brazils, a country that offers its citizenry one of the best medical health care systems in the world yet fails so many in need.

Claims that poor health services resulted in deaths in Itai and PFC prisons were common among Nigerian inmates, as well as incarcerated couriers sent by Nigerian cocaine traffickers in various countries. The death of female courier Nke, which happened in mid-2011 in PFC, is one example. Inmate Lita called her Nigerian "business associate" to send a courier to SP; in this case, Nke was sent to carry about three kilograms of cocaine. However, Nke was arrested at the SP Airport, convicted, and sentenced to six-year imprisonment, meaning that the sender and her courier ended up in the same prison. Whereas Lita knew this, Nke did not. First, this illuminates the working of Nigerian traffickers from inside a Brazilian jail. It also explains the role of strikers in the trafficking chain to the extent that the recruited courier, Nke, did not know for whom she worked. Despite becoming friends in jail, Lita concealed the facts from her. She stated to me, "I did not want her to know; it is the nature of the business! But it matters nothing any longer because Nke died in prison about four months ago" (Lita, personal communication, December 28, 2011).

As Lita told it, Nke went to the church, came back to the pavilion, and thereafter collapsed. She was taken to the prison clinic, but the doctor was unavailable, and medicine was out of stock. She was administered the pain reliever paracetamol, but Nke died. Because the cause of Nke's death could not be determined, inmates believed she died of voodoo and witchcraft, demonstrating the ongoing role of traditional beliefs among Nigerian inmates and associates. Lita added: "I think so because she did African traditional religious believe *Macumba* or *Voodoo* in prison. She tried every-thing just to get out of prison safe, having being [*sic*] denied progressions. One time I saw four plastic knives tied together with a red piece of cloth in our cell. It was smelled like shit. I do not know how it came in there. I called Mari and other girls. I also called the inmate Mama Africa who after praying threw the symbol away" (Lita, personal communication, December 28, 2011).

Mama Africa, or Chi, is a 60-year-old Nigerian inmate whom I interviewed in PFC. Inmates frequently accused her of witchcraft. Chi related feelings of isolation and developing mental problems, stating, "I cannot stand these accusations any longer. When someone dies, they would say that me, *Mama Africa*, killed the person. Because of this, I do not sleep at night. They call me witch and all that" (Chi, personal communication, December, 2011). Older women in African society are often accused of being witches because there are poor, troubled, rejected, or bereaved particularly in the context of prison life. Witchcraft accusations usually occur when people suffer one or more material or intangible losses. In Nigeria, illnesses, financial troubles, and a range of other misfortunes are associated with witchcraft. Both the late Awosade and Chi were relatively powerless, emotionally vulnerable, and unable to fight back when accused of practicing witchcraft. They are widely imagined to be jealous, bitter, and envious. The notion of witchcraft could mask real psychological issues: Chi claimed to hear voices and complained of disturbances even when no one else was present. Chi stated: "I have night-mare. I am tortured mentally because my photo was regularly shown on the TV in Brazil for carrying cocaine. I hear voices about it always and critics."

In the absence of real professional counseling, traditional beliefs fill the void. Fewer than 15% of inmates have access to educational or work opportu-nities, and health services are often deficient. Rio's Public Defenders' Office reported that in that state alone, 266 people died in detention in 2017, most of such treatable conditions as diabetes, hypertension, or respiratory ailments (HRW 2019). Nigerian inmates told me they wait up to 12 months for a doc-tor's appointment. In a confinement where good health care is lacking, some inmates turn to traditional medicine and rituals. What is missing is the train-ing, primarily in terms of the Nigerian inmate's reintegration, since the prison staff should act as educators and rehabilitators.

5.6 STAY IN BUSINESS IN JAIL

In Brazilian prisons, communication is restricted for Nigerian inmates. During closed regime, inmates receive phone calls once in six months for the duration of about an hour. Most prison officials do not speak English, making it difficult to communicate when family members call. As a result, prison officers may or may not send for the called person. In lieu of such a gamble, some inmates opt to pay up to USD1,400 in PFC for a cell phone or up to USD20,000 in Itai prison to stay in business while incarcerated. Whereas a Nigerian *Oga* or "Big man" trafficker could afford this, small-scale traffickers frequently pool money to buy a cell phone together. This motivates small-scale cocaine traffickers to work harder while inside. Prohibited items are smuggled in and sold through the activities of the PCC criminal faction in jails (see Mingardi 2007) or prison officers in exchange for kickbacks. Through this symbiotic relation between the legitimate and illegitimate world, the activities of the Nigerian cocaine traffickers and associates continue from prison. One dealer, Rija stated, "I bought my phone for BRL$1,800. I hide it in my pussy mostly. One time I slept with it for 72 hours. Sometimes it was for weeks. It hurts like mad" (Rija, personal communication, December 28, 2012). Guards enter the cells regularly and use metal detectors to check or scan clothes; they search inmates naked but not inside body cavities.

Telephones are important because inmates want to remain connected with friends and relations. For instance, Lita arranged for her courier Nke to be sent to SP from inside prison. Those who cannot afford a handset often buy a SIM card and rent phones from others. Inmates are careful about the right time to make calls. Those with phones remain vigilant because the warders can enter any time. Mana stated: "They found my phone hidden in the toilet. They seized it, and I was sent into *castico* or isolation for 30 days. Long enough to think about how to buy another phone. My contact outside paid USD$3,000 for each of the three cell phones I bought from Brazilian inmates. In prison you can buy everything, including drugs" (Mana, personal communication, December 22, 2011).

Affluent Nigerian inmates said that they succeeded in jail by collaborating with their Brazilian and Latin American inmates. However, those caught are punished accordingly. They may lose their job and remission or place in school and might be sent to solitary confinement for a period. Though it seems an easy way to circumvent harsh jail conditions, wardens patrol the corridors, walking bare footed to listen to conversations, and inmates often betray one another. Still, most opt again to take the risk to stay in business.

In this regard, it is wishful thinking that inmates no longer do business from the inside. On the contrary, most tend to do their best in keeping what they had already established. Being in prison robs inmates their freedom, yes, but at the same time, it offers inmates the chance to make new and strengthen existing trafficking contacts.

In the Nigerian international context, being inside had little effect on those who had solid partners, relatives, and family members to run their deals. If the principal trafficker is inside, his subordinates might cheat him but not in

an absolute sense. He is updated with movements of goods, prices, and profits or losses. In all, incarcerated Nigerian traffickers still direct their cocaine
deals from inside. Prison offered them the opportunity to consolidate friend-
ships with Latin American and inmate members of PCC in SP. They stay in
business because of the mutual relationship existing between them and the
custodians in varied hubs worldwide.

Chapter 6

Cocaine Hoppers and the Culture of Cocaine Trade and Consumption in China

This chapter will attempt to provide insight into the nature of the involvement of the Nigerian traffickers in China by first highlighting the background and influx of African and Nigerian traders into China. China's main trade hub for these traders is Guangzhou, Guangdong Province. Following the termination of superpower competition and emergence of economics as a key determinant of foreign policy (see Garnaut et al. 2018; Payne and Veney 1998), with the growing Sino-Africa trade interests, China, and Guangzhou in particular, attracted many Africans in the 1980s and 1990s, with Nigerians topping the list. Globalization increased the migration of peoples to places where they may have opportunities for a more comfortable life, including Nigerian international cocaine traffickers. Enthusiasm toward the new trend of illicit cocaine traders is driven by the desire to escape poverty and economic hardship, and fueled by the perception many Nigerians have of the West and Asia as countries where financial success comes easily.

China is becoming increasingly popular as a destination for foreigners. For instance, a survey of global expats in October 2014 found that China was ranked as the third most popular destination for expats in the world, exceeded only by Switzerland and Singapore. Experts attributed the increasing popularity to the growth of China's national strength and improved global image. One major reason for this is the move from attracting financial capital to attracting human capital, in line with China's national talent plan. The plan recruits experts to fill technical jobs that drive innovation and growth in China's economy. It calls for more foreign students to study in the country and to increase the number of foreign permanent residents in China (see Zhou 2017; Lie 2015). China's GDP growth was 6.6% in 2018 as United States' 2.9% (World Bank 2019b). Its real GDP in purchasing power parity overtook that of the United States and was estimated to be almost USD20 trillion in 2016. The size of the new middle class in China is fastest growing in the world, swelling from 39.1 million people or 3.1% of the population in 2000 to roughly 707 million or 50.8% of the population in 2018 (see Center for Strategic and International Studies [CSIS] 2021; Morreale et al. 2018; *The Economist* 2016). As such, many businesses are eager to penetrate the Chinese market. Economic booms go together with increase in consumption of recreational drugs and cocaine is no exception, as it happened earlier in other countries such as Spain, Italy, or the United States.

Nigerian cocaine traffickers follow the goods—in this case illicit cocaine—placing themselves strategically in production and transit areas like Brazil as well as destination countries in new Asian markets. China is essential for several reasons, notably its billion plus population and growing middle class. Cocaine is a recreational product for the wealthy, who are increasing in number in China and who admire Western culture. With an increase in cocaine trafficking and consumption, control will be difficult. China holds an important place in international commerce in Africa and Latin America that are transit and production hubs of cocaine, respectively.

In this regard, we will look at the Nigeria's "old school" and "new generation" relationship with cocaine trafficking in Guangzhou. Most old-school traffickers recall how they were warmly welcomed and respected in the first influx of immigration as compared to the stigmatized image they suffer following new arrivals since the early 2000s. Furthermore, this chapter will uncover Nigerian traffickers' social practices that say much for the research. We shall also discuss their involvement in cocaine trade and related crimes within these contexts from traffickers themselves, since they have the ability to both corroborate as well as contradict published information by researchers and law enforcement officials.

6.1 *I DEY GO CHINCO* (I AM GOING TO CHINA)

Contrary to the widespread view regarding the influx of Nigerians into China, interviews reveal that Nigerian traders were sought out by their Chinese business partners to come to China for long-term business relationships. For instance, the entrepreneur, Joe, expressed: "The Chinese sought out Nigerian importers of various goods those days. It was normal for Chinese embassy staff coming to my office and persuading me to come and take visa to China. Because I designed shoes and sandals, and they produced it in China. This led my having joint venture business with my partner" (Joe, personal communication, May 20, 2011).

In an attempt to outdo their Chinese competitors, Nigerian traders often journeyed to Guangzhou to do business directly. India, Thailand, and

Malaysia were other key countries for traders, but many took their businesses to China.

On the one hand, as many Chinese intellectuals say, they are trying to do something good about their county's political and financial interest in Africa (see Ngomba 2007). On the other hand, all-pervading global media accounts about the rise of China, and word-of-mouth accounts about "greener pastures" and "new land of opportunity" continue to attract many Nigerians to Guangzhou. Nonetheless, China could be a welcoming, friendly, and yet risky.

China has a sizeable domestic drug consumption market. At the turn of the twentieth century, there were between 21.5 and 25 million people dependent on opium. Addiction and addicts had not been eliminated as said during Mao's regime, noted Patrick Tibke's (2017) "Drug Dependence Treatment in China." Drug addiction persists as demonstrated by the number of officially registered drug addicts, about 2.51 million in 2016, according to the National Narcotics Control Commission report. That is an increase of about 6.8% annually. Of these addicts, the majority were aged from 18 to 35 years old. Critics suggest that the number of addicts is actually much higher. A key reason for this is that dark numbers are endemic to illicit activities, and China is no exception.

On the other side are the errors in criminal records that include those of exclusion and incompleteness as well as those of inclusion and superfluity. Agozine (2003, 103–111, 215) questions the privileging of facts and values by Habermas (1996) and raises issues with Baudrillards's (1996) perfect-crime-as-no-crime thesis. He pointed to the interdependence of fact and fiction in the social construction of knowledge. Where dark numbers exist, we should find exaggerated official statistics of crime in accordance with Cohen's (1972) amplification of deviance thesis and Hall et al.'s (1978) idea that media crime news serves as a morality play inherent to policing the crisis in response to negative attention. Furthermore, the hyperrealism of Baudrillard (1996) underlines the notion that social theory or law or morality is not simply a question of the tensions between facts and norms, or of telling the truth, the whole truth and nothing but the truth, but one of the coexistence of fact and fiction.

Official figures only include drug users whose details are known to Chinese public security organizations. A resurgence in drug-related problems remains a concern because of China's vicinity to drug cultivation and production areas in the Golden Triangle (GT), Golden Crescent, and Golden Azalea. In addition, drug addiction in China is considered a personal failure; addicts are highly stigmatized, and drug addiction does not receive public sympathy or priority in government funding, according to Pan Suiming (2018) who observed that surveys on drug taking reveal that there are many more users than official estimates acknowledge, and policies need to be adjusted accordingly.

Furthermore, drug addiction is no longer restricted to the border areas. The Chinese government publicly acknowledges the phenomenon in all provinces and major urban areas. China is no longer just a transit country; it has a sizeable addict population, notwithstanding stepped up control by the government. Chinese police arrested 168,000 suspects for drug offenders and solved 140,000 drug-related criminal cases in 2016 (*Xinhua News* 2017). But, if the number of users is in the tens of millions, as researchers suggest, then the number of arrests is a drop in the bucket.

In Hong Kong, cocaine is ranked fifth highest among the reported drug abusers in 2016 (Central Registry of Drug Abuse [CRDA] 2017). Observers at the grassroots level noted the official figures significantly underestimate both the scale and rising levels of cocaine addiction. It is popular among young professionals and drug abusers under 21, and male users are more common than female. Cocaine has become so popular in China that it has become the second most common addiction treated. Researchers found that demand-focused prohibitive actions by law enforcement agencies have unintended adverse consequences, and China is not unique in this. Spatial displacement, substance displacement, policy displacement, creation of black markets, and marginalization of drug users are some of the unintended adverse consequences observed also in Europe (Martin and Anette 2016; European Monitoring Centre for Drugs and Drug Addiction [EMCDDA] 2015). Likewise, scholars in other places have found that prohibition and tighter control over some drugs has prompted drug abusers to switch to taking other drug substitutes (Gupta et al. 2015; Rolles and Kushlick 2014). In the case of China, this could explain the trend away from heroin consumption toward cocaine.

6.2 COKE ENTERS

Among Nigerian traders in Guangzhou, I came across several university graduates and dropouts, former street hawkers, and members of Nigerian cocaine trafficking that followed the "good" cocaine: small scale, strikers, and dealers. China provides possibilities for Nigerian traffickers in continuous search of new markets and new clients to increase the supply, true to form for the globalization of crime and drug trafficking. Similar to the way migrating to Western countries was popular in Nigeria, Asia became a new attraction. Interviews suggested that to travel, some had a small amount of capital raised by family or relatives who sold property; others borrowed directly from close friends and acquaintances under various agreements. Yet, several knowingly or unknowingly risked engaging in the illicit cocaine trafficking through friends and contacts that arranged the trip. In this regard, getting Chinese visas through *man know man* or *long leg* (Nigerian expression for the unofficial way) is typical amid Nigerians in Guangzhou. The shop owner, Yadu, stated: "Do not forget China resembles Nigeria in some ways. The 'connection man' here has 'connection man' in Nigeria, and together they will connect all; China 'L' visa is available for about N300,000 naira [about USD$2,000], single entry" (Yadu, personal communication, May 21, 2011).

Entering China's economy has its challenges. This evokes Mathews and Yang's (2012) concept of *high-end globalization* and *low-end globalization*. Generally, globalization is associated with globally recognized brands like Apple, Samsung, or Huawei. However, many people encounter globalization not through this "high-end globalization." For instance, ordinary Nigerians who want to purchase a smartphone would not go to an Apple or Samsung showroom in Lagos that would be considered high-end. Instead, they buy a cheap Chinese-made imitation at the street market for few U.S. dollars equivalent. This ordinary Nigerian experiences the contemporary global interconnectedness through "low-end globalization."

This process enhances flow of people and trade across borders, small amounts of capital, and informal, semilegal, or illegal transactions: "It is goods such as this that bring global communication to the developing world, even if that involves copyright infringement and customs bribery." For this reason, policymakers in the developed world should acknowledge the benefits of low-end globalization to underdeveloped-world consumers and create legal spaces for this trade to be done safely (see Mathews 2018).

It is worth noting that semilegal or illegal transactions are not limited to low-end globalization. This recalls the notion of blurred borders of formal and informal economies as discussed previously. It implies that the informal economy is to the formal economy what low-end globalization is to high-end globalization. But today's world is linked and lines blurred. No autonomous national economies exist but rather a single global economy in which the illicit drug trade is part. As an important driver and facilitator, globalization has a significant effect on illicit drug markets. Cocaine hoppers harness these developments and achieve similar benefits to those in the legal economy.

China's opening-up policy evolved into a combination of "bringing in" and "going out." China attracted foreign direct investment from developed countries and encouraged outbound investments from its public and private sectors in underdeveloped countries. Perhaps the emphasis by Suzhou Industrial Park Administrative Committee (2004) recollects this view that during the process, China also took in corrupt Western ideas and lifestyles with corrosive and damaging effects upon Chinese society. Or better recalled with Deng

Xiaoping's comment that when you open the window, you'll let in air as well as flies and mosquitoes, but ways to handle this exist.

6.2.1 Old School and New Generation Influx

Africans and Nigerians make up an outstanding group of foreign residents and transitory populations in Guangzhou. There is a lack of reliable data regarding their numbers, nationalities, and activities because official figures are secret or unknown as many foreigners are undocumented. The publicity regarding Africans in Guangzhou has led to varied claims, which range from 20,000 to 200,000 (see Mathew et al. 2017; Castillo 2014; Bodomo 2012). Regardless of their status, the Nigerian government estimated the size of the Nigerian community in China to be about 10,000. Over 70,000 Nigerians arrived in Guangdong Province alone in 2016 for business, tourism, education, and health care, said the Nigerian Consul-General in Guangzhou (see *Vanguard* 2018). It is an influx that is influencing certain areas and changing the fabric of Guangzhou. Some residential and business areas of the city, such as Dongpu, Dengfeng Jie, and Yongping Jie, have been designated "Chocolate Cities," in a clear allusion reminiscent of so-called Chinese *ethnoburbs*—a term first coined in 1997 by Wei Li in a paper on the Chinese in Los Angeles (see Li 1998; Morais 2009).

The inrush of Africans evokes Gilles's (2015) "Social Construction of Guangzhou as a Translocal Trading Place" where place is no longer a single locality, but becomes a complex of localities or a translocality produced by the diverse forms of connections, interactions, and practices of the actors (Gielis 2009, 280). It also calls to mind Mathew's (2015) inquiry on Africans as cultural brokers in Guangzhou, and how those who by virtue of their skin color may be seen as the "most foreign of the foreign" by many Chinese, learn to adjust to life in China (11).

Pioneer Nigerian traders living in Guangzhou, those who arrived in the 1990s, refer to themselves as the old school, to differentiate from those semi-settled and newly arrived in the mid-2000s. Most discuss disillusionment following an influx of Nigerians that changed their reputation in the city. This threatens their intention to contribute positively to the development of Nigeria and establish small-scale industry there in future—a dream undermined by the Nigerian state crisis, as discussed in chapter 2. As the number of those overstaying visa validity increased, some were pushed to survive as illegal aliens—cocaine trafficking being a prominent means of this. This situation became worrisome for law-abiding Nigerians at large, who suffered stigmatization. Shop owner, Kedu, stated: "We fought for Nigeria community to exist today because newcomers wanted to take it over as a base for their criminal activities. They formed gangs such as *Bagger* and *Eiye* with which they engage drug trafficking, extortion, armed robbery, kidnapping, and murder in Guangzhou. I am not happy these guys are messing things up for all Nigerians. They even sell cocaine on the streets here" (Kedu, personal communication, May 20, 2011).

Potential profits have attracted criminal organizations such as the NBM, a Nigerian cultist group (also called the Black Axe movement, Aiye, or confraternities), which were initially selective university student associations based on the Oxbridge model. First created at the UI in 1952 for the promotion of local identity, Aiye and other secret organizations multiplied in a matter of years, and eventually becoming part of cocaine hoppers in countries including Brazil, Italy, Malaysia, and China. Cohen (2019, 40) found that as confraternities were increasingly manipulated by military juntas to fight left wing or pro-democracy organizations on university campuses, they transformed into secret societies involved in arsons, markets taxations, human trafficking, and drug trafficking.

Nigerians in Guangzhou are aware of the extent to which drug trafficking by a few has stigmatized them all, regardless of the fact that the illicit trade in opium, heroin, and cocaine was already well established in China prior to their arrival. Lo and Kwok (2012) wrote on how triad societies respond to socioeconomic change. They found that triad society, or *Hung Mun*, is a well-established, cohesive branch of Chinese criminal organizations focally aimed at monetary gain. Prosperity in China fostered the expansion of triad activities due to increasing demand of legal and illegal services in Chinese communities. Connectedly, triad societies have changed from a rigid territorial base and cohesive structure to more reliance on flexible and instrumental social networks (see Lo and Kwok 2012). Triads are involved in a wide range of licit and illicit businesses, including wholesale and retail markets, brothels, extortion, drug trafficking, and money laundering. In the early 2000s, there were 294 active youth gangs in Hong Kong under the control of 19 triad societies (Lo 2002). Leading triad gangs are the 14K, the Sun Yee On, and the Wo Shing Wo. It is estimated that there could be as many as 100,000 triad members currently operating in Hong Kong, according to Blundy (2017).

The booming drug trafficking business in China could be attributed to an existing domestic drug consumption market and thriving drug narcotics business in China.

A thriving drug narcotics business arose as traffickers developed alternative routes to the lucrative Chinese market. For instance, the largest cocaine seizure in Lagos involved two Chinese entrepreneurs, as discussed in chapter 4.5.1. Hong Kong authorities confiscated 537 kilograms of cocaine in the first 10 months of 2018, a 78.4% increase on the same period in the previous year. Among the traffickers arrested was a former Hong Kong bank manager. Officers seized 80 kilograms of cocaine (valued at around USD16.2

million) hidden in grape shipment from Peru (see Lo 2021). In another drug busts, Hong Kong Police seized about 567 kilograms of cocaine in various localities. Traffickers used diverse methods to avoid detection, including concealment in engine oil and brake fluid containers. The arrest of eight offenders included of a U.S. citizen, five Mexicans, a Colombian woman, and her Chinese husband demonstrated the transnational nature of Chinese participation in the global cocaine trade. In April 2010, the disappearance of a Dutch-Chinese man led to the confiscation of 372 kilograms of cocaine from a village house in Hong Kong. In another case, authorities seized 70 kilograms of cocaine from Peru in Shanghai. The Ministry of Public Security admitted that cases of cocaine entering China from South America have been on the rise, and as a result, they have strengthened cooperation with foreign antidrug control agencies (see Bacchi 2014).

6.2.2 "Open Talk" Cocaine

Nigerian traffickers frequent several popular locations where Africans entertain themselves in Sanyuanli, Dengfeng, or the surrounding Xiaobei. The area is a site where transnational African flows meet with Chinese from various provinces and ethnic groups. It is a neighborhood where the local and transnational converge for business and entertainment. When not threatened by the presence of law enforcement agents, Nigerian cocaine traffickers talk freely about their activities. They call relatives or business partners in Nigeria, Ghana, Uganda, SA, and Brazil. From an ethnographic point of view, spending time with my contacts in various settings including dance clubs and bars encouraged informal conversations and semi-in-depth interviews that provided relevant data from direct and indirect players in the illicit trade. Knowledge of various languages enabled this author to participate in and comprehend conversations.

The centrality of conversation has connections to issues related to my research. Intentionally or unintentionally with jokes, boasting, quarrels, and threats, Nigerian traffickers expose what they do, how, with whom, when, where, and price in language unfamiliar to outsiders. Conversely, when things are said in Pidgin English, the topic of conversation changes when strangers approach. For instance, while Aki was talking about taking precautions regarding "runs and scores" (meaning cocaine deals), he did not hear when Azu asked to change the topic because a Chinese couple stood close by. Nigerian trafficker and ex-inmate, Azu, cautioned: "Brother, continue the story in native please. Did you not hear what I asked you? *Basket* Mouth! Please change the story because they are around. Are you a 'like a bike without brakes? Here is not Europe; we are in China, *you wan wahala* (Do you want trouble)?" (Azu, personal communication, April 26, 2012).

Azu tried to remind Aki that he should be careful talking openly about cocaine dealing because of the presence of outsiders. I was trusted because my contacts introduced me to them.

This is reminiscent of my conversations with one U.S. sociologist, KK, released on December 14, 2013, after serving seven months in White Cloud District Detention Centre (WCDDC) in Guangzhou for taking a large sum of money from a colleague at a Chinese University where he taught. In several extensive interviews via Skype and email correspondences, KK told me about his experience with Nigerian inmates incarcerated for drug trafficking offenses in WCDDC. He was not trusted initially. KK stated:

> My Nigerian friends were leery at first. Being American that speaks Chinese, they thought I worked for the police. But later that will ease; they opened up because my close Nigerian friend "Biyi" told them, "You can trust Mr. KK." For example, "DD" felt quite accomplished after having come from such a challenging background. From a mule swallowing and carrying up to one kg of drug in his stomach he had saved enough money to purchase his own stock and developed a lucrative customer base of users and smaller dealers. He maintained and pursued his dream of being a drug kingpin while in WCDDC (KK, personal communication, November 29, 2014).

Because they spent eight months together, they had enough time to establish a sense of trust. They talked freely with KK when not threatened by the presence of outsiders.

In several settings during the fieldwork, Nigerian traffickers talked about their experiences and boasted to elevate their status as tough guys who survived the hard life of prison. On such occasions, those without jail experience were somehow belittled or not taken seriously when they spoke. Nevertheless, they tried to share their experience by telling stories of friends, acquaintances, friends of friends, or sometimes of relatives. This way, they contributed to conversation, but it is not the same as someone with direct experience. Yet, the more they conversed, the more they risked divulging sensitive information to outsiders.

6.3 RECRUITMENT, TRAVEL, CONTROL, AND DELIVERY

The involvement of Nigerian traffickers in China is demonstrated by the arrest of offenders being made public. It highlights the extensive network of the Nigerian drug traffickers operating in China. All through my fieldwork, Nigerian traffickers talked about their counterparts in Guangzhou. KK stated:

> I had large amount of extended interaction with Nigerians while incarcerated, majority involved in the heroin trade. I encountered a variety of Igbo involved

in all facets of the drug trade from local to international—from simple to death penalty cases. Two out of ten I know well are serving death sentence. While in Army hospital for three weeks, I met several others from Detention Three where about 300 Nigerians were. In the hospital, they brought people from the airport suspected of swallowing cocaine or heroin. I spent my entire days with them talking. They helped me and helped them too. Together we helped ourselves in the brutal detention center (KK, personal communication, November 29, 2014).

A Nigerian ex-convict, who was freed in early 2015 after serving two years in different jails in Guangzhou, told me that more than 400 Nigerian inmates were in detention there and WCDDC. Several are men in their early twenties, some of whom were on death row. Nigerian cocaine traffickers, in China as in other arenas, use various methods in the illicit cocaine trade, involving players from large-scale importers to small-scale traffickers, as well as strikers, couriers, and part-time couriers. The interplay between these participants in Nigeria and in production and transit hubs provides a steady supply of cocaine to their associates globally, China is no exception.

6.3.1 Courier Approach: "My Darling"

Interviewees suggested that Nigerian international cocaine traffickers can easily recruit drug couriers because of the socioeconomic factors discussed previously. Female traffickers, in particular, are often exploited, made to carry drugs unwittingly or drawn into the trade by boyfriends or husbands. Women from other African countries, including Tanzania, SA, and Zimbabwe, are often recruited because they have easier access to entry visas to China. For instance, the Nigerian trafficker, Aki, alleged that in February 2012 undercover police in Guangzhou traced and arrested a Nigerian cocaine trafficker. Aki stated: "His Ugandan female courier arrested at the airport implicated him. His wife from a Southern African country recruits female couriers" (Aki, personal communication, December 29, 2012).

In March 2011, the Chinese wife of a Nigerian in Guangzhou was arrested for drug trafficking, as was her sister. The three of them had traveled to Nigeria together and the couple wed there. On their return trip, the husband concealed cocaine in their luggage. Using business appointments as an excuse, he departed in Singapore while his wife and her sister continued to China and were apprehended. The two women said they did not know about the packaged drugs in their luggage. The husband had intentionally stayed in Singapore waiting to return while the deal was completed successfully.

While having drinks with friends and listening to stories about making quick money, Noko, a Nigerian trafficker, disclosed that his Chinese girlfriend brought in some "market" from Malaysia five days ago, "She brought back cool 3.5kg of 'white' [cocaine] concealed in bottom bag. My 'spirit' [a Chinese friend or customer] picked it up from the airport and brought her to my place. Oh, I love. My honeymoon, *Oyoyo* [beauty]" (Noko, personal communication, May 22, 2011). Realizing that others could hear, he decided to quit the topic. Though Noko did not want to talk further, my contact later informed me that his courier had a "problem" (meaning he was arrested) in a neighboring country. In addition, Noko had forgotten that he told me when I met him a year prior that he had reliable contacts in Brazil and in several drug hot spots in Asia, including Thailand, Malaysia, Macao, and Hong Kong where his associates are active. For attractive financial reward, couriers are available. Noko expressed: "I pay my courier USD$6,000 per kilo to bring it from Brazil. She makes 10K if she brings in two and that is much as they could earn in years in China. I pay her half of the money up front and the rest when she delivers. I treat her good! She has mastered it well because she takes antidiarrhea medicine to prevent going to toilet during the trip" (Noko, personal communication, May 22, 2011).

The "mules" of the Nigerian networks have been widely reported on. From 1995 to 1998, for example, 20 "white mules" belonging to one of these organizations were arrested in Brazil. A police investigation showed that a Nigerian responsible for the network purchased the cocaine in Bolivia for between USD1,000 and 2,000 per kilogram, and deployed Brazilian or Bolivian smugglers to transport it to SP in batches of 10–15 kilograms. There it was packed and shipped under the control of a European "mule." The "white mules" received between USD1,000 and USD2,000 in compensation, in addition to plane tickets. For some, this is an opportunity to travel for free (Mingardi 2001).

Noko's girlfriend, likewise, recruited others willing to take the risk for such lucrative gains. Some female couriers are also unaware that their Nigerian boyfriends deceive or sweet-talked other women into undertaking the same risk. The use of drug couriers is a dominant pillar of Nigerian trafficking globally. It shows that similar conditions that frustrate individuals into the illicit trade in Nigeria are equally found in societies around the world. In this aspect, China is not unique, except when things go wrong.

6.3.2 Postage Method: Try Your Luck

Nigerian traffickers in Brazil and other countries in Latin America deploy the postage method to smuggle small quantities of cocaine concealed in various items using private or institutional mailing services. With the improved measures of control such as X-ray machines, special scanners, and sniffer dogs, the interception rates for this method of transporting the drug are uncertain. Usually, the quantities sent are relatively small, which is the reason Nigerian traffickers refer to it as the "try your luck" method. However, while many succeed, some are discovered, as was the case of Nigerian trafficker, Ndi, in China.

One afternoon in April 2011, the telephone rang, and it was a contact in China who gave me the surprising news that the police apprehended Ndi for cocaine trafficking. This happened about six months after another Nigerian, Fefe, was arrested in November 2010, as we shall discuss later. These cases were extra motivation for the fieldwork in China in May and June 2011. In his late twenties, Ndi entered China in the mid-2000s and was lucky to have contact with respectable people who helped secure him a teaching job in southern China. He received a salary of about CNY5,000 (about USD780) monthly, which is slightly more than the minimum salary in China.

A write-up on *Work and Life in China* noted that teaching English in China can pay between CNY6,500 and CNY18,000 (2019). That's about USD920–2,500 per month, depending on qualification, city, education level, and experience. Depending on the number of hours worked, the average salary kindergarten teachers can expect is around CNY8,000–12,000, about USD1,200–1,800 (Mitchell 2019). Many teaching contracts also provide housing and other benefits, including return travel to one's home country. However, many non-native English speakers, like Nd, have no option other than accepting to work for a lower salary. This is due in part to the demand for native speakers but also due in part to pervasive racism in China and the preference for white Westerners who are perceived as professionals, even if they lack qualifications. Kele had this to say: "Surprisingly Ndi was talking about couriers coming and going. I warned him to stop and not to think about drug trafficking. Otherwise he must stop coming to me. He assured me he was not into it. So, I was shocked when his cousin informed me Ndi was arrested because of cocaine posted from Malaysia to a Chinese girlfriend's address. I was speechless" (Kele, personal communication, April 28, 2012).

Ndi subleased a room in his flat to a man from a West African country, who had been in China for about two weeks. Ndi asked him to collect a parcel from his Chinese girlfriend's home address. Unaware the parcel contained hundreds of grams of concealed cocaine sent by Ndi's associates in Malaysia, he was lucky as he could not find his way to the address. Ndi decided to collect the parcel himself. Unaware of the girlfriend's undercover police activity, Ndi was arrested for the act. His family asked Kele to contact a lawyer for Ndi. Kele added: "I refused to do it. I asked the guy if he could imagine what a disgrace at school where Ndi was teaching? In addition, I reminded him we have discussed many times with Ndi about Fefe or others arrested for trafficking. So, I really could not take it, they knew the consequences. Ndi was not supposed to derail, even though he complained of financial problem at home. I think that something blindfolds these guys or what?" (Kele, personal communication, April 28, 2012).

Nigerian traffickers look for girlfriends who will also work as drug couriers. The lawyer, Jian, noted "they deliberately sought Chinese women as girlfriends and lured them to trafficking cocaine" (Jian, personal communication, May 26, 2011).

According to the Chinese law, people convicted of smuggling, selling, transporting, or producing more than 50 grams of cocaine or heroin can be sentenced to death in China. One contact in Guangzhou informed me that law enforcement agents in Xiamen in mid-June 2013 arrested his acquaintance, a Cameroonian teacher, in connection with about 290 grams of cocaine sent by mail. The clothes in the package were filled with cocaine, parceled from Brazil using the girlfriend's work address, but ultimately, they were uncovered. The teacher was arrested at Xiamen University. These interceptions show the perseverance of Nigerian traffickers and partners using this method to smuggle small but steady quantities of cocaine and other drugs.

It is a method used by small-scale exporters, amateur traffickers, and local consumers with friends or contacts in source countries. Risks can be lowered by many simple measures: faking the sender and the origin country, concealing the cocaine within protective materials or disguising it with special products, faking the recipient by writing a false name, simulating ignorance, or using the safer addresses of employers or friends who are unaware of the illicit content.

6.3.3 Nigerian Street Dealers: "Your Happiness is my Business!"

Nigerian cocaine traffickers are involved in "street pharmaceuticals" as they call it, or, more formally, selling petty quantities of cocaine in Guangzhou and beyond. After the police cracked down in 2009, the practice was displaced, and dealers went underground. Nigerian cocaine traffickers often perform deals inside the clubs, as I observed during fieldwork. They generally started with soft drugs they said were for personal use as a strategy to start conversation and later informed potential customers that cocaine and/or heroin were available. One conversation went as follows:

KK: In certain clubs, sometimes I would be seating with a group of friends. They would come and first put two or three grams of hash in the middle of the table as a gift or sample. Even some had business card printed, with name and phone number. Some had their name cards printed, with phone numbers on it. One said to me, "Mr. K, your happiness is my business."

Qs: While in jail, what did Nigerian inmates tell you were their reason for taking such risks knowing that if caught they could be executed?

KK: Of course, every person is different. I cannot speak for everybody. In most cases I do not know. But I will tell you about one guy. He put it to me like this "that if I am successful, I have the chance to send my children to school. If I do not may be my family is in poverty for many generations." It's that simple. To me they would have to know because it was so open. (KK, personal communication, December 6, 2014)

In another setting, the Nigerian cocaine trafficker, Ach, said to Kele: Ach: I noticed you called me yesterday. I went to meet my "spirits," [customers] in Shenzhen. Man must keep hassling. I put my telephone off because I did not want guys to disturb. Only my Hong Kong telephone was on.

Kele: Yes, I called to arrange seeing you. Ach, you and hassling! I saw you were rushing often to toilet like someone suffering from running stomach. Did she give you or you gave her?
Qs: He or she? Once I noticed Ach went to the toilet twice in few minutes and thereafter his friend who stood next to him.
Ach: That is life, my brother! I went to settle some matter. It is the more you look the less you see, because I collected from a female courier who carried it in her private part, and handed it over to my customer. That's it! The hole from where she brought in the toilet is not important, the money is. (Ach, personal communication, April 28, 2012)

Ach said his friends are seasoned dealers and have contacts for local couriers. Even in a dancing bar, between drinks, dancing, and conversation, transactions are completed. Interviewees said that marijuana grows wild like weeds in some rural areas in China. Hashish has long been a favorite with the pipe-smoking elderly. Cocaine and designer narcotics like ecstasy are increasingly available in party settings. Heroin use was traditional (Zhang and Chin 2016), but night clubs and karaoke bars are hot spots for methamphetamines and ketamine (Li et al. 2017). Ach and his associates are successful because they follow in the footsteps of existing drug trafficking businesses and wholesale markets that have become fragmented. They work with counterparts who recruit couriers for about USD350–600.

The couriers undertake the riskiest tasks in the trafficking business and are most likely to make mistakes that lead to their arrest. Those behind the scene who hire the mules and coordinate trafficking operations are better insulated from the actual trafficking activities. Ach and his associate choose a busy place to distract attention and agree upon signs to communicate and transact deals. To minimize the risk further, they choose the place for ad hoc appointments carefully, away from CCTV cameras.

6.4 *ARABANKO* GUANGZHOU (MAXIMUM ENJOYMENT GUANGZHOU)

6.4.1 Chic Parties, Escorts, and Cocaine

Introduced by one of my contacts, Titi and Raka were East African sex workers in Guangzhou whose trust I earned, and eventually they agree to an in-depth interview. Lured into prostitution like several others from Rwanda, Uganda, Tanzania, Cameroon, and Burundi, they arrived in China a few years before our meeting. Why would sex workers risk drug trafficking? Both women asserted they were pressured into drug trafficking to pay off racketeers.

Raka remarked: "You are right brother, no problem. I had to pay my madam at least CNY300 [about USD40] per week till I finished USD6,000 debt. This is a pressure that caused me to risk drugs especially when I saw someone who did it coolly and made money to upset her debt. Also, I have been asked severally by some guys to do it" (Raka, personal communication, April 28, 2012).

At that rate, it would have taken Raka years to pay off her debt.

Titi added to this, saying:

Look it is a common thing here in Guangzhou for girls like us to be approached by some Nigerians or Ghanaians or whoever, for that. While socializing, guys will buy you drinks and food and all that. You get to know each other and that is how it starts. Then they will ask if you have visa and when it will expire and so on. When my friend [Raka] was traveling to Beijing two weeks back, one guy approached her for it, and she refused. Also, they have tried me many times. They will always ask you to carry it to places like Shanghai, Shenzhen, and Beijing among others (Titi, personal communication, April 27, 2012).

Titi expressed that at least five men approached her in 2011 to carry drugs, but she refused. However, about three months prior to our discussion, she fell in love with the Nigeria boyfriend she met at a bar in Guangzhou.

Titi said: "I know he has money, but I was not sure how he makes it. I doubted if it was only from sending some goods sometimes to Nigeria, as he said. But at a time, it did not matter anymore. He was buying good clothes and other things for me. I so much liked the guy that I was in love with him. Maybe he had used voodoo on me, or what?" (Titi, personal communication, April 27, 2012).

However, while having dinner with his Chinese friends in a chic restaurant one day, he asked if she ever heard about cocaine. Titi responded yes, but that she had never seen it or touched it before. He told her she could make fast money by collaborating with a local female courier in delivering something to some people. Titi told me, "This is another point that weaken me because I thought, if local woman does it, why couldn't I?" (Titi, personal communication, April

27, 2012). Raka and Titi underestimated the risk by delivering cocaine pellets body-packed in their vaginas to contacts at private parties. When asked how many times she has risked delivering cocaine, Titi replied:

> I did it about four times to finish my bills. Then I stopped because enough was enough. That is why I am telling all this now. One day, the lady and I were on our way to deliver. But the police stopped the taxi driver for alcohol control. I had the "thing" in my private part. I was uncomfortable because it was causing some pains. So, I was praying to get to the destination quickly and offload it. Believe me, I was almost dead when the police asked for my passport. Luckily my visa was OK. That was it for me! That was enough! Nonetheless each time I got the money, I could not believe it. One time, I got paid USD$1,000 for delivering 100 grams. In fact, I could not think of how many men I had to fuck to be able to make that much. Each time I did it, I totally refused to think at that moment. I kept praying and God helped me, because some individuals from my country were executed for it. However, one thing was that, it did not happen often. Because the guy I worked for sometimes disappears for months and then reappears again (Titi, personal communication, April 27, 2012).

Part-time couriers, like Raka and Titi, felt comfortable talking with me because I highlighted my encounters in KL, Hong Kong, Shanghai, or Beijing for instance. At least two Philippines and a Chinese girl I met through contacts said that their Nigerian friends had approached them to carry cocaine to Shanghai. Chatting with three Nigerians, two South Africans, and a Cameroonian, I observed that dealing in drugs, including cocaine, is a way to make ends meet for some that seemed willing to accept the risk. In this regard, Beijing, Hong Kong, and Shanghai are similar to KL and others in that they are outlets for Nigerian illicit cocaine entrepreneurs and associates—reinforcing the concept of deviant globalization. It is an economic, moral, and legal concept that flourishes at the node of ethical difference, regulatory, and law enforcement inefficiencies.

Wherever there is a fundamental disagreement about what is right as well as a connection to the global market, cocaine hoppers arise to meet the unfulfilled demand. In meeting collective desires, deviant entrepreneurs see the differences in notions of public good, morality, and health as bankable market opportunities. Neoliberalism's wide-open, market-oriented rules might govern globalization, Gilman et al. (2011) wrote, but the game gets played on a morally inconsistent field. Contrary to some dominant notions of globalization that portray it as a process that annihilates differences across space (Tomlinson 1999; Papastergiadis 2000), deviant globalization underscores the continued importance of spatial differences in the structure of the global economy (10).

The pathways of deviant globalization flows are established not only by the border security and state authority but also by technical education and technological connectivity, job opportunities, as well as the amount of natural resources and entrepreneurship that a country possesses, which generate comparative advantages for deviant entrepreneurs. They move through cities—from the inner cities of the United States to the *favelas* of Rio de Janeiro to the *banlieues* of Paris to the urban slums from Dakar to Lagos. They flow "along the cocaine supply route that links the mountains of Colombia to São Paulo and the waterways of West Africa to noses in the Netherlands," and through the mainstream financial establishments—"from Wall Street to London to Tokyo's Nihonbashi District" (Gilman et al. 2011, 11). Deviant globalization could be found almost everywhere and connected to the global economy.

6.4.2 Body Package: Front and Back

Body-packing of small quantities of cocaine from 10 to 100 grams is an attractive option for women in otherwise dire situations. They function as cocaine couriers in Guangzhou and beyond. At a party organized by friends of Titi and Ach, I came in contact with a female courier from the Philippines who stated: "Make sure it is well packed and take it in front or back, for a short distance delivery. God has made private parts, vagina, anus, etc. So, use it! When you are frustrated and desperate, it could be way out. You just do not think to be unlucky because it is a life and death kind of feeling. I did it because it got to the point of no return" (Lies, personal communication, May 22, 2011).

In this regard, it is about making ends meet and staying alive. Dealers are only concerned with delivering the product to its users, regardless of how it was transported by the couriers. In addition, Titi and her friends sometimes arranged for additional part-time sex work to coincide with their deliveries. One African sex worker stated: "They pay us well, so why not? Western and Chinese men like African girls, too. Guys are guys, no matter from which country. They drink, and they like having fun. In such places, some use cocaine or other type of drugs in tablet forms and some smoke marijuana. Before, I thought ganja [marijuana] was something Afro only. But no way, they like it here too. Thereafter, all they desire is maximum enjoyment" (Afse, personal communication, May 22, 2011).

Guangzhou has a ready market. According to "Tracing Consumption Patterns of Stimulants, Opioids, and Ketamine in China by Wastewater-Based Epidemiology," methamphetamine and ketamine were the dominant illicit drugs used in Guangzhou, followed by cocaine (see Zhang et al. 2019; Liu et al. 2021).

Interviewees suggested that getting cocaine to Hong Kong paid better. To the inquiry about how much he sells 100 grams of cocaine for in Hong Kong, Ach stated:

Ach: About USD$8,500. The money is sweet!

Qs: How come you are not afraid? After all some individuals have been apprehended and executed.

Ach: This is internal deal. Crossing international boarder and all that is riskier
without pre-arranged contacts. It is less risky with local couriers, because they
are less noticeable. But internal is cooler and deals are run underground, calcu-
lated and well packaged to the "spirits."

Qs: Why are they called spirit?

Ach: Because they could be unnoticed. They come, do it *sharp sharp* [fast] and
disappear like spirits. Everybody talk about Nigerians and all that, but not about
the big guys, Chinese and Westerners or Asians. They do it in big quantities.
Guys are ready to pay whatever to have good stuff. So, they are spirits and we
are servicing them! Though this country is awful with punishment, settlement
with cash instantly is also possible with some koti [police].

QS: Do you mean kickbacks work here?

Ach: Bros, what happens in Naija [Nigeria] in this sense, happens here too! But
what we are doing is like a battlefield. I want to stop it by God's grace (Ach,
personal communication, April 28, 2012).

Ach is no exception in alleging that some Chinese police could be as corrupt as their counterparts in Nigeria. While this allegation lingers, Nigerian
cocaine traffickers maintained that Guangzhou is like Lagos where all sorts
of drugs are available.

Guangzhou's similarity to Lagos exposes the features exploited by Nigerian
traffickers covertly supplying small quantities of cocaine to its users. In this
way, Lagos also resembles Beijing because Nigerian traffickers maintain
that regardless of crackdowns, street dealing still regenerates. A stroll down
Beijing's trendy nightclub district in Sanlitun panoramically reveals an inti-
mate and concentrated network of Africans and associates brazenly peddling
narcotics without fear of arrest, both an affliction and convenience to foreigners patronizing the busy boulevard. I observed that in this atmosphere, small
quantities of cocaine ranging from 5 to 20 grams are tightly sealed and sold.
It is delivered to cocaine users in different ways, including body-packed in
the anus or vagina, worked into lady's handbags, wigs, and removable shoe-
heels. Delivering small quantities generates sufficient profits at minimum risk
because it does not involve international movement. In this regard, female
couriers delivering cocaine from one place to the other are available within
the traffickers' network.

Therefore, it is a misleading notion that the phenomenon disappeared following crackdowns. The strong repression made the Nigerian traffickers act
more carefully. Dealing might no longer happen rampantly on the streets, but
it still occurs covertly in private environments.

6.5 SWEET AND SOUR GUANGZHOU: CHINESE
REACTION TO NIGERIAN COCAINE TRAFFICKERS

This section will bring focus into the restrictive criminal justice policy measures in reaction to Nigerian international cocaine trafficking. By discussing the Nigerian cocaine trafficker, Fefe, we shall investigate a drug trafficking hearing in a Chinese court and the tendency toward repetition amid Nigerian cocaine traffickers, thereby recalling the concepts of edge work, the emotions of crime, and the neutralization approach deployed.

Just as Chinese immigration abroad has exacerbated recent social tensions in Africa and other places, the influx of large numbers of foreigners, particularly Africans, into China is altering the social fabric of cities such as Guangzhou, Hong Kong, and Macau, and proving to be a headache for the authorities. Experts have explored the social construction of deviance, examined the idea of policing the crisis in response to negative attention, and the important role played by *moral panics* (Cohen 1972; Goode and Ben-Yehuda 2009; Chibnall 1977; Hall et al. 1978; Greer and McLaughlin 2017). Greer and McLaughlin (2017) emphasized that the media play a crucial role in moral panics. Cohen's (1972) Mods and Rockers in 1960s Britain traced the spiraling social reaction to youth subcultures through initial intolerance, media stereotyping, increased surveillance, labeling and marginalization, and deviancy amplification that seemed to justify the initial concerns.

The media "can both constitute as well as inflame and even generate public concern" about threats (Goode and Ben-Yehuda 2009, 90). In particular, media-driven images of the new trend Nigerian drug traffickers and related crimes could increase public panic, placing immense pressure on authorities to ensure public safety. Representations of victims of drug-related crimes spread the anxiety of drug overdose, suggesting that everyone was equally likely to be a victim. Death counts are objective givens or visible numbers that can be manipulated for claims-makers; the count gives them a reality to play with (Goode and Ben-Yehuda 1994). The news media is one of the key repositories for and creators of public knowledge. Chibnall (1977) wrote that the news media can create issues and define the boundaries of debates. They can organize opinion and develop worldviews by providing structures of understanding into which isolated and unarticulated attitudes and beliefs may be fitted. News media provide interpretations, symbols of identification, collective values, and myths which are able to transcend the moral boundaries within a society (226).

Hall et al. (1978) asserted that the media publicize what significant events that are taking place and "offer powerful interpretations of how to understand these events" (57). Crime news serves as a morality play "in which the 'devil' is both symbolically and physically cast out from the society by its guardians—the police and the judiciary" (66). For Hall et al., the news media orchestrate moral panics as a key ideological means through which "the 'silent majority' is won over to the support of increasingly coercive measures by the state and lends its legitimacy to a more than normal' exercise of control" (42). In all, Chibnall (1977) underlined that journalistic "commonsense" will place news values above other interests, including state interests, in selecting and constructing news (9–10). For Chibnall (1977) news power is understood primarily as professional practice; for Hall et al. (1978) it is ideological practice; and for Cohen (1972) it is social practice (Greer and McLaughlin 2017).

These works suggest that examining the way the media fashions certain episodes reveals how particular characteristics are emphasized, including volatility, values, and exaggerations. The involvement of a few Nigerians and their associates in cocaine and other drug-related offenses made headlines in China, giving a negative image to other African immigrants and the Chinese. For example, it caused uneasiness among locals as some neighborhood committees banned Africans from living in residential complexes.

However, the majority of Nigerians in Guangzhou also condemn the activities of the criminals. They do not deny the wrongdoings of those they are associated with because of nationality. Denial could be seen giving too little importance to the problem. They are not against taking sides: they are critical of cocaine trafficking and related crimes, but turning a blind eye is a risky process. "We are immersed in reality, but we choose to ignore it when it is convenient to do so," said one Nigerian trader in Guangzhou (Nigeria shop owner, personal communication, April 28, 2012). Nonetheless, as bad news spread quickly following the activities of Nigerian cocaine traffickers, Nigerians endured the attention of law enforcement agents and restrictive policies.

6.5.1 Yeye Naija (Delinquent Nigerian)

The illicit drug trade and other offenses committed by a relatively small number of Nigerians, which includes illegal overstay of visas, engagement in the commercial sector without valid permits, murder, and vandalism, attracted the attention of the public and law enforcement agents as demonstrated by the number of arrests made public, which may not be conclusive. A Nigerian activist group, *Liberty Writers Africa* (2019), claimed that over 6,000 Nigerians are subjected to inhumane situations in Chinese prisons. Another unofficial source, *Patriotic Citizen Initiatives*, alleged no fewer than 8,000 Nigerians are confined in Chinese prisons based on immigration offenses including invalid traveling documentations, overstaying, smuggling, and so on. Family members and friends of inmates in Chinese prisons worry as rumors spread that Nigerians in Chinese prisons have made allegations of mysterious deaths and organ harvesting (Oladimeji 2016). Recent data from Wale Oloko, the consul-general of the Federal Republic of Nigeria in Guangzhou, estimated about 600 Nigerians are in various prisons in Guangdong Province for overstaying their visas and for other offenses (*The Guardian Nigeria* 2018). Determining the number of Nigerians in Chinese prison is difficult mainly due to the difficulty of researching a covert activity, and no study of any sort has yet been conducted specifically on Nigerian involvement in international cocaine trafficking. As we shall see later, many Nigerian inmates used false documents and as such are not documented as Nigerians.

Many Nigerians were languishing in Chinese prisons convicted for drug offenses. Another apprehended Nigerian courier excreted 1,410.9 grams of cocaine and faced death penalty (see Anyagafu 2017). Analysis of fieldwork information showed that in 2008–2009, Nigerian traffickers were openly selling cocaine on the streets and molesting people. They fought and stabbed each other, scattering cocaine on the streets in the Dungpu area of Guangzhou and other places. Passersby were at risk of assault and violence, and young women were at risk of being sexually assaulted. This violence subsided following the 2009 crackdown by law enforcement.

Curious about opinions concerning Africans, and Nigerians in particular, I interviewed English-speaking Chinese individuals, including owners of bars frequented by Nigerians, waiters and waitresses, traders in the Tangqi mall and other store keepers, university students and lecturers, taxi drivers, and tenants in gardens or estates where my contacts lived. Apart from an intense dislike for drug traffickers, several Chinese remarked that they found the Nigerian culture of sharing a flat with many people disturbing because they are generally noisy, disobedient, and play music too loudly. They also could not understand the Nigerian lifestyle of fighting on the streets, in hotels, bars, and clubs, or the habit of drinking outside until the early morning hours. Their attitude and crimes irritate the Chinese and fellow Nigerians. Didi asked: "Why wouldn't the police handle us otherwise? Should you expect the public to give *yeye naija* drug gangs red carpet treatment? Those who carry guns and machete to kill themselves and murder others, cut into parts, and put in the fridge?" (Didi personal communication, November 28, 2009).

In this regard, interviewees recalled that there were at least eight known murder cases and several unknown, committed by cultish cocaine traffickers. In the case Didi referred to, a courier was killed, cut into pieces, and packed in a fridge. The perpetrators locked the flat and disappeared.

Another courier was found dead with a broken head, after the killers took the drugs and left the flat. In early February 2011, the body of a South African cocaine courier was dismembered, packed in suitcases, and dumped in a Nanhai swamp. This information stems from a recorded confession of the culprits, which the writer obtained from the Nigerian community leadership during fieldwork. The killing was not limited to Nigerians or Africans; it was alleged that a Chinese woman also became the victim of a similar heinous crime. This was a killing that changed things for all Nigerians in the city. Didi stated:

> Bros! Things dey happen for Chinco! You sabi say Naija killed one Chinese woman, some years ago? Dem wan parcel am to Naija for ritual. Na that one make Chinese hate us and police de panel beat Naija man like a car wey get accident. [Translated: Brother, things happened in China! Did you know that some Nigerians killed a Chinese woman some years ago? They wanted to parcel her to Nigeria and use for ritual, it's rumored. This case made the Chinese here to hate us; and it is reason why the police choose to panel-beat us like a car that got damaged in an accident] (Didi, personal communication, November 28, 2009).

Subsequent to these incidents and despite being an otherwise diverse, cosmopolitan city, things became much more difficult for Nigerians as they were increasingly confronted by the law enforcement agents.

6.5.2 Restrictive Policy Measures

Immigration policy has become flashpoint issue in many wealthy countries, and the issue of allowing in and absorbing existing immigrants has become increasingly controversial and politically divisive. These days, policies in developed countries concentrate on attracting mostly highly skilled individuals and leaving behind low skilled. In the UK, under the Resident Labor Market Test, skilled jobs still must be advertised domestically for 28 days to enable citizens of the EU/European Economic Area and those who already have the right to work in the UK to apply first. Since October 2019, many more people come under the Shortage Occupation List, where the Resident Labor Market Test is not required (Workpermit 2019). Australia is stumbling with acute skill shortage. Many jobs are going unfilled as employers are unable to find the skilled workers with specialized skills. A recent report by Deloitte published that nearly 243,200 jobs lay vacant in May 2019. The report concluded there will be more than two million openings in education, health, professional services, and government services workers in the near future. The message remains that immigrants have an economic and social utility for their destination countries. For instance, immigrants' productivity raises the U.S. GDP by an estimated USD37 billion per year (West 2011). In 2016, 40.2% of companies listed in the Fortune 5000 had at least one founder who was either an immigrant or the child of an immigrant. "These companies employed nearly 19 million people in 2014 and generated USD$4.8 trillion in revenue—or one out of every seven dollars generated by U.S. businesses" (Kosten 2018).

In this regard, the Law of the People's Republic of China on Control of the Entry and Exit of Aliens promulgated in 1985 is the basis of Chinese immigration legislation. The law has been amended to introduce harsher regulations and penalties, which led to police crackdowns in cities such as Guangzhou and Beijing on the "three illegals" by foreigners: unlawful entry to China, unauthorized employment, and illegal residence in China. The campaign is being publicized through posters showing a clenched fist "striking hard" on illegal activity (Lefkowitz 2013; Chodorow 2012).

Dissimilar to Western countries that have distinctive laws to regulate the management of transnational immigrants, regulations only sporadically appeared in Chinese legal instruments concerning entry and exit administration and the use and invitation of foreign investment. Zhang Jijiao, researcher with the Institute of Ethnology and Anthropology, told *Xinhua News* in 2010: "This reflects how China's transnational migration management has long been focused on the legitimacy of entry and exit out of economic considerations. In the long run, however, it is far from enough as immigrants into the country also have other demands that need to be addressed, especially relating to ethnic culture and customs, employment and education" (*The Economic Times* 2010).

The Chinese permanent residency permit is deemed the "hardest to get in the world" (Lefkowitz 2013), as it targets attracting exclusive, highly qualified foreign talent. This implies that disadvantaged African traders in Guangzhou without higher education and valued professions run into soaring barriers and discourses that frame them as a threat. Indeed, the barriers designed to reduce or prevent African migration in a "borderless world" have more to do with hegemonic politics and less to do with any real danger. The Chinese People's Consultative Conference (2008) made the case for a strong control on immigrants in Guangzhou, pointing to the way foreigners with poor manners and low "quality" (*suzhi*) or values cause anxiety among urban Chinese.

It is the othering of sub-Saharan Africans, who because of their phenotypical appearance calls to mind the undesired foreigner. Aspects of African cultural brokers' own ambivalent relationships with China, strong tie to Muslim and Christian religious beliefs and sub-Saharan Africa's stalled development, contribute to their marginalization abroad. It shows how bias about skin color and physical characteristics is still common in China. There, blackness is constructed as being foreign and incompatible with local Guangzhou or greater Chinese identity. And jokes reinforce negative media representations of Africans as a threat to social order in South China (Lan 2017). For example, in 2016 China, there was a shocking detergent commercial about a black man and a young Chinese woman flirting: "As he leans in for a kiss, she thrusts a detergent capsule in his mouth and bundles him into a laundry machine.

She sits atop the machine as the man spins and screams inside until, to her apparent delight, out pops a handsome Chinese man dressed in a clean, white t-shirt" (Griffiths and Lu 2016).

Black Africans in Guangzhou are sometimes viewed as inferior to Chinese—a form of racism based on skin color, nationality, and economic status.

In history and literature, Chinese attitudes to foreign contact often demonized the foreigner. Skin color performed an important function of social differentiation in demonological terminology. They thought foreigners were barbarians or devils, which could be "white devils" (*baigui*) and "black devils" (*heigui*) (Dikötter 1992, 38–39). This recalls David Ho's (1985) concept of *culturocentrism*, the prejudice against non-Chinese, "A conviction as to the pliable endurance and superiority of Chinese civilization (in its spiritual, but not material, aspects), and a tendency to apply Chinese values without question in judging other races" (224). In traditional Chinese society, skin color does not indicate any immutable biological characteristics, and yet, as Yuan Gao (1989) wrote in a *New York Times* article, fair skin is generally associated with higher social status while dark skin is associated with dirt, poverty, stupidity, and low status.

Willard Waller averred that the term *social problem* implies a value judgment that indicated not merely an observed phenomenon but the state of mind of the observer as well (Waller 1936). Becker's term "deviant career" in his classic text, *Outsiders* (1963), emphasized that deviance lies not in the act itself but in the process by which society labels certain acts as deviant. He elucidated further in moral entrepreneurs the notions of "rule creators" and "rule enforcers" as well as the double-blind facing rule enforcers (Becker 1963, 157)—to justify rule enforcers' existence and their employment, they must demonstrate to others that a problem exists and show that their attempts at enforcement are effective and worthwhile. I take up the role of moral entrepreneurs or *claims-makers* as expressed by Loseke (1999). When these values are transgressed, it invokes social problem games and strategies for solution. Loseke describes it as an episode, often triggered by alarming media stories and reinforced by reactive laws and public policy, of exaggerated or misdirected public concern, anxiety and fear or anger over a perceived threat to social order—for instance, from Nigerian cocaine traffickers and undocumented individuals engaging in unregistered commercial activities or informal economic activities in Guangzhou.

Moral entrepreneurs or *claims-makers* exaggerate the problem to make local events seem like those of pressing national concern and an index of decline of morality and standard. Best (1997) highlighted that the media does not only restate such claims. News stories are constructed in line with conventions, restraint, and agendas of the media. These factors vary across time and settings, resulting in increased efforts at control which in turn lead to further marginalization and stigmatization of deviants; this leads to more calls for action, more police action, and so on into a *deviancy amplification spiral* (Cohen 1972).

Whereas it diminishes portrayals of China and its growing soft power in Africa, it also calls to mind the concepts of othering and Young's conceptualization of inclusion and exclusion. It justifies some tougher measures. For instance, a foreigner who works illegally may be given a fine of CNY5,000 (USD700) to CNY20,000 (USD2,800) or imprisonment from 5 to 15 days in serious cases, whereas prior rules allowed fines not exceeding CNY1,000 (USD140) and no detention, which clearly were not very strong deterrents. The Public Security Bureau (PSB) carries out inspections of businesses for immigration law compliance without giving the employer prior notice. A fine of CNY10,000 (USD1,400) may be imposed for every foreigner illegally employed, up to a maximum of CNY100,000 (USD14,100); prior rules allowed for fines not exceeding CNY50,000 (USD7,000) (Chodorow 2012).

In addition, the PSB of Dengfeng has bilingual English-Chinese notices in restaurants, cafés, and hotels where foreigners congregate, warning visitors about the penalties for drug trafficking, violence, robbery, and prostitution. As these notices are difficult to find in areas of the city hosting significant non-African foreign populations, it strengthens the view of structural discrimination and racism amid Africans in China. For instance, Bodomo (2012) averred that cases of overt discrimination against black people are common, particularly in interactions with the police, resulting in crackdowns by Beijing police, and in Guangzhou, the provincial government introduced a regulation in May 2011 to encourage the public to report violations involving foreigners, including illegal entry, overstaying, working without permits, or doing business without licenses. The PSB asserted that foreigners who did not have permanent residence and a job were more likely to engage in illegal activities. Whereas, we shall discuss cocaine hoppers' culture of cocaine trade and police control later, let us zoom in on the case of a Nigerian trafficker in a Chinese criminal court.

6.5.3 Nigerian Cocaine Trafficker, Fefe

In November 2010, a Nigerian who used his Chinese girlfriend as a courier was arrested for trafficking 903.36 grams of cocaine via mailed post. The International Criminal Police Organization then notified the PSB of Amoy about drug smuggling activities by an African criminal network, which Fefe was part of, operating in Shanghai, Taicang, and other parts of China (TV People 2011).

During my fieldwork in China in 2009 and 2010, for instance, I observed how Fefe and others chattered and contradicted themselves on issues of capital punishment and conationals executed in China; the consequences of cocaine trafficking for family members, girlfriends, or landlords; and whether to quit or stay involved in the trade after having made a decent amount of money. In such settings, blinded by the social construction of their reality, when confronted by friends and acquaintances who foresaw the risk, traffickers downplayed its consequence, assured nothing would happen. My Chinese contact attended the court hearing of Fefe in Shanghai. What follows is analysis of fieldwork information regarding this direct participant of Nigerian international cocaine trafficking.

6.5.4 Good Lawyer, Save my "Pikin" (Child)

One afternoon in late 2010, my telephone rang. It was an update because, in trying to keep current with happenings regarding Nigerian international cocaine traffickers in Lagos, Guangzhou, or KL, I regularly made calls to contacts and informants. For important cases, I asked to be paged so that I could call back immediately, as in this case. Fefe was to travel to Indonesia to visit his girlfriend, who recently relocated back home on completion of her studies in China. Unable to reach him, she called Kele, who stated: "I told her I was with Fefe last weekend, and that I will reach her back. But not been able to reach him, I called a couple of friends to inquire. Abu related that Fefe went to collect his "market" [cocaine]. Then I called another guy that told me Shanghai police arrested him. After I confirmed it from another Fefe's girlfriend in Shanghai, I informed the one in Indonesia. She was silenced. Fefe is very stupid guy" (Kele, personal communication, November 11, 2010).

His arrest came unexpectedly, but not surprisingly in keeping with the tumultuous life of a cocaine trafficker. Neither was it unique because in the course of this research, such was the case for several Nigerian traffickers in other countries like Brazil, Italy, and Nigeria. When he was arrested, his friends contacted me to look for a good lawyer in attempt to save his life. However, China has strict rules in this regard. Biyi, an ex-inmate of WCDDC Guangzhou, stated: "A Nigerian man served 18 months in White Cloud District Detention Centre in Guangzhou and was released mid-2014. He was part of a scam where they tricked someone to wire funds to an account, and he went to the bank to collect. The lawyer his friends hired was denied access because of in China only family members are allowed to arrange lawyers for convicted inmates" (Biyi, personal communication, September 17, 2015).

A dominant opinion among Nigerians in China is finding a good lawyer to defend arrested offenders is very difficult. This feeling comes from the high expectations, disappointments, and wishful thinking based on experience wherein state-appointed advocates did not succeed in preventing long prison sentences or execution. Fefe's court hearing took place almost a year after his arrest. A Chinese English translator was provided by the court to enhance communication. According to the Criminal Law of the People's Republic of China, Fefe shall be held responsible for the crime of drug smuggling, trafficking, and illegal possession. Article 347: "A person who smuggles, traffics in, transports or produces drugs, regardless of the quantity, shall be demanded for criminal responsibility and imposed criminal punishment. A person who, under any of the following circumstances, smuggles, traffics in, transports or produces drugs, shall be sentenced to fixed-term imprisonment of fifteen years, life imprisonment or death and concurrently to confiscation of property" (http://www.procedurallaw.cn/english/law/200807/t20080724_40992.html)."

Fefe was indicted for deploying two Chinese girls to receive posted parcels containing concealed cocaine. Caught on the spot with 50 grams of cocaine, the police searched his temporary accommodations in different towns and seized a total of 3,000 grams (3 kilograms) of cocaine. As shown in the video that was made public, police recovered other personal belongings of Fefe, including a stethoscope, telephones, bus and train tickets, banknotes in CNY and USD, several credit cards, laptops, and watches. What follows are some inquires and responses during the hearing that might provide insight into the workings of Nigerian international cocaine trafficking through the contradictions and offender's social construction realities, in line with certain criminological concepts, namely techniques of neutralization, edgework, and emotional arousal.

6.5.5 Considerations

The 33-year-old Fefe entered China in 2006 as a businessman, using a Ghanaian passport and a fake name. Confronted by the prosecutor, he admitted not being a Ghanaian citizen. It is common for Nigerian cocaine traffickers to use passports from other countries. This supports the fact that there is a dark number of Nigerians involved in international trafficking and the actual figure of Nigerians and inmates in China or elsewhere cannot be accurately known. A Nigerian trafficker arrested in Mumbai had fake money, seals, visa stickers, and 155 passports from different countries, including Lesotho, Ghana, Botswana, UK, Germany, SA, and China (see Goel 2012).

In addition to trafficking, Fefe cheated several individuals in Hong Kong and his Chinese girlfriend out of approximately CNY260,000, or about USD40,000, in early 2010. This claim was reiterated by several interviewees. Recall that in the right atmosphere, the Nigerian international trafficking activities remain an open secret, even in countries where the offense attracts capital punishment.

In *The Seductions of Crime*, Katz (1988) emphasized the aesthetic and emotional appeal of the criminal experience, challenging the dominant theories of crime, including the routine activities theory, control theory, and rational choice theory, which take for granted offender motivation. These theories appear to lack curiosity and conceptual resources needed to adequately understand how and why people are compelled to commit crimes (Haan and Loader 2002). Katz considered extensively the "foreground" of criminality: the immediate, interactional interplay through which a deviant activity takes shape and the "magical" excitement of committing crimes to which the Nigerian global cocaine trafficking is no exception. In this view, motivations for criminal behavior lie in the foreground of immediate experience, such as luring and compelling, which are intrinsic in cocaine trafficking. Interactions and micro dynamics leading up to them have more to do with the rewards of the crime experience itself than the "background factors," such as deviant material and social conditions, their psychological development, and life events (Lyng 2004; McLaughlin and Muncie 2005). In other words, to comprehend the thrill criminals experience by committing crimes, one should grasp how deviants try to deal with and/or overcome certain moral emotions like disgrace, arrogance, mockery, righteousness, defilement, skepticism, and vengeance (Katz 1988). However, the effects of the criminogenic environment are push and pull factors that frustrate many hopeless individuals into cocaine trafficking.

The Nigerian context has fostered the new trend cocaine trafficking in line with Lemert's (1951) and Becker's (1963) "important advances towards a full social theory of deviance" (Taylor et al. 1973, 139) by concentrating on the interaction processes between those who commit an act labeled as deviant and the reaction of society to that behavior and the deviants themselves. Lemert averred that societal reaction to an initial act of deviancy (*primary deviation*) is crucial to the subsequent self-definition of the deviant and can lead to *secondary deviation*.

I observed that some Nigerian traffickers neutralize their stigmatized image by accepting it and using it as motivation instead. Self-filling prophecy is the danger that as a negative label or reputation becomes strongly and overtly applied to an individual, it may develop into part of that individual's identity. This can create further deviance due to resentment not only of the norms being violated but also the social structures themselves levying penalties. When a person begins to engage in deviant conduct or develops a concept of identity based upon it as a means of defense, attack, or adjustment to the overt or covert problems created by the consequent societal reaction to the individual, this deviation becomes secondary (Lemert 1951), as is the case with many Nigerian cocaine traffickers. As one respondent put it, "If people always call me the chick robber, I will then steal a big fowl" (Tito, personal communication, October 27, 2016).

Techniques of neutralization and other emotional coping mechanisms are often shared, as with other social strategies, both with people inside and outside the deviant milieu.

Didi stated: "Brother, as you are aware of, I am one of the two persons close to Fefe, outside his criminal friends. He used to come and seek advice concerning non-criminal things like renewal of visa or resident permit and so on. He tried to talk me into 419 scam and cocaine trafficking, but I refused. In reply he said I was *mugu* [stupid] that did not want to make money, and I asked him, 'If I was *mugu,* why do always come to me for advice?'" (Didi, personal communication, May 23, 2011).

Another respondent very familiar with Fefe added: "He talked about having "markets" [cocaine] in his flat often. I warned him of the consequence, to think about the punishment and putting people that rented the flat to him in problem. I asked him to quit cocaine trafficking; after all, he had made money from it. 'Nothing would happen, I know what I am doing,' he said" (Ody, personal communication, May 23, 2011).

In this view, drug traffickers tend to be arrogant. Most said they know what they are doing. It is also not surprising that he went from scamming to cocaine trafficking. Examining more closely the nature of Nigerian illicit cocaine trafficking unveils its intricate linkage of emotions, sentiments, ambiguity, mobility, trust, distrust, reprisal, and contemporary mainstream and private businesses.

6.5.6 Striker's Game

A principal feature of Nigerian international cocaine trafficking is the role of the middleman function, as discussed previously. As a broker in China, Fefe arranged supply from his contacts in a country in South America and kept his local distribution and selling channels intact. Fefe gave his girlfriend's address to a contact in South America who dispatched several packages containing kilograms of cocaine concealed in wooden photo frames to his girlfriend. On receiving the parcel, he would forward it to a third person in Nigeria, a business associate. When asked what kind of business the contact was doing in Nigeria, he replied, "I don't know because he only told me he comes to China to do business with Chinese partners" (Translator Jian citing Fefe, personal communication, April 29, 2012). However, it is known that he sold cocaine to his customers in China, as well.

In his work, *Crime, Edgework and Corporeal Transaction*, Lyng (2004) emphasized that edgework refers to emotionally charged and adrenaline-fueled acts and offenses including criminal activities, where someone thoughtfully tries to arrive at and negotiate the physical edge of daring, hoping to arrive beyond social strictures and reflective consciousness to accomplish a certain degree of self-actualization. Furthermore, Matza's (1969) *Becoming Deviant* draws attention to the boundary circumstance which offenders face in illicit situations, "the 'invitation edge' that splits the 'outside' and 'inside' of a deviant activity" (147).

Likewise, an additional explanation of this phenomenon is offered by Lofland's (1969) *Deviance and Identity*; he emphasized that "playing with the invitational edge of deviance often carries a 'positive sense of adventure, excitement and enchantment'" (104–105). Individuals involved in moments of illegal edgework construct resistance doubly. In the first place, by combining such instances of soaring risk with precise practical artistry, actors invent an identity—a sense of skilled self that refuses to accept the usual humiliation of inferior status and deskilled, estranged labor. Second, to succeed in extremely dangerous contexts of criminalization, offenders find an amplification of the edgy excitement of illicit activity, such as cocaine trafficking in China.

Seen from this angle, the resilience of Nigerian cocaine traffickers in China implies that these concepts' intense and often ritualized moments of pleasure and excitement define the experience of subcultural membership and seduction into continued participation, even regions where drug trafficking is punishable by death. While edgework pushes offenders toward the deviant act, denial techniques allow them to relinquish acceptance and responsibility of the act. In line with these concepts, when confronted by the prosecutor after being found with over 3,000 grams of cocaine, the defendant, Fefe, and his advocate had the following reactions:

Chief Judge: The defendant, you can defend yourself, as well as be defended by the advocate. Do you understand?

Defendant: Ok. I have never been selling any drugs in China, and I never want to do this, as well. For my friend in Shanghai, we were merely friends, and I had never been doing any business with him. I've been to his place for only twice. I'm not his boss at all. Those packages are not mine; I've already told the police.

Advocate: In my opinion, the defendant's action should be considered as "illegal holding drugs," instead of "drug smuggling." In addition, I want to remind the court, the doubtful point of the source of the 3,000 grams of cocaine in his room in Wenzhou. Were all the drugs belonging to the defendant?

Chief Judge: From your point of view, the amount of the drugs the defendant had been illegally holding is 3,000 grams?

Advocate: No. Only the drugs seized on the spot; not including those in the house in Wenzhou. (Translator Jian citing *Chen v. Lee*, April 29, 2012)

Whereas Fefe's girlfriend admitted to receiving parcels and acknowledged paying about CNY300 a total of six or seven times to colleagues who received packages on her behalf, Fefe all denied responsibility. He refuted having any knowledge of the cocaine or having sent her to receive packages of smuggled items. Another crucial feature highlighted is the prominent role played by modern technology in enhancing the activities of the Nigerian international illicit cocaine trade. Fefe and his girlfriend met online, and she had a formal job in a company. This is a widespread strategy amid Nigerian traffickers. An important strategy in trafficking is the ability to recruit couriers. Anybody who provides couriers is remunerated financially. Several traffickers deploy their girlfriends and acquaintances as couriers because they are perceived as naïve, and they do it for little payment.

By having girlfriends employed in formal jobs, or enrolled as students, Fefe's illegal activity could be executed without much suspicion. Claiming to live in Hong Kong for business purposes was another reason he gave to entice his girlfriend to receive some "samples" from abroad. Therefore, exploiting this gray area, he gave the girlfriend's address to his partners in South America and secured a safe landing for the parcel in China. However, receiving repeated packages through a recipient company not in possession of adequate license drew the attention of the authorities. Another important aspect underlining the activities of the Nigerian international cocaine trafficker is mobility. Many Nigerian traffickers keep separate residences for goods and money in case of a police bust or robbery by dishonest acquaintances or customers.

6.5.7 Narrow Escape: Enter the Dragon

In search of the Nigerian Dream, Fefe and those like him spent money at will despite having no formal job or real trading business in Guangzhou. He proudly talked about his house in his hometown; his plan to complete a four-story building in Nigeria by December 2011; how he sent USD15,000 or USD20,000 through traders on business trips to China; and a four wheel-drive vehicle he bought for his mother in Nigeria. Interestingly, he said that he spends about CNY50,000 (USD7,000) on kickbacks yearly to renew his permit to stay in China. His openness about cocaine trafficking and his achievements, regardless of the consequences, recalls Riemer's (1981) view on traditional conceptualizations that deviance has rarely "been considered a spontaneous, 'just for the hell of it' activity. In which the participants engage simply for the pleasure it provides" (39). O'Malley and Mugford's (1994) believed that even where pleasure has been considered, it "has appeared in traditional criminologies as perhaps 'obvious' explanatory variable on the category and experience of pleasure in enhancing criminal arts" (209). Nonetheless, things fell apart for him as the hearing ended:

Chief Judge: Stand up the defendant! According to the Criminal Procedure Law of China, you have the right to make a final statement. What would you want to say?

Fefe: I have been to a lot of countries, and China is only one of them. I have never been selling any fucking drugs and committing other crimes. I just come to China for doing my business. Those drugs founded in my bag were just for my own to use. But I had not taken them yet. If I really did something wrong, I beg for the court's forgiveness.

Chief Judge: Now the judgement is ended. Bring the defendant back to jail. (Translator Jian citing *Chen v. Fefe*, April, 2, 2012)

Fefe applied neutralization techniques up to the last minute of the court hearing. First, he employed a denial of injury tactic, indicating that no one was hurt, because the cocaine was for his personal use. Second, he denied the existence of a victim, by expressing that he had not yet taken the drugs. Last, he showed remorse or shame, in keeping with the behavior of repentant criminals, for committed acts with respect for those who obey the law (Sykes and Matza 1957). In February 2012, the verdict concluded Fefe's penalty: the death penalty was suspended for two years.

Nigerians were happy that Fefe escaped execution, unlike many others, and many hoped that he will be freed at some point in time. His lawyer performed well because Fefe's family spent tens of thousands of dollars on his defense; a state lawyer would not have likely achieved the same result. Likewise, in Nigeria, Brazil, and Malaysia, those who cannot afford reputable lawyers are destined to lose their hearings. As KK told me, among the invaluable services that the U.S. Consulate rendered to him, was helping secure competent legal representation. He stated:

Good legal representation was absolutely necessary because translations are erratic, and any attempt at correction or to clarify the PSB turned to intimidation stating any discrepancies would lead to problems. As calmly as possible, I stood my ground but later learned my clarification never entered their official Chinese version. Such help would cost, at least, USD$10,000 to get a competent firm, to start, and the total could easily rise to USD$30,000. Furthermore, even if inmates are allowed CNY500, my lawyer Danny produced a receipt dated the day after my intake [4/15] showing where my University had deposited CNY500. I had asked everyday about these funds and had been told they didn't exist (KK, personal communication, December 6, 2014).

Fefe is now one of the many Nigerians in China's prison convicted for drug offenses. He demands money be sent each time he calls friends such as MK and DK in Guangzhou. He needs money to feed because upon arrest his money and possessions were confiscated.

6.6 HIS TAKE: A HARSH PRISON LIFE

Burdened by some of the same deficiencies as Brazilian prisons in terms of overcapacity and pretrial detention, conditions in Chinese detention centers and prisons are much worse. For instance, KK told me that he was in a cell as big as a handball court with zero furnishings (the toilet was a hole in the corner) with about 30 prisoners, all sleeping on the concrete floor without blankets or pillows. The room was so crowded that most inmates slept on their sides with arms draped over each other. There was no bail, no visitors, and no communication. The heat, hunger, and harassment from Chinese inmates were harsh. For instance, the Nigerians Ndy and Ropa had death penalty cases. The former is imprisoned, alleged to have paid a Chinese national to smuggle drugs from Nigeria. Whereas no solid proof was provided, he had still been in detention for two years—one year until court and then after another year, still with no judgment. Ropa was caught with 2 kilograms of heroin and a homemade gun. The age on his passport was disputed, and after seven years he had his case appealed and hoped to have his sentence commuted to life instead of death.

Fefe, Ndy, Ropa, and many others incarcerated in China used passports from other African countries. Though this would appear to be an inventive way to avoid detection, for those who are caught, it's often a deadly choice. For instance, four of the eight male drug traffickers who were executed by Indonesian government on April 29, 2015, were Nigerians. Two traveled on false passports, from Ghana and Spain, as we shall discuss ahead. KK added:

> I was told by my Nigerian inmate friends that the reason most Nigerians use other country passports is because the Chinese government limits the number of passports to Nigerians due to a patterned history of illegal activities. That was the reason given—although TJ mentioned some may be hiding their identities because of drug crimes in other countries. In one setting when drug trafficker inmate XX inquired about his case, the *Zhu Guan* [guard] standing tall, affirming total control stepped toward him. Looking down not revealing his feeling, or what would come next, he mercilessly stated, "Mr. XX, you have no country! I'm the only one who can help you! I am your GOD!" I thought to myself—surely, he said, "I am your Guard!" If not, in such desperation we both would have laughed out loud. He went on to state that the Niger Embassy had denied his being a citizen and thus he had no embassy aide. XX was silent and in the only demonstration of weakness I ever saw, a few tears shed, running parallel with his tattooed cheek (KK, personal communication, December 6, 2014).

Nigeria in many cases is unable to protect its citizenry, and its embassy remains credited with denying much needed assistance to its people. Normally, embassies and consulates serve as a means to notify families and supporters of inmates and ongoing cases. With almost zero communication, many do not remember telephone numbers of beloved ones or their home address. Africans in China on fraudulent passports have been denied embassy services and were cut off from loved ones or possible support.

According to KK, inmates from small countries with limited embassy services are lucky to get a phone call from their embassy in Beijing. In contrast, being an American spared KK the harshest of punishments. Other foreigners sometimes waited for over a year without a court date or outside communication. Likewise, most of the Chinese prisoners had simply disappeared from the outside world without their family knowing if they were dead or alive. A Nigerian ex-convict stated, "Prisoners on death row are shackled. Sometimes they just pick someone up and you will not see the person again" (Biyi, personal communication, September 17, 2015).

In WCDDC, Nigerian prisoners begin working on their first day of detention regardless of the circumstances. Each person was required to assemble at least 3,000 Christmas lights working up to 10 hours a day without payment. This maltreatment is supplemented by beatings from prison guards, and from cell gang leaders who pushed work production through a series of rewards and punishments. KK explained to me: "Kuai-dian' (means 'faster'), anything from slow work production to a 'wrong look' results in physical punishment like a slap to the head or kick to the ribs. If slow production persisted or a prisoner back talked, the regime would bring them to the front of the cell for a series of kicks, blows, and punches. The most common punishment was withholding the daily ration of two hand-rolled cigarettes and food rations cut in half. Such prisoners were solitary confinement, being chained to the floor, flogging with Christmas light cords, and left for 2 to 3 days without food" (KK, personal communication, June 12, 2014).

The People's Republic of China employs several forms of corrections for people who have been arrested, including so-called reeducation through labor. Drawing upon the Soviet Union's infamous gulag, Mao Zedong established *laogai* (reform through labor [RTL]) labor camps to punish convicted criminals, and *laojiao* (reeducation through labor) camps to incarcerate alleged class enemies and petty criminals without the time and evidentiary burdens of a trial (Dotson and Vanfleet 2014). These crimes are so broadly defined that essentially authorities can arrest almost anyone (Wu et al. 2008, 6). As noted by the Criminal Reform Handbook PRC Ministry of Justice (1988): "Ours is a socialist state exercising the democratic dictatorship of the people. As one of the tools of the people's democratic dictatorship, our Laogai facilities, representing the working class and the working people of our country, exercise dictatorship over a minority of elements who are hostile to socialism, thus safeguarding our socialist system" (3).

The Laogai facilities of the CJS are facilities also of special enterprises, a system of forced labor camps that spans China's territory—from the highly industrialized prison factories of the eastern coastal cities to the isolated, fenceless farms of the west. Whereas Chinese officials and others tout the so-called legal reforms, these reforms have not delivered real changes to the Laogai system, and the camps are more prevalent than ever. Yet RTL epitomize, "A formal sentence to confinement in a prison farm or factory. The Chinese government officially dropped this term, but it remains in widespread usage, and the practice continues" (Dotson, and Vanfleet 2014, 3). For instance, a 2013 report published by the U.S. Department of State estimated that China has 681 prisons, holding 1.64 million inmates, and researchers identified about 1,422 forced labor facilities of all types in China (Wu et al. 2008).

Uyghur Human Rights Project's write-up of October 2019 published that East Turkistan is the source of over 80% of the total cotton produced in China, heavily subsidized by the Chinese government. The region is also known to use detainee labor in the form of cheap or entirely unpaid Uyghur labor. A general manager of a textile industry in the Uyghur Region stated to state-sponsored media, "With the support of the government, we have already 'recruited' more than 600 people" since the founding of the new factory in 2017, and, "We have generated more than USD$6 million in sales. We plan to reach 1,000 workers by the end of this year. We plan to provide jobs to 1,500 people by the end of 2019" (Byler 2019). Invariably, the Laogai prison camps are among the most extensive and repressive prison systems in the world. According to *Laogai Research Foundation*, an estimated 40–50 million Chinese have fallen victim to the system throughout its history (Wu 2010). Laogai products are produced with largely unpaid, forced labor, creating a competitive cost advantage over legitimately manufactured products utilizing fully paid labor.

In all, the fundamental task of our Laogai facilities is punishing, reforming, and organizing criminals in labor and production, thus creating wealth for society (Criminal Reform Handbook 1988). The superior, prison cadre within the prison, according to Mao, plays a key role in guiding the inmates and the success of thought reform. Due to lax enforcement and evasion of existing laws and agreements, Laogai products continue to be a profitable, yet largely hidden part of the international economy, including the United States (Wu 2010). Notwithstanding, Chinese authorities said that conditions have improved in the Laogai and Chinese judicial systems, the ideology behind the institution persists. Exploitation of prisoners, including Nigerian inmates, under horrific conditions remains widespread.

The first Mao's advocated RTL document, issued in 1957, sought through thought education in labor centers to resocialize the "bad elements," from social order disturbers to self-supportive persons (Biddulph 2007, 69); at the same time, RTL also targeted some special "social illnesses," including drug offenses (Herschatter 1997, 305). One reason for this is that profitable prison companies help to fund the operations of both local and national government. Prison labor enterprises producing high-tech goods such as semiconductors and optical instruments are the most profitable, each earning an estimated annual revenue of tens of millions of USD and paying hundreds of thousands of USD annually in taxes to the Chinese government (Dotson and Vanfleet 2014; Kempton and Richardson 2009).

6.6.1 Business On

If the primary aims of imprisonment are rehabilitation and reduction of recidivism to crime, then, contemporary exploitation of inmates in Chinese prisons and other places seems to have the opposite effect. Nigerian inmates and others worked without pay—essentially slave labor—producing Christmas lights and other goods sold globally. Critics insist that Chinese prison inmates are brutally exploited for big business, generating billions for multinational enterprises. *Australian Financial Review* reported Dongguan's forced labor under cruel conditions, exploited indirectly by among others Qantas, British Airways, Emirates, Swedish giant Electrolux, and Fortune 500 Company Emerson. Annual output value of prison labor in the RTL system for 1990 was CNY2.5 billion, which is about 0.08% of the nation's total industrial and agricultural production output value for the year. Equally Emerson, a New York Stock Exchange-listed company, has 135,000 employees and had worldwide sales of USD24.4 billion in 2012 (Murray and Grigg 2013).

Perhaps the primary aims of imprisonment are rehabilitation and reduction of recidivism to crime. Many failed businessmen and ex-convicts are prominent in illicit trade in China (Chin and Zhang 2007).

Yet China defends its RTL policies. According to Reform of Criminals through Labor, reasons for using forced labor as means to reform criminals who are able to work include: assisting criminals to realize that social wealth does not come easily, fostering work ethic, helping inmates overcome bad habits such as sloth and hedonism, and giving them a sense of social responsibility and law-abiding spirit in addition to improving self-discipline. Some advocates for such practices also suggest that labor helps inmates overcome depression, indolence, and thoughts of escape or suicide, common to monotonous prison life. Lastly, it is a means of acquiring productive skills and knowledge necessary for adapting to normal social values and earning a respectable living for inmates after prison life, which doubles as a deterrent to crime. China's recidivism rate seems to prove this. Recidivism is a broad term that refers to relapse of criminal behavior, which can include a range of outcomes, including rearrest, reconviction, and reimprisonment (Butorac and Gracin 2017). On the one hand, China boasts one of the lowest recidivism rates in the world, with only 6–8% repeat offenders (People's Republic of China 1992). In contrast, Nigeria has a high recidivism rate of above 60% (Otu 2015), which generates substantial cost to society in the form of cost to the victim, additional police and justice expenditures, cost of incarceration, loss of human and social capital, and loss of production while incarcerated. Recently released prisoners often represent a high-risk group compared to other offenders contributing to overall societal criminality and violent crimes (Andersen and Skardhamar 2014), with about one-fifth of all crimes in any year being committed by those released from custody (Petersilia 2011). Hence, proponents of RTL argue that reducing recidivism can potentially make a large contribution to public safety.

Researchers emphasized that China's low recidivism rate could be attributed to key features like low levels of residential mobility, high levels of informal social control, and crime prevention. Jiang et al. (2010) noted that this includes a "total society strategy" through which the government "mobilizes a variety of social forces, such as political, economic, cultural, judicial, educational, and the media, to prevent crime and keep social order" (461). It is a horizontal mechanism through which Chinese authorities and organizations, including criminal justice agencies, youth leagues, women's federations, employee unions, the media, and grassroots organizations, are all required to participate in social and crime control. For example, when offenders are sent back to their communities, local residents help monitor them (Jiang et al. 2014). To reduce recidivism, the Chinese government adopted a policy requiring those inmates who were evaluated as likely to commit crime again and who had no place to return, to stay within a prison for employment after they finished their sentences. For instance, in 1960 Guangdong Province, about 70% of 1,791 prisoners who finished their sentences remained in prison for their employment (ibid., 78). Another key feature of Chinese corrections that differentiates it from the Western controls system is the "total person approach" in which an offender's values, attitudes, and behaviors are all controlled. As Xin Ren noted: "[The] most important distinction, perhaps, is the efforts of the Chinese state to control both the behavior and the minds of the people. Social conformity in the Chinese vocabulary is not limited to behavioral conformity with the rule of law but always moralistically identifies with the officially endorsed beliefs of social standards and behavioral norms" (Ren 1997, 6).

On the other hand, China regards all statistics related to the Laogai as state secrets. It is difficult to trace Laogai products and data (Wu 2010). In 1991, the Ministry of Economic Relations and Foreign Trade and the Ministry of Justice jointly issued a circular entitled, "Reissue of Regulations Prohibiting the Export of Products Made in a Reform-through-labor Programme." The Chinese government is strict on this point, and any violations of these regulations are dealt with severely (People's Republic of China 1992). In response to the pressure to eradicate RTL, the Chinese government acknowledged official plans to abolish the Laojiao labor camp system following the Third Plenum of the 18th Party Congress held in November 2013. However, we all enjoy things like Christmas lights and plastic earbuds. These are most likely made by prisoners in China.

Several drawbacks exist to using recidivism rates as indicators of success. Auty (2019) noted that (1) recidivism rates underestimate the true amount (and cost) of crime in society, as a not all crime is reported or solved due to dark number; (2) recidivism rates do not reveal if the new offense committed was more or less serious than the previous one; (3) they only capture instances of failure and do not take into account successes; and (4) recidivism rates do not reflect what we know about desistance theory (i.e., pathways out of crime often involve sidesteps and missteps). In all, comparisons between prison regimes internationally remain difficult considering changes in prison populations, policy, and reporting practices. Furthermore, what is crime could vary from one country to another.

Nigeria and Brazil's criminal codes include neither the death penalty nor a life sentence for drug trafficking. In theory, every inmate will reemerge into the outside world. Most do so brutalized, lacking skills and ostracized by a society with high unemployment, inequality, and a punitive attitude toward criminals. That pushes recidivism rates above 60%, starting the ghastly cycle anew (IBA 2010). On the other hand, research has found that prisoners, who gain professional skills while in prison and those who earn a decent wage for their work, are far less likely to end up back behind bars, especially in a country like Brazil with zero social safety-net programs to compensate for the missing income. Their recidivism rate is less than 7%, compared to 64% of the state's general prison population (Friedmann 2014). Whereas Nigerian inmates in Chinese WCDDC work for free, their counterpart interviewees in PFC prison in Brazil earn about BRL466.50 or USD229.65 monthly. They petitioned the authorities to allow them to send money home to pay their children's school fees in Nigeria. That makes a big difference in preventing a future deviant generation.

What the exploitative jobs of inmates in China did not provide was a wage substantial enough to support their families and to save for postprison life, nor did it offer job training that would help ex-convicts pursue goals after prison.

6.7 STRIKE TO BAD REPUTATIONS: A SURVIVAL STRATEGY

This section will focus on the Nigerian community's response to Nigerian international cocaine trafficking. It provides insight into measures they took to engage local authorities in constructive dialogue, which opened up opportunities for its members to achieve a respectable life through commercial activities, thereby dissuading Nigerian cocaine traffickers and reducing would-be drug traffickers.

The businessmen and women I encountered talked about their appreciation for changes that had been made in the city. They could now work freely without being harassed by Nigerian street drug dealers and delinquents. In this sense, many in Lagos are no longer skeptical of visiting Guangzhou. With its subtropical and tropical climate, touristic appeal, and trees on the pathways of San Yuan Li streets where most of them do business, the environment of Guangzhou exemplifies the attractiveness they would love to have in Nigeria. Nonetheless, many strains exist on their relationship with their host society, and one wonders what is behind this feeling and transformation? Some Nigerians have taken the initiative to disprove the stigma that Nigerian people are all cocaine traffickers.

By setting up a new Nigerian community in China, the pioneers of this initiative took it upon themselves to disprove negative Nigerian stereotypes by constructing a new image to more accurately reflect Nigerian culture. They built traditions to be emulated by other Nigerians in Guangzhou. This initiative was undertaken to exert a level of social control, with hopes of lowering deviant activities in the society. Guangzhou is not unique; Nigerians everywhere expressed that those representing them abroad are disconnected with Nigeria's own citizens. It is a mindset that will not change unless the government itself changes and individuals change their attitudes.

Some of the interviewees in Guangzhou, such as Emmanuel Osy, Dadi, and Mark, felt the then-exiting Nigerian community in China, which formed in 1999, was stigmatized by the bad reputation of certain members. Having made developed positive relationships with authorities in Guangzhou, they opted to redeem the Nigerian community for the benefit of all, despite opposition from some Nigerians standing in the way of reform. Why should some Nigerians stand against reforming the community and curbing deviant activities? These were direct and indirect members of Nigerian cocaine trafficking circles who profited from the atrocities committed by their cult gangs. However, pioneers of the reform initiative persisted, driven by the desire to gain respect and standing in the community.

Realizing how important their business relationship with the host country was to them, they saw the law enforcement crackdowns in 2009—aimed at getting Nigerian dealers off the streets in Guangzhou—as a chance to collaborate with the authorities and improve their status and livelihood. The crackdowns resulted in death and displaced dealers, pushing them into other areas. Despite these efforts and the reported arrests of many Nigerian traffickers, authorities in Guangzhou acknowledged that "although there are increased efforts to monitor the movement of foreigners living in Guangzhou, in reality there is little we can do" (Chin and Zhang 2007, 39).

The initiatives taken by the Nigerian community in response to the 2009 crackdown can be viewed on three issues inherent to place-making processes: the ways in which they intersect with their host country, structures of belonging that are built through organizations and communities, and strategies for settlement and mobility. They needed to counteract institutional barriers to their presence in China. Confronted with these processes, a delegation was sent to the Nigerian Embassy in Beijing. This included officers from the Immigration Office of Guangzhou. They discussed their plan to unite Nigerians to assist in reducing and preventing the deviant activities of small number of Nigerians. By engaging the Nigerian and Guangzhou authorities in a constructive discussion, the delegates formalized the formation of a new Nigerian community in Guangzhou. As we shall see later, it inspired trust among its members, clarified their purpose, aligned strategies, and implemented plans to achieve their aims.

Engaging law enforcement officials in the conversation underscores the view that Covey (2008) espoused in the article, "A Whole New Mind-set on Fighting Crime" that communities must make a conscious moral choice to end crime. That choice can be very difficult. As *Midwest Writing Centers Associaton* (MWCA 2007, 3) recalled, "At every crossroads on the path that leads to the future, tradition has placed 10,000 men to guard the past."

Letting go of ineffective crime-fighting methods can be hard. Many of the methods that once produced results are failing now because the problems themselves have changed. So, it is with fighting crime and violence. Covey's (2008) emphasized that a raft of overwhelming social issues: drugs, violence, welfare, and homelessness besiege our communities, which collectively affect everyone's prosperity. Notwithstanding the serious financial impact of drug trafficking, turning a blind eye had its consequences because much of the burden is borne by tax payers. The Nigerian community realized that a new approach was required if they were to have any impact on the social issues plaguing the community in Guangzhou.

Criminal activities of Nigerians acting individually or in conspiracy with others, devoid of formal organizations, were interpreted as activities of organized crime groups. This has affected efforts to control their activities in various countries. In addition, foreign governments and experts concerned with this new trend have failed to appreciate the economic, political, and social forces that have influenced a large number of Nigerians and their involvement in crimes. While the early nineteenth-century model of a central police organization was, as Garland (2001) pointed out, preventive, over time it became more focused on crime detection, in favor of punishment after the event, as opposed to prevention beforehand. This was partly a Benthamite project of utilitarian rationalization and partly a political project of asserting central control over the disorderly populations of the industrializing metropolis where revolution was most feared. Such steps toward centralized punitive regulation of the poor through paramilitary police organizations were eventually taken almost everywhere, though often much later (Braithwaite 2003).

6.7.1 Dealers, Off the Streets

Contrary to the view that sees Nigerians as an incoherent people, the Nigerian community instead embraced a proactive, problem-solving approach that focused on prevention, in which it is everyone's responsibility to promote safety. This change cannot be made without a plan. The four imperatives of leadership created to work against the negative effects of cocaine trafficking were to inspire trust, clarify purpose, align systems, and unleash talent. Running through each of the four crucial points are the three threads already discussed: initiative, partnership, and prevention. Within this preventive view, the Nigerian community representatives approached local authorities to discuss ways of solving the problem collaboratively. It was an inside-out approach to the problem.

Disparate Nigerian groups previously fragmented along ethnic lines united to form the new Nigerian community. They elected Emmanuel Osita Ojukwu (who died on February 4, 2021) as president of the Nigerian community in Guangzhou and other executives to head it with a mandate. And through constructive discussion, the new community pledged to respect the Nigerian Community's Statute and China's constitution. First, the leaders of Nigerian community in Guangzhou defined their purpose and led members to prevent and limit deviant activities, including drug trafficking, fraud, armed robbery, kidnapping, and murder. Second, engagement within the Nigerian community led to the formation of a vigilant group of market coordinators to curtail Nigerian street dealers of cocaine and other drugs. At the Nigerian community's behest, a team of about 60 volunteer members drove the streets addressing Nigerian and African drug dealers to respect themselves and get off the street. They stressed the fact that there would be no refuge for dealers and defiance would be reported to the police. They asked for compliance and participation in the efforts against trafficking.

Late Emmanuel "Ossy" Ojukwu and his team created a mechanism that enabled Nigerian entrepreneurs to work hard and cooperate independently with their Chinese counterparts. The representative of the volunteers, Igwe, stated to me, "They complied. People nodded their heads in agreement and gave their word. They got the message and above all, they knew we are all Nigerians, and that we knew who they were. *Naija sabi Naija* [Nigerian knows Nigerian]" (Igwe, personal communication, May 27, 2011). Regarding the fact that Nigerian cocaine traffickers did not seem worried about execution for drug trafficking, Igwe stated:

> That is their business. They are aware of the implication because every business has its risks. It seems they know how to deal with it because, it's like armed robbers in Nigeria, who knows he/she will be shot if caught; yet they do it. I don't understand them, do you? We should not allow these *Yeye* [delinquent] Nigerians to break our balls also in China! As traders, China allows us to partially establish here, so they should not make things worse. Here is not Europe or the U.S. where you become citizens. May be one day. For me, here *na home too oh* [here is also home] (Igwe, personal communication, May 27, 2011).

Ultimately, Emmanuel Ojukwu signed an "amnesty agreement" with the local PSB, promising to assist the police with immigration control in return for the promise that overstayers would be allowed to return to China legally after paying their visa-related fines (Lefkowitz 2013). The leaders of the Nigerian community in Guangzhou implemented their strategic plan, and as a result, most gangs were driven way from Guangzhou, and Nigerian crimes were reduced, including drug trafficking.

This recalls the widespread reaction amid Nigerian and African entrepreneurs in Guangzhou regarding their feeling of fluid status in China and desire to attain immigrant status. Aware that China is not an easy country to permanently immigrate to, the initiative taken by the Nigerian community to create a permissive environment to live and function despite their transitory status contests geographically bounded notions of "at homeness." Sometimes "home" becomes embodied—a project that is carried and reproduced on the move. In other words, Nigerians in Guangzhou are contributing to developing constructions of their nation-state that encompass those residing abroad—or deterritorialized nation-states (Basch et al. 1994).

By reflecting in terms of transnational mobility instead of migration, both the regularities and irregularities of human transnational movement are incorporated. Transnational mobility dares the telos of examination and methodological research in structural studies of migration, and resonates with the trenchant critiques of the bounded and static categories of nation, community, place, and state offered by several theorists like Appadurai (1996, 2006); and by those theorizing the formation of translocal identities and networks such as Castells (1997) and Hall (1991). A transnational mobility perspective also demonstrates the convergence of previous theorizations on transnationalism, translocality, mobility, networks, and assemblages. The lives of Africans in Guangzhou depend on multiple and constant interconnections across international borders, and their public identities are configured in relationship to more than one nation-state. They forge and sustain simultaneous multistranded social relations that link together their societies of origin and settlement. They construct and reconstruct their concurrent embeddedness in more than one society.

Whereas Igwe's inquiry recalls the discussion in previous chapters regarding the Nigerian state crisis, it underlines that despite its financial proceeds, edgework, the emotions of crime, and neutralization techniques are part and parcel of the push and pull features of cocaine or drug trafficking. On the one hand, this shows the zeal with which law-abiding Nigerians wanted to curtail the bad image and negative consequences suffered due to the crimes committed by conationals in Guangzhou. On the other hand, it demonstrates the resilience of Nigerian traffickers, as they still sell cocaine in bar areas of Guangzhou. However, the Nigerian community wanted their interests and future protected. This evokes the discussion in previous chapters regarding "old school" and "new-arrival" Nigerians in Brazil. Successful Nigerians have long-term Chinese visas (or permission to stay) and serve as brokers between African traders and Chinese factories, whereas those who are least successful overstay their visas and risk arrest and deportation. However, belonging to the old or new generational group does not make one immune to cocaine trafficking. For instance, Fefe was well established in both his business and personal life. Nigerians incarcerated in China include individuals with valid residence permits and married with children. The negative consequences affect everyone, and so everyone in the new Nigerian community fights against it.

6.7.2 Cultism, Cocaine, and Violence

In SP, the new trend illicit cocaine traders used traditional Nigerian secret societies to enhance their activities, whereas, in Guangzhou they used cultism, and cult gangs have killed several couriers and businessmen.

Prior to the police crackdown in 2009, many Nigerians could not walk freely in Guangzhou without been attacked because Nigerian cocaine traffickers formed criminal gangs or cults like *Eiye*, *Bagger*, and *Tutu* who would rob merchants and passersby. Surrounding the victim, some put cocaine on the person's bag or pocket and accused him or her of drug trafficking. Several businessmen and women were kidnapped, robbed, and brutalized (see, figure 6.1).

Emma Ossy stated to me in Guangzhou: "Guangzhou was a hell because they killed more than a few Nigerians" (Emma Ossy, personal communication, May 24, 2011).

The same cultism experienced in Nigerian universities spread to Guangzhou. Each gang had up to one hundred members. Although their primary interest was trafficking, they were also kidnapping, extorting money, and killing rival Nigerian cocaine traffickers and couriers in Guangzhou and neighboring cities to secure their stronghold on trafficking.

Missing or disappeared couriers were a common topic among Nigerian cocaine traffickers in Lagos, Amsterdam, and KL. Some attributed the

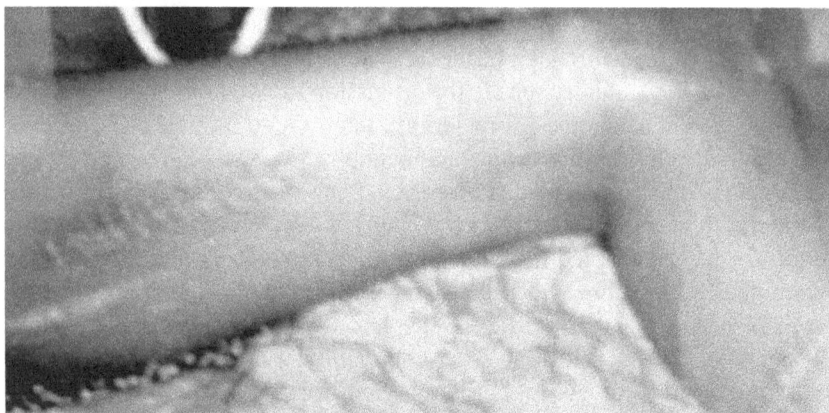

Figure 6.1 Picture of Nigerian Cocaine Traffickers' Violence (Guangzhou). *Source:* Nigeria community Guangzhou 2011.

missing couriers to delays of departure or transit; several suspected the courier ran away with the drugs; and others wondered if the person was arrested by police. In Guangzhou, several Nigerian drug couriers were killed, left in flats, and the ingested cocaine was robbed from their bodies. For example, in February 2011, six Nigerian cocaine traffickers extracted ingested cocaine pellets by dismembering the body of a courier and dumping it in the swamp of River Nanhai (Emma Ossy, personal communication, May 24, 2011). The crime was uncovered when people saw two suitcases in the river and alerted the police. Igwe stated: "The law enforcement agents arrested a Nigerian entrepreneur in Guangzhou, alleged that one of his workers was linked to the crime. The community took up responsibility to intervene because the police succeeded in arresting two out of the five suspects; whereas the rest escaped. Called upon its members to assists, the offenders were identified and apprehended by the vigilant team, interrogated, and handed over to the police" (Igwe, personal communication, May 24, 2011).

The offenders admitted involvement and detailed their modus operandi and personal backgrounds, which revealed more of the nature of Nigerian cocaine traffickers. Whereas some members were traders, others were school and university dropouts from middle-class families in Nigeria. For example, Ogy, one of the men convicted in this case, came from a good family; his father was a medical doctor in Nigeria. Nevertheless, criminogenic circumstances at home and abroad drove Ogy toward trafficking. Nkam, another man implicated in this crime, stated in a recorded video in possession with the writer: "Abu paid us USD$8,000 in total. Nonetheless, because he did not have USD$8,000 complete on that day, he promised to pay us next day.

But that did not go down well with us, so they asked to be paid with goods [cocaine] instead. So, Abu paid us USD$4,000 cash and gave us 11 pellets or balls of cocaine to make it up. Shared as follows; Oina got one ball of cocaine and CNY2,000 for watching out. We shared the rest equal between us" [Aky, Kis2, Ogy] (Recorded video, personal communication, May 24, 2011).

Ogy and his accomplices were handed over to law enforcement authorities in Guangzhou. The offenders said that a lack of legitimate documents to work led them into cocaine trafficking and related crimes, deploying Sykes and Matza's (1957) neutralization technique of denial of responsibility and the appeal to higher loyalties.

In 2009, one Nigerian businessman was robbed of USD450,000 on arrival at Guangzhou airport. A Nigerian staff member at a money transfer office in Guangzhou had passed on information about the man's arrival in Guangzhou, the gang followed him from the airport, and robbed him. Telling a similar story, Igwe showed me pictures taken of a man that showed knife cuts all over his body. Igwe added: "This man was taken home by a Chinese girl, who later same night called *Eiye* cult members that accused the guy of cocaine possession and of snatching their girlfriend. They robbed the man USD$3,000. We have worse cases and pictures. As you aware off, we got the offenders and interrogated them here, and handed over to the authorities" (Igwe, personal communication, May 24, 2011).

This is the kind of evidence community volunteers used to bring criminals to justice when handing them over to the police. I contacted Bonife, a famous Nigerian musician who was attacked by a cult gang in China, and interviewed him in Lagos. Bonife added: "They beat me up in Guangzhou for speaking out against their atrocities and rituals. They were cocaine traffickers who robbed and murdered. I was tired of Guangzhou, so I relocated to Nigeria, from where I continued with my music. I will be traveling to Guangzhou within few days to release a new album. Guangzhou is different these days thanks to the new generation Nigerian leadership that curtailed the bad guys. Yet, some carry drugs to China, after undergoing all sorts of rituals" (Bonife, personal communication, October 12, 2011).

My in-depth conversation with Bonife echoed many aspects underpinning Nigerian illicit cocaine trafficking: cultism, religious beliefs, and calls on supernatural power in pursuit wealth regardless of the means.

6.7.3 Renewed Opportunities and Choices: Unbundling "Immobility"

The Nigerian community confronted the state of immobility of conationals by approaching the authorities in the neighboring town of Foshan-Nanhai, which wanted a police crackdown similar to that in Guangzhou. They did not want to see the policy of raiding homes and shops of Nigerians implemented, but instead preferred to document Nigerians and Africans in Foshan with membership ID cards of Nigerian community members in Guangzhou. Since a lack of valid permits to engage in commercial activities was indicated as a major factor motivating people into criminal activity, the ID would allow them legitimacy. The authorities gave the proposal a chance. There was an overwhelmingly positive response to the initiative, and as a result a majority of Nigerians were able to earn their living as traders in Canal Market in Guangzhou, following the initiative taken in Foshan-Nanhai. Igwe added, "About 1000 individuals participated, and we are still busy with it. Each person goes into agreement with the community not to get involved in crime and to be his brother's keeper in this sense" (Igwe, personal communication, May 24, 2011).

By empowering or expanding community initiatives, Nigerians were able to get "unstuck" and move toward a more legitimate direction. The Nigerian community in Guangzhou has kick-started a community shift from hopelessness to expanding horizons of new choices, shifting the social culture and assuring its entrepreneurial support. If someone committed a crime and there was evidence of the crime, the community reported the offender to authorities. However, while Nigerians contributed to social pressures that would reduce crime and trafficking, Nigerian cocaine trafficking continues regardless. And so, the bottleneck remains, as raids by the police continue in an effort to control crime. Authorities think in terms of crime detection and punishment, but in the course of raiding, many innocent individuals are affected. This evokes the notion that people are not born democratic and decent; civility is something we must learn in a structured way (Braithwaite 2011). This is the reason the Nigerian community has adopted the strategy of giving drug traffickers the opportunity to quit and to engage in legal, mainstream activity. Nigerian ex-trafficker, Atamu, expressed: "I joined *Eiye* and sold cocaine, heroin, and marijuana on the streets to survive. *Eiye* cultist used to send them to kidnap cocaine couriers and traders rob their drugs and money. It was difficult to survive in Guangzhou. That's why I was frustrated into joining cults. It was just as in Nigeria, isn't it? Now things have changed in Guangzhou. I have a legal business, and I like it" (Atamu, personal communication, May 25, 2011).

Atamu and others who turned their lives around could become volunteers of the community as a correctional measure. By so doing, the person offered an apology openly to the community and promised not to offend again.

This relates to the notion of shame management, which contends that restorative justice interventions are well suited to the task of managing and working constructively with the shame that all parties experience in situations of crime and conflict. It considers the degree to which offending is shamed and whether that shaming is reintegrative or stigmatic. Braithwaite (1989) defined reintegrative shaming as disapproval that is respectful of the person, is terminated by forgiveness, and does not label the person as evil nor allows condemnation to result in a master status trait. This traditional African concept, widely practiced in among the Igbos in Nigeria and in many African countries, envisages that the practice of reintegrative shaming will result in less offending. Conversely, stigmatizing shaming is not respectful of the person, is not terminated by forgiveness, labels the person as evil, and allows them to attain a master status trait. The reintegrative shaming theory predicts that this latter type of shaming results in greater levels of offending. It focuses on the evil of deed rather than on the offender as a redeemable individual.

I observed on some occasions that representative of the community and executives worked till early morning hours resolving issues. When dealing with issues such as reported disputes, delinquent acts, and crimes against the community, the offender was called to report at the community headquarters, at number 90 Jinfu Da Sha, Qifu, Baiyun, in Guangzhou. If an offender does not appear willingly, they may be apprehended by community volunteers, confronted, and sanctioned by the community.

Many Nigerians said that criminals had persisted for so long because no one stopped them, neither the authorities nor the community. In response, the community volunteer team rounded up about 126 cult members and handed them over to the authorities, while others fled to Nigeria or other countries. Having largely eradicated cultism and violence and reduced street dealing, the Nigerian community in Guangzhou worked toward successful mediation to prevent deviant activities.

6.7.4 Impact and Policy

In the course of my fieldwork in Guangzhou, I observed several arguments and disputes in connection with traders who became victims of business deals that caused the loss of their only available capital. They were left feeling powerless and in debt. Without some knowledge of Mandarin, traders can be easily cheated by Chinese merchants deceiving the oblivious African buyers before them (Mathews and Yang 2012). The risk of fraud is high as Nigerian traders have few sanctions to apply against Chinese business partners who do not deliver on promised goods, services, or payment (Haugen 2012).

Faced with such a situation, many turned the fight to another front. For instance, Aga related that he was frustrated into cocaine trafficking to pay back debt after a Chinese agent duped him USD3,000. Aga added: "I hated myself in China! Left with USD3,000 debt, an acquaintance introduced me to risk. I sold cocaine and brown [heroin] and so on. I did it out of hopelessness. I saw it as the only chance because I could not go to the bank to borrow, neither from a friend none from my parents who have nothing. I made some money from it and paid off my debt. I made start capital. Now I have a good business. I thank God for saving me from troubles. I learnt my lesson in China!" (Aga, personal communication, May 25, 2012).

This recalls several others who asserted that they were lured to cocaine trafficking as a means of repaying debts or raising capital for starting businesses. With the measures in place now, the Nigerian community could have assisted through their official contacts. For example, pulling out a file from his bookshelf, the president of the Nigerian community pointed to two current cases, which involved about USD80,000 and USD100,000, respectively. Things become difficult due to the state of immobility caused by Chinese visas. Visas are easy to acquire in Nigeria, but when one still has business to do, extending it becomes difficult. Cocaine trafficking is a risky way out for Aga and those in a similar position. However, thanks to intervention by community representatives, many cases of cheating or bad business deals between Nigerians or Chinese and Nigerians have been resolved with dialogue instead of violence or the need for criminal activity.

This initiative in Guangzhou has not only gradually influenced new thinking in their host society but also in Nigeria. For instance, it is now possible for Nigerian traders to get a two-week extension for their visas to allow them finish protracted transactions. In an unprecedented move, the present Nigerian administration, following the footsteps set by former president Olusegun Obasanjo, has opened its consulate in Guangzhou, thereby closing the wide gap between Nigerians and the home government.

The Nigerian community's action draws attention to the concept of *justice reinvestment*. Justice reinvestment arises from the observation that if cost-effective ways of reducing crime exist than what is currently on offer, the social resources saved from the implementation of a successful intervention will outweigh the costs (Fox et al. 2013). It is a multistage process that provides a framework for local agencies to work together to identify and reduce the drivers of criminal justice costs. In this view, the Nigerian community sought to assist local authorities in developing measures and policies to improve the prospects of individual cases and in particular places. They adopted a strategic approach to the prevention of offending and reoffending by collecting and analyzing data to inform commissioning decisions. Their approach recognizes the potential to create a more law-abiding society in a more effective and less costly way than the traditional detect/convict/punish approach.

Envisaged in this model is a reduction in the crime rate, as justice reinvestment proposes moving resources spent on punishment of offenders to programs designed to tackle the underlying problems, which gave rise to the criminal behavior (see Allen 2011). Solve the sources of crime rather than its causes recommended Reiman and Leighton because pathways to crime are less direct and more complicated than simple cause and effect. We know that sources of crime include unemployment, poverty, and inequality, which breed alienation from social institutions and reduce the likely rewards of going straight (2017, 35–37). Prison produces more crime than it prevents (Alexander 2012). Ex-cons burdened with the stigma of prison records, rarely trained in a marketable trade, find their lives often continue to be characterized by violence, joblessness, substance abuse, and family breakdown. A U.S. Bureau of Justice Study using data of inmates released in 2005 found that 67.8% were rearrested within three years and 50% returned to prison (Durose et al. 2014, 1).

When one is situated in a state of immobility, illegal status leads to illegal actions. Nigerian community called on the Chinese reformists for assistance. Indeed, the former Nigerian president Obasanjo commented that China was a role model for Africa, "This is the 21st century, and China will lead the world. And when you are leading the world, we want to be close behind you. When you are going to the moon, we don't want to be left behind" (Alden 2007, 69).

In redrawing the line, the Nigerian community in Guangzhou exemplifies the relevance of social culture and positive leadership in contributing to the prevention of cocaine and drug trafficking. Cocaine and other drug traffickers must no longer tarnish the image and reputation of innocent Nigerian traders in Guangzhou.

Chapter 7

Involvement in Southeast Asia, the United States, the United Kingdom, and the Netherlands

This chapter will focus on the activities of the new trend Nigerian drug traffickers in various countries internationally.

Following their success in China and in search of new markets where they might go undetected, Nigerian drug traffickers sought to spread their networks. Growth in reputation, sophistication, and international ties bolstered expansion. Countries in proximity to the GT—where most of the world's opium originated from the 1950s to 1990, before Afghanistan's opium production surpassed that of Myanmar (formerly Burma)—were a good fit for Nigerian traffickers (Renard 1996).

Mainland SEA, while not major drug trafficking hub in comparison to Brazil or China, but it does have a substantial drug consumer market. For instance, heroin and methamphetamine are produced in Myanmar and trafficked or consumed regionally or exported overseas. Cocaine hoppers source drugs from Myanmar for transport to other countries including Japan, Australia, the United States, and Europe. They also traffic Latin American cocaine into the SEA region. As a result of these illicit activities, an estimated 650 Nigerians are on death row in prisons across SEA, most on drug-related offenses (Onyekwere 2017).

7.1 MALAYSIA

In the 1960s, Nigeria established bilateral cooperation with Malaysia. In this period, Malaysia planted its first palm seeds from Nigeria. It is pertinent to note that as of 2017, Indonesia was the largest producer and exporter of palm oil in the world, followed by Malaysia and Thailand; Nigeria ranked fifth (Index Mundi 2018). Economic growth in both nations made them lands of opportunity for Nigerians in search of greener pastures and better education. The exact number of Nigerians residing in either country is unknown.

Unofficial sources from representatives of various Nigerian community organizations in KL and Malacca told me there could be tens of thousands of Nigerians living in Malaysia. As of 2016, there were about 13,000 Nigerian students in the country (Bello et al. 2017). As of August 2016, 35% of the 350 foreign students in Malaysia arrested for drug trafficking were Nigerians (see *Free Malaysia Today* 2017). Modeled on the British education system, the English-speaking environment, and affordable tuition fees made Malaysia an attractive alternative for higher learning as Nigerian institutions deteriorated. Culturally, Malaysia is a good fit for many Nigerians because Islam is the official religion of the state. Most parents believe that with the practice of Islamic culture, their children will be better off, as they will not be influenced by immoral Western lifestyles. But Malaysia is not the promised land that many hoped it would be. Many experience the struggle of family separation, sociocultural adjustment, exploitation by landlords and their agents, stigmatization and stereotypes against Africans, and financial difficulties. The number of Nigerians imprisoned in Malaysia is uncertain. The director of Sungai Buloh Prison told me there were 400 Nigerians inmates there, most convicted for drug trafficking offenses (Ingh, personal communication, 2012). And as many as 81 Nigerians were on death row in Malaysia as of 2016 (Adebayo 2016).

7.1.1 Fatu-matter: Malaysian Courier

Fatu was one of several Malaysian female couriers I came across in SP. A former university undergraduate, she was arrested and jailed in Brazil in 2008 for cocaine trafficking. Fatu was sentenced to five years in prison—a much lighter sentence than what she may have faced in her home country of Malaysia, which still supports the death penalty in some drug-related crimes. Abandoned by her family and following a breakup with her boyfriend, Fatu wanted to get out of Malaysia at any cost. She was recruited by her friend's Nigerian boyfriend who often used other girls as couriers. Fatu stated:

> They sent me to Madrid in Spain to meet their friend, a woman by name DS and the boyfriend NJ who lived in Italy. After the boyfriend of a Malaysian girl refused to travel to Argentina to carry cocaine, because the country was judged too risky for couriers then, I optioned to be sent because I just wanted to travel after my heart was broken. They changed and asked me to travel to Brazil instead. They gave me EUR4,000 euro for ticket, hotel, and so on. But cash mattered less. To cover up things prior to departure, I told my brother I needed money to pay my passport and travel. He gave me USD6,000. So, money was not my problem to start with. On arrival in São Paulo, I checked into a hotel and

informed DS in Spain. On the departure day after one week, the guy brought the cocaine that was packed in a kind of cloth that I wore. . . . I did not ask how much because money did not interest me. I was 21 years old. I just wanted to travel. That was what I told the judge and that was my reason for traveling. I told the judge that I know where they people that sent were in Spain and that I am ready to go with the police there (Fatu, personal communication, January 3, 2013).

However, Fatu believed that she was set up as a fall guy, which is a tactic sometimes used by traffickers employing the shotgun approach, discussed earlier:

At the airport, I recognized I was the only one wearing a thick cloth. However, I got my boarding pass and I was almost gotten in the plan when an undercover policewoman asked if I was Malaysian and to see my passport. Glancing through my passport, she asked me to follow her for a control. After searching my hand-luggage she asked me to pull off my jacket. She asked what it was? Jokingly, I said that I do not know what it was. They took me inside and someone kept calling me on the phone, until one of the police guys took the call. The first thing he said was 'she is here already.' I came to understand the setup game played by some Nigerian connection men that arranges that cocaine for couriers, as well as passing information to their police friends. They share the drugs and send the small couriers to prison. I feel I was used (Fatu, personal communication, January 3, 2013).

Personal gains for couriers are low compared to the risks they assume. Interviews in SP suggested that most couriers recruited by Nigerian traffickers are not only Nigerians but include South Africans, Senegalese, the Democratic Republic of the Congolese, Europeans, and Asians. These couriers are considered "low cost" mules. Some remain in Brazil and become integrated into licit society, while "others are longing to go back to their countries after their experience. They are offered a trip back to their country along with a thousand dollars and have to transport a luggage or items in their own luggage" (Cohen 2019, 39).

The issues caused by drug trafficking are not the exclusive control of producing or major consuming countries. Globalization—interdependent economies and the opening of endless trade routes—has made all countries susceptible to international crime. Instead of being criminalized, Fatu and her ilk could be regarded as victims of a kind of human trafficking.

Many Malaysians serving sentences in foreign prisons for drug-related offenses were often students or youths, often ignorant, uneducated, or from poor families. The same is true for Nigerians arrested in Malaysia; according to Malaysian authorities, of the 137 Nigerian drug offenders arrested between January and August 2016, 38 were students (*The Sun Daily* 2017). Easily manipulated, many become victims lured by money, gifts, and exciting vacations. Though making fast money remains the motive for most individuals engaged in cocaine trafficking, I found that other pressures play important roles as well, as the above case demonstrates. Though young and naïve, Fatu was intelligent and educated. She was pushed into the drug trade following inadequate family guidance, relational disappointment, and the search for escape. After finishing her jail sentence in SP, Fatu returned to Malaysia, where she is struggling to find a good job.

7.1.2 Societal Reaction and Government Response

The Malaysian trader, Sheik, was one of many who asserted Africans, particularly Nigerians, preyed on their women and used them for criminal purposes. His view of Nigerians as criminals and parasites was bolstered by media portrayals related to Malaysia's war on drugs. The government used the war on drugs as a bailiwick to justify higher taxes and repressive policies. Yet, those measures have seen results: police busted major drug syndicates from Nigeria, Iran, Brazil, Venezuela, Afghanistan, and China. In 2016, Malaysian police apprehended more than 1,000 traffickers who had imported tons of drugs, including roughly 368 kilograms of cocaine in the last seven years. Of the 798 Nigerians arrested, 426 had entered the country as private university students (*The Straits Times* 2016). These figures also expose an illicit drug trade embedded in the negative consequences of present-day globalization.

Malaysia has made major strides in eradicating poverty, but ongoing migration from rural to urban areas has increased urban poverty, and excessive urban growth leads to escalating economic and social costs, for example, unemployment, rising cost of living, drugs, crime, and social problems (see Chamhuri et al. 2016). With the growing economy, wealthy middle class, and bubbling tourism, narcotics use has become fashionable. Malaysian authorities acknowledged the number of drug addiction cases increased by 14% in one year, reaching 30,847 in 2016. They also deemed narcotics a major threat to the country's safety and security, as drug use has led to theft and murder, as so often happens (see Bernama 2017).

A study done by Universiti Utara Malaysia showed that the government spent 8.65 billion Malaysian Ringgit (about USD2.09 billion) in direct and indirect costs to tackle drug issues in 2009. Fear of crime and drugs evoke calls for greater intervention by law enforcement, and in response, the National Anti-Drugs Agency increased the number of its operations by thousands compared to 2017 (Zainal 2018). The government also enacted six new drug laws with extremely harsh punishments for narcotic traffickers. For example, the quantities of narcotics that trigger a mandatory death penalty in Malaysia are as follows: cocaine 40 grams, heroin 15 grams, methamphetamine 50 grams, marijuana 200 grams, and morphine 15 grams (Leechaianan and Longmire 2013). Whereas soft drugs such as marijuana are being decriminalized, drug-assisted treatment for hard drugs is being implemented to combat public health risks in places like Portugal, Switzerland, the UK, and the Netherlands. For instance, heroin is being prescribed for use under medical supervision as part of successful programs to treat long-term users of illicit opioids (EMCDDA 2012).

7.1.3 Corruption We Hail

Limiting endemic corruption which fuels illicit drug trafficking remains a priority. Among interviewees, police were the number one public servants to whom bribes were paid in Malaysia (Transparency International-Malaysia 2017). Malaysians themselves perceive the police as the most corrupt institution in the country. Bribes and irregular payments are sometimes exchanged in return for obtaining favorable court decisions. One former Malaysian prime minister, Najib Razak, was recently arrested over the multimillion-dollar looting of a state investment fund (*BBC* 2019). Abuse of power occurs at all levels in Malaysia.

Newburn and Webb (1999) averred that systematic police corruption happens when individual corruption events are duplicated regularly into arrangements. Wong Chen (2017) wrote on the Royal Malaysian Police and the negative public perception it carries. Wong Chen found that corruption involving organized crime syndicates was serious as it involves long-term schemes, large amounts of money, and the collusion of senior police officers. Criminal operators of this variety were seldom caught, although the illicit activities they were engaged in, including drug trafficking, could be relatively easily detected and acted upon, but were not because of bribes paid by suspects to investigating officers or bribes solicited by the investigating officers. Such bribes involved money, reselling drugs, and pilfering money held under police custody. It is all considered another cost of doing business.

For Malaysian-based Nigerian traffickers, it was critical to have a "Godfather" and grease the palms of police officers, particularly when their couriers were apprehended. Interviewees said that Nigerian drug barons paid between USD14,000 and USD28,000 to Malaysian police for the release of a courier. Bribes were a small percentage of their overall profits. Such are the rewards of successful deals that traffickers are often seen in nightclubs spending thousands of dollars—even going so far as to rinse their hands with champagne. They succeed because the networks and the modus operandi in Malaysia render a win-win situation for the players involved.

The police force risks losing the trust of the public in Malaysia. Even those who were deported have sometimes been able to bribe their way back into the country. Such was the case of one interviewee, Hipo. Busted by police and deported to Nigeria in 2014 for an immigration offense, Hipo paid USD2,000 to a "connection man" who arranged a visa and fast-tracked his reentry to Malaysia. Several other interviewees asserted that kickbacks paid to corrupt law enforcement agents allowed them to avoid arrest. Others said their "insider" informed them ahead of dangers or police raids. It's an untenable arrangement that thrives on the social, economic, and geopolitical struggles of the region.

7.2 THAILAND

Historically, Thailand served as a transit country, moving drugs from the rugged hills of Myanmar and Laos to world markets in East Asia, Australia, North America, and Europe. Recently, Thai authorities reported an increase in the availability of cocaine within Thailand consumed by foreigners and affluent Thais (see INCSR 2017). The Thai Office of the Narcotics Control Board (ONCB) confiscates many kilograms of cocaine yearly (INCSR 2016; ONCB 2015). Drug use is pervasive in private residences, entertainment spots, and popular tourist destinations in various provinces. In 2015, the majority of drug addicts who accessed treatment in Thailand were under 24 years old, including children under 15 (see Kanato et al. 2017).

Thailand's well-developed banking system among countries in the GT helped consolidate its function as the main hub for financiers. Thailand is also a primary hub for Nigerians in SEA. About 4,000 Nigerians are in Thailand, and the community is fast growing. Many believe that Nigerians use Thailand as a base for financial scams or the illicit drug trade, as those arrested for such crimes are overrepresented in the Thai media. But as in other countries in the region, the majority of Nigerians choose to live in Thailand to conduct genuine business and enjoy respectable lives. They have contributed positively to the Thai economy. Nigerians have opened successful restaurants, catering in particular to other expatriates longing for a taste of home, and others have established businesses for the import and export of jewelry, gemstones, and textiles. According to the Thai Ambassador to Nigeria, trade between both countries was estimated to reach USD3 billion in 2018. Nigeria is one of the world's largest importers of Thai rice.

Whereas many Nigerians have made legitimate and socially acceptable achievements, others have chosen to exploit the opportunities afforded to them in their host country. Cocaine hoppers in Thailand traffic in cocaine but also heroin and synthetic drugs. Interviewed suggest that Thai-based Nigerian drug dealers sell on the streets and in nightclubs in Bangkok. They often sell small quantities of drugs, including cocaine, ecstasy, and marijuana. The postage method is also popular in Thailand and may be sourced from countries like the Netherlands, Belgium, Brazil, and other Latin American countries. These drugs are for the Thai market, as well as neighboring countries including Japan, Malaysia, or China. A somewhat unique method in Thailand is the use of couriers embedded on group tours abroad. This ensures a steady influx of drugs trafficked under the guise of legal tourism. This led Japanese police to seek help from Thai law enforcement to track down a Nigerian drug trafficking gang connected with Thai female couriers they busted in Japan (*Thai BPS* 2018).

7.2.1 Thai Couriers

Tapa, who was serving an eight-year jail sentence in SP for carrying about two kilograms of cocaine, was one of the eight female couriers from Thailand I interviewed in 2012 and 2013. She knew about 30 other female couriers from her country and many other countries in SEA who were convicted in SP for the same offense. After her business college education and attempted university studies, Tapa started a business center and beauty salon, but thereafter she derailed into drug trafficking, including cocaine. What follows are extractions from the conversations with Tapa that shed light on her transition into cocaine trafficking and its consequences. Hers is a case study representative of the many women lured into international trafficking:

> My Nigerian boyfriend introduced me to [cocaine trafficking]. I met him through my cousin that had a Nigerian boyfriend, as well. My ex had a cargo business to Africa but under he was doing drugs trade. I was about 18 or 19 years old and in love with him. He took me regularly out for eating and buying expensive things for me, sometimes spending about USD2,000 daily. He was rich. I wondered. Then he took me to an apartment he rented, where he kept cocaine and heroin. "You could stay away from me if you would prefer," he said. But I did not mind it. Because prior to meeting him, my girlfriend and I were already selling *yaa baa* [methamphetamine pills, aka madness drug] in my college. I got into drug trafficking because I just wanted to have my own money. After I met him, I started selling cocaine. He showed me drug and I said I want to deal. So, it was 50/50 partnership. We buy from Brazil or Argentina. We sent girls to carry it. He has contact in these countries. They carry three or five killograms back. We bought for USD2,000 per kilogram. We sell back in Bangkok for USD20, USD30 or even USD60,000 dollars depending on the class of buyers (Tapa, personal communication, January 3, 2013).

Most Nigerian international cocaine traffickers assert that couriers are aware of the risk involved with the illicit trade, accepting financial gains when successful but rebuffing responsibility when things go bad. It was remarkable that Tapa, who came from a middle-class family in Thailand, opted to partner with her Nigerian boyfriend in the cocaine business. Like

Tapa, many stated clearly that they joined the trafficking trend willingly, contrary to the perception of deceit by Nigerians.

Thailand is being confronted with the need to embrace humane and effective approaches to drug enforcement and control. While Nigerian cocaine hoppers are credited with trafficking cocaine through airports in Thailand and neighboring countries, South American and Chinese trafficking groups are involved in larger-scale cocaine smuggling through Thailand, typically for further export to China and Australia.

7.2.2 Control: Thai Naija, Siamese

Thai law enforcement officials are known to rip through areas of Bangkok hosting African immigrants, demanding passports and using sniffer dogs to search out illicit drugs. That is the reason why Jedan dislikes going to places such as Ramkhamhaeng Road and Sukhumvit Road, which are sites of frequent mass arrests and media frenzies. Several hundred Nigerians were arrested and detained in and around Bangkok during a bust by the Thai authorities in early October 2011 (Agbakwuru 2011). The death of Nigerians in prison custody, coupled with the Nigerian government's careless attitude, caused peaceful protests by the Nigerian diaspora in Thailand. O'Beni, a Nigerian contact living in the Netherlands, was saddened hearing that his cousin died in prison in Thailand, "I spent much money paying his lawyer to save him because he promised to quit drug trafficking. But all in vain now" (O'Beni, personal communication, December 6, 2016). He is one of many Nigerians who have had a relative or friend die while serving time in prison for drug trafficking. In 2017, Nigeria's ambassador to Thailand revealed that about 1,000 Nigerians are in Thai prisons for drug trafficking (Iroanusi 2017), but that statistic is likely speculation, as Ambassador Nuhu Bamalli did not directly engage prison authorities nor Nigerian inmates—another failing of the Nigerian government to uphold the duties of their office.

The Thai Narcotics Act B.E. 2522 of 1979 and subsequent amendments guarantee harsh punishment for offenders if the quantity of illicit drugs possessed is over the prescribed. For example, possession of 100 grams of cocaine earns imprisonment fromone to 10 years and/or a fine of between 10,000 baht (USD320) and 100,000 baht (USD3,200); heroin and methamphetamine possession over 100 grams warrants the death penalty or a life sentence; and 10 kilograms of marijuana garners imprisonment from two to five years and/or a fine of between 20,000 and 150,000 baht (Narcotic Laws of Thailand 2007; Kanato et al. 2016).

Thailand's stringent approach to a social and economic-driven illicit drug trade has had its consequences. The drive to make Thailand a drug-free land within three months resulted in an infamous war on drugs and extrajudicial killings that left more than 2,000 people dead. Thai police said that most killings were the result of drug dealers silencing potential informants (Windle 2015). The Thai government barely addressed concerns around the high death toll (HRW 2004). Thailand's ONCB asserted that crackdowns and their narcotics suppression policy aimed for qualitative improvements; however, a higher trend of arrest and human agony is the real result. In 2015, Thailand's prison population rose to 284,499. Thai antidrug control agents hailed this as an accomplishment, alongside disrupting the financial cycle of major traffickers and confiscating assets valued at millions of baht. But it is worrying that Thailand imposed 216 new death sentences, including 24 foreign nationals as of 2016, despite the fact that the abolition of the death penalty is part of the Third National Human Rights Action plan due to be implemented by 2018 (Amnesty International 2016).

Doubly worrying is that official corruption remains widespread, notwithstanding efforts made by the government to control it. In *Corruption and Democracy in Thailand*, Phongpaichit and Piriyarangsan (1999) noted endemic corruption at the highest level. In the past, officials were traditionally not paid salaries but were expected to remunerate themselves by taking a cut from the revenues they collected, 10–30%, and extracting fees for services performed (McFarlane 2000). In the traditional Thai value system, merit is derived from power, which in this way forms a basis for patron-client relationship in political society. Presenting gifts to high officials is common, and Thais do not see that as a form of corruption. Such corruption is compounded by the existence of influential provincial businessmen called *Jao Pho* (godfather), who function above the law (Mhuentoe 2013; Warsta 2004). As in Nigeria, aspects of culture that used to be legitimate under the traditional patronage system are clearly considered problematic in the modern legal system.

Likewise, the growing divide between the urban middle class and poor rural people perpetuates the patron and client tradition. And as in other countries discussed in this work, public servants in Thailand often earn low wages. If they cannot make a sufficient living, they will have greater motivation to get their share of the cake, so to speak, especially when Thai police officers are paid about 6,000 baht (USD185) a month, which is well below the national average. Affected officers rely on the "support of their communities" to make the wage livable—meaning payments from the gold shops they protect, fines they issue, and commissions from brothels (Jennings 2018).

In their research on factors affecting the effectiveness of police performance in the Metropolitan Police Bureau in Thailand, Tengpongsthorn (2017) applied Herzberg's two-factor theory: motivator factors and hygiene factors (40–41). The research found that the hygiene factor regarding salary had the lowest level of satisfaction. In other words, inappropriate compensation could have a negative impact on the effectiveness of their work performance. Police officers agreed that sufficient compensation would support them to work more effectively. Drug trafficking persists because huge profits are earned in the process, corrupting many local authorities including police and customs agents. As Tapa stated: "It is illegal to offer a bribe just like prostitution is illegal, but it is rampant in Thailand. Business is good because some Thai police take bribe. *Naija* people for Thailand *sabi am* well (Nigerians in Thailand know it well). My ex-boyfriend said, '*Thai* and *Naija* (Nigerians) are *same same* because money talks'" (Tapa, personal communication, January 3, 2013).

Nigerian drug traffickers crown in Thailand because those willing to pay engage those willing to accept kickbacks in return for turning a blind eye to illicit drug trafficking.

7.3 THE UNITED STATES AND THE UNITED KINGDOM

This section will focus on the activities of cocaine hoppers in the United States and United Kingdom. While the Nigerian diaspora in the United States stands out as role model of leadership for immigrants among 15 immigrant communities analyzed by the Rockefeller Foundation-Aspen Institute Diaspora Program (RAD 2015), the activities of "bad eggs," that is, Nigerian drug traffickers, involved in multiple crimes damage Nigerian's otherwise sterling reputation there. Despite efforts by the diaspora to distance itself from trafficking and other crimes, cocaine hoppers continue to operate in two important pioneer countries of the drug trade. The United States and its allies established drug control policies on an international scale. However, this was compromised by ineffectiveness to control the illicit cocaine market. That led to Nigerian drug traffickers clinching in the traditional drug market in the United States and exploiting new horizons offered by attractive UK market connections, in coordination with or subservient to dominant organized crime groups already involved.

The United States has a long history of aiding and abetting, or at the very least, neglecting, drug trafficking and use—from the CIA's involvement in the Iran-Contra Affair, trafficking cocaine into the United States and leading to the crack epidemic, to allegations of turning a blind eye to drug traffickers in SEA during the Vietnam War, and even heroin trafficking by Mujahidin rebels in Afghanistan to support the Afghan resistance to the Soviet Union's occupation in the 1980s (see Feiling 2009; Steinberg 1982). Hard drug trafficking through Nigeria into the United States in the 1950s, intertwined with the work of secret intelligence agencies (including an Italian intelligence officer and Lebanese trafficking syndicates), paved the way indirectly for Nigerian traffickers.

The practice by police of selling drugs obtained during official seizures continues today. In a review of police corruption by the UK Home Office, Newburn (2004) listed the main methods used by corrupt police. These included "shakedowns": protection of illegal activities to ensure their continued operation; "the fix": undermining criminal investigations and proceedings; and the acceptance of a bribe for not following through on a criminal violation, that is, not making an arrest, not filing a complaint, or not impounding property. Scholars have emphasized that the policing of illegal drug trade is one of the key drivers of police corruption (Van de Bunt 2004). In the United States, serious efforts at reducing police corruption have taken place within the last 50 years in Los Angeles, Oakland, Kansas City, and New York City; unfortunately, the success of these efforts seems to be short term. The characteristics of the drug market make it vulnerable to corruption: it is usually "secretive, duplicitous and quasi-legal"; the use of informants is widespread; it is extremely difficult to regulate; the "war on drugs" rhetoric often increases pressure on officers for results; securing sufficient evidence to convict is often difficult; officers may be required to occasionally use drugs in the course of their work (as part of undercover operations); and very large sums of money may be available to the corrupt officer (Miller 2016, 29).

The United States and the United Kingdom are also some of the most lucrative markets because demand is high. Today in the United States, cocaine users can buy purer cocaine at cheaper price (DEA 2017). One in twenty American adults ages 18–25 used the drug in 2015. According to the Global Drug Survey 2019, Scotland is ranked number one for cocaine use globally, at 12 days a year. Brazil, Italy, Portugal, Denmark, and England tied Canada for second place (Hristowa 2019).

Researchers found that about 16% of new cocaine users will develop cocaine dependence within 10 years (Kilmer and Midgette 2017). Moreover, drug overdose cases involving cocaine (or in combination with opioids) have increased in the United States (UNODC Executive summary 2017). In the UK, high levels of youth unemployment alongside cuts to social and other services under austerity, illegal economies have become one of the only income-generating opportunities for those who would otherwise have to negotiate life with little or no income. In the latest survey, cocaine is now the next most commonly used drug after cannabis among adults aged 16–59 (Crawford et al. 2017; Home Office 2016). Beyond the wider drug trends, price, purity, and availability are considered to be important drivers of drug use over time in UK.

7.3.1 United Naijas (Nigerians)

The exploitative, transatlantic slave trade, which the UK played major role in, forced millions of Africans to the United States. Both countries are still important destinations for Nigerians, as constant instability pushes many to immigrate. For instance, Dr. Nnamdi Azikiwe arrived in the United States in 1925, studied at Howard University, and on his return to the country, became the first president of Nigeria (Igwe 2015). Role models such as him have paved the way for others. In 2015, there were about 376,000 U.S.-based Nigerians (RAD 2015), and about 200,000 in the UK (The Migration Observatory 2017). According to the Central Association of Nigerians in the UK, as many as two million Nigerians reside in the country. However, estimates are flawed by the dark number.

At the international level, the negative image from crimes committed by Nigerian criminal networks seems to overshadow the achievements of the law-abiding majority. The United States' Nigerian diaspora ranked the best educated of the 15 groups in the RAD program's most recent analysis. A far greater share of the Nigerians first and second generation earned undergraduate degrees—more than the general U.S. population—were more than twice as likely to have secured an advanced degree, and substantially more likely than the general U.S. population to be in the labor force. Notwithstanding, they have only a slightly higher median annual income than the general U.S. population (RAD 2015). Likewise, the UK is home to highly educated Nigerian professionals and entrepreneurs (see Akhilomen 2016).

However, emigration out of Nigeria has come at a cost to the country: "brain drain," meaning the most educated and able have left to employ their skills abroad. On the one hand, the diaspora provides substantial remittances to Nigeria, which plays a major role in development at local levels. For instance, between 2011 and 2014, the Nigerian diaspora remittance was estimated at USD63.17 billion, which makes the second biggest source of foreign exchange earnings for the country after the oil industry. The U.S.- and U.K.-based Nigerian diaspora are the largest source of remittance inflow (RAD 2015; World Bank 2015). On the other hand, these remittances include those from the illicit drug trade, financial fraud, and other crimes. Recent arrests of Nigerian scammers in LA, Atlanta, and Maryland are examples. What is clear is the effect of the ill-gotten wealth metamorphosed in Nigeria, as so-called role models flaunted their extravagant lifestyles, fancy homes, luxury vehicles, and designer clothes. These only served to increase the pressure on those left behind, dreaming of a better life, pushing them toward financial scamming, human trafficking, and the illicit drug trade.

7.3.2 Bad Eggs or Good Eggs in a Bad Omelet?

Cocainehoppers' specialty of swallowing (*suicide*) or rectum insertion (*kele*) small quantities of drugs have contributed to labeling Nigerians as bad eggs globally; however, it is not uncommon for Nigerians at the top of the trafficking chain to be individuals of privilege and influence, such as senators, former officials of the NDLEA, and diplomats. Cocaine hoppers often commit other crimes related to their trafficking endeavors, most frequently fraud and human trafficking. Make no mistake, Ach told me, "basically you must have your finger in 'this and that' to get a piece of the cake" (Ach, personal communication, April 28, 2012). Money raised from scamming victims or from underage prostitution is invested into trafficking drugs.

But the notion of cocaine hoppers as strictly "bad eggs" overlooks the fact that drug trafficking seems the only option for many youths affected by the political and economic crises in Nigeria who look to U.S. and U.K. markets as a way out of poverty. Owo, an experienced striker, had succeeded several times as a courier before getting caught, "I have been doing this shit from 1982 till in 1984 when I was caught in the United States. I served time at Jefferson Dekker Juvenile Prison, in New Jersey because I faked my age on the passport" (Owo, personal communication, December 16, 2012). Owo was caught at JFK airport in New York for trafficking 600 grams of cocaine concealed in a photo frame after his friend, TY, who was caught with 800 grams of cocaine, implicated him. Both were sentenced to two years but served 18 months. On the topic of this betrayal, Owo remarked:

> It was very surprising and sad to be betrayed this way by a friend. His reason was that he did not want to go to prison alone in the United States. He was afraid. He needed a companion to survive in there, he said, that's why he implicated me. I was very mad with him. I felt like killing him sometimes, especially the first week and month. On the one hand, one mind said I should really find a way and kill him. But on the other hand, another mind asked me not to do it. I kept contemplating this dilemma. I kept asking myself how was it possible for him to do what he did. I myself would have not done it to anybody. I learnt a lot after this bad experience. The question was, is there anything like a trustworthy someone? Can anyone really be trusted? (Owo, personal communication, December 16, 2012).

In the world of trafficking, there can be no real trust in the absolute sense because good friends can and do betray one another. Indeed, as we've seen, even lovers betray each other. Nevertheless, in the cocaine business it is a need that partners achieve a level of trust—even if that trust is tenuous.

I traced TY who resides in Europe now. He acknowledged what happened. Life, he said, is full of mistakes. Now TY is a changed man. At 51-year-old, he was smartly dressed for our meeting and said he has put drug trafficking behind him, "Ain't do that shirt no more and ain't going to Naija no more. I've paid my price, and gradually I've got my life together. That's what is important to me" (TY, personal communication, August 10, 2013). Owo was not as lucky as TY. His experience with the U.S. prison system changed him also but not for the better:

> In a way, I came back more frustrated and angry because the prison made me more hardened. Worst because I made a lot friends in the prison. I met a lot of American both black and white in there, and learnt a lot about cocaine, heroin, crack and speed. I got experienced to the paranoia caused by crack. The uneasiness caused by crack cocaine and the fear that translates or causes violent acts out there (Owo, personal communication, December 16, 2012).

Owo has suffered immensely as a result. The violence crack unleashes is evident. He kept scratching his body, neck, nose, arms, and legs. As far as cocaine is concerned, as discussed previously, he went into prison as a novice and came out as a professional. However, he also learned some skills in marketing and tailoring. In Owo's words, "I came to know the rules: don't betray, don't lay, or they will kill you" (Owo, personal communication, December 16, 2012).

7.3.3 Small Fish in a Big Pond

Contemporary criminal groups operating in the United States are many and range from small- to moderately-sized, loosely fused groups that distribute drugs at low level and mid-levels, and Nigerians are among the drug and money laundering organizations operating in the United States. The Sinaloa Cartel's leader, alias *El Chapo*, was extradited to the United States in 2017, but his associates made cocaine easily obtainable in high drug consumption areas throughout the United States compared to the previous year (DEA 2017). In Florida and Miami, cocaine smugglers were a more ruthless group: "A saying began to circulate in the 1980s: a pot deal is done with a handshake; a coke deal is done with a gun" (Zimmerman 2006, 94). Nigerians cannot compete with the cartels or other large-scale traffickers in these markets. Instead they rely on using strong and weak ties within their networks, trafficking mainly small potions and brokering medium quantities of drugs in U.S. and U.K. markets. Tito explained to me in this way, "Better to avoid them. Otherwise, it is you and them and gun. Powerless you! They are serious gang members with serious guns. That is why it's a small, small, business. Think!" (Tito, personal communication, March 6, 2017).

African criminal groups identified by the Federal Bureau of Investigation in several major metropolitan areas in the United States are predominantly Nigerian. They are especially active in Baltimore, Chicago, Houston, New York, Newark, Los Angeles, Atlanta, and Washington, D.C. For example, Temitope Ayoni Olaiya (aka "Tammy"), a Nigerian woman was sentenced by U.S. Attorney's Office Eastern District of Virginia on February 28, 2020, to 10 years in prison and ordered to pay over USD377,000 in restitution for a 'triple threat' of criminality: trafficking cocaine from Brazil into the United States, involvement in bank fraud scheme, and fraudulent claims submitted to Medicaid for reimbursement. The 40-year-old Tammy recruited men from the greater Washington, D.C., area to act as drug mules and sent them to SP where they picked up cocaine concealed in the lining of soft-sided briefcases or attaché cases. Experienced cocaine striker opened bank accounts in the couriers' names, assisted them in obtaining passports and visas, and booked their travel arrangements. Antidrug control officers confiscated almostseven kilograms of cocaine at three different U.S. airports from three separate couriers recruited by Tammy (United States Department of Justice. U.S. Attorney's Office, Eastern District of Virginia 2020, 2019).

Nigerians use decentralized, loosely structured networks, as opposed to the stringent hierarchical model of the Italian Mafia. Research on drug distribution networks revealed that large drug shipments are most often conducted by small and highly organized groups (Bichler et al. 2017), while suppliers are loose groups of people involved in many different areas (Pearson and Hobbs 2001). Nigerians who have settled in Latin America and the Caribbean are also primary actors sending couriers into the United States and the United Kingdom. They use private networks to buy or sell drugs in private settings and often conduct business in coded native languages.

7.3.4 Britico, no Wahala (Britain, no Problem)

Cocaine hoppers have used their comparative advantage of proximity to Europe and extensive networks to traffic drugs into the UK's lucrative market. Groups involved in serious and organized crime in the UK are heterogeneous in terms of personal characteristics, offending histories, and trajectories, and they have different ethnic and national origins (Francis et al. 2013). Cross-ethnic partnerships have also been documented (Ruggiero and Khan 2006; von Lampe and Antonopoulos 2018). In addition to more traditional, hierarchically structured groups, the UK is also home to criminal groups with loose structural organization, more typical of a network than a family. In other words, they tend to be individuals who decide to engage in ad hoc criminal activities and dissolve afterward. The opening of borders in the EU as well as the instability in the Balkans enhanced opportunities for new criminals in the UK. They built on the Italian and Spanish organized crime groups, which inspired by the French Connection, seeded their drug trafficking and money laundering in England. The illicit heroin market is mostly controlled by Turkish and Pakistani organized criminals; however, cocaine supply and distribution are predominantly in the hands of Albanian groups and Jamaican "Yardie" gangs (Her Majesty's Government 2013). If the UK authorities identified the main threats originating from organized crime groups to include terrorism, people smuggling, human trafficking, financial fraud, and drug trafficking, then Nigerian criminal networks should be included.

Nigerian drug traffickers transport drugs using speedboats and ships from secret departure points in Lagos, often operating under the cover of darkness. They coordinate with officers on the ships, sometimes employing naval officers or military soldiers in transit or destination countries (see Ibagere 2000). Nigerian nationals have increased their involvement in the cocaine trade to the extent that they are now on an equal footing with Latin Americans in their ability to source, finance, and transport both bulk and "little and often" quantities of cocaine to Africa and Europe. In several interviews, I asked if it was possible to control hundreds of vessels from Europe, the Americas, and Asia to service Nigeria's "container economy"? Lamba told me, "When you have good connection, *Britico no Wahala* [Britain no problem]" (Lamba, personal communication, November 8, 2017).

By establishing hubs around Europe, cocaine hoppers secured a position that enables them to traffic small but steady quantities of cocaine into the UK—like the extensive infrastructure network built by Amazon to outcompete other delivery businesses. Leku is one such cocaine hopper—he has seen it all. Confident in his networks, Leku used scheduled flights departing from various international airports in SSA and Latin America to traffic cocaine into the Netherlands. He and associates deployed "passive couriers" who were not liable to rigorous checks to carry cocaine concealed in varied forms and hidden in various parts of the aircraft. He could sell in the Dutch market because Amsterdam's drug market attracts many tourists, but if the cocaine is brought into the UK, Leku makes much more. In the UK market, he earns at least GBP50 per gram. Sending multiple couriers and cutting the cocaine to about 60–70% purity increases profits further.

7.3.5 Nigerian Inmates in the United States and the United Kingdom

Recent data made public showed that about 534 Nigerian nationals (485 men and 49 women) were serving time in British jails as of 2017, most convicted for drug offenses. That figure jumped to over 750 Nigerians in British jails the following year. Nigerians account for one in 20 of all foreign prisoners, putting the country fifth on the table of nations whose citizens have been jailed in the UK. In a bid to relieve overcrowding, authorities have engaged the Nigerian government in a compulsory prisoner transfer agreement to increase the number of prisoners who are transferred (*The Sun* 2018)

In the United States, the CJS holds more than 2.3 million people in its correctional institutions. Every year, about 636,000 people walk out of prison gates, but people go to jail over 11 million times annually (Wagner and Rabuy 2016). The most commonly prosecuted drug offenses carry mandatory minimum penalties, under 21 U.S.C. §§ 841 and 960 provisions (Pryor et al. 2017, 10). Under both provisions, a five-year minimum penalty and a maximum term of 40 years applies, while larger amounts increase the penalty to 10 years, with a maximum of life imprisonment. Under both provisions, for instance: a sentence of five years applies for possession of 100-gram heroin or 500-gram powder cocaine or 28-gram crack. A sentence of five years for cocaine powder requires possession of 500 grams—100 times more than the quantity of crack for the same sentence. Most of those who use cocaine powder are white, middle-class or rich people, while mostly blacks and Latinos use crack (see Peláez 2019).

Considering people in state and federal prisons by race and ethnicity in 2017, more than 60% of the people in prison were people of color.

Black men are six times as likely to be incarcerated as white men, and Hispanic men are 2.7 times as likely. For black men in their thirties, about one in every 12 is in prison or jail on any given day (The Sentencing Project 2017, 5).

The incarceration rate does not reflect actual rates of use. National evidence on drug use shows that African Americans and whites use illegal drugs at about the same rate. A recent study on "Race and Wrongful Convictions in the United States" revealed that drug crime exonerations are even more racially concentrated: 55% have black defendants and 24% white defendants. Gross, Possley, and Stephens found that African Americans are about five times as likely to go to prison for drug possession as whites, and judging from exonerations, innocent black people are about 12 times more likely to be convicted of drug crimes than innocent white people (2017, 16–17). Few low-level drug convictions result in exoneration, regardless of innocence, because the stakes are too low: In Harris County, Texas, however, there have been 133 exonerations in ordinary drug possession cases in the last few years. These are cases in which defendants pled guilty and were exonerated after routine lab tests showed they were not carrying illegal drugs. Sixty-two percent of the Harris County drug-crime guilty plea exonerees were African American in a county with 20% black residents (ibid., iii, 18–20). Researchers concluded that a key reason for the racial disproportion in convictions of innocent drug defendants was that police enforce drug laws more vigorously against black people than against members of the white majority, despite strong evidence that both groups use drugs at equivalent rates (21). Black people are more frequently stopped, searched, arrested, and convicted, including in cases where they are innocent. The extreme form of this practice is systematic racial profiling in drug law enforcement.

The number of Nigerian diaspora in prison in the United States is unknown. For instance, out of a total population of federal inmates, U.S. nationals top the list of inmates. They are followed by Mexicans, Colombians, Dominicans, and Cubans. Nigerian inmates will increase as federal prosecutors recently made public that 80 people in Los Angeles, and dozens in Atlanta, most of them Nigerians, have been charged in the United States with being part of a widespread conspiracy that stole millions of dollars from businesses and elderly individuals through a variety of scams and laundered the money (Federal Bureau of Prisons 2017; Almasy 2019; Department of Justice U.S. Attorney's Office Northern District of Georgia 2020).

Drug-related offenses and financial scams are among the major reasons why Nigerians are deported. For instance, in June 2018, the U.S. government deported 34 Nigerians over offenses, including drugs, homicide, and fraud (Aliyu 2018). In 2016, the NDLEA received 204 Nigerians, made up of 197 males and 7 females, deported on drug-related offenses from several countries that include Thailand, 43; the United States, 38; China, five; Indonesia, three; the United Kingdom, three; and Brazil, one. In the same year, the antidrug agency confiscated illicit drug money from traffickers of about EUR300,000 and USD90,000 among other currencies (NDLEA 2016/2017, 33).

Of the 229 Nigerians deported from various countries in January 2015 for drug offenses, 37 were from the United States (*Pulse.ng* 2015). Likewise, in the Netherlands, several Nigerians have been extradited to the United States to face charges for crimes committed against U.S. citizens.

Nigeria is now a breeding ground for militant organizations and Islamic terrorist groups. The United States and various international organizations have linked Boko Haram to trafficking cocaine and heroin across West Africa as means for financing their activities. A 2017 UNODC report refers to the trial of members of the organization in Chad that revealed they were involved in the drug trafficking. In November 2009, a Boeing 727 (aka "Mali drug-plane") landed in the middle of the Malian desert. Later when the soldiers arrived, they found the plane empty and burned. The aircraft that took off from Venezuela was loaded with about nine tons of cocaine, valued around USD225 million. U.S. DEA officers believed the cocaine was taken north from Mali and eventually smuggled into Europe through connections with local al-Qaeda barons (Write 2014; Cohen 2019).

Abject poverty—driven by the majority of the population's exclusion from the benefits of their natural resources—is among underlying reasons why the MEND launched some of its most audacious attacks on foreign oil companies and contractors working in the Niger Delta. They claimed responsibility for the double bombing which killed 12 people and wounded dozens during Nigeria's 50th Independence anniversary on October 1, 2010. MEND's leader, Henry Okah, was arrested in SA, convicted and sentenced to 24 years in prison (*Vanguard* 2013). Nigerian terrorism is now a threat inside the United States and the United Kingdom, as well. A federal judge sentenced a 25-year-old Nigerian, Umar Farouk Abdulmutallab, to life in prison for trying to blow up a U.S. airliner bound for Detroit on Christmas Day in 2009 with a bomb hidden in his underwear. In the UK, two British-born converts to Islam were convicted for killing a British soldier who was run over with a car and then stabbed in London on May 22, 2013. Michael Adebolajo and Michael Adebowale were both of Nigerian ancestry and Christian families living in London. Adebolajo will spend life in prison and Adebowale received a sentence of at least 45 years (Smith-Spark et al. 2014).

Ironically, domestic terrorism is an additional reason many Nigerians desperately attempt to enter the United States or the United Kingdom to seek a better life. Illegal aliens from Nigeria constituted almost one-quarter of the total immigrants that crossed the Mediterranean to arrive Italy in 2016 (*Premium Times* 2017), most of them said they were running away from Boko Haram or the Niger Delta crisis. Once in Italy, undocumented Nigerians move to other destinations, including the United States, United Kingdom, and the Netherlands. During fieldwork, many undocumented Nigerians told me that they became drug couriers as a means of reaching their desired destination, and if caught and convicted, life in prison was better than the one they left behind in Nigeria.

7.4 THE NETHERLANDS

The Netherlands is a preferred center for the redistribution of cocaine in Europe. Moreover, the country faces a shortage of police officers due to low salary incentives and declining public image. Nigerian drug traffickers in the Netherlands were also aware that ad hoc police busts are limited and selective because the priority was antiterrorism. As a result, the Netherlands is a one-stop shop for traffickers, serving as a destination, transit, and production country in one, especially in the case of synthetic drugs and cannabis. Authorities in the UK acknowledged the Netherlands is among the major transit countries for cocaine entering the country. British-based organized crime groups have invested abroad, including in the Netherlands, and, in particular, have laundered illicit proceeds elsewhere—both in Europe and beyond (Siddle 2013; Hobbs 1998). Rather than controlling certain regions or certain sectors of the economy, criminal groups use the legal infrastructure and legal commodity and money flows.

As the Netherlands is an important logistical node in Europe, Amsterdam's Schiphol Airport and well the port at Rotterdam act as revolving doors for traffickers. The Netherlands also has several smaller airports and landing strips where almost no inspections take place. This is ideal for cocaine hoppers who wish to move larger quantities across borders. For example, the court in Rotterdam sentenced a former customs officer, Gerrit G., to 14 years in prison for involvement in two drug transports in November 2014 and April 2015 (Boerman et al. 2017). These transports involved a total of 3,400 kilograms of cocaine. In the port of Rotterdam, customs officers, container company staff, and truck drivers have become an essential link in the Dutch established drug trafficking chain. This of course has resulted in allegations of corruption and a number of arrests.

There is criminal phenomenon of 'undermining' in the Netherlands, infiltration of underground world into urban life or the emergence of 'freezones,' as acknowledged by the Dutch police (Politie 2019, EMCDDA 2019, 55). Economic sectors are used to commit or to conceal crimes or to spend criminal proceeds (Kruisbergen et al. 2012). Dutch law enforcement asserted that about 10 tons of cocaine is seized in the Netherlands annually, which represents only 10–15% of the total import and export of the 19 EU member states (Boerman et al. 2017, 40). Traffickers persist in the attractive EU market where about 119 tons of cocaine was consumed in 2017. And the minimum estimated value of the retail market for cocaine in the same year was around EUR9.1 billion. This represents almost a third (31%) of the total illicit market in drugs and makes it the second largest, after cannabis (EMCDDA 2019, 130).

Belgian authorities suspect that some 70–80% of the cocaine trafficked into Antwerp is destined for the Netherlands, where the average consumer price is stabilized at EUR50 per gram and wholesale price of cocaine at about EUR25,000 per kilogram. Navigating an illicit drug market in which the high levels of inelastic demand and high prices create a very lucrative industry, and those involved in extorting or protecting dealers can make substantial sums doing so.

Chapter 8

Controlling International Cocaine Hoppers in Nigeria, Brazil, China, and Indonesia

This chapter focuses on issues regarding curtailing the new trend illicit drug traffickers. It will zoom in on Nigeria where sound antidrug laws exist but not the will and means for effective control. Cocaine hoppers persist in spite of the threat of harsh prison sentences, capital punishment, and police cultures defined by corruption and extortion in Brazil, China, and Indonesia. With no large, organized crime structure, ad hoc drug traffickers rely on indirect actors that the ongoing drug war is unable to control despite costing billions annually.

8.1 PROBLEM OF CONTROLLING NIGERIAN TRAFFICKERS IN NIGERIA

Drug trafficking is illegal in Nigeria. The NDCMP 2015–2019 and the enactment of Decree 48 of 1989 led to the establishment of NDLEA, responsible for controlling prohibited drugs. The Money Laundering Decree No. 3 was enacted in 1995 to monitor laundering of drug trafficking proceeds through financial institutions. The Economic and Financial Crime Act No. 20 led to the establishment of the EFCC. Also, Nigeria's legislation on drug control revolves around the UN International Conventions on drugs. In 2012, NDLEA and the U.S. DEA signed a memorandum of understanding to establish a vetted unit to exclusively work with DEA (INCSR 2014).

These strict measures were meant to reduce illicit drug issues by apprehending, prosecuting, and sentencing drug producers, traffickers, and users. The antidrug agency has intensified efforts of screening Nigerians going to drug source countries before they are given visa. This is to ensure that only persons with legitimate businesses have the opportunity to travel to those

243

countries. These measures legitimize the antidrug control agency but most importantly serve to justify budgets, though no single law enforcement agency has adequate resources to combat the sophisticated international criminal networks operating in the country. The agency has also been applauded for its robust relationship with international partners. NDLEA receives aid in the form of training and equipment from foreign donors including the United States, France, and Germany. And joint projects aimed at the interdiction of illicit flows at selected airports in Africa, Latin America, and the Caribbean have led to significant seizures of drugs, cash, and the enhancement of law enforcement (NDLEA 2018a, b).

The impression is that the war on drugs has made progress in curtailing Nigerian drug trafficking. But many traffickers have evaded control, as cocaine hoppers have demonstrated their capacity to traffic drugs into, through, and within the borders of Nigeria. They show the magnitude of the drug trade and its internationalization that places Nigeria at the very center of one of the most dynamic drug routes in the world. That has resulted in overcrowded prisons in deplorable conditions and corrupt judiciary and law enforcement, among other consequences. Nigeria, like the United States, has committed itself to mass incarceration as one of its main crime control strategies. It is a *penal harm movement*, which advocates helplessness and other stringent measures aimed at punishing offenders, with the hopes of both incapacitating offenders and deterring current and future offenders (Clear 2007). Prisons are not seen as a last resort nor places for rehabilitation. Rather, prisons are now used for all manner of offenders, both serious and minor, where the goal is to deterrence or even revenge. The overarching consequence has led to more people currently behind bars.

8.1.1 Deplorable Prison Conditions

Nigeria's Prison Service noted the total inmate population was about 72,194 prisoners, with 98% being male inmates, as of April 2018. A majority of inmates are awaiting trial, resulting in severe overcrowding in a prison system meant officially for about 50,000. As of June 2014, about 1.7% were juvenile prisoners and approximately 0.3% were foreigners (Institute for Criminal Policy Research; Australian Government DFAT 2018).

Nigeria abolished capital punishment for drug offenders but has not addressed related human right abuses. Prison and detention center conditions remain life threatening; detainees were reportedly subjected to extrajudicial execution, torture, inadequate sanitary conditions, and medical treatment. The U.S. Department of States, Country Reports on Human Rights Practices (2016) noted that prison officials, police, guards, and other security force personnel often denied inmates food and medical treatment to punish them or extort money. The Administration of Criminal Justice Act (2016) provided for alternative sentences other than prison custody, such as community service, parole, and suspended sentences; however, penal and judicial authorities opted not to use alternatives to incarceration for nonviolent offenders. In all, prison overcrowding is a thorn in the flesh which is bedeviling Nigeria.

Connectedly, there is a high rate of recidivism among inmates because prisons lack trained professionals for addressing problematic behaviors of inmates. And despite reforms regarding occupational training, skill acquisition hygiene, and educational opportunities existing on paper, in reality, few if any measures have been taken to implement these reforms.

Acknowledging the inexorable link between sound prison management and the prevention of corruption, experts assessed risks and developed a mitigation plan. Good and practical applications of the Nelson Mandela rules and measure should include: First, improving the integrity of staff (training, codes of conduct, etc.); second, strengthening accountability (detection, investigation, and sanctions); and third, building transparency and oversight through independent monitoring, awareness, and consultation (UNODC 2017b, 26; Penal Reform International 2018, 32).

The Nigerian prison system is in a crisis. Nigeria bragged recently that six "ultramodern" prisons will be opened across the country. But there is little incentive for reform because prisons are big business in Nigeria, generating billions of naira annually. There is gross embezzlement at all levels in Nigeria—billions of dollars meant to fight Boko Haram or pay salaries of civil servants are misappropriated—including from the prison system.

Regarding on inmates convicted for drug offenses, a Nigerian judge stated to me that those who deal in hard drugs should serve their full sentence. Unsurprisingly, wealthy citizens tend to escape incarceration. The state of the Nigerian prisons today is a reflection of the state of criminal justice administration and the country itself. In a prison system where everything has a price tag, rich inmates receive visitors in the offices of very senior prison officials and can even arrange sorties outside the prison walls. The NDLEA once arrested a drug trafficker at Kano airport who had been convicted and sentenced for drug trafficking and was supposed to be in prison, but he, like many others, spent that time anywhere but the prison. Between the court officials and the warders so much can be arranged.

8.1.2 Corrupt Judiciary and Antidrug Enforcement

A dominant view amid Nigerians, during fieldwork, is that it is difficult for citizens to obtain legal redress through the Nigerian court system. A recent research study on Justice Needs and Satisfaction in Nigeria found 72% of Nigerians seek information or advice mainly from their social network, relatives, and friends. Legal aid is largely unavailable, and 10% of problems reach a lawyer. People are inactive in their legal disputes because of negative expectations and financial pressure (Hiil 2018). Nigerian courts are overwhelmed during court proceedings by delays and the unreasonable length of proceedings. Inordinate delays in the prosecution of cases have made litigation a very expensive and tortuous process for victims of human rights abuses and the poor (International Commission of Jurists 2012).

Nigerian courts suffer from significant inefficiency and backlog of cases due to a lack of resources and corruption. For Elechi and Otu (2015), judges in Nigeria operate as an island in the comity of judges worldwide. Yet, Nigerian judges attend overseas trainings and workshops yearly, giving them ample opportunity to update and exchange views with counterparts in various countries. For instance, the Lagos State Judiciary 2017 Judges Retreat in Amsterdam focused on the theme "Preserving Judicial Independence in a Period of national Transformation." It also gave the 61 judges in attendance the chance of interaction with Nigerian judge Osuji (now ICC's president) and colleagues at the International Criminal Court in The Hague. Another series, "Financial Crimes: Money Laundering and Terrorism Workshop for Judges," which I organized for 14 Honorable Federal High Court Judges in Rome in August 2017, focused on organized crime and drug money, as well as changing mentalities to address integrity among Nigerian judges. Similar projects have aimed at criminal justice cooperation and investigation to enhance capacity to effectively counter organized crime along the cocaine route, including Nigeria (Cocaine Route Programme 2020).

Corruption from within is possible because of Nigerian attitudes toward the issue. It is worrisome that one insider told me his desire to be transferred to a major Nigerian city where he could preside on "better cases," such as drug trafficking, that offer greater opportunity for taking bribes to influence judgment. "I need cash to pay school fees for my children, and to purchase electricity power generator so as to work at home," he said (DD, personal communication, March 24, 2018). Most judges write their judgments by hand, and electricity supply failure in the offices and at home is the norm. Yet, Nigeria is blessed with scorching sunlight daily; solar power could power the whole Ministry of Justice edifice and much more. Similarly, in the security and justice sectors, human and financial resources are not commensurate with the demands of Nigerians. One then wonders what a total allocation of N18,269,519,380 as of 2016 meant to the Federal Ministry of Justice (FMOJ Budget, Federal Ministry of Nigeria 2016 Appropriation Act). Nigerian citizens face long delays and receive requests from judicial officials for bribes to expedite cases or to obtain favorable rulings.

Likewise, the NDLEA acknowledge its inefficacy. Several officials told me that Nigeria's prime antidrug control agency suffers from poor logistics and hiring gaps. Nigeria prefers foreign experts over Nigerian experts—likely because of misguided bias. It's the embedded "exclusion game" that underpins kleptocracy and mediocracy in Nigeria. Yet, antidrug control organizations point out that lack of adequate personnel capable of intelligent-led operations and reliable staff are amid the crucial bottlenecks undermining work in Nigeria. As embezzlement reigns, money meant for operations disappear. Persistent corruption and impunity open the flood gates for drug traffickers and other criminals. In illicit drug policing in Nigeria, Udama (2013) wrote that there has been a complex as well as a negotiated relationship between the business of illicit drugs traffickers and the duty of policing drugs.

The response from law enforcement and the CJS has, as a result, became skewed in favor of managing small threats and unable to manage the big ones. Despite strict anti-corruption laws, authorities can point to only a few notable convictions. For instance, the Court of Appeals in Lagos overturned the conviction of Bello Lafiaji, the former chairman of the NDLEA, who was sentenced to 16-year imprisonment for abuse of office and conspiracy involving USD164,000 in drug trafficking money. The appeals court ruled that there was insufficient evidence to convict Lafiaji and, therefore, quashed all charges of fraud and abuse of office against him (see *Street Journal* 2011b). High-level corruption that goes unpunished sends the message that cocaine traffickers can carry on with impunity in Nigeria.

8.2 *NAIJAS* AND BRAZILIAN POLICE CULTURE

Having discussed in chapter 5 the Brazilian reaction to Nigerian cocaine traffickers and the criminal justice response to Nigerian cocaine trafficking, let me highlight briefly that Brazil and Nigeria have much in common, not only in the noticeable difference between rich and poor but also regarding corruption. I observed that in both countries there was a police culture of accepting kickbacks, bribery, and street corruption of collecting money from cocaine traffickers.

In Nigeria, police routinely stopped drivers who had committed no traffic infractions, refusing to allow a car to continue until the driver paid a bribe. If extortion is the unlawful use of one's position or office to obtain money through coercion or threats, then 72% of Nigerians surveyed said corruption has increased considerably over the past two years, and 92% considered police—as an institution—affected by corruption; more than 75% admitted to paying a bribe to the police in the last 12 months (Business Anti-Corruption Portal 2014). Almost all Nigerians believe the police is corrupt, making it the most corrupt institution in Nigeria. Police officers continue to operate with impunity (GAN Business Anti-Corruption Portal 2017a).

The Nigerian police force terrorizes more people than it protects. Ebbe (2012) and Shaw (2003) averred that at its foundation, the National Police Force was intended to only protect the colonial masters who set it up, which underlines its contemporary attitude to policing. The stringency, disdain, and brutality with which most have discharged their duties over the years has worked to harm society and the public confidence in police to enforce law and order. It is a consequence of decades of disregard by military regimes that marginalized the police to prevent competition.

During an in-depth conversation with 10 Nigerian police officers, they told me that they must collect bribes to survive because their salary is insufficient to take care of nuclear and extended families.

Likewise, successful Nigerian cocaine traffickers said that they had the "right" social capital within the police in SP to succeed in the illicit trade. They bought confiscated cocaine from police in Brazil. Nigerian traffickers MNF expressed: "SP is like Nigeria. Regular quality cocaine comes from my good paddies within the *Eke* [Python or police]. They have dream like any other and how could they meet up. I give my guys cash handout even when without giving me market [cocaine]. Apart from maintaining family, the need to maintain their lovers. I invest in the friendship, we help each other" (MNF, personal communication, December 20, 2011).

Many interviewees asserted that their success in the illicit trade is due to the existence of kickbacks and collaboration with police. Like all criminal organizations, international trafficking cannot exist without links to the repressive apparatus of the countries where it operates. Recalling our discussion in chapter 5.5.2, "In the first case, that of Nigerians, these links are limited to corruption. Investigations undoubtedly show that African traffickers have continued (or are still active) because the police are turning a blind eye to their activities," concluded Mingardi (2001) regarding money and the international drug trade in SP. Corrupt payments and more indirect forms of mutual tolerance are used alongside the use of force as bargaining chips. These cycles are shaped by various factors, including the shifting dynamics of illegal markets, criminal organization, and policing tactics (Richmond 2019). For instance, Brazilian authorities apprehended over 115 members of Pure Third Command, Red Command (Brazil's oldest criminal group), and military police officers in connection with laundering BRL1 million (USD250,858). Officers were taking approximately BRL2,000 (USD500,809) to BRL5,000 (USD1,252) a week for trafficking and mediating between police and criminals by negotiating the sale of information, weapons, and drugs (Cengic 2019).

Such collaboration delivers cocaine at somewhat lower than the market price, as the officers want to dispose of seized cocaine quickly. In this regard, the same mechanism that paves the way for successful drug trafficking in

Nigeria or Sub-Saharan Africa also works in Brazil. For this reason, transporting illegal goods by road is seen as less of a risk.

Brazil is known for endemic corruption. Brazilians acknowledge corruption as the flaw that systematically undermines the country's economic development. Luiz Inácio Lula da Silva, former Brazilian president, was jailed for 12 years for corruption. It is a noxious state of affairs in which the establishments supposed to combat corruption are infected with it. This recalls that the military police, trained and organized by the military, police and patrol the streets. The plainclothes civil police are the bureaucratic arm of the public security system. Both forces may arrest suspects caught in the act of committing a crime or pursuant to an arrest warrant issued by a judge (see IBA 2010). Both are vulnerable to corruption.

Mingardi's (2001) work identified the types of relationships between foreign criminal groups involved in drug trafficking and local Brazilian criminal organizations. In this view, Nigerian international cocaine traffickers cannot manage without the cooperation of influential local people, whether they are criminals, state officials, or employees in Brazil or beyond. In 2014, for instance, a shipment of 874 kilograms of cocaine heading to the Democratic Republic of Congo was seized in Paraguay. It belonged to Jorge Rafaat Toumani who was killed in 2017 by the organized crime group PCC (Cohen 2019). In January 2013, Venezuela's antinarcotics authorities arrested six men including four Nigerians for smuggling seven kilograms of cocaine on public transport from Maturin to Delta Amacuro, a notorious departure hub for cocaine from Latin America to West Africa. In 2012, Argentine customs agents confiscated a 530-kilogram cocaine shipment on a cargo plane bound for Nigeria (Pachico 2013). This further demonstrates the borderless activity of Nigerian traffickers and their associates in Latin America.

The same mechanism fostering the success of Latin American cocaine traffickers in Nigeria exists for Nigerian traffickers to exploit in Brazil. In all, I observed that the achievement traffickers resulted from the existence of a police culture accepting of kickbacks, bribery, street corruption, and extortion by unscrupulous law enforcement agents.

8.3 CONTROLLING COCAINE HOPPERS IN CHINA

China is among the countries that still issue capital punishment sentences for drug offenses, though reforms have led to a reduction in the number of death sentences and executions. In fact, Beijing continues its tradition of mass executions for drug traffickers to commemorate the UN International Day against Drug Abuse and Illicit Trafficking each year on June 26 (*Xinhua* 2013). And, as with many policies and events inside China, the number of death row inmates remains a closely guarded state secret. However, cocaine hoppers' activities in China have demonstrated that the death penalty is not an effective deterrence to an embedded societal problem.

8.3.1 Police Street Culture: China Gives, China Takes

Standing opposite Tong Tong shopping mall while chatting with one respondent, Osina, in April 2012, about eight undercover police apprehended Africans on the street and inside the McDonald's restaurant in the mall. While Nigerians and other Africans without valid documents fled the scene, Osina did not because he is a legal alien in China. He called friends to alert them of the raid so that people could stay inside their stores or hide. While stopping and searching individuals, police asked for passports and visas; those who could not present their documents were sent to the police office. Two African women were apprehended. One Nigerian escaped from the McDonald's restaurant by jumping the steps. Thereafter, I inquired what the problem was from a police officer rushing to join his colleagues. He replied, "Nigeria man problem, visa finish, drug!" (Officer, personal communication, April 26, 2012). These are the generalities and stereotypes believed by many Chinese police. However, as ex-inmate interviewee KK stated, a raid by Guangzhou police in the Yuexiu District in August 2013 resulted in the arrest of 168 Nigerians suspected of drug trafficking and illegal overstay, but "several individuals detained had nothing to do with drug trafficking" (KK, personal communication, December 6, 2014). Despite targeting real offenders, normal traders could become victims of unscrupulous law enforcement agents. Aki, who rented a store in the market through his Chinese associates for CNY2,000 per month added: "Though few bad apples among us engaged in drugs and all that, majority of us are good. These guys should stop raiding everybody for God's sake. These days, they stop cars to check and arrest Nigerians, despite Nigerian community's efforts to prevent crimes among Nigerian and achieving good results. They just take money from us. Oh Nigerians! What prisoners we are! First our so-called leaders lash all sorts of violations and hold us as prisoners in the country, and now Chinese also treat us the way they want" (Aki, personal communication, May 21, 2011).

Aki's dismay is common among Nigerians. Chaki, another trader, stated:

> I ran way when I saw them coming even if my visa is still valid for one month. Some of them are false. They are making money from us by asking for immediate settlement. Some will arrest you even though you have visa. They will tell you, "China give, China takes." They will find one way or the other to take you away and ask you pay before getting to the office. Threatening your visa will not be renewed and claiming that you could be selling drugs, you are put under

pressure to negotiate settlement with them. Then they will ask you to call your friends to bring money. Even one of them gave me his telephone to call my friend with. I paid CNY3,000 to free myself. On the way back, I was rearrested by another group of undercover police and had to pay another CNY2,500 after they refused to set me free. This is China, sometimes worse than in Nigeria (Chaki, personal communication, April 27, 2012).

Chaki's claim is not unique. If an overstaying trader is caught, he will often attempt to bribe the policeman, sometimes to no avail (Mathews and Yang 2012, 113). This implies that life for Africans is becoming more complicated. A sense of fascination with the newcomers has given way to instances of racism, police harassment, and an increasingly stringent and corrupt visa system that has contributed to a rise in illegal immigrants. Whereas entry visas are easier to get in Nigeria, a combination of tighter regulations and corruption has made visa renewals more difficult and expensive in China. Most Nigerians asserted that Chinese agents and middlemen ask commission that has inflated the cost of renewals to about CNY35,000 or USD5,000. Many limited their movement to and from their shops due to the uneven and arbitrarily implemented legal framework concerning immigrants in China, which created opportunities for corruption. Solicitations for money from police on or off duty who checked passports and visas were a common nuisance (Haugen 2012). In this regard, events happening in China evoke incidents that go beyond corruption in Malaysia, Brazil, or China, and these claims are not only made by Nigerians, "Regularly the police would do 'passport sweeps' checking all foreigners' passports. In practice, they checked mostly people with dark skin. Same thing with urine tests in clubs. It was clearly racist" (KK, personal communication, November 29, 2014).

In another incident, police raided and arrested a trader in Canal Market in Sanyuanli area. A crowd of Nigerian traders confronted them and rescued the handcuffed boy. Whereas some suggested taking him to Nanhai to cut the handcuffs off, others preferred he be taken to the Nigerian community representative who pleaded with them to stop fighting the police. He suggested instead that they should have paid the fine or allowed the boy to be taken to the police station as required by law. Didi rebuffed this, pointing out the double standard for Chinese living in Nigeria: "The irony is Chinese have spoiled business for our people at home. They also own shops in the markets in Nigeria. If a trader brings moving sample of goods and orders a quantity, Chinese sends five container loads of the same to his partner in Nigeria, who will then sell the item cheaper. Thereby displacing even those coming to buy here. This is why Nigerians raise their voices" (Didi, personal communication, November 29, 2010).

Chinese media reported that around 70 of the 100 Chinese citizens arrested for living or doing business in Nigeria illegally have been released after negotiation with the Nigerian authorities. In the course of their repatriation, the

Chinese embassy urged an estimated 20,000 Chinese citizens residing in the country to become more integrated into Nigerian society by observing local laws and communicating more with local people (*China Daily* 2012).

8.3.2 Corruption: Two to Tango

I observed three Nigerians having a dispute over money one evening close to Huanshi Dong Lu in Guangzhou. While a fourth man was trying to mediate, I heard one of them saying loudly to two others about to step into a three-wheel taxi, "I will show you that I am a street guy. Share the money and 'market' alone. Guys will deal with you in KL," he warned before leaving. The fourth man stated to me: I just tried to stop them from fighting. They are a disgrace to us all. I do not know them; otherwise, I could report them to the Nigerian community for fighting on the street. I think the dispute was about sharing drug money, as you must have heard, too. The other one told me that they were renting a flat together, which they lost because they could not pay the rent. They were almost busting each other here, and I do want that to happen in my presence (Ata, personal communication, May 25, 2011).

It's a familiar situation. Dealings in "street pharmaceuticals" by Nigerian international cocaine traffickers are common knowledge. Interviewees, Ping and Lee, told me that while in Guangzhou with their European visitors, Nigerian drug traffickers approached them asking if they wanted drugs—cocaine, ecstasy, or marijuana. I heard similar stories from English and German tourists I met in Guangzhou during fieldwork. Responding to an article about Chinese drug addicts in Shenzhen, commenter Mao420 noted: "Every night Nigerians are selling all kind of drugs opposite Garden Hotel in front of policemen. I have seen with my own eye. They openly ask any foreigner on the street. Someone should go and make a blog about this. I asked one Nigerian how he manages to sell his drugs without police interference; he said 'they get their cut'. So, it is always the police who are the culprit. Why don't they get executed?" (Fauna 2011).

China is no exception regarding endemic corruption and embezzlement. In 2011, the People's Bank of China reported that close to 18,000 public officials had embezzled and smuggled abroad almost CNY800 billion (USD125 billion at the time) between the mid-1990s and 2008 (UNHCR 2012). And just as in Nigeria and Brazil, organized crime in China, including drug trafficking and corruption, has attracted international attention and publications. A number of sources pointed to links between organized crime groups and local government public servants, criminal justice officials, and police in China (Dwyer 2020; Wike et al. 2016; Lo and Kwok 2012; Broadhurst 2012; Stratfor 2008). Official corruption is a major concern. President Xi Jinping's anti-corruption efforts led to the arrests of many Communist Party officials, accused of corruption. About half (49%) the Chinese public stated corrupt officials were a very big problem in the country, while another 34% believed they were a moderately big issue (Wike et al. 2016).

Organized crime was embedded in Shanghai already in the early twentieth century when the city's leaders were the police chief and director of the office in charge of confiscating opium (Stratfor Global Intelligence 2008). Because organized criminals use bribery or threats to entice government officials to partake in syndicate activities or to obtain protection from them to take control of a particular trade amid other interests. The result is the existence of a "protective umbrella," through which criminal syndicates connect with officials and offer them luxurious gifts, including overseas travel and simple bribery in exchange for protection in legal and illegal business activities. Because of the absence of the rule of law and corruption, protective umbrellas have developed rapidly alongside China's booming economy (Siegel and van de Bunt 2012). This hinders anticrime efforts as the patron-client networks connect high-ranking police officers, local officers, and court judges with criminal elements (see Shiu-Hing Lo 2009; Broadhurst 2012). At the highest level of political corruption is the practice known as *maiguan maiguan*, or the selling of government posts to criminals or action by government officials to protect criminals. Because organized crime has a grip on local politics in China and because local politics control law enforcement and communication to higher-ups in the Chinese bureaucracy, the central government has found it difficult to crack down on criminal groups. This is compounded by the principle of *guanxi*, a standard in Chinese culture that puts personal relationships and commitments above everything else, including the law. It is defined as the "personal relationship and reciprocal obligation developed through a particular social network" (Lo 2010, 853). In Williams and Godson's (2002) view, guanxi relationships "provide a basis for the global activities of Chinese criminals" (330). Similar to its counterparts in Nigeria or Brazil, the Chinese justice system is not immune to reform shortcomings within the public security bureau and the police, which could undermine its work.

The vast power enjoyed by regional and local public security forces stems partly from the official Communist Party's policy of encouraging decentralized control over the police—a practice rooted in Mao Zedong's directive that security work must emphasize party leadership and accept direct leadership by party committees (see Tanner and Green 2007). Although the *tiao-kuai* system theoretically vests vertical (*tiao*) power in higher level public security administrative bodies, superior police departments one level up are only permitted to assist local governments by making suggestions that officials are supposed to consider. Public security departments are strictly bound by horizontal (*kuai*) power exercised by party committees. Consequently, the central government has less control over local police forces than it does over other administrative agencies governed by binding vertical (*tiao*) power. The reality of public security officials serving almost parallel to powerful government officials exacerbates problems of accountability further (Wu and Goodrich 2014).

Observers point out that it would be unrealistic to ask the government to spend all its money on drug enforcement activities. Nationwide, about 17,000 police officers are assigned to drug enforcement details. Each provincial police agency typically has its own drug enforcement division, and so do most large municipal or county police agencies. Small county police agencies normally fold their drug enforcement functions into their criminal investigation divisions. However, regarding official corruption in drug enforcement, Chinese officials acknowledged its share of the problem, but said that in comparison to other developing countries, particularly those in Latin America, China is running a relatively clean operation (Chin and Zhang 2007). For instance, Chinese authorities punished more than 210,000 officials for corruption in the first half of 2017, according to the Communist Party's corruption watchdog. This included 38 senior officials from ministries and provincial administrations and more than 1,000 at the prefecture levels. Former Interpol president, head of the China Coast Guard, and vice minister of public security was sentenced to 13-year imprisonment for corruption. Meng Hongwei pleaded guilty to using his position to solicit more than USD2 million in bribes between 2005 and 2017 (Dwyer 2020).

But the Chinese belief in moral order is based on the concept that human nature is essentially good and that most people can be changed by education. This key emphasis in the Chinese justice system is placed on rehabilitation and reeducation of offenders for offenses that undermine social order and morality such as using narcotic drugs (Li 2010). The Chinese philosophy of rehabilitation is based on the idea that order is inherent in the process of existence itself: that which causes and that which is caused are not finally distinguished (Hall and Ames 1995). Therefore, the justice system integrated education and re-indoctrination of the offender into the sanctioning phase. However, the emphasis on rehabilitation in China does not impede severe punishment for extremely serious offenders. Harsh penalties are seen as justified for these offenders because their crimes have damaged social cohesiveness and collective interests of society (Jiao 2001). "Presently, there are more than 500 Nigerians serving jail terms for drug trafficking and over 200 languishing in jail for illegal residence in China," stated one Nigerian Envoy in China (Anyagafu 2017). However, cocaine hoppers demonstrate dark numbers are endemic to illicit activities, and China is no exception.

China is controlling drug trafficking; however, corruption and the street culture of unscrupulous police officers undermines control and enhances the illicit trade. China's huge population, a rising wealthy middle class, growing drug consumption, and above all illegal drug trade estimated at billions of dollars make China an attractive market for traffickers.

8.4 CONTROLLING COCAINE HOPPERS IN INDONESIA

Drug trafficking is illegal in Indonesia, and offenders are severely punished. The paradox is Indonesian drug laws are among the strictest in SEA; yet the use of illegal drugs is relatively high in some parts of the country. Like its neighbors in the GT, lack of resources undermines efforts by the Indonesian antinarcotics agency, BNN, to monitor the country's extensive coastline border.

Indonesia's laws regarding narcotics aim to eradicate illicit drug trafficking, help drug abusers, and promote drug use for therapeutic and scientific purposes. Possessing small amounts of some illicit drugs that are legal in other countries can lead to lengthy sentences and expensive fines, and penalties increase rapidly with the quantity of narcotics one possesses. Punishment for trafficking drugs is extremely severe: five to 15 years and fines of IDR 10 billion (USD716,000) even for small amounts and the death penalty for quantities exceeding allowed quantities (Aquino 2017; Silvestrini 2014). For example, in January 2015, Indonesia executed several Nigerians for alleged drug offenses. Among them, 50-year-old Martin Anderson, accused of being part of a local drug ring, was arrested for possessing about 1.8 ounces (about 0.05 kilograms) of heroin (Ezeamalu 2017). The wife of another said that a judge offered to sentence him to prison rather than death if he paid a bribe of 200 million Rupiah (then about USD22,000), but since he was only a courier, he did not have the money for the bribe.

In Indonesia, unlike in Malaysia, capital punishment for drug-related offenses is based on case-specific circumstances and the judges' opinions. For example, a 14-year-old Australian boy arrested at Komang salon in South Bali for possessing 3.6 grams of marijuana was sentenced to only two months in prison, despite the fact that the maximum penalty for the amount he possessed could have been several years (Marcus 2011). The judges recognized the teenager's age as a mitigating circumstance and allowed for a shorter sentence. However, this fluidity in the law creates opportunities for corruption within the law enforcement and the judiciary, as we shall see later.

Nigerian drug traffickers recognize that, while Indonesia's antinarcotics laws are harsh, business is possible because Indonesia is like Nigeria insofar as it suffers from endemic corruption. But despite the involvement of elites, law enforcement officials, and judges in the illicit narcotics trade, Indonesian authorities often choose to make an example of foreign drug offenders in their jurisdictions. Prisons across the country housing Nigerians and other foreigners are proof of this.

8.4.1 Kill to Deter?

Article 6(2) of the International Covenant on Civil and Political Rights (ICCPR) acknowledged abolishing the death penalty worldwide and that it may be imposed only for the most serious crimes. The term most serious remains controversial across all countries due to social, religious, and political culture; however, the international bodies have agreed that they tend to limit capital punishment to intentional crimes with deadly outcomes (e.g., homicide), evoking an implicit consensus that the meaning of most serious under ICCPR is restricted to crimes that directly result in the loss of life (Leechaianan and Longmire 2013). Still, the lack of a definitive statement regarding what constitutes the most serious crimes makes it difficult to determine if drug trafficking falls within the category. This has led to arbitrary application of the death penalty and gross human right violations in countries that retain the death penalty—even though it does not deter drug crimes, nor does it protect people from drug abuse.

On June 26, 2008, two Nigerians were killed by firing squad to mark the UN International Day against Drug Abuse and Illicit Trafficking. One interviewee described the event as follows, "When the time comes, after any final wishes have been granted, the prisoner is taken to a field to stand in front of 12 gunmen. A single shot is fired from each rifle, carefully aimed at the chest. If that does not kill the prisoner, the commander will fire a point-blank shot to the head" (Gelling 2008). This was how it went for Samuel I. Okoye and Hansen A. Nwaliosa and many others killed recently. Indonesia's president Joko Widodo has instructed law enforcement officers to shoot drug traffickers, "Be firm, especially to foreign drug dealers who enter the country and resist arrest. Shoot them because we indeed are in a narcotics emergency position now" (Reuters 2017a).

Capital punishment for drug offenders appears to have been introduced with little consideration for other threats to the social or moral fabric of the country, such as the lack of fair trials, the risk of executing the innocent, and different standards for serious crimes across borders (Amnesty International 1995). For example, the amount of heroin possession triggering the death penalty in Singapore is 15 grams of pure heroin (equivalent to 750 grams of normal heroin). This compares with 15 grams of normal heroin in Malaysia and 20 grams of normal heroin in Thailand. Furthermore, 200 grams of cannabis can trigger the death penalty in Malaysia, compared to 500 grams in Singapore. Since a capital drug crime in one country might only be a minor offense in another country, the absence of consistency among retentionist countries in the amounts of illicit drugs that trigger the death penalty leaves a questionable definition of whether drug trafficking and related offenses are legitimately considered to be among the most serious crimes. Not only does this disparity weaken any potential utilitarian purpose for the use of the death penalty, but it also demonstrates the arbitrary nature of any policy considering drug offenses among the list of the most serious crimes (Leechaianan and Longmire 2013; Lines 2007). The death penalty as a sanction in drug-related cases is especially abhorrent in countries that cannot guarantee a fair trial. In Indonesia and Malaysia, international standards and safeguards for fair trials have been diminished for suspected drug offenders, which has resulted in offenders being wrongly sentenced and executed as a result of false accusations. Moreover, foreign nationals may not be familiar with the laws of the country where they are tried, and they will have difficulty understanding the charges against them or participating in the proceedings if facilities for interpretation are inadequate. For instance, Humphrey Jefferson Ejike ("Jeff") was convicted and sentenced to death in 2004 for a drug trafficking offense. He was not allowed access to a lawyer for five months—including during his arrest, interrogation, and detention—in a clear breach of international law, as well as Indonesia's own Criminal Procedure Code. Jeff, like several others, asserted that he was repeatedly beaten during interrogation and threatened with being shot if he refused to sign papers "confessing" to possession of heroin or if he refused to implicate others. According to his legal team, Jeff was unjustly killed. Raynov Tumorang stated, "The government does not respect the ongoing legal process on Jeff's case. . . . There is strong evidence of torture, and he was not given a fair trial. Racism towards our client can be seen in the court decision" (IANS Jakarta 2016). A U.S. study showed that white people on death row were more likely to have their sentences commuted than blacks. For both groups, those who had private counsel, who devoted more attention and energy to client's cases, were more likely to have their executions commuted than condemned persons defended by court-appointed attorneys (Wolfgang, Kelly and Nolde 1969, 309). National Academy of Sciences reported "a conservative estimate of the proportion of false conviction among death sentences in the United States" was 4.1% (Gross, Barbara, Chen and Edward 2014).

African Americans are only 13% of the American population but make up a majority of innocent defendants wrongfully convicted of crimes and later exonerated. Researching racial disparity for three types of crime that produce the largest numbers of exonerations in the Registry—murder, sexual assault, and drug crimes—Gross et al. (2017) found that African Americans constitute 47% of the 1,900 exonerations listed in the National Registry of Exonerations (as of October 2016), and the great majority of more than 1,800 additional innocent defendants who were framed and convicted of

crimes in 15 large-scale police scandals and later cleared in "group exonerations." This supports Agozino's (1997) claims of Victimization-As-Mere-
Punishment and Victimization-In-Punishment. The key point of VAMP is
not the uncomplicated one that the CJS makes mistake, but the critical one
that the system also institutionally violates the right of some people due
to the ways that power relations are structured within the system (12, 157,
162). Equally known as over-criminalization or excessive punishment relative to the nature of the offence, VIP (14, 159) recall imprisonment of some
convicts for offenses that other defendants with similar or severe previous
records could get noncustodial sentences or shorter jail sentences, get better
treatment in prison, and the militarized policing of certain groups of suspects when other groups engaged in similar activities could be more civilly
policed. As demonstrated on January 6, 2021, predominantly white rioters,
supporters of Trump, stormed the U.S. Capitol in Washington with ease. "If
Rioters were Black, 'Hundreds' Would have Been killed" (Bose and Brice
2021).

Dark numbers imply that we don't know the number of false criminal
convictions, for murder or any other crime. Most remain hidden—false convictions far outnumber exonerations—and we have too little information to
estimate that hidden figure (Gross et al. 2014).

In Indonesia, likewise, recent evidence uncovered by the ombudsman
of maladministration showed the government denied the legal rights of the
executed Humphrey Jefferson Ejike (Reuters 2017b; Amnesty International
2018).

Furthermore, increasing the severity of penalties tends to drive up drug
prices, playing into the hands of organized crime and hardened criminals
seeking greater profit and unafraid of violence in pursuit of it. Endemic corruption in Indonesia has meant that drug couriers or drug users are put to
death while those higher up in trafficking operations avoid apprehension and
punishment, often through the use of bribery. In 2002, police busted Iwan
Thalib, a notorious Bali drug dealer, and found 80,000 ecstasy tablets, 600
grams of cocaine, one kilogram of heroin, and various machines that linked
Thalib to running an ecstasy factory from his home (Silvestrini 2014, 9).
Iwan Thalib paid his way to a shorter sentence: "the police who executed the
raid on his house halved the number of pills they reported found, and another
cut of cash caused the drugs manufacturing charges to be dropped". He
avoided the death penalty and was sentenced to 13 years for drug possession,
whereas the more unfortunate Nigerian, Emmanuel, was the first person to be
sentenced to death for drug charges in Bali after he was found carrying 400
grams of heroin at Denpasar's Ngurah Rai International Airport. Emmanuel
had been caught with less than a quarter of the drugs Iwan Thalib was found
with, but because he lacked money for bribes, he received the death sentence.

Despite the reality that the death penalty does not work as a deterrent, a majority of Indonesians still believe the opposite. Retribution and deterrence are the principal justifications for capital punishment given in any survey of popular opinion about the death penalty (Hodgkinson et al. 2010). A survey found that majority of Indonesians support the death penalty for drug offenses, believe that drugs "destroy the young generation," and that the punishment has a deterrent effect (Simandjuntak 2015). This attitude stems in part from media representations and government statements that lead the public to think of drugs as a problem originating outside of Indonesia and brought into the country by foreigners, portraying Indonesian drug users as victims of foreign perpetrators. The portrayal of the death penalty as a struggle against foreign influence seemed to have helped in consolidating support for capital punishment among Indonesians, reinforced by expressions such as "war against drugs" and "foreign negative influence" (ibid., 7).

Retentionist countries usually justify the use of practices that do not fully follow the international human rights norms through the notion of cultural relativism. Originating in the field of anthropology, cultural relativism is used in international law to describe a "cultural chasm" in which irreconcilable differences preclude the pervasive realization of substantive international law and morality. It implies that different cultures have different traditions; thus, each culture's human rights traditions are valid because they should be judged according to the culture from which they have sprung, and not according to western-derived, international law norms (Wyman 1997; Sinha 1996). Asian and Islamic governments and the like, stung by criticism of their human rights practices—like the use of capital punishment for drug trafficking crimes—have been quick to adopt cultural relativism as their rationale for not fully implementing international human rights norms.

Appraisable capital punishment has been designated an "alternative sentence" in the Criminal Code revision bill currently awaiting passage in the Indonesian House of Representatives. Article 89 of the bill states, "The death penalty will be imposed as an alternative and as a last resort to protect society" (Anti-Death Penalty Asia Network 2018). Hopefully, convicts who receive the death penalty will be given a 10-year probation period, after which their sentence may be commuted to a life sentence or to a 20-year prison sentence at the discretion of the law and human rights minister.

8.4.2 Graft: A Fight

In Indonesia as in Nigeria, corruption is the norm, not the exception. Holloway (2008) noted that like with many things in Indonesia, surface impressions conceal a much more complex world beneath the surface. Numerous lawyers, judges, businessmen, and politicians have been charged with corruption;

even Corruption Court judges are charged with corruption. The Law on Eradication of Criminal Acts of Corruption criminalizes major acts of corruption. Giving or accepting a bribe is a criminal act punishable by a fine of up to USD110,000 and imprisonment of up to 20 years. Embezzlement, failure to report corrupt activities, and gifts to public officials are punishable by Indonesia's Criminal Code. But poorly enforced corruption legislation results in widespread corruption, as confirmed by Transparency International (2017) and GAN Business Anti-Corruption Portal (2017b). While formally independent, Indonesia's judiciary is rife with corruption and is subject to political influence; bribes are taken at all levels of the judiciary, including in court verdicts and appeal courts.

The *Jakarta Post* reported a Constitutional Court chief justice, Akil Mochtar, was charged with accepting bribe in exchange for fixing a court ruling (2013). Law enforcement confiscated cash in the form of Singapore and U.S. dollars, worth about Rupiahs three billion (USD267,000) from Mochtar's house, and marijuana and ecstasy pills in his office at the Constitutional Court. Mochtar was later confronted with his own words regarding the need to cut the fingers off corruption convicts off for a maximum deterrent effect; Mochtar lost his temper and slapped the journalist who confronted him this way. In 2014, Mochtar was found guilty and received a life sentence for corruption (*Indonesia Investments* 2016). Arrests such as this are not uncommon.

The Corruption Eradication Commission (KPK) makes its decisions on who to investigate and which investigations to prosecute. It is also true that part of the KPK investigators came from the Indonesian National Police, which is one of the most corrupt government bodies in Indonesia (Kouwagam 2013). The Indonesian police are plagued by corruption, and bribery is widespread. Police officers solicit bribes on every level, ranging from traffic violations to criminal investigations. In a survey conducted in 2017, two out of five people in Indonesia perceived most or all of the police to be corrupt, and one in four Indonesians reported having paid a bribe to the police services in the previous 12 months (Global Corruption Barometer 2017).

Many interviewees during fieldwork felt that Nigerians were singled out by the KPK. Rumor spread fast in the diaspora that Alpha, a trafficker, was arrested at his apartment in Depok during a raid by immigration officers. In the process, they confiscated methamphetamine and marijuana estimated at about USD450,000 (N104 million). Friends were relieved when Alpha was sentenced in 2015 to life imprisonment, despite the prosecution's push for the death sentence. Some said that friends had contributed enough money for paying kickbacks to save his life. But in dramatic turn of events, the chief prosecutor considered mounting appeal to obtain the death sentence against Alpha. Law enforcement and the judiciary are increasingly obstinate in the pursuit of justice, or more likely, kickbacks: Foreign affluent recreational users in Bali had thought that if arrested with a small quantity of drugs, they could buy a "get out of jail free card" for few thousand U.S. dollars. "Now, if caught with a joint or few ecstasy pills at home, the fee to avoid the problem leaving your lounge room had jumped to between USD$30,000 and USD$50,000. Police, average wage was less than USD$200 a month, were winning the lottery just by kicking in doors" (Bonella 2012, 224).

As a result, prisons are overcrowded as minor offenders are unable to bribe their way out of jail time. At the start of 2017, there was a reported total prison population of about 210,682 inmates in Indonesia in prison system meant with an official capacity designed for almost half that, noted World Prison Brief's Indonesia data (WPB 2018). One such prison, Kerobokan, colloquially known as Hotel K, holds up to 1,315 local and foreign prisoners, crammed into a correctional facility designed for 350 inmates. There, more than 60% of the inmates are incarcerated for drug offenses (Coconuts Bali 2020; Neubauer 2017). Corrupt prison staff provide wealthier inmates with drugs, outings, prostitutes, escort them on daytime excursions to Bali's beaches, and even assist in escapes; those who cannot grease the palms of prison staff are often exploited and mistreated. Prison guards extort money from inmates for basic services and family visits. Overcrowded prisons, poor hygiene, and ventilation problems lead to various infectious diseases and in some cases, death according to the U.S. Department of State's Indonesia 2017 Human Rights Report (2017). Indonesia lacks an adequate number of professional officers, and overcrowding results in almost 90% of Indonesians convicted of a felony offense being sent to prison, as opposed to being given a suspended sentence or fine. Furthermore, the trend grows because, as Indonesian criminologist, Adrianus Meliala, said, "The punitive attitude among Indonesian society is high, and judges follow that" (*The Jakarta Post* 2018).

8.5 COST OF ENFORCEMENT

The war on drugs is an expensive operation. The direct costs in some countries include not just ordinary policing but extensive military and paramilitary operations. The arrest, detention, criminal justice processing, and incarceration of millions of persons each year, including people charged with minor, nonviolent drug infractions, are very costly to national and subnational budgets. Some suggested that pursuing a "drug-free society," which remains the stated goal of drug policy in many countries, and enforcing global prohibition costs at least USD100 billion yearly. And far from eliminating use, supply, and production, as many as 250 million people used drugs worldwide in 2015, contributing to a global market with a conservative annual turnover of above USD300 billion contemporarily (UNODC 2017; Mejía and Csete 2016). In the United States, for instance, data from the National Drug Control Strategy Reports showed the total expenditure on drug law enforcement by the United States has been estimated at over USD1 trillion over the last 40 years (Lyman 2017). In the UK, the key focus of enforcement is to reduce crime and restrict availability. A formal review noted the strategy did nothing of the sort, has no prospect of doing so, and in crucial respects, actually made things worse. Yet, the UK government spends GBP1.6 billion a year enforcing drug laws with little effect on street prices or availability, all the while fueling drug market violence, and harming the young and vulnerable through criminalizing them (Cowburn 2017).

8.5.1 Win-win

Beneficiaries of the illicit international drug trade and the war on drugs include drug barons, law enforcements, politicians, and the private sector. The influx of cash has helped create an opaque security industry open to corruption at every level. As a result, what is considered a crime is increasingly determined more by corporate and political interests than any sense of morality or ethics.

Politicians, of course, benefit from appearing "tough on crime." Intractable adversities such as poverty, marginality, deprivation, alienation, and ethnic tensions can conveniently be attributed to drugs as an alien evil. Applying U.S. Bureau of Justice Statistics' data from 2002 through 2014, Rabuy and Kopf (2015) show the commonality of low incomes of incarcerated prisoners before they were locked up. They pinpoint that the U.S. prison system is overcrowded with people who have been shut out of the economy and who had neither a quality education nor access to good jobs. In 2014 dollars, the incarcerated had a median yearly income of USD19,185 before their incarceration, which is 41% less than nonincarcerated people of similar ages.

"Our society has, in the name of being tough on crime, made a series of policy choices that have fueled a cycle of poverty and incarceration. We send large numbers of people with low levels of education and low skills to prison, and then when they leave just as penniless as they were when they went in, we expect them to bear the burden of legally acceptable employment discrimination" (ibid. 2015).

Connectedly, the United States has become a nation consumed with anxiety, worried about terrorism, rogue countries, Muslims, Mexicans, and Nigerian immigrants (Zakaria 2008). Since crime became public enemy number one in the 1960s, successive governments, perhaps with the exception of Jimmy Carter's administration, the wars on crime and drugs have sacrificed once-sacred civil liberties (Reiman and Leighton 2017, 12–20). Today, nearly

2.5 million Americans live behind prison bars while tens of millions more live in gated communities (Dilulio 2010). In the past 80 years, nearly every political persuasion and type of government has endorsed drug prohibition (Levine 2002). Why?

In the twentieth century, drug prohibition spread from the United States to every country in the world, for a number of reasons. First, drug prohibition spread so successfully because of the enormous economic, political, and military power of the United States. Second, many different kinds of governments throughout the world supported drug prohibition because they found that police and military resources marshaled on behalf of drug prohibition could be used for many nondrug-related activities. Third, drug prohibition also gained substantial popular support in many countries because drug demonization crusades and antidrug ideology were rhetorically, politically, and even financially useful to many politicians, the media, schools, the police, the military, religious institutions, and some elements of the medical profession. Fourth, the spread of drug prohibition was aided by the twentieth century's romantic or utopian ideologies about coercive state power, making the fight against "drugs" the one topic on which politicians of all stripes could usually agree. Finally, drug prohibition gained great legitimacy throughout the world because it was seen as a UN project. All forms of drug prohibition, from the most criminalized to the most decriminalized, probably have involved at least some explicit drug demonizing. In general, drug demonization and drug prohibition reinforce each other (Levine 2002, 172).

Despite the United States' investment of billions of dollars to improve security and stability in Colombia, the country remains the dominant producer of cocaine and in the DEA's National Drug Threat Assessment for 2017 is the primary source of seized in the United States (Beittel 2017). In many ways, the drug war subsidizes drug production and distribution. Narcoterrorism, violence perpetrated by drug traffickers to protect and advance their economic interests, often in cooperation with terrorist organizations, is big business. Estimating how much money involved is difficult; however, recent data suggests the illegal, armed groups, the FARC and Bacrim, in the great majority of cases sell cocaine at a range between USD2,300 and USD3,000 per kilogram, contributing to an estimated market value of cocaine produced in Colombia of about USD820 million or nearly 0.2% GDP (Gaviria and Mejia 2016; Ramírez 2017). In Nigeria, many disenfranchised youths have joined Niger Delta militants or Boko Haram, which use illicit drug proceeds to finance terror in Nigeria. They have reportedly helped drug traffickers to smuggle heroin and cocaine across West Africa, and arrested members admitted in court they were regularly involved in the trafficking in and consumption.

Another beneficiary of illicit drug trafficking is law enforcement that receives tax money to fight traffickers. This creates a staggering footing in which the "good guys" and the "bad guys" have a mutual interest in guarding the state of affairs. In New York City, the crack scare that so gripped the press in the 1980s came to a swift end once police had been granted the resources to take back the city's streets. That done, the coverage of drug use and drug markets became onerous and unhelpful. After that, then mayor Rudy Giuliani adopted a policy of withholding information about drug-related homicides and counterdrugs operations from the press, and drug stories fell off the front pages. Feiling (2009) noted that if cocaine is no longer the cause for concern it once was, it is because the ritual punishment of the guilty is complete, the government has run out of ideas to curtail the supply of cocaine, and too many people like things the way they are.

Because the prison systems of many countries are profit-making enterprises—from building and staffing prisons to security systems to medical record keeping and psychiatric counseling—there is a strong incentive to fill them and keep them filled. In fact, private prisons and elements of the "criminal justice industrial complex" make money from the system as it is, so they consciously lobby to protect and improve their profits. According to the National Academy of Science on incarceration:

> "By the mid-1990s, the economic interests—including private prison companies, prison guards' union, and the suppliers of everything from bonds for new prison construction to Taser stun guns—were playing an important role in maintaining and sustaining the incarceration increase"(Travis, Western and Redburn 2014, 126).

In the United States, for instance, the number of people jailed on drug charges has skyrocketed since the 1980s, and over 2.3 million people are incarcerated in U.S. prisons and jails. Considering people in state and federal prisons, by race and ethnicity, in 2015, more than 60% of the people in prison today are people of color (see Wagner and Rabuy 2017b). At year-end 2019, there were 1,096 sentenced black prisoners per 100,000 black residents, 525 sentenced Hispanic prisoners per 100,000 Hispanic residents, and 214 sentenced white prisoners per 100,000 white residents in the United States (Carson 2019).

The face in the criminal justice's carnival mirror is often a black face. It's an image that dates back decades. Drawing from Lombroso's theory of the born criminal, Albert Hooton (1939) was looking for biological basis of criminology. He analyzed 17,000 people in the United States to determine if they had any of the 125 characteristics that supposedly disposed people to criminality. He suggested that it is desirable to control "the progress of human evolution by breeding better types and by the ruthless elimination of the inferior types, if only we are willing to found and to practice a science of human genetics" (cited in Barkan 1992, 106–107). In this vein, the Nazis, and many states in America with the support of the Supreme Court, forcibly sterilized tens of thousands of citizens who were deemed feeble-minded (Agozino 2003, 34). Retired police chief, Anthony Bouze's *How to Stop Crime* stated, "Crime is mostly a black and poor young man's game" (1993, 57). A 1995 survey asked respondents to "close your eyes for a second, envision a drug user and describe the person. Ninety-five percent pictured someone black," noted Alexander Michelle's *The New Jim Crow* (2012, 160).

Data on racial discrimination in sentencing elucidates such prejudices. Reiman and Leighton (2017, 67), citing U.S. Uniform Crime Report 1974 in which black people made up 11.4% of the population but accounted for 34.2% of arrests for Index crimes, noted that the typical criminal, to start with, a *he*. Of the 8.8 million people arrested for crimes in 2014, 73% were males, and 80% of those apprehended for violent crime were men. Next, *he* is young. Thirty-six percent of men arrested for crimes were under 25 years old, and the same applies to violent crime, 37%. Also, he is predominantly urban. Furthermore, *he* is predominantly black: in 2014, blacks made up 13% of the U.S. population but made up 38% of violent crime and 28% of all criminal arrests. And finally, he is poor.

Cassia Spohn (2000) noted the notorious "100 to 1" disparity between sentences for possession of cocaine in powder, common in the wealthy neighborhoods, and crack cocaine, common in poor ones. From 1986 until 2010, U.S. federal laws required a mandatory five-year sentence for crimes involving 500 grams of powder cocaine (about a pound) or 5 grams (around one-sixth of an ounce) for crack cocaine. Consequently, around 82% of those convicted for federal crack offenses were black, and approximately 8% were white (455, 481). The Fair Sentencing Act of 2010 decreased the 100:1 disparity to 18. The National Academy of Sciences panel on incarceration stated that the racial "disparities are enormous" for incarceration, capital punishment, and life sentencing (Travis et al. 2014, 91).

The long-run trends in incarceration of drug offenders in the United States are worrying. The public largely favors a strong criminal justice response, but its actual impact on drug use is minimal. Drug law violations are no longer universally considered criminal offenses, and many have questioned if incarceration is the right response. Effects on families, minority communities, and general well-being are serious issues, as is reintegration into society after release from prison. U.S. incarceration rates in general have grown dramatically, and now greatly exceed those of other Western countries—indeed, they surpass any in history. Among the reasons why the United States is an outlier are sentencing policies such as mandatory sentencing, "truth in sentencing" and "three strikes" policies, and, in particular, increasing drug-related incarceration (Caulkins and Chandler 2006; Tonry 1999). For example, the spread of mandatory sentences for drug possession meant that "from 1980 to 1997, the number of violent offenders doubled, the number of nonviolent offenders tripled, and the number of drug offenders increased eleven-fold" (Schiraldi 2002).

The cost of incarcerating drug offenders runs into billions of dollars yearly (Pearl 2018); the socioeconomic cost, as well as the individual cost (i.e., personal disadvantages in home and career), caused by the incarceration of millions of people is not included in this number. The huge costs serve to enrich the booming security and prison systems profit-making enterprises. In following the money of mass incarceration, Wagner and Rabuy found that it is a business attracting yearly total cost of about USD182 (Wagner and Rabuy 2017). Above all, it maintains a system that does not definitively improve public safety, but, instead, destabilizes communities, harms families, and derails the lives of individuals.

Furthermore, international drug trafficking is enabled by access to financial institutions that reap enormous profits doing business with drug traffickers. Traffickers often siphon assets into foreign banks in countries like Switzerland, Isle of Man, Cayman Islands, and Liechtenstein that have bank secrecy laws. Following the Money Laundering Act of 1986, however, traffickers could no longer hide their cash with a simple bank deposit, and as a result, several banks have been implicated in drug money laundering. For example, BCCI was implicated in drug money laundering activities in Nigeria; in 2010, Wachovia Bank, which laundered about USD378.4 billion for Mexican drug traffickers, paid U.S. federal authorities USD110 million in forfeiture and received a USD50 million fine for failing to monitor cash which was used to transport 22 tons of cocaine; and the British multinational bank, HSBC, agreed to pay U.S. regulators USD1.9 billion as a settlement after it was found to have laundered billions in cash for drug cartels and terrorists (Vulliamy 2011; Thomas 2012).

8.5.2 Opportunity Costs

An important facet of the war on drugs is to restrict production and supply through crop eradication or interdiction, and by that, either directly reducing availability or deterring use by heightening prices. But in an essentially unregulated market in which the laws of supply and demand are dominant, increasing prices only serves to increase the profit incentive for new producers and traffickers to enter the market; supply then increases, prices fall, and a new equilibrium is established. Connectedly, enforcement pressure on one production area or transit route, at best, simply displaces illegal activity to new ones, making any gains localized and short-lived. As Rolles et al. (2012,

29) noted, the well-documented "balloon effect" displaces coca production from one country in Latin America to another and transit routes from the Caribbean to West Africa and Mexico, with often devastating results. The general risks of involvement in the illicit drug trade, coupled with unscrupulous profiteering on the part of suppliers, lead to astronomical price markups. For comparison, there is about a 400% markup from farm gate to consumer in the price of a legal drug, coffee, whereas the percentage price markup for illegal drugs can run into multiple thousands (Wilson and Stevens 2017, 2). Packer (1968) noted almost five decades ago that efforts at prohibition lead directly to a "crime tariff" on prohibited substances that is essentially a state-imposed tax that goes directly to organized crime.

According to International Programs and Drug Policy Research Center, more than 90% of the value added (gross profit) of cocaine is generated at the distribution stage of the illicit drug industry. For instance, taking 2014 figures, powder cocaine at 0.25 pure gram retailed for USD218 (Kilmer et al. 2014). This represents a significant profit margin considering a retail price of less than USD5 a gram in places like Cartagena, Colombia (Pino, personal communication, June 5, 2015). Wholesalers and retailers reap big portions of the retail price of cocaine. Although the farmers who cultivate illegal crops are by no means rich and are exposed to considerable risks, the drug crops provide better returns than most licit crops, as well as being more easily stored and transported (compared to fresh fruit or vegetables, for example). Drug profits have been so inflated by the failed war on drugs that three-quarters of all drug shipments would have to be interdicted and seized to reduce the present profitability of the drug trade (UNODC 2017).

Consequently, there is the potential for entire sectors to come under the unique control of illegal enterprises. As development in Nigeria and several countries in the region demonstrate, especially during difficult economic times, with high inflation and interest rates, the masses and legitimate businesses struggle to obtain the cash they need to survive. By contrast, cash is not a problem for those with access to drug money. In this scenario, drug money has the potential to create unfair competition. In the process, legitimate businesses, without access to illicit funds, may be forced out of the market. Drug traffickers who make use of frontline legitimate businesses know that where such big money is involved, even respectable citizens can be induced to condone the source of the money.

8.6 GLOBAL VILLAGE GONG

The ongoing war on drugs has demonstrated its weakness in defining and teaching about morality and ethics in a combat devoid of enemies.

Unfortunately, current prohibition thrives on ignorance of drugs and misplaced faith in the power of the law to regulate human vice. Imagine that cigarettes and alcohol were once labeled and criminalized. The less people know about drugs, the more concerned about them they tend to be. For instance, in Nigeria older people are concerned about the dangers that drugs pose to young people, but were often unable to distinguish the risk involved in taking cocaine or smoking marijuana. Often people are worried about violence and reprisals from local dealers. Even in the Netherlands, which decriminalized drug possession, rival drug gangs have been linked to several murders. A recent research that collected some standardized comparable data on homicide in several European countries found that about 50% of the homicides committed across the Netherlands (2012–2016), Finland (2014–2015), and Sweden (2013–2014) were drug related. The homicides also took place in public settings such as parks, roads, bars, restaurants, and hotels more often than other homicides. The victims of drug-related homicides were more often male, under the age of 45 (EMCDDA 2019, 46). Crime and violence animate the unpopularity of drugs in the popular imagination.

Lawmakers assert that because drugs users are deluded by the drugs they take, they are unable to recognize the harm that they do to themselves. Society has a moral obligation to intervene, against the will of the drug user if need be, to save him from his own worst impulse.

Furthermore, upholders postulate that prohibition is the best framework for dispensing medical treatment to those who want to stop taking drugs and managing those who cannot or will not stop taking drugs (Feiling 2009). However, this is not the case as was evidenced in polls conducted in 1999 France. Eighty-five percent of respondents agreed that criminal penalties should be imposed on consumers of heroin and cocaine; 70% thought that cannabis smokers should face penalties. But when the question was reframed to emphasize the rights of the user, one-third of interviewees agreed that the prohibition of cannabis was an infringement of the right to use one's body as one saw fit (EMCDDA 2000).

Today, Canada is the second country in the world, after Uruguay, and the first major world economy to legalize recreational marijuana. The Netherlands led the way with its "normalizing drug policy, conceiving of the drug problem as a social problem and finding a solution by gradually reversing the social construction of the drug problem through a process of reduction of significance and (moral) interest" (Cohen 1994). Akin to decriminalization, normalization in this view does not only require the reduction of secondary harm and attractions of illegal substances, but it also implies that the social and political rewards of the drug prohibition system itself are to be discarded (Leuw and Haen-Marshall 1994). In line with normalization, no extrinsic moral or political interests should be served with the regulation of psychoactive substances.

The Dutch alternative drug policy, despite international criticism, stands out in tearing down the wall around the social construction of drugs. Enacted in 1976, the Opium Act created a formal distinction between soft drugs, like marijuana and hashish, and hard drugs. It also introduced a "two-track" policy: a medical approach to addicts and a criminal justice-oriented (repressive) approach to large-scale dealers of hard drugs (Manja et al. 2003). In the Netherlands, the use of drugs was viewed as a deviant behavior that was part of a youth culture. Following discovery in the late 1960s that most cannabis users were "normal people," normalization policy made such behavior less stigmatizing. In other words, attacking deviant behaviors with punitive measures could intensify them, and make reintegration of the person to a socially accepted lifestyle difficult (Boekhout van Solinge 1999). And while most countries struggle with overcrowded prisons, the Netherlands has the opposite problem: a shortage of people to lock up. In the last few years, 19 prisons have closed down and more will follow (Weller 2017). Shorter prison sentences, better rehabilitation, and a decreasing crime rate in the country are among the reasons leading to empty cells and why the Netherlands now has one of the lowest incarceration rates in Europe. Additionally, less than 10% then return to prison after their release. In comparison, England's overall proven reoffending rate was almost 30% in 2016 (Wartna et al. 2017). In the United States, overall, 68% of released state prisoners were arrested within three years, 79% within six years, and 83% within nine years ("Watkins's Update on Prison Recidivism" 2018). As the deputy governor of Norgerhaven, a high-security prison in the northeast of the Netherlands stated: If somebody has a drug problem, we treat their addiction; if they are aggressive, we provide anger management; if they have got money problems, we give them debt counseling. So, we try to remove whatever it was that caused the crime. The inmate himself or herself must be willing to change, but our method has been very effective (Ash 2016).

Above all, lenient law enforcement existed. Dutch police to act on the basis of the so-called expediency principle, meaning that repressive intervention is not an automatic response to illegality. Applied in its positive variant: laws and rules were enforced if there is risk or actual occurrence of individual and societal harm. This relaxed style of policing is supported by official guidelines that police should follow (Korf 1995, 53–63).

Calls are growing for the decriminalization and normalization of drugs. As frustrations with the drug problem and current drug policies rise, growing numbers of political leaders, law enforcement officials, drug abuse experts, and common citizens are insisting that a radical alternative to current policies be fairly considered: the controlled legalization or decriminalization of drugs (Nadelmann 1991). The global drug prohibition is in crisis, and the fact that it is at long last becoming visible is one symptom of that crisis (Levine 2002).

In the long run, the more criminalized and punitive forms of drug prohibition almost certainly are doomed. In the short run, the ever-growing drug-law and drug-policy reform movements make it likely that criminalized drug prohibition will find itself confronted with new opponents, also in Nigeria, as discussed in chapter 1.

Dr. E. K. Rodrigo, a psychiatrist with more than 30 years' experience in Sri Lanka, the UK, and Bermuda, emphasized that legalization of drugs would work in the same way as alcohol and tobacco. In "Let's Talk About a Revolution" interview on Bermuda Sun, he explained that a controlled legal drug trade would help people who were using drugs to do it more safely, thereby mitigating law enforcement costs (see BDA Sun n.d. 2005–2020). Prevention is most important, high taxation, high-minded education, and effective treatment programs are what count (International Alliance for Responsible Drinking [IARD] 2015). Teaching children better methods of dealing with stress, and with anger, and create possibilities for disadvantaged children to acquiring life skills are crucial to discovering more pleasurable activities in life than from taking drugs.

This prediction is already becoming a reality in many countries, including the Netherlands, Switzerland, Germany, Portugal, Canada, Spain, and the UK. In 2003, for example, Canada decriminalized possession of small quantities of marijuana and started embracing "safe injection centers for the use of hard drugs" (Hughes and Stevens 2010, 1001). The *harm reduction* concept has spread very fast in recent years and has now become the basis for a rational and pragmatic drug policy in almost every EU country and several others like Australia, New Zealand, Canada, Brazil, and the United States. Practices such as decriminalization of consumption, leniency in law enforcement toward cannabis and toward possession of other drugs for personal use, and needle exchange programs are common.

However, a key fact is that almost all nations are signatories to the UN antidrug treaties and the bedrock of the current international control system. By employing rhetoric stating drugs are a "grave threat to the health and wellbeing of all mankind," the 1998 UNGASS echoed the foundational 1961 convention of the international drug control regime, which justified eliminating the evil of drugs in the name of the health and welfare of mankind. As noted by Bruun et al.'s (1975) *The Gentlemen's Club*, "The limits of action in the drug field are, like in many other fields, set by the lines of political relationships prevailing in the world at large." Upholders of the regime can therefore exert considerable pressure on nations to conform to the established norms of behavior regarding control policies. As such, no country has been able to withdraw politically from global drug prohibition. Open defection from the drug prohibition regime would result in severe consequences. As discussed in chapter 1, Nigeria was labeled a narco-state and faced damaging repercussions including economic sanctions, aid cutoffs, and diminished standing in the international community.

However, the gong sounds increasingly in most other countries, and many prominent politicians, public health professionals, and police officials who are strong defenders of drug prohibition also have supported reform and harm reduction. Recently, the UN General Assembly adopted the outcome document of its 2016 special session on the world drug problem. Several nonmandatory recommendations focused on demand and supply reduction, the availability of controlled substances for medical and scientific purposes, human rights issues, international cooperation, and new challenges (UN Commission on Narcotic Drugs 2018; Csete et al. 2016). They considered control of illicit drugs, an important part of social policy that has been fraught with controversy, as inconsistent with human rights norms, and for which scientific evidence and public health approaches have arguably played too limited a role.

This work underscores a movement within drug prohibition that shifts drug policies from the criminalized and punitive end to the more decriminalized and openly regulated end of the drug policy continuum—moving drug policies away from severe punishment, capital punishment, coercion, and repression, and toward tolerance, regulation, and public health. Research shows the legalization and regulation of drugs can and does work. "People often say 'How would you legalize these drugs?' You can just go, "the legal production and usage of these drugs already exists" (Csete et al. 2016), and the pioneers of the drug trade are in control of legal manufacture, importing, exporting, and stocking.

According to recent report of the International Narcotics Control Board, Peru is the only country in the world legally exporting coca leaf, and the United States is the only country which imports Peru's coca leaf—about 133 tons in 2016—which it uses to extract flavoring agents and manufacture the drug as a by-product (INCB 2017). The report also noted that of the estimated 76.1-kilogram global licit cocaine manufactured in 2016, almost 95% was produced in the United States, and close to 5% was manufactured by China. The UK and other countries then import the finished product from America.

Britain exported 57 kilograms of legal cocaine in 2016, far ahead of the next biggest exporter, the Netherlands, which shipped out 13.7 kilograms the same year. As Embury-Dennis noted in his article on April 17, 2018, Britain also imported 330 kilograms of legal cocaine in the same year, about 83% of global demand, and accounted for almost half of cocaine consumption for medical purposes (90 kilograms). The largest stocks of cocaine were held by the United Kingdom, then the United States, Japan, and Switzerland (Embury-Dennis 2018).

This kind of data has prompted campaigners to call on governments to regulate the drugs trade. Under prohibition, control of the drug market defaults to unregulated and untaxed criminal profiteers, meaning governments forgo a substantial potential source of income. Waterfeld (2011) highlighted the Netherlands' quasi-legal cannabis markets; the Dutch coffee shops that pay about EUR315 million in tax annually, and turnover of approximated EUR1.6 billion. Harvard economists found that legalizing and regulating drugs in the United States would save roughly USD47.9 billion per year in government expenditure on drug enforcement. Drug legalization would yield about USD58.8 billion annually in tax revenue, assuming legal drugs are taxed at rates comparable to those on alcohol and tobacco. The total effect of drug legalization on government budgets would be approximately USD106.7 billion in combined savings and additional revenue. That is about 8% increase from the estimates in the 2010 Cato study. Furthermore, nearly 60% of budgetary gains would come from legalizing heroin and cocaine (Miron 2018; Miron and Waldock 2010).

Global reform regarding prohibition of drugs is on the rise. Upholders presumed prohibition would decrease illicit trafficking, consumption, and related crimes and health issues. Critics are convinced prohibition has only little effect on trafficking and consumption, but has insurmountable excesses inherent to the phenomenon.

Chapter 9

Findings and Conclusion

Cocaine Hoppers has addressed a number of issues regarding Nigerian involvement in global cocaine trade. It has principally focused on the genesis of cocaine in Nigeria and trafficking activities in the areas of brokerage and importation of cocaine from South America. Also highlighted was the role of onward transshipment and the distribution internationally. This chapter summarizes the conclusions in relation to the primary research questions:

1. What is the role of Nigeria and Nigerians in the international cocaine trade?
2. What are the mechanisms behind the success of Nigerians in the global cocaine trade?
3. What is the involvement of Nigerians in Brazil, a cocaine export country, and in the global destination countries discussed in the book?
4. And how can this involvement be explained?

This research was conducted based on the fact that much is known about Nigeria and its long and complicated history as a country, but very little information is available on the involvement of Nigerians in the cocaine trade outside the information provided by drug enforcement agencies and the CJS. Little is known about who the Nigerian drug traffickers are, how they became involved in this illegal trade, and why they chose to enter into this life. The general consensus is they have large criminal networks or are drug barons working in partnership with South American cocaine cartels; however, this is hard to demonstrate directly as Nigeria remains a no-go area for criminological researchers.

In this regard, the research method was implemented in line with the anthropology and sociology of deviance and carried out by interviewing more than 250 people and observing participants in the criminogenic environment. Hence, it was based principally on different types of qualitative data received in Nigeria and in various countries abroad, including the Netherlands, Malaysia, Hong Kong, Mainland China, and Brazil. The primary data is based on empirical observations and is complemented with secondary data in related fields: academic work, media publications, and reports from international institutions and organizations on Nigerian international cocaine traffickers.

Attempting to bridge this knowledge gap, I used concepts from various fields of knowledge such as criminology, economics, and sociology, each of which inspired different parts of the work. In some cases, theories exist that refer to macro perspective in terms of economic political power, and in some cases, it refers to micro level in terms of othering or social learning theories. These notions were instrumental as they helped explain social processes and interactions directly and indirectly related to Nigerian cocaine trafficking.

My findings are different from the dominant images of "Nigerian drug barons and their cronies" patterned after sophisticated transnational criminal organizations, because the research revealed that Nigerian traffickers principally engage in ad hoc transaction operations involving licit and illicit arrangements, in which actors and businesses are connected in flexible and changeable forms. I found that the Nigerian cocaine trade engages a wide range of enterprises and persons, including legitimate companies, law-abiding family members or friends, and a pool of collaborators and service providers that are vital to the business as they are "detached" from it. As a Nigerian researcher, I was allowed an insider viewpoint. On the one hand, I had insight into the social context and was better able to understand the workings of traffickers both in Nigeria and abroad. On the other hand, I did not always have sufficient distance from the group I studied, risking becoming assimilated or too close to maintain objectivity. Consequently, this is a blind spot where self-evident practices or beliefs could develop. I have strived to advance an unbiased balance between the insider and outsider approach, by reminding myself of the difference between "understanding" and "accepting" the respondents' truths, which remained crucial in achieving the insider perspective.

Hence, hopefully, my work has contributed to the discussion by providing insights into Nigerians' involvement in the global cocaine trade, as well as its consequences for Nigeria and the world. Drawing briefly from cocaine's pioneer trade background, it has discussed the illicit cocaine trade in Nigeria and traced Nigerian traffickers' efforts in traditional markets and newer, emerging markets.

9.1 THE ROLE OF NIGERIA AND NIGERIANS IN THE GLOBAL COCAINE TRADE

The role of Nigerians in international cocaine trade is the brokerage of small, medium, and large quantities of South American cocaine trafficked from Brazil especially, a major exporter nation (UNODC 2018b), into Nigeria and international markets. Nigeria's role is enhanced by the country's central location and ease of access, which in terms of movement, fosters transshipment of cocaine in several ways. First, Nigeria's proximity to cocaine producing nations across the Atlantic Ocean offers a comparative advantage for Nigerian and South American drug traffickers in terms of movement, as shipment from Brazil to Nigeria takes about 19 days, and from SA to the Gulf of Guinea is about two days or a six-hour flight. Second, in terms of transshipment, I found that the role of Nigerians in the global cocaine business is based on a high number of potential participants. This work distinguished the major actors into six groups: (1) *Oga* ("big man") large-scale smugglers, (2) small-scale traffickers or entrepreneurs, (3) strikers, (4) "suicide birds" or couriers, (5) part-time couriers or "freelance" traffickers, and (6) retailers. Actors can play different roles in different stages of cocaine trafficking.

The role of Nigerians is not limited to Nigeria. I found that the social organization of Nigerian cocaine trafficking, network, and actors, existing in many countries in SSA, offers excellent transport and criminogenic environments for imported cocaine to be repacked and reexported to markets abroad. Nigeria's proximity to cocaine production/export countries in Latin America has contributed to the involvement of Nigerians in the illicit global cocaine trade. The data received in this research shows that different actors either intentionally or unintentionally downplay its danger or see their activity as momentary trade transactions with an acceptable level of risk. This recalls Sykes and Matza's (1957) technique of neutralization by denial of responsibility, denial of injury, denial of victim, condemnation of the condemners, and the appeal to higher loyalties, when things go wrong.

Nigerian drug traffickers' involvement extends beyond trafficking cocaine to involvement in financial crimes, human trafficking, and illicit goods smuggling. Money raised from scamming victims or underage prostitution is invested in trafficking illicit drugs and vice versa, according to what works and where. It could be said that Nigerian traffickers are brokers dwelling in and moving from one country to another, buying and selling the illicit drug, and, therefore, are called "cocaine hoppers."

9.2 MECHANISMS BEHIND THE SUCCESS OF NIGERIANS IN THE GLOBAL COCAINE TRADE

Though the involvement of Nigerians in the illicit global trade is demonstrated by the resilience of Nigerian traffickers, I maintain that they are not more successful people than Colombians, Mexicans, Italians, Spanish, Portuguese, Dutch, or British. Nevertheless, Nigerians are relatively successful because they have some advantages based on historical, socio-geopolitical, economic, and cultural factors.

Historically, first of all, Nigeria's relationship with slavery and colonialism has been grounded in the illicit trades. The RCC is among the core slave traders and colonial imperialists, along with Britain, the United States, the Netherlands, France, Spain, and Portugal, which forced, sold, exploited, and brutalized Africans during slavery in the Americas (Global Black History 2020; Gates 2011; Rodney 1973). The philosophy of "civilizing Africans" disguised colonial accumulation of wealth. Enlightenment philosophers' works should carry a warning to African readers: "Beware, this work can damage your racial self-esteem," suggested Soyinka (1988).

Ironically, industrial exploitation of the coca leaf fostered the international illicit drug trade. The slave trade happened centuries ago, but its spillover effects on the lives of Africans and Afro descendants are still felt. The phenomenon of embedded discrimination is compounded by endemic poverty, marginalization, criminalization, and "Victimization-As-Mere-Punishment" (Agozino 1997). The rise of "internal colonialism" demonstrates the need for decolonization—hence African and African descendant's demand for restitution and reparations for the crimes of slavery, colonialism, and imperialism (Black Lives Matter 2020).

British colonial authorities in 1934 experimented with the cultivation of the coca plant in Nigeria. In addition, Nigeria's connection with the new world resulted in globalized Nigerian descendants. This explains why Nigerian traffickers are not out of place in the Americas and in SEA. Development in Nigeria has shed light on state complicity in drug trafficking. This legacy left by the elites led to the emergence of heroin in Nigeria, and attracted South American drug lords, and cocaine culture in Nigeria.

The second set of indirect mechanisms concerns a number of socio-geopolitical issues in Nigeria that foster crime, including the illicit cocaine trade. To start with, Nigeria's inability to shake off its neocolonial mentality fostered a divisive society, with low levels of trust, solidarity, reciprocity, and empathy.

This enhanced the development of strong local identities and feeble national identity. It may be asserted that Nigeria is a country, but not a nation in the logic of having an identity that generates cohesion among its citizenry. This resulted in political instability that plunged Nigeria into a civil war (1966–1970). Directed largely at the civilian population, this in turn led to high levels of crime, as its aftereffects ruptured the fabric of society and its institutions. In addition, *Cocaine Hoppers* explicated that Nigeria's geopolitical factors, such as natural resources, modern infrastructure, knowledge base, and good connections, are crucial for traffickers' success in illicit activities. Nigerian cocaine traffickers thrive due to the availability of good infrastructure including roads, airports, and seaports, and because Nigeria's extensive borders, riverine waterways, and coastline remain mostly unguarded and porous.

An additional mechanism underscoring the success of Nigerian cocaine traffickers is related to political factors concerning issues of governance and social control, which have affected the Nigerian political economy, productive structure, culture, and institutional developments. This is characterized by dysfunctional institutions, organized crime, endemic corruption, and weak rule of law.

I argue that since Nigeria gained its independence, democracy and leadership have suffered in terms of sufficient governance, consequently, resulting in worrying dysfunctional institutions and multiples of socioeconomic and political issues. Primarily, a weak central state and civil society resulted in failure of leadership, which crippled institutions' abilities to perform core functions like providing public services and support effectively. These excesses resulted in a continuous political power struggle, sectarian violence, and terrorism among other problems, providing a criminogenic environment for development and success of the new trend cocaine trade. Furthermore, mechanisms behind the success of Nigerians in the global cocaine trade cannot be explained without economical features that made it possible. Nigeria's richness in natural and human resources, economic mismanagement of the oil and gas revenues, failed structural adjustment programs, and continuous political contestation marked the decline of the Nigerian state, resulting in undiversified economy, noninclusive economic growth, deficit quality education, soaring poverty and population growth, inequality, unemployment, and relative deprivation.

Nigerian traffickers' success also relies on Nigerian organized crime groups. These organizations are embedded in the political, economic, and sociocultural fabric of Nigeria. The involvement of high-ranking officials and the Nigerian state under military regime in drug trafficking won Nigeria the reputation of "the hub of African narcotics trafficking." Therefore, the achievements of Nigerian international cocaine traffickers draw on the mechanisms that institutionalized corruption; organized crime and society are linked, because the illegal world has a meaningful relationship with the legal world. In this way, Nigerian traffickers recall to mind Ruggiero's (1996) fundamental concept that organized crime can only reproduce itself if it develops external relationships with corporate crime, the state, street crime, and society at large.

The third set of mechanisms fostering the success of Nigerian cocaine traffickers concerns cultural features related to social control, anomie (Merton 1938; Durkheim 1964), and low law observations, which engulfs other subcultural notions such as reversed social capital and othering. In combination, these views directly and indirectly enhance the new trend cocaine trade in pursuit of the Nigerian Dream. Powered by the endemic culture hooked on worshipping money, wealth, and status regardless of means, this dream draws on a state of ethical normlessness or deregulation. Findings from my interviews reveal that Nigerian global cocaine trafficking is a reaction to the perceived pressure of the Nigerian Dream. The transformation in social structure and ethos exalted individual competition and offered incessant and impossible goals, leading many into criminal activity in pursuit of wealth and status. I also contend that the low level of obedience to the law in Nigeria is embedded in executive lawlessness, which has resulted in economic crimes being defined merely as activities that generate income and wealth. Because widespread informal economy and smuggling activities are common, breaking laws became socially acceptable and habitually encouraged. In other words, criminal activities were accepted as normal and justified because of inequality, poverty, and social exclusion.

Furthermore, antidrug laws and measures to combat drug trafficking remain inconsequential if they are devoid of the political will and human capacity to implement them. The impunity enjoyed by Nigerian drug lords stems from their skill in neutralizing the work of law enforcement agents and the CJS, as they use the "language of money" in Brazil (Huguet and de Carvalho 2008), "protective umbrella" (Lo and Kwok 2012) in China, and "long leg" in Nigeria to keep their businesses running. My findings show that Nigerian cocaine traffickers rely on support from public officials and the relative weakness of street-level police. Their activities are bolstered by an asymmetric balance of power between the extralegal spaces occupied by coercive criminal groups and the formal legal space of law and state power. I claim that a key mechanism behind the success of Nigerian traffickers remains that the offense hardly attracts punishment when it involves the elite, particularly in Nigeria, which often misleads younger, low-level operators into a false sense of security. Elite stakeholders' participation in cocaine trade paved the way for vulnerable individuals, who have few alternatives, to engage in illicit acts.

Globalization and technology have also contributed to the rise of Nigerian cocaine traffickers. International travel is affordable and easy, and advances in telecommunications have been vital to conducting trafficking operations.

Deals involving thousands or even millions of naira or dollars are closed by pure verbal communication. Scanning a large number of travelers or bulky goods for illicit items remains difficult for law enforcement and border control agents.

In all, I found that these historical, socio-geopolitical, economic, and cultural factors act in combination to foster the involvement of Nigerians in the global cocaine trade.

9.3 DECRIMINALIZATION AND REGULARIZATION

Drawing on practical and ideological goals, the nations of the world constructed a global system of drug prohibition. The 1998 UN General Assembly justified eradicating the "evil" of drugs in the name of "the health and welfare of mankind." However, I assert these international agreements do not relate in reality to how drug prohibition itself might affect public health. Additionally, the violence associated both with illicit drug markets and with policing remains traumatic. The cost of incarceration of enormous numbers of people for minor, nonviolent offenses weighs heavily on societies. The misuse of the important social tool of the CJS to discriminate against racial and ethnic minorities is a pressing reason for change in the current drug prohibitive policies.

Early prohibitions on drug use were constructed by lawmakers with moral objections to drug use, but their objections were informed by bias, racism, and political and corporate interests. The "war on drugs" and "zero-tolerance" policies that grew out of the prohibitionist consensus are now being challenged on several areas, including their health, human rights, and development consequences. As a result, there is a gradual deconstructing of worldwide drug prohibition. It is presumed that drugs such as cocaine, heroin, or methamphetamine are automatically addictive; however, majority who use them do so recreationally and do not become dependent. Legalization and regularization would be the key step in making people more aware of the less harmful forms of drugs and the safest ways to use them.

Next step, physicians should be allowed the rights to prescribe drugs such as cocaine and heroin to chronic users. For instance, heroin-assisted treatment aimed to combat public health risks caused by street use, already happening in several countries—including Portugal that in 2001 decriminalized the possession of all drugs for personal use, and the Netherlands, Switzerland, the UK, Germany, and Canada—prescribe heroin for use under medical supervision, as part of successful programs to treat long-term users of illicit opioids. Effectiveness and the useful lessons for managing problematic forms of drug use as a public health challenge, rather than a criminal justice one saves money. The generally successful outcomes are also reflected in the shifting public opinion. The EMCDDA (2012) concluded that heroin-assisted treatment can lead to "substantially improved" health and well-being of participants; "major reductions" in their continued use of illicit heroin; "major disengagement from criminal activities," such as acquisitive crime to fund their drug use, and "marked improvements in social functioning." These findings disprove the view by those who asserted that the most dangerous people in America are those who believe in legalizing drugs. They discredit also the view of those who defend laws against drugs: compulsive drugs were criminalized because they are harmful; they are not harmful because they were criminalized (Barbour 2000). These findings also bring a renewed call for the abolition of the death penalty for drug offense.

The legalization of drugs could work in the same way as alcohol and tobacco. As with cannabis now, people would apply for official permit to sell cocaine or heroin. Governments would no longer be bothered with pursuing illicit drug offenders, and it would be a controlled, legal trade. In a general market, those who develop problematic cocaine use would benefit from services similar to those that exist for alcoholics, and compulsive drug users would in all likelihood need those services for a much shorter period of time than most alcoholics. No drugs should be allowed to be marketed— available but not advertised or promoted—just as governments have regulated the distribution and marketing of tobacco and alcohol. There are also training programs and age minimums required for people who serve alcohol, designated drive schemes, and courses to educated drinkers about the risks of drinking too much. High taxation, high-minded education, and effective treatment programs are what count (Rolles et al. 2012; IARD 2015). Legalization and regularization of drugs will open a world of opportunities. By making the illicit legitimate, cocaine hoppers, Jamaican *Yardie*, Italian *Ndrangheta*, Mexican and Colombian drug cartels, and their associated criminal authorities will go bankrupt as retail prices of illicit drugs drop.

Future policy changes should consider that legalization combined with taxation and regulation is more effective than decriminalization, meaning repealing criminal penalties against possession but retaining them against trafficking. First, legalization eliminates arrests for trafficking in addition to eliminating arrests for possession. Second, legalization saves prosecutorial, judicial, and incarceration expenses; these savings are minimal in the case of decriminalization. And third, legalization allows the taxation of drug production and sale, meaning increased tax revenue and decreased government expenditures (Miron 2018).

Many citizens are breaking the law because of their drug use. Illegal drugs confront users with much higher harms because they are made dependent on criminal market. However, the punitive approach to combating drugs fundamentally disrupts relationships between individual citizens and the state. In addition, it contributes to the marginalization of drug users and justifies criminalizing people who do not actually harm others. Fortunately, increasing number of nations are experimenting with different ways of legally regulating the drug market because a "drug-free world" is both unrealistic and unsafe—unrealistic, in that prohibition has not eradicated drug use and unsafe because prohibition causes mass incarceration and executions in contravention of international law. It fosters the spread of dangerous viruses, drives human rights abuses for drug offenders, and contributes to the drug-related deaths that in 2015 stood at about 450,000 people around the world (UNODC 2018). In all, legalization and regularization are vital steps in the right direction for drug policy reform, and national governments should liberate themselves from the constraints of old-fashioned and punitive framework.

9.4 *NAIJAS'*: SAME PHENOMENON, DIFFERENT PICK

In spite of harsh drug policies and the threat of long imprisonments in America, Nigerian criminal networks traffickers persist in the United States. Sub-Saharan criminal networks in several major cities in the United States are predominantly of Nigerian origin. Cocaine hoppers traffic drugs from Africa, Europe, and Asia into the United States and use inner-city associates to distribute drugs in urban neighborhoods. The illicit drug trade continues to thrive, with expanding markets in cocaine, heroin, and synthetic drugs (UNODC 2018). The number of Americans who try an illicit drug has been increasing since 1970. One in twenty American adults ages 18–25 used cocaine in 2015 (Miroff 2017). Each year, U.S. law enforcement makes about 1.5 million drug arrests and more than 80% are for possession only. Drug Policy Alliance (2017) noted in the executive summary that by any measure and every metric, the U.S. war on drugs has been a catastrophic failure. U.S. government policies which are designed to be tough on people who use and sell drugs have helped overfill prisons, branded millions of people as criminals, and exacerbated drug-related death, and suffering.

Wrongful convictions in the United States evidenced that drug crime exonerations are even more racially concentrated. Of the many costs that the war on drugs inflicts on black communities, the practice of deliberately charging innocent defendants with fabricated crimes, as well as those unjustly executed may be the most shameful. Designed to fail, drug policy has not reduced drug use, nor substantially reduced or eliminated crime. Acting as a "carnival mirror" that weeds out crime of the well-offs in line with the Pyrrhic defeat notion (Reiman and Leighton 2017), be it in the United States or Nigeria, the CJS yields benefits to those in positions of power that amount to victory for the few at the expense of the masses.

In all, removing criminal penalties for drug use and possession will save billions of dollars that can be used to provide effective health interventions for those who need them, while focusing criminal justice resources on serious public safety problems.

In spite of the threat of long imprisonments, sanctions, deportation, and fines, cocaine hoppers persist in Brazil and China. Above all, I assert that their success in China, as in Indonesia and Malaysia, demonstrates the perseverance and resilience in trying to arrive at and negotiate the physical "edge" of daring, endurance, and hope to accomplish self-actualization. They show that playing with the invitational edge of cocaine trafficking in the United States, Brazil, or China often carries a sense of adventure, excitement, and enchantment. I found that an overwhelming majority of cocaine traffickers chose their path because of the constraints of low-paid, legitimate jobs on the one hand and the promise of huge financial reward from the widespread informal or illicit economies on the other hand.

However, much of the Nigerian diaspora has tried to distance itself from criminal elements. Indeed, many have established themselves abroad and earn a respectable living through legal commercial activities. In areas like Guangzhou, the Nigerian community made a conscious choice that focused on prevention, where it is everyone's job to deter engagement in drug trafficking. Their leadership initiative in Guangzhou has kick-started the Nigerian community and organizational shifts from hopelessness and despair to expand new horizons. The Nigerian community used the widespread African concept of shame management, restorative justice interventions, and reintegrative shaming that resulted in less offending by not stigmatizing offenders (Braithwaite 2003). Their approach, which reduces participation of their conationals in cocaine trafficking, elucidates the relevance of implementing programs designed to tackle the underlying problems that contributes to the involvement of Nigerians in the international cocaine trafficking.

This work shows that Nigerians can change, and Nigerian involvement in the global cocaine trade can be reduced by adequate governance and community-led interventions, which could be achieved through the initiative of motivated Nigerian leaders. Reverse the making of crime big business in Nigeria. The Nigerian community in Guangzhou introduced change by creating "a stairway to reform" from micro to macro level. I say that this is an inside-out approach starting from below with "role model leadership" to the top. This hope resides now with Buhari's performance. Hopefully, we will see renewed development in Nigeria with inclusive transformative politics to curtail collateral damage. The cost of the imposed war on drugs calls for scrutiny as the international assistance has failed to produce expected results. Nigeria cannot afford the war on drugs, which is void of real enemies. We should reinvest the billions spent on a fruitless "war" by legalizing and regulating the cannabis market. This can be done while adhering to the rule of law and delivering on adequate socioeconomic public goods. Harm reduction alternatives would provide treatment to drug users in Nigeria and pave the way for an informed, healthy Nigeria and a thriving economy, as many other countries are doing.

Buhari's government must create an enabling environment to attract more Nigerian diaspora and foreign investments in the country to enhance development and enable people to achieve a good standard of life. When correctly followed, the "stairway to reform" could mitigate the attraction to cocaine trafficking. The Nigerian community's approach to reducing cocaine trafficking and crimes among its conationals in China is an example to be emulated by other countries and communities facing the harms around illicit drug trafficking.

The negative image from crimes committed by Nigerian criminal networks should not be allowed to overshadow the achievements of the law-abiding majority of Nigerian professionals and entrepreneurs. U.S.-based Nigerian diaspora are the best educated immigrant communities in the country. A far greater share of the Nigerian first and second generation individuals earned undergraduate degrees than the U.S. population overall; they are more than twice as likely to have secured an advance degree; and they are substantially more likely than the general U.S. population to be in the labor force (RAD 2015).

A new world order implies that there will be no "narco-state" and less risk of "government by theft" in Nigeria as a result of a collective action. This is a key reason why a change of mentality is an inevitable foundation for real development of the country and reducing Nigerian involvement in international cocaine trafficking. I claim that the "giant" of Africa, Nigeria, has developed but not in the direction desired. It is solipsism, fake morality, mediocrity, and the dominant criminogenic environment in Nigeria that condone crime and involvement in the global drug trafficking, but it is not too late to change.

Bibliography

Abiona, Opeyemi, Mojisola Oluwasanu, and Oladimeji Oladepo. 2019. "Analysis of Alcohol Policy in Nigeria: Multi-Sectoral Action and the Integration of the WHO 'Best-Buy' Interventions." *BMC Public Health* 19: 810.

Abizadeh, Arash. 2011. "Hobbes on the Causes of War: A Disagreement Theory." *American Political Science Review*, 105(2) (May 2011): 298–315.

Abubakar, Mohammed. 2017. "Why Nigerian Varsities Rank Low Globally." *The Guardian*, March 29, 2017. https://guardian.ng/news/why-nigerian-varsities-rank-low-globally

Achebe, Chinua. 2012. *There Was a Country*. New York: Penguin Group Publisher.

Adebayo, Adejobi. 2016. "81 More on Death Row in Malaysia, 15 in Indonesia as Nigeria is Executed for Drugs." *This Day Live*, November 19, 2016. https://www.thisdaylive.com/index.php/2016/11/19/81-more-on-death-row-in-malaysia-15-in-indonesia-as-nigeria-is-executed-for-drugs

Adebayo, Shayo. 2018. "SERAP Exposes Huge Scale of Corruption Going on Inside Nigerian Universities." *Posterity Media*, February 9, 2018. https://posteritymediang.com/serap-exposes-corruption-inside-nigerian-universities

Adedeji, Arowolo A., Arowolo E. Adefunke, and Adaja I. Joseph. 2016. "Trend Analysis of Students Dropout Rate and the Effects on the Social and Educational System in Nigeria." *International Journal of Latest Research in Engineering and Technology*, 2(4): 8–16.

Adesina, Segun, Akinyemi Kunle, and Kayode Ajayi, eds. 1983. *Nigeria Education: Trends and Issues*. Ile Ife: University of Ife Press.

Adeso, Bamidele S. 2020. "CBN Pays $4.45 Billion External Debt to World Bank, Others in 2-Month." *Nairametrics*, March 24, 2020. https://nairametrics.com/2020/03/24/cbn-pays-4-45-billion-external-debt-obligation-to-world-bank-others-in-2-month/

Adiele Pius O. 2017. *The Popes, the Catholic Church and the Transatlantic Enslavement of Black Africans 1418–1839*. Hildesheim: Georg Olms Verlag.

Adler, Patricia A., and Peter Adler. 1987. *Membership Roles in Field Research.* Newbury Park, CA: Sage.

Afigbo, Adiele E. 1972. *The Warrant Chiefs: Indirect Rule in Southeastern Nigeria, 1891–1929.* London: Longman Press.

Afigbo, Adiele E. 2006. *The Abolition of the Slave Trade in Southeastern Nigeria, 1885–1950.* New York: University Rochester Press.

Africa Research Institute. 2016. "Buhari, Nigeria and the IMF: Echoes from the Past." *Africa Research Institute*, June 29, 2016. https://www.africaresearchinstitute.org/newsite/blog/buhari-nigeria-and-the-imf-echoes-from-the-past/

Agbakwuru, Johnbosco. 2011. "700 Nigerians in Thai Prisons, Others Dead." *Vanguard*, October 5, 2011. https://www.vanguardngr.com/2011/10/700-nigerians-in-thai-prisons-others-dead/

Agbo, Nats. 1996. "Chairman Bamaiyi." *Newswatch*, January 22, 1996. 8–11.

Agence France-Presse (AFP). 2012. "Ex-President Slams Brazil's Tough Anti-drug Bill." *Agence France-Presse*, December 26, 2012. http://www.druglawreform.info/en/newsroom/latest-news/item/4233-ex-president-slams-brazils-tough-anti-drug-bill

Agnew, Robert. 1985. "On Testing Structural Strain Theories." *Journal of Research in Crime and Delinquency*, 24(4): 281–290.

Agozino, Biko. 1995. "Methodological Issues in Feminist Research." *Quantity and Quality*, 29(3): 287–298.

Agozino, Biko. 1997/2018. *Black Women and the Criminal Justice System: Towards the Decolonisation of Victimisation.* New York: Routledge.

Agozino, Biko. 2003. *Counter-Colonial Criminology: A Critique of Imperialist Reason.* Pluto Press.

Ajaja, Patrick O. 2012. "School Dropout Pattern among Senior Secondary Schools in Delta State, Nigeria." *International Education Studies*, 5(2): 145–153.

Ajayi, Ola, and Bukola Ifegbayi. 20015. "$20trn Stolen from Nigeria's Treasury by Leaders—EFCC-." *Vanguard*, March 25, 2015. https://www.vanguardngr.com/2015/03/20trn-stolen-from-from-nigerias-treasury-by-leaders-efcc

Akçomak, Semih I., and Bas ter Weel. 2008. "The Impact of Social Capital on Crime: Evidence from the Netherlands." Discussion Papers 3603, Institute for the Study of Labor (IZA), July 2008. http://ftp.iza.org/dp3603.pdf

Ake, Ayodeji. 2018. "Nigeria: Tobacco Consumption Contributes 12% Deaths from Heart Diseases." NHF. *This Day*, May 17, 2018. https://www.thisdaylive.com/index.php/2018/05/17/tobacco-consumption-contributes-12-deaths-from-heart-diseases-says-nhf/

Akhilomen, Austine. 2016. "Nigerians Living in England." *Nigerian Reporter*, April 30, 2016. http://nigerianreporter.com/2016/04/30/nigerians-living-in-england

Akinwotu, Emmanuel. 2020. "'Just Stop Killing Us': Young Nigerians Rise Up Against Brutal Police Force." *The Observer*, October 24, 2020. https://www.theguardian.com/world/2020/oct/24/just-stop-killing-us-young-nigerians-rise-up-against-brutal-police-force

Akpan, Ime. 2010. "Edo Politician Arrested for Drug Trafficking." *Allafrica*, May 17, 2010. http://allafrica.com/stories/201005190624.html

Akpede, Benedicta. 2019. "Despite Increasing Budgetary Allocation, Nigerian Prisons Remain in Squalor." *Dataphyte*, September 13, 2019. https://www.dat aphyte.com/development/governance-development/despite-increasing-budgetary-allocation-nigerian-prisons-remain-in-squalor

Akyeampong, Emmanuel. 1996. *Drink, Power, and Cultural Change: A Social History of Alcohol in Ghana, c.1800 to Recent Times*. Oxford: James Currey.

Akyeampong, Emmanuel. 2005. "Diaspora and Drug Trafficking in West Africa: A Case Study of Ghana." *African Affairs*, 104(416): 429–447.

Alabi, Tope. 2014. "Youth's Unemployment and Crime Control: An Analysis of Nigerian Experience." *European Scientific Journal*, 10(2): 1857–7881.

Alden, Chris. 2007. *China in Africa*. London: Zed Books.

Aldrich, Michael. 1997. "Medicinal Characteristics of Cannabis." In *Cannabis in Medical Practice: A Legal, Historical, and Pharmacological Overview of the Therapeutic Use of Marijuana*, edited by Mary Lynn Mathre, 33–55. North Carolina: McFarland & Company Publishers.

Aldridge, Stephen, David Halpern, and Sara Fitzpatrick. 2002. "Social Capital." Performance and Evaluation Unit Discussion Paper. London: Cabinet Office. http://www.strategy.gov.uk/down-loads/seminars social-capital/social capital.pdf

Alemika, Etannibi O., and Chukwuma, Innocent C. 2000. "Police-Community Violence in Nigeria." *Centre for Law Enforcement Education and National Human Rights Commission*. Lagos: CLEEN. http://smtp.cleen.org/police-violence.pdf

Alexander, Michelle. 2012. *The New Jim Crow: Mass Incarceration in the Age of Colorblindness*. New York: The New Press.

Ali, Ali A. G., Tesfaye Dinka, Ibrahim A. Elbadawi Ahmed, Augustin Fosu, Alan Gelb, and Kupukile Mlambo. 2000. "Can Africa Claim the 21st Century?: Main Report (English)." Washington, DC: World Bank Group. http://documents.world-bank.org/

Aliyu, Abdullateef. 2018. "US Deports 34 Nigerians Over Homicide, Drugs, Others." *Daily Trust*, June 21, 2018. https://www.dailytrust.com.ng/us-deports-34-nigerians-over-homicide-drugs-others-257331.html

Al Jazeera. 2018. "Peru: The New Cocaine Kingdom." *Al Jazeera*, July 22, 2018. https://archive.org/details/ALJAZ_20180722_060000_Peru_The_New_Cocaine_Kingdom

Allen, Chris, and Jan Burgess. 1999. "Africa and the Drug Trade." *Review of African Political Economy*, 79: 5–11.

Allen, Rob. 2011. "Justice Reinvestment: Making Sense of the Costs of Imprisonment." *Criminal Justice Matters*, 71(1): 41–42.

Almasy, Steve. 2019. "Feds Indict 80 People in Massive Web of Scams Tied to Nigerians." *CNN*, August 22, 2019. https://edition.cnn.com/2019/08/22/us/nigeria-scams-indictments/index.html

Alves, Lise. 2014. "São Paulo Guarulhos Airport Opens Third Terminal." *The Rio Times*, May 13, 2014. http://riotimesonline.com/brazil-news/rio-business/São-paulo-guarulhos-airport-opens-third-terminal

Amin, Samir. 1974. *Accumulation on a World Scale: A Critique of the Theory of Underdevelopment*. New York: Monthly Review Press.

Amini-Philips, Chinyere, and Chukwuma Ogbuagwu. 2017. "Corruption and Administration of Higher Education Institutions in Nigeria." *World Journal of Social Science*, 4(2): 12–17.

Amnesty International. 1995. "The Death Penalty: No Solution to Illicit Drugs." *ACT 51/002/1995*. Amnesty International. https://www.amnesty.org/en/document s/ACT51/002/1995/en/

Amnesty International. 2016. "Urgent Action: Imminent Round of Execution in Indonesia." *UA: 179/16 Index: ASA 21/4542/2016 Indonesia*. Amnesty International. https://www.amnesty.org/download/Documents/ASA214542201 6ENGLISH.pdf

Amnesty International. 2018. "Moratorium on the Death Penalty in 2018 Within Reach." Press Release April 12, 2018, 05:40 UTC. Amnesty International. https:// www.amnesty.id/moratorium-death-penalty-2018-within-reach/

Ana-Caj. 2017. "South Africa Should Be Eternally Grateful to Nigeria." *IOL*, February 27, 2017. https://www.iol.co.za/news/politics/south-africa-should-be-e ternally-grateful-to-nigeria-7955145

Andersen, Synøve N., and Skardhamar Torbjørn. 2014. "Pick a Number: Mapping Recidivism Measures and Their Consequences." Oslo: Statistics Norway Discussion Papers 772: 3–29, March 2014. https://www.ssb.no/en/forskning/dis cussion-papers/_attachment/166596

Anderson, David, and Neil Carrier. 2009. "Khat in Colonial Kenya: A History of Prohibition and Control." *The Journal of African History*, 50(3): 377–397.

Andrés, Amado P. de. 2008. "West Africa Under Attack: Drugs, Organized Crime and Terrorism as the New Threats to Global Security." UNISCI Discussion Papers No. 16, 203–228. January 2008. https://www.ucm.es/data/cont/media/www/pag-72 513/UNISCI%20DP%2016%20-%20Andres.pdf

Anti-Death Penalty Asia Network. 2018. "Indonesia: Proposed Law that Keeps Death Penalty as 'Alternative Sentence', 10 Year Before Execution with Possibility of Commutation. Compromise Reached on Death Penalty." *Anti-Death Penalty Asia Network*, January, 12, 2018. https://adpan.org/2018/01/12/indonesia-proposed-la w-that-keeps-death-penalty-as-alternative-sentence-10-year-before-execution-with -possibility-of-commutation/

Anyagafu, Vera S. 2017. "Nigerian Excretes 1410.9 Grams of Cocaine, Faces Death Penalty in China." *Vanguard*, August 20, 2017. https://www.vanguardngr.com/20 17/08/nigerian-excretes-1410-9-grams-of-cocaine-faces-death-penalty-in-china/

Anyanwu, Ogechi. 2010. "Experiment with Mass University Education in Post-Civil War Nigeria, 1970–1979." *Journal of Nigeria Studies*, 1(1): Fall 2010.

Appadurai, Arjun. 1996. *Modernity at Large Cultural Dimensions of Globalization*. Minneapolis: University of Minnesota Press.

Appadurai, Arjun. 2006. "The Right to Research." *Globalization, Societies and Education*, 4(2): 167–177.

Aquino, Michael. 2017. "Drug Laws in Bali and The Rest of Indonesia." *Tripsavvy*, September 19, 2017. https://www.tripsavvy.com/drug-laws-in-indonesia-1629332

Aradeon, David. 1996. "The Unmaking of Tradition: The Preface to Architecture." *African Quarterly on the Arts,* 1(3):72–85.

Araujo, Ana L. 2011. "Forgetting and Remembering the Atlantic Slave Trade: The Legacy of Brazilian Slave Merchant Francisco Felix de Souza." In *Crossing Memories: Slavery and African Diaspora*, edited by Ana L. Araujo, Mariana P. Candido, and Paul E. Lovejoy, 79–103. Trenton, NJ: Africa World Press.

Arhin, Kwame. 1983. "Rank and Class Among the Asante and Fante in the Nineteenth Century". *Journal of the International African Institute*, 53(1): 22.

Arias, Enrique D. 2006. *Drugs & Democracy in Rio de Janeiro: Trafficking, Social Networks, and Public Security*. Chapel Hill: The University of North Carolina Press.

Ash, Lucy. 2016. "The Dutch Prison Crisis: A Shortage of Prisoners." *BBC News*, November 10, 2016. https://www.bbc.com/news/magazine-37904263

Asiyai, Romina I. 2015. "Improving Quality Higher Education in Nigeria: The Roles of Stakeholders." *International Journal of Higher Education*, 4(1): 61–70.

Asuni, Tolani. 1964. "Sociopsychiatric Problems of Cannabis in Nigeria." *UNODC Bulletin, 1964/01/01: 1728*. https://www.unodc.org/unodc/en/data-and-analysis/b ulletin/bulletin_1964-01-01_2_page003.html

Australian Government Department of Foreign Affairs and Trade (DFAT). 2018. "DFAT Country Information Report Nigeria." Australian Government, March 9, 2018. http://dfat.gov.au/about-us/publications/Documents/country-information-re port-nigeria.pdf

Auty, Katherine M. 2019. "Open Peer Review." A Systematic Review of Criminal Recidivism Rates Worldwide: 3-Year Update [Version 1; Peer Review: 1 Approved, 2 Approved with Reservations], by Denis Yukhnenko, Shivpriya Sridha, and Seena Fazel. 2019. *Wellcome Open Research*, 4(28).

Aviram, Hadar. 2014. "CCC Visit to a Maximum Security Prison in Brazil." *California Correctional Crisis*, August 28, 2014. http://californiacorrectionscrisis. blogspot.com/2014/08/ccc-visit-to-maximum-security-prison-in.html

Aziaki, Steve S. 2003. *Inequities in Nigerian Politics, The Niger Delta Resource Control, Underdevelopment and Youth Restiveness*. Yenagoa: Treasure Communications Resource Ltd.

Babbie, Earl. 2001. *The Practice of Social Research*, 9th edition. Belmont: Wadsworth.

Bacchi, Umberto. 2014. "US DEA Helps China Make $7m Cocaine Bust in Shanghai." *International Business Times*, August 29, 2014. http://www.ibtimes.co .uk/us-dea-helps-china-make-7m-cocaine-bust-shanghai-1463146

Bailey, Kenneth. 1994. *Methods of Social Research*, 4th edition. New York: The Free Press.

Barbour, Scott. 2000. *Drug Legalization*. Farmington Hills, MI: Greenhaven Press.

Barkan, Elazar. 1992. *The Retreat of Scientific Racism. Changing Concepts of Race in Britain and the United States Between the World Wars*. Cambridge: Cambridge University Press.

Barker, Neave. 2017. ""Kleptocracy Tour" Highlights London Money-laundering." *Aljazeera*, September 28, 2017. https://www.aljazeera.com/news/2017/09/klepto cracy-tour-highlights-london-money-laundering-170928102917563.html

Barrientos, Armando, and Hulme, David, ed. 2008. *Social Protection for the Poor and Poorest: Concepts, Policies and Politics*. Palgrave Macmillan.

Basch, Linda G., Nina G. Schiller, and Cristina S. Blanc. 1994. *Nations Unbound: Transnational Projects, Postcolonial Predicaments and Deterritorialized Nation-States*. London: Routledge

Bateman, Joseph. 2013. "Brazil Poised to Pass Harsh, Rights-Violating Drug Law." *International Drug Policy Consortium*, May 30, 2013. https://idpc.net/alerts/2013 /05/brazil-poised-to-pass-harsh-rights-violating-drug-law?setlang=fr

Baudrillard, Jean. 1996. *Perfect Crime*. London: Verso.

Bauman, Zygmunt. 1998. *Work, Consumerism and the New Poor*. Buckingham: Open University Press.

Becker, Howard S. 1963. *Outsiders: Studies in the Sociology of Deviance*. New York: The Free Press.

Beckett, Edward F. S. J. 1996. "Listening to Our History Inculturation and Jesuit Slaveholding." *Studies in the Spirituality of Jesuits*, 28/5- November 1996. https:// ejournals.bc.edu/index.php/jesuit/article/view/3964

Beittel, June S. 2017. "Colombian: Background and US Relations." Congressional Research Service Report 7-5700. 2017. November 14, 2017. https://fas.org/sgp/crs /row/RL32250.pdf

Bello, Ismail, Mohammad F. Ottman, and Mohd D. K. B. Shariffuddin. 2017. "An Appraisal of Malaysia-Nigeria Foreign Economic Relations." *European Academic Research*, 1:751–765.

Bello, Moses A. 2017. "Principles and Practice of Succession Under Customary Law." *Customary Court of Appeal*, FCT-Judiciary Abuja, March 22, 2017. http: //nji.gov.ng/images/Workshop_Papers/2017/Refresher_Judges_and_Kadis/s4.pdf

Benjamin, Nancy, Kathleen Beegle, Francesca Recanatini, and Massimiliano Santini. 2014. "Informal Economy and the World Bank." Policy Research Working Paper 688, May 2014. The World Bank. http://documents.worldbank.org/curated/en/416 741468332060156/pdf/WPS6888.pdf

BDA Sun (Bermuda Sun). 2005–2020. "Let's Talk About a Revolution." *Bermuda Sun Ltd*, April 10, 2020. http://www.bermudasun.bm/Content/NEWS/News/Ar ticle/Let-s-talk-about-a-revolution/24/270/27831

Bernama. 2017. "Drug Addiction Cases in M'sia Shot Up 14 Percent in 2016." *New Straits Times*, March 1, 2017. https://www.nst.com.my/news/2017/03/216259/drug -addiction-cases-msia-shot-14-cent-2016

Bernstein, Henry. 1999. "Ghana's Drug Economy: Some Preliminary Data." *Review of African Political Economy,* 26(79): 13–32.

Best, Joel. 1997. "Secondary Claims-Making: Claims About Threats to Children on the Network News." In *Social Problems in Everyday Life: Studies of Social Problems Work*, edited by Gale Miller, and James Holstein, 73–95. Greenwich CT: JAI Press.

Bevan, David L., Paul Collier, and Jan W. Gunning. 1999. *The Political Comparative Study Economy of Poverty, Equity, and Growth Nigeria and Indonesia*. Edited by Deepak Lal and Hla Myint. A world Bank Comparative Study. New York: Oxford University Press.

Bewley-Taylor, Dave, and Martin Jelsma. 2014. *The Rise and Decline of Cannabis Prohibition. The History of Cannabis in the UN Drug Control System and Options for Reform*. Amsterdam: Transnational Institute (TNI).

Bharadwaj, Ashish. 2014. "Is Poverty the Mother of Crime? Empirical Evidence of the Impact of Socioeconomic Factors on Crime in India." Economic Analysis Working Papers (2002–2010). *Atlantic Review of Economics, (2011–2016)* 1: 1–1.

Bichler, Gisela, Aili Malm, and Tristen Cooper. 2017. "Drug Supply Networks: A Systematic Review of the Organizational Structure of Illicit Drug Trade." *Crime Science*, 6(2):1–232.

Biddulph, Serah. 2007. *Legal Reform and Administrative Detention Powers in China*. Cambridge University Press.

Biersteker, Thomas J. 1993. "Nigeria, 1983–1986: Reaching Agreement with the Fund." In *Dealing with Debt: International Financial Negotiations and Adjustment Bargaining*, edited by Thomas. J. Biersteker, 133–152. Boulder, Colorado: Westview Press.

Bjerk, David, and Caleb Mason. 2014. "The Market for Mules: Risk and Compensation of Cross-Border Drug Couriers." IZA Discussion Paper, No. 8224. Bonn, German. May 2014. http://ftp.iza.org/dp8224.pdf

Black Lives Matter. 2020. "These Three Words." *Black Lives Matter*, January 28, 2021. https://blacklivesmatter.com

Blalock, Hubert M Jr. 1967. *Toward a Theory of Minority-Group Relations*. London: John Wiley.

Blundy, Rachel. 2017. "A Brief History of Hong Kong's Triad Gangs." *South China Morning Post*, February 4, 2017. https://www.scmp.com/news/hong-kong/law-crime/article/2067890/brief-history-hong-kongs-triad-gangs

Bodomo, Adams. 2012. *Africans in China: A Sociocultural Study and Its Implications for Africa-China Relations*. Amherst, NY: Cambria Press.

Boekhout van Solinge, Tim. 1999. "Dutch Drug Policy in a European Context." *Journal of Drug Issues*, 29(3): 511–528.

Boerman, Frank, Martin Grapendaal, Fred Nieuwenhuis, and Ewout Stoffers. 2017. *National Threat Assessment Organised Crime 2017*. Driebergen: Central Intelligence Division. https://www.politie.nl/binaries/content/assets/politie/algem een/nationaal-dreigingsbeeld-2017/2017-national-threat-assessment-organised -crime.pdf

Bonacich, Edna. 1973. "A Theory of Middleman Minorities." *American Sociological Review*, 38(5): 583–594.

Bonella, Kathryn. 2012. *Snowing in Bali*. Australia: Pan Macmillan.

Bosanquet, Nicholas, and Peter B. Doeringer. 1973. "Is There a Dual Labour Market in Great Britain?" *Economic Journal*, 83(330): 421–435.

Bose, Nandita, and Makini Brice. 2021. "If Rioters were Black, 'Hundreds' Would have Been killed: Washington Reflects on Capitol Rampage." *Reuters*, January 08, 2021. https://www.reuters.com/article/us-usa-election-inequality-idUSKBN29D1 HM

Bourdieu, Pierre. 1993. *Sociology in Question*. London: Sage Publishing.

Bourdieu, Pierre, and Loic J. D. Wacquan. 1992. *An Invitation to Reflexive Sociology*. Chicago: University of Chicago Press.

Bouze, Anthony. 1993. *How to Stop Crime*. New York: Plenum.

Bovenkerk, Frank. 2001. *Misdaadprofielen*. Amsterdam: Meulenhoff.

Bovenkerk, Frank, Dina Siegel, and Damián Zaitch. 2003. "Organized Crime and Ethnic Reputation Manipulation." *Crime, Law and Social Change*, 39: 23–38.

Bovenkerk, Fank, and Yesilgoz, Yucel. 2004. "Crime, Ethnicity and the Multicultural Administration of Justice." In *Cultural Criminology Unleashed*, edited by Hayward, Jeff, Keith Morrison, and Wayne Mirrison, Mike Presdee, 81–96. London: Glasshouse Press.

Bovin, Rémi. 2010. "Le Monde à L'envers? Vers une Approche Structurelle du Trafic Transnational de Drogues Illicites." *Déviance et Société*, 34: 93–114.

Bowles, Samuel, and Herbert Gintis. 2002. "Social Capital and Community Governance." *Economic Journal of the Royal Economic Society*, 112: 419–436.

Brahmbhatt, Milan, Canuto Otaviano, and Vostroknutova Ekaterina. 2010. *Dealing with Dutch Disease (English)*. Economic premise; no. 16. Washington, DC: World Bank. http://documents.worldbank.org/curated/en/794871468161957086/Dealing -with-Dutch-disease

Braithwaite, John. 1981. "The Myth of Social Class and Criminality Reconsidered." *American Sociological Review*, 46(1): 36–57.

Braithwaite, John. 1989. *Crime, Shame and Reintegration*. Cambridge, UK: Cambridge University Press.

Braithwaite, John. 1992. "Poverty, Power and White-Collar Crime." In *White-Collar Crime Reconsidered*, edited by Schlegel, Kip, and David Weisburd, 124–145. Boston: Northeastern University Press.

Braithwaite, John. 2003. "Principles of Restorative Justice." In *Restorative Justice and Criminal Justice: Competing or Reconcilable Paradigms*, edited by Andreas von Hirsch, Julian V. Roberts, Anthony E. Bottoms, Kent Roach, and Mara Schiff, 1–20. Oxford: Hart Publishing.

Braithwaite, John. 2011. "Partial Truth and Reconciliation in the Longue Durée." *Contemporary Social Sciences*, 6(1): 129–146.

Braun, Michael. 2009. "Confronting Drug Trafficking in West Africa." U.S. Senate, Subcommittee on African Affairs, Committee on Foreign Relations. Washington, DC. June 23, 2009. http://www.gpo.gov/fdsys/pkg/CHRG-111shrg52925/html/ CHRG 111shrg52925.htm

Brecher, Jeremy, Tim Costello, and Brendan Smith. 2000. *Globalization from Below*. Cambridge, MA: South End Press.

BBC (British Broadcasting Corporation). 2012. "Former Nigeria Governor James Ibori Jailed for 13 Years." *BBC*, April 17, 2012. http://www.bbc.com/news/world-africa-17739388

BBC (British Broadcasting Corporation). 2014. "Business: Nigeria Becomes Africa's Biggest Economy." *BBC*, April 6, 2014. http://www.bbc.com/news/business-26 913497

BBC (British Broadcasting Corporation). 2019. "Najib Razak: Malaysia's Former PM and His Downfall Over Alleged Corruption." *BBC*, August 13, 2019. https:// www.bbc.com/news/world-asia-22338100

BBC (British Broadcasting Corporation). 2020. "Cocaine and Guinea-Bissau: How Africa's 'Narco-State' is Trying to Kick Its Habit." *BBC*, May 28, 2020. https://ww w.bbc.com/news/world-africa-52569130

BBC (British Broadcasting Corporation). 2020. "Nigeria Protests: President Buhari Says 69 Killed in Unrest." *BBC*, October 23, 2020. https://www.bbc.com/news/world-africa-54666368

Broadhurst, Roderic G. 2012. "The Suppression of Black Societies in China." *Trends Organ Crime*, 16: 95–113.

Brown, Carolyn A., and Paul E. Lovejoy, ed. 2010. *Repercussions of the Atlantic Slave Trade: The Interior of the Bight of Biafra and the African Diaspora*. New Jersey: Africa World Press.

Brown, Stacy M. 2018. "The Major Role the Catholic Church Played in Slavery." *Amsterdam News*, September 18, 2018. http://amsterdamnews.com/news/2018/sep/18/major-role-catholic-church-played-slavery/

Bruun, Kettil, Lynn Pan, and Ingemar Rexed. 1975. *The Gentlemen's Club: International Control of Drugs and Alcohol*. Chicago: University of Chicago Press.

Bunt, Henk G. van de. 2004. "Police Corruption in the Netherlands." In *Police Corruption. Challenges for Developed Countries*, edited by Mohammad Amir, and Stanley Einstein, 413–433. Huntsville: Office of International Criminal Justice.

Bunt, Henk G. van de., Dina Siegel, and Damián Zaitch. 2014. "Organized Crime as a Socially Embedded Phenomenon." In *The Oxford Handbook of Organized Crime*, edited by Letizia Paoli, 321–339. Oxford: Oxford University Press.

Burduş, Eugen. 2010. "Fundamentals of Entrepreneurship." *Review of International Comparative Management*, 11(1) (March 2010). https://pdfs.semanticscholar.org/af33/e2030635898ded757cbdef4930d868a9d006.pdf

Busari, Stephanie, and Bukola Adebayo. 2018. "Sex-for-Grades Scandal: Nigerian Professor Sacked." *CNN*, June 20, 2018. https://www.cnn.com/2018/06/20/africa/nigeria-university-sacks-lecturer-sexual-assault/index.html

Business Anti-Corruption Portal. 2014. "Brazil Country Profile: Business Corruption in Brazil." *Business Anti-Corruption Portal*, July 2014. http://www.business-anti-corruption.com/country-profiles/the-americas/brazil/snapshot.aspx

Butorac, Ksenija, Dijana Gracin, and Nebojša Stanić. 2017. "The Challenges in Reducing Criminal Recidivism." *Public Security and Public Order*, 2017(18). https://bib.irb.hr/datoteka/912525.Butorac_et_al.pdf

Bybee, Ashley N. 2012. "The Twenty-first Century Expansion of the Transnational Drug Trade in Africa." *Journal of International Affairs*, 66(1), Transnational Organized Crime (FALL/WINTER 2012): 69–84. https://www.jstor.org/stable/24388252

Byler, Darren. 2019. "How Companies Profit from Forced Labor in Xinjiang." *Living Otherwise*, October 11, 2019. https://livingotherwise.com/2019/10/11/how-companies-profit-from-forced-labor-in-xinjiang

Byrne, John. 2010. "Halliburton Reportedly Agrees to Pay Nigeria $250 Million to Drop Bribery Charges Against Cheney." *The Raw Story*, December 14, 2010. http://www.rawstory.com/2010/12/halliburton-reportedly-agrees-pay-nigeria-250-million-drop-bribery-charges-cheney-firm/

Caldeira, Teresa P. R. 2001. *City of Walls: Crime, Segregation and Citizenship in São Paulo*. University of California Press.

Caldeira, Teresa P. R., and John Holston. 1999. "Democracy and Violence in Brazil." *Comparative Studies in Society and History*, 41(4): 691–729.

Cantens, Thomas, Ireland Robert, and Raballand Gael. 2015. "Introduction: Borders, Informality, International Trade and Customs." *Journal of Borderlands Studies*, 30(3):365–380.

Carson, Ann E. 2019. Prisoners in 2019. U.S. Department of Justice Office of Justice Programs, Bureau of Justice Statistics, October 2020, NCJ 255115. March 06, 2021. https://www.bjs.gov/content/pub/pdf/p19.pdf

Carson, Johnnie. 2012. "Countering Narcotics Threats in West Africa." Testimony of Assistant Secretary Johnnie Carson, Bureau of African Affairs U.S. Department of State, Before the Senate Drug Caucus, May 16, 2012. Accessed January 25, 2019, https://www.drugcaucus.senate.gov/sites/default/files/Amb%20Carson%20Testimony.pdf

Cassidy, John. 2020. "The Great Coronavirus Divide: Wall Street Profits Surge as Poverty Rises." *The New Yorker*, October 16, 2020. https://www.newyorker.com/news/our-columnists/the-great-coronavirus-divide-wall-street-profits-surge-as-poverty-rises

Castells, Manuel. 1997. *The Power of Identity*. Blackwell.

Castells, Manuel, and Alejandro Portes. 1989. "World Underneath: The Origins, Dynamics and Effects of the Informal Economy." In *The Informal Economy*, edited by Alejandro Portes, Manuel Castells, and Lauren Benton. Baltimore, MD: Johns Hopkins University Press.

Castillo, Roberto. 2014. "Feeling at Home in the "Chocolate City": An Exploration of Placemaking Practices and Structures of Belonging Among Africans in Guangzhou." *Inter-Asia Cultural Studies,* 15(2): 235–257.

Caulkins, Jonathan P., and Sara Chandler. 2006. "Long-Run Trends in Incarceration of Drug Offenders in the US." *Crime & Delinquency*, 52(4): 619–641.

Cengic, Imelda. 2019. "Brazil Cracks Down on Gangs and Corrupt Government Agents." *OCCRP*, August 16, 2019. https://www.occrp.org/en/daily/10493-brazil-cracks-down-on-gangs-and-corrupt-government-agents

CSIS (Center for Strategic and International Studies). 2021. "How Well-off is China's Middle Class?" China Power. *CSIS* 2021. https://chinapower.csis.org/china-middle-class/

CIA (Central Intelligence Agency). 1984. "Nigeria: Transit Point for Southwest Asian Heroin." Sanitized Copy Approved for Release 2010/11/01: CIA-RDP85T00287R001200620001-2. *CIA* Directorate of Intelligence, November 6, 1984. *CIA*, November 25, 2019. https://www.cia.gov/library/readingroom/docs/CIA-RDP85T00287R001200620001-2.pdf

CIA (Central Intelligence Agency). 2020. "The World Factbook: Population Below Poverty Line. Country Nigeria." *CIA*. Accessed April 23, 2020. https://www.cia.gov/library/publications/the-world-factbook/geos/ni.html

CRDA (Central Registry of Drug Abuse). 2017. "Central Registry of Drug Abuse Sixty-Sixth Report 2007-2016." Hong Kong: Narcotics Division, Security Bureau, Government of the Hong Kong Special Administrative Region. *CRDA*, March 02,

2019. https://www.nd.gov.hk/pdf/report/crda_66th/Chapter1%20Exe%20sum%2 0(66th).pdf

César, Rubem. 2012. "Brazil's "Drug Law: It's Time to Change" Campaign Collects Over 50,000 Signatures in Three Days." *Open Society Foundations*, July 26, 2012. https://www.opensocietyfoundations.org

Chamhuri, Siwar, Ferdoushi Ahmed, Ahmad Bashawir, and Md S. Mia. 2016. "Urbanization and Urban Poverty in Malaysia: Consequences and Vulnerability." *Journal of Applied Sciences*, 16(4): 154–160.

Chase-Dunn, Christopher K., and Peter Grimes. 1995. "World-Systems Analysis." *Annual Review of Sociology*, 21: 387–417.

Chibnall, Steve. 1977. *Law and Order News: An Analysis of Crime Reporting in the British Press*. London: Tavistock.

Chin, Ko-lin, and Sheldon X. Zhang. 2007. "The Chinese Connection: Cross-border Drug Trafficking Between Myanmar and China." U.S. Department of Justice, Document No. 218254. https://www.ncjrs.gov/pdffiles1/nij/grants/218254.pdf

Chin, Yee-Whah W., and Lim Ee-Shiang. 2018. "SME Policies and Performance in Malaysia." ISEAS Economics Working Paper, No. 2018-3, July 2018. https://ww w.iseas.edu.sg/images/pdf/ISEAS_EWP_2018-3_ChinLim.pdf

China Daily. 2012. "Nigeria Releases Around 70 Chinese, FM Spokesman Says." *China Daily*, May 24, 2012. http://usa.chinadaily.com.cn/world/2012-05/24/cont ent_15381960.htm

Chodorow, Gary. 2012. "New Exit-Entry Law Enacted by China's Congress." *Lawandborder.com,* August 29, 2012. https://lawandborder.com/wp-content/uplo ads/2012/07/GC-Article-on-New-PRC-EEAL-2012-08-29.pdf

Chowdhury, Amira. 2019. "The Story Behind Brazil's Prison Crisis." *Penn Political Review*, August 11, 2019. https://pennpoliticalreview.org/2019/08/the-story-behin d-brazils-prison-crisis/

Christiansen, Catrine, Mats Utas, and Henrik E. Vigh, eds. 2006. "Navigating Youth, Generating Adulthood Social Becoming in an African Context." *Nordiska Afrikainstitutet*, Uppsala 2006. http://www.engagingvulnerability.se/wpcontent/ uploads/2016/03/Finnstrom2006_NavigatingYouthwhole_book.pdf

Chukwu, Chinyere L., and Ehigiamusoe E. Lato. 2016. "Perception of Students on 'Sorting' in Nigerian Universities." *Multidisciplinary Journal of Academic Excellence*, 16(1):1–12.

Clear, Todd R. 1977. *Imprisoning Communities: How Mass Incarceration Makes Disadvantaged Neighborhoods Worse*. New York: Oxford University Press.

Cobas, Jose A. 1987. "Ethnic Enclaves and Middleman Minorities: Alternative Strategies of Immigrant Adaptation?" *Sociological Perspectives*, April 30(2), 143–161.

Cocaine Route Programme. 2020. "Activities and Achievements So Far." *Cocaine Route Programme*, June 16, 2018. http://cocaineroute.eu

Cockayne, James, and Williams Phil. 2009. "The Invincible Tide: Towards an International Strategy to Deal with Drug Trafficking Through West Africa." *International Peace Institute*, October 2009. https://www.ipinst.org/wpcontent/up loads/publications/west_africa_drug_trafficking_epub.pdf

Coconuts Bali. 2020. "Nearly Half of Kerobokan Prison Inmates Tested 'Reactive' for Coronavirus: Official." *Coconuts Bali*, October 22, 2020. https://coconuts.co/bali/news/nearly-half-of-kerobokan-prison-inmates-tested-reactive-for-coronavirus-official/

Cohen, Corentin. 2019. "Development of the Brazilian Drug Market Toward Africa: Myths, Evidence and Theoretical Questions." *Journal of Illicit Economies and Development*, 1(2): 134–144.

Cohen, Peter D. A. 1994. "The Case of Two Dutch Drug Policy Commissions. An Exercise in Harm Reduction 1968–1976." Paper Presented at the 5th International Conference on the Reduction of Drug Related Harm, March 7–11, 1994. Addiction Research Foundation: Toronto. Revised in 1996. https://pure.uva.nl/ws/files/971668/2218_cohen.case.html

Cohen, Stanley. 1972. *Folk Devils and Moral Panics*. London: MacGibbon and Kee.

Coleman, James S. 2000. "Social Capital in the Creation of Human Capital." In *Social Capital: A Multifaceted Perspective*, edited by Partha Dasgupta, and Ismail Serageldin, 13–39. Washington, DC: World Bank.

Collier, Paul, Anke Hoeffler, and Catherine Pattillo. 2001. "Flight Capital as a Portfolio Choice." *The World Bank Economic Review*, 15(1): 55–79.

Constitution of the Federal Republic of Nigeria 1999, as amended to 2010. UN Women. Global Gender Equality Constitutional Database. March 20, 2021. https://constitutions.unwomen.org/en/countries/africa/nigeria

Consultancy.eu. 2019. "Europe Blooms to World's Largest Legal Cannabis Market." *Consultancy.eu*, February 4, 2019. https://www.consultancy.eu/news/2307/europe-to-become-the-worlds-largest-legal-cannabis-market

Cooper, Robert. 2002. "The New Liberal Imperialism." *The Guardian*, April 7, 2002. http://www.theguardian.com/world/2002/apr/07/1

CFR (Council on Foreign Relations). 2013. "The Global Regime for Transnational Crime." *CFR,* June 25, 2013. http://www.cfr.org/transnational-crime/global-regime-transnational-crime/p28656

Courtwright, David T. 2001. *Forces of Habit: Drugs and the Making of the Modern World.* Cambridge, MA: Harvard University Press.

Covey, Stephen R. 2008. "A Whole New Mind-Set on Fighting Crime." *International Association of Chiefs of Police Chief*, October 20, 2012. http://www.policechiefmagazine.org/magazine/index.cfm?fuseaction=display_arch&article_id=1687&issue_id=122008

Cowburn, Ashley. 2017. "Government Accused of 'Squandering' £1.6bn a Year on Anti-Drug Policy." *Independent*, August 7, 2017. https://www.independent.co.uk/news/uk/politics/anti-drug-policy-government-16-billion-theresa-may-usage-levels-illicit-illegal-a7881356.html

Cox, Donald, and Marcel Fafchamps. 2006. "Extended Family and Kinship Networks: Economic Insights and Evolutionary Directions." https://web.stanford.edu/~fafchamp/CoxFafchamps_FirstDraft.pdf

Coyle, Andrew, Catherine Heard, and Helen Fair. 2016. "Current Trends and Practices in the Use of Imprisonment." *International Review of the Red Cross*, 98(903): 761–778.

Coyne, Christopher J., and Abigail R. Hall. 2017. "The Continued Failure of the War on Drug." *CATO Institute*, Number 811. April 12, 2017. https://www.cato.org/site s/cato.org/files/pubs/pdf/pa-811-updated.pdf

Crawford, Catherine, Rhia Gohel, Miranda Heneghan, Fay Thomson, and Crag Wright. 2017. "United Kingdom Drug Situation: Focal Point Annual Report 2016." *UK Focal Point on Drugs*, March 1, 2017. https://www.gov.uk/government/publi cations/united-kingdom-drug-situation-focal-point-annual-report

Csete, Joanne, Adeeba Kamarulzaman, Michel Kazatchkine, Frederick Altice, Marek Balicki, Julia Buxton, Javier Cepeda, Megan Comfort, Eric Goosby, … Christopher Beyrer. 2016. "Public Health and International Drug Policy." *The Lancet*, 387(10026) (April 2, 2016):1427–1480.

Currie, Eliott. 2013. *Crime and Punishment in America*. New York: Picador.

Dagne, Ted. 2005. "Nigeria in Political Transition." *Congressional Research Service. The Library of Congress*, June 3, 2005. https://fas.org/sgp/crs/row/IB98046.pdf

Daily Times. 1994. "NDLEA Stinks—Bamaiyi." *Daily Times*, February 18, 1994.

Dambazau, Abdulrahman B. 2009. *Criminology and Criminal Justice*, 2nd Edition. Ibadan: Dalog Prints and Packaging Limited.

Danaan, Victoria V. 2018. "Analysing Poverty in Nigeria Through Theoretical Lenses." *Journal of Sustainable Development*, 11(1): 20–31.

Decorte, Tom, and Damián Zaitch. 2016. *Kwalitatieve Methoden en Technieken in de Criminologie*. Leuven: Acco.

De Lucca, Denis. 2015. "Jesuits and Fortifications: The Contribution of the Jesuits to Military Architecture in the Baroque Age." *The Catholic Historical Review*, 101(3):661–662.

Devitt, James. 2020. "The Reckoning is Real": On Slavery, the Church, and How Some 21st-Century Institutions Are (Finally) Starting to Talk About Reparations." February 3, 2020, https://www.nyu.edu/about/news-publications/news/2020/f ebruary/-the-reckoning-is-real---on-slavery--the-church--and-how-some-21.html

Dikötter, Frank. 1992. *The Discourse of Race in Modern China*. HK: Hong Kong University Press.

Dilulio, John J. Jr. 2010. "Rethinking Crime–Again." *Democracy*, 16(Spring 2010):46–57. https://democracyjournal.org/magazine/16/rethinking-crime-again/

Dolan, Loretta. 2017. *Nurture and Neglect: Childhood in Sixteenth-Century Northern England*. London: Routledge.

Dotson, John, and Teresa Vanfleet. 2014. *Prison Labor Exports from China and Implications for U.S. Policy*. U.S.-China Economic and Security Review Commission Staff Research Report. July 9, 2014. https://www.uscc.gov/sites/def ault/files/Research/Staff%20Report_Prison%20Labor%20Exports%20from%20C hina_Final%20Report%20070914.pdf

Dowdney, Luke. 2003. *Children of the Drug Trade: A Case Study of Children in Organised Armed Violence in Rio de Janeiro*. Rio de Janeiro/2003: 7Letras. http:// resourcecentre.savethechildren.se/sites/default/files/documents/3261.pdf

Drug Policy Alliance. 2017. *It's Time for the U.S. to Decriminalize Drug Use and Possession*. Drug Policy Alliance, July 2017. https://www.drugpolicy.org/resource /its-time-us-decriminalize-drug-use-and-possession

Dunaway, Gregory R., Francis T. Cullen, Velmer S. Burton JR V. S., and Timothy D. Evans. 2000. "The Myth of Social Class and Crime Revised: An Examination of Class and Adult Criminality." *Criminology*, 38: 589–632.

Durham, Deborah. 2004. "Disappearing Youth: Youth as Social Shifter in Botswana." *American Ethnologist*, 31(4): 589–605.

Durkheim, Emile. 1964. *The Rules of Sociological Methods*, 8th edition, translated by Sarah A. Solovay and John H. Mueller and edited by George E.G. Catlin. New York: Free Press.

Durkheim, Emile. 1965. *Essays in Sociology and Philosophy*. Edited by K Wolff. New York: Harper & Row.

Durose, Matthew R., Alexia D. Cooper, and Howard N. Snyder. 2015. "Recidivism of Prisoners Released in 30 States in 2005: Patterns from 2005 to 2010." U.S. Department of Justice, *Bureau of Justice Statistics*, April 2014. Accessed March 04, 2021. https://www.bjs.gov/content/pub/pdf/rprts05p0510.pdf

Dwyer, Colin. 2020. "Former Interpol President Sentenced to Prison in China for Corruption." *NPR*, January 21, 2020. https://www.npr.org/2020/01/21/798121397/former-interpol-president-sentenced-to-prison-in-china-for-corruption

Ebbe, Obi N. I. 2012. "Organized Crime in Nigeria." In *Traditional Organized Crime in the Modern World: Responses to Socioeconomic Change*, edited by Dina Siegel and Henk van de Bunt, 169–188. New York: Spring.

Ebbe, Obi N. I. 2013. *Comparative and International Justice Criminal Systems. Policing, Judiciary and Corrections*, 3rd edition. Boca Raton: CRC Pres.

Ebbe, Obi N. I. 2016. *State Crimes Around the World: A Treaties in the Sociology of State Deviance*. Dubuque: Kendall Hunt.

Ehigiator, Kenneth. 2010. "How Couple Used Twins to Export Drugs 7 Times Before Arrest, by NDLEA." *Vanguard*, April 26, 2010. http://www.vanguardngr.com/2010/04/couple-used-twins-to-export-drugs-7-times-before-arrest/

Ekeopara, Chika A. 2012. "The Impact of the Extended Family System on Socio-Ethical order in Igboland." *American Journal of Social Issues & Humanities*, 12(4): 262–267.

Elechi, Oko, and Smart E. Otu. 2015. "Nigeria: Legal System of the Ebonyi State." In *Trends in the Judiciary: Interviews with Judges Across the Globe, Volume 2 (Interviews with Global Leaders in Policing, Courts, and Prisons) 1st Edition Kindle Edition*, edited by David, Lowe, and Dilip K. Das, Section 11. Boca Raton London New York: CRC Press.

Ellis, Stephen. 2009. "West Africa's International Drug Trade." *African Affairs*, 108(431): 171–196.

Embury-Dennis, Tom. 2018. "UK is the World's Biggest Exporter of Legal Cocaine and Heroin, Show New Figures." *Independent*, April 17, 2018. https://www.independent.co.uk/news/uk/home-news/uk-drugs-cocaine-heroin-exports-imports-international-narcotics-control-board-report-a8308891.html

Eteghe, Daniel. 2016. "Ojukwu's Niece, Others Arrested in 2.24 kg Drug Bust." *Vanguard*, January 12, 2016. https://www.vanguardngr.com/2016/01/ojukwus-niece-others-arrested-in-2-24kg-drug-bust/

EIHA (European Industrial Hemp Association). 2018. "Position Paper on: Reasonable Regulation of Cannabidiol (CBD) in Food, Cosmetics, as Herbal Natural Medicine and as Medicinal Product." *EIHA*, Hürth (Germany), October 2018. http://eiha.org /media/2016/10/18-10-EIHA-CBD-position-paper.pdf

EMCDDA (European Monitoring Center on Drugs and Drug Addiction). 2000. *Report to the EMCDDA. France Drug Situations 2000.* OFDT and EMCDDA, December 2000. http://www.emcdda.europa.eu/attachements.cfm/att_34648_EN _NR2000FranceEN.PDF

EMCDDA (European Monitoring Center on Drugs and Drug Addiction). 2012. "Country Legal Profiles the Netherlands. Development of Legislation." EMCDDA, March 19, 2012. http://www.emcdda.europa.eu/html.cfm/index5174EN.html?p luginMethod=eldd.countryprofiles&country=NL

EMCDDA (European Monitoring Center on Drugs and Drug Addiction). 2015. "New Psychoactive Substances in Europe. An Update from the EU Early Warning System." EMCDDA Lisbon, March 2015. http://www.emcdda.europa.eu/publica tions/rapid-communications/2015/new-psychoactive-substances_en

EMCDDA (European Monitoring Center on Drugs and Drug Addiction). 2019. "EU Drug Markets Report 2019." EMCDDA. Luxembourg. https://www.europol.europ a.eu/publications/

Eusebius, Achugo, and Clement C. Chigbo. 2014. "Empowering, Regulating and Controlling Apprenticeship in Nigeria for Employment and Development." *International Journal of Research in Applied, Natural and Social Sciences*, 2(6):219–232.

EIR (Executive Intelligence Review). 1986. "Why Nigeria Turned Down the IMF Loan." *EIR*, 13(8) (February 21). https://larouchepub.com/eiw/public/1986/eirv1 3n08-19860221/eirv13n08-19860221_053-why_nigeria_turned_down_the_imf.pdf

Ezeamalu, Ben. 2015. "Kashamu's Arrest: We've Received Formal Extradition Request—NDLEA." *Premium Times*, May 23, 2011. http://www.premiumtimesng .com/news/headlines/183551-%E2%80%8Bkashamus-arrest-%E2%80%8Bwe%E 2%80%8B%E2%80%8Bve-received-formal-extradition-%E2%80%8Brequest-% E2%80%8B-ndlea.html

Ezeamalu, Ben. 2015. "16 Million Nigerians Use Indian Hemp, 7 Million on Cocaine—NDLEA." *Premium Times Nigeria*, November 18, 2015. https://www .premiumtimesng.com/news/more-news/193448-16-million-nigerians-use-indian- hemp-7-million-on-cocaine-ndlea.html

Ezeamalu, Ben. 2017. "Despite Recent Killings, Another Nigerian Attempts Drugs Trafficking to Indonesia." *Premium Times*, April 8, 2017. http://www.premiumti mesng.com/news/headlines/228332-despite-recent-killings-another-nigerian-at tempts-drugs-trafficking-indonesia.html

Ezeudu, Florence O., Nkokelonye Cyprian U., and Adigwe Joseph C. 2013. "Science Education and Challenges of Globalization in Igbo Nation." *US-China Education Review B*, 3(2): 116–127.

Fafchamps, Marcel, and Susan Lund. 2003. "Risk Sharing Networks in Rural Philippines." *Journal of Development Economics*, 71: 261–287.

Fajnzylber, Pablo. Daniel Lederman, and Norman Loayza. 2002. "What Causes Violent Crime?" *European Economic Review*, 46(7): 1323–1357.

Fanon, Frantz. 1963. *The Wretched of the Earth*. Harmondsworth: Penguin.

Fanon, Frantz. 1965. *A Dying Colonialism*. Translated Haakon Chevalier. New York: Monthly Press.

Farah, Douglas. 2012. "Fixers, Super Fixers and Shadow Facilitators: How Networks Connect." *International Assessment and Strategy Center*, April 23, 2012. http://www.strategycenter.net/docLib/20120423_Farah_FixersSuperFi xersShadow.pdf

Fatokun, Samson O. 2016. "Predicting the Market Share of a New Airport in Multi-Airport Cities: The Case of Lagos." PhD diss., and Theses 192. Embry-Riddle Aeronautical University Daytona Beach, Florida. May 2016. https://commons.erau .edu/cgi/viewcontent.cgi?article=1191&context=edt

Fauna. 2011. "Chinese Drug Addicts Living Under Shenzhen Overpass." *China Smack*, August 9, 2011. https://www.chinasmack.com/chinese-drug-addicts-living-under-shenzhen-overpass

Federal Bureau of Prisons. 2017. "Statistics Inmate Citizenship." *Federal Bureau of Prisons*, November 25, 2017. https://www.bop.gov/about/statistics/statistics_in mate_citizenship.jsp

Federal Government of Nigeria. 1958. *The Role of the Federal Government in Promoting Industrial Development in Nigeria*. Lagos: Government Printer.

Federal Ministry of Justice. n.d. *FMOJ Budget. Federal Ministry of Nigerian 2016 Appropriation Act*. Federal Ministry of Justice. Accessed July 06, 2018. http:// www.justice.gov.ng/index.php/fmoj-downloads/other-documents/fmoj-budget

Feiling, Tom. 2009. *The Candy Machine. How Cocaine Took Over the World*. Penguin Books: London.

Ferrell, Jeff. 2005. "The Only Possible Adventure: Edgework and Anarchy." In *Edgework: The Sociology of Risk-Taking*, edited by Stephen Lyng, 75–88. London and New York: Routledge.

Ferrell, Jeff, Mark S. Hamm, Peter Adler, and Patricia A. Adler. 1998. *Ethnography at the Edge: Crime, Deviance, and Field Research*. Northeastern University Press.

Finn, Peter C. 1974. "The Slaves of the Jesuits of Maryland". M.A. in History Thesis presented at Georgetown University, May 1974. http://hdl.handle.net/10822 /1044615

Folarin, Sheriff F., Ilemobola P. Olanrewaju, and Yartey Ajayi. 2014. "Cultural Plurality, National Integration and the Security Dilemma in Nigeria." *Covenant University Journal of Politics and International Affairs,* 2(1): June 2014. https://jo urnals.covenantuniversity.edu.ng/index.php/cujpia/article/view/122

Forest, James J. F. 2012. "Confronting the Terrorism of Boko Haram in Nigeria." Joint Special Operations University. Report No. 12-5. Florida: JSOU (U.S.). May 2012. Accessed April 13, 2020. https://www.hsdl.org/?view&did=715583

Forrest, Tom. 1982. "Brazil and Africa: Geopolitics, Trade, and Technology in the South Atlantic." *African Affairs*, 81(322) (Jan): 3–20.

Forrest, Tom. 1995. *The Makers and Making of Nigerian Private Enterprise*. Lagos: Ibadan Spectrum Books.

Fox, Chris, Kevin Albertson, and Kevin Wong, 2013. "Justice Reinvestment and Its Potential Contribution to Criminal Justice Reform." *Prison Service Journal* 207: 34–46.

Fox, Louise, and Thomas P. Sohnesen. 2013. "Household Enterprises in Sub-Saharan Africa: Why They Matter for Growth, Jobs, and Livelihoods." World Bank Policy Research Paper No. 6184. World Bank, Washington, DC. https://openknowledge .worldbank.org/handle/10986/12038

Francis, Brian, Leslie Humphreys, Stuart Kirby, and Keith Soothill. 2013. *Understanding Criminal Careers in Organised Crime Research Report 74*. Home Office, October 2013. https://assets.publishing.service.gov.uk/government/upl oads/system/uploads/attachment_data/file/246392/horr74.pdf

Free Malaysia Today. 2017. "81 Nigerians on Death Row in Malaysia, Says Report." *Free Malaysia Today*, August 13, 2017. http://www.freemalaysiatoday.com/ca tegory/nation/2017/08/13/81-nigerians-on-death-row-in-malaysia-says-report

Friedmann, Alex. 2014. "Recidivism Performance Measures for Private Halfway Houses in Pennsylvania." *Prison Legal News*, September 19, 2014. https://www .prisonlegalnews.org/news/2014/sep/19/recidivism-performance-measures-private -halfway-houses-pennsylvania/

Fukuyama, Francis. 2001. "Social Capital, Civil Society and Development." *Third World Quarterly*, 22(1): 7–20.

Gaffey, Conor. 2017. "Nigeria's Anti-Corruption Agency Finds $43 Million in Cash at Lagos Apartment." *Newsweek*, April 13, 2017. https://www.newsweek.com/ nigerian-anti-corruption-43-million-cash-lagos-apartment-583481

GAN Business Anti-Corruption Portal 2017a. "Brazil Corruption Report." *GAN Integrity*, June 2017. https://www.ganintegrity.com/portal/country-profiles/brazil/

GAN Business Anti-Corruption Portal 2017b. "Indonesia Corruption Report." *GAN Integrity*, June 2017. https://www.ganintegrity.com/portal/country-profiles/indonesia/

Gao, Yuan. 1989. "What U.S. Is Doing for Human Rights in China; It's Just Jealousy." *The New York Times,* March 18, 1989. Sec. 1, 26. https://www.nytimes. com/1989/03/18/opinion/l-what-us-is-doing-for-human-rights-in-china-it-s-just-je alousy-764689.html

Garnaut, Ross, Song Ligang, and Fang, Cai, ed. 2018. *China's 40 Years of Reform and Development: 1978–2018*. China Update Book Series. Acton: ANU Press, http://dx.doi.org/10.22459/CYRD.07.2018

Garland, David. 2001. *The Culture of Control: Crime and Social Order in Contemporary Society*. Chicago: University of Chicago Press.

Gates, Henry, L. Jr. 2011. *Black in Latin America*. New York; London: NYU Press.

Gaviria, Alejandro, and Daniel Mejía, ed. 2016. *Anti-Drugs Policies in Colombia: Successes, Failures and Wrong Turns*. Nashville: Vanderbilt University Press.

Geelhoed, Flore. 2012. "Purification and Resistance: Glocal Meanings of Islamic Fundamentalism in the Netherlands." PhD diss., Erasmus University Rotterdam, The Netherlands. January 13, 2012. https://repub.eur.nl/pub/31685/

Gelling, Peter. 2008. "Indonesia Widens Use of Death Penalty." *The New York Times*, July 11, 2008. https://www.nytimes.com/2008/07/11/world/asia/11iht-indo.1.1 4421132.html

Geschiere, Peter, and Birgit Meyer. 1998. "Globalization and Identity: Dialectics of Flow and Closure." *Development and Change,* 29: 601–615.

Gesley, Jenny. 2016. "Decriminalization of Narcotics: Netherlands." *Library of Congress Law*, February 01, 2021. https://www.loc.gov/law/help/decriminalizatio n-of-narcotics/netherlands.php

Gielis, Ruben. 2009. "A Global Sense of Migrant Places: Towards a Place Perspective in the Study of Migrant Transnationalism." *Global Networks*, 9(2): 271–287.

Gilles, Angelo. 2015. "The Social Construction of Guangzhou as a Translocal Trading Place." *Journal of Current Chinese Affairs*, 44(4): 17–47.

Gilman, Nils, Jesse Goldhammer, and Steve Weber, ed. 2011. *Deviant Globalization: Black Market Economy in the 21st Century.* New York, NY: Continuum.

Gitlin, Todd. 1995. *Twilight of Common Dreams.* New York: Henry Holt.

Global Black History. 2020. "The Role of the Roman Catholic Church in Slavery." *Global Black History.* https://www.globalblackhistory.com/2015/11/the-role-of- the-roman-catholic-church-in-slavery.html

Global Corruption Barometer. 2017. "People and Corruption: Asia Pacific." *Transparency International*, February 21, 2018. https://www.transparency.org/ whatwedo/publication/people_and_corruption_asia_pacific_global_corruption_ba rometer

Godfrey, Brian J. 1999. "Revisiting Rio de Janeiro and Sao Paulo." *Geographical Review*, 89(1): 94–121.

Goel, Sandeep. 2012. "A Nigerian National, Member of an International Drug Trafficking Syndicate Arrested." *Delhi Police North East District*, March 03, 2012. Press Release. Accessed March 19, 2020. delhipolice.nic.in/home/backup/01-03 -2012.doc

Goode, Erich, and Ben-Yehuda Nachman. 1994. *Moral Panics: The Social Construction of Deviance*, 2nd edition. Cambridge, MA: Blackwell.

Goodenough, Patrick. 2014. "Boko Haram Recruitment: Kerry Blames Poverty." *CNS News,* May 7, 2014. https://www.cnsnews.com/news/article/patrick-goode nough/boko-haram-recruitment-kerry-blames-poverty

Gootenberg, Pual, ed. 1999. *Cocaine: Global Histories.* New York: Routledge.

Gould, David J., and Jose Amaro-Reyes. 1983. "The Effect of Corruption on Administrative Performance." World Bank Staff Working Papers Number 580, Management and Development Series Number 7. The World Bank, October 31, 1983. http://documents.worldbank.org/curated/en/799981468762327213/pdf/multi -page.pdf

Graham, Ousey C., and Matthew R. Lee. 2013. "Community, Inequality, and Crime." In *The Oxford Handbook of Criminology Theory*, edited by Cullen, Francis T., and Cullen and Pamela Wilcox, 352–369. New York: Oxford Press.

Granovetter, Mark. 1983. "The Strength of Weak Ties: A Network Theory Revisited." *Sociological Theory,* 1: 201–233.

Granovetter, Mark. 1995. "The Economic Sociology of Firms and Entrepreneurs." In *The Economic Sociology of Immigration: Essays on Ethnic Entrepreneurship*, edited by Alejandro Portes, 128–165. New York: Russell Sage Foundation.

Green, Penny. 1996. "Drug Couriers: The Construction of a Public Enemy." In *Drug Couriers. A New Perspective*, edited by Penny Green, 1–20. Howard League Handbooks 11. London: Quartet Books.

Green, Penney, and Ward Tony. 2004. State Crime: Governments, Violence and Corruption. London: Pluto Press.

Greenwood, Louise. 2010. "Are Africa's Commodities an Economic Blessing?" *BBC Africa*. http://www.bbc.com/news/business-10710488

Greenwood, Peter, and Allen Abrahamse. 1982. *Selective Incapacitation.* Santa Monica, CA: The Rand Corporation.

Greer, Chris, and Eugene McLaughlin. 2017. "News Power, Crime and Media Justice." In *Oxford Handbook of Criminology*, 6th edition, edited by Alison Liebling, Shadd Maruna, and Lesley McAra, 260–283. Oxford: Oxford University Press.

Griffiths, James, and Shen Lu. 2016. "Outrage Erupts Over "Racist" Detergent ad." *CNN*, May 28, 2016. https://www.cnn.com/2016/05/27/asia/chinese-racist-detergent-ad/index.html

Grix, Jonathan. 2001. *Demystifying Postgraduate Research.* Birmingham: University of Birmingham University Press.

Gross, Samuel R., Maurice Possley, and Klara Stephens. 2017. "Race and Wrongful Convictions in the United States." *National Registry of Exonerations*, March 7, 2017. http://www.law.umich.edu/special/exoneration/Documents/Race_and_Wrongful_Convictions.pdf

Gross, Samuel R., O'Brien Barbara, Hu Chen, and Kennedy Edward. 2014. "Rate of False Conviction of Criminal Defendants Who are Sentenced to Death." *PNAS*, 111(20): 7230–7235.

Gupta, Vikram K., Priya Bansal, Amanpreet Kaur, and Gurmeet Singh. 2015. "Pattern of Shifting of Substance Abuse Among Drug Addicts Undergoing Treatment at DDCS (Drug Deaddiction Centers) in Punjab." *Journal of Evolution of Medical and Dental Sciences*, 4(37): 6546–6550.

Haan, Willem de, and Ian Loader. 2002. "On the Emotions of Crime, Punishment and Social Control." *Theoretical Criminology*, 2(3): 243–253.

Habermas, Jürgen.1996. *Between Facts and Norms.* Cambridge: Polity.

Hacienda, Terry. 2017. "Colombia President Compares Drug War to Riding a Stationary Bike." *The Fresh Toast*, November 7, 2017. https://thefreshtoast.com/cannabis/colombia-president-compares-drug-war-to-riding-a-stationary-bike/

Hall, Stuart. 1988. *The Hard Road to Renewal: Thatcherism and the Crisis of the Left.* London: Verso.

Hall, Stuart. 1991. "Old and New Identities, Old and New Ethnicities." In *Culture, Globalization and the World-System*, edited by Anthony D. King, 41–68. Houndmills: Macmillan.

Hall, David L., and Ames Roger T. 1995. *Anticipating China: Thinking Through the Narratives of Chinese and Western Culture.* SUNY Press.

Hall, Stuart, Chas Critcher, Tony Jefferson, John Clarke, and Brian Roberts. 1978. *Policing the Crisis: Mugging, the State and Law and Order.* London: Macmillan.

Harris, Kamala D., and Joan O'C. Hamilton. 2009. *Smart on Crime.* San Francisco: Chronicle Books.

Hart, Keith. 2001. *Money in an Unequal World: Keith Hart and His Memory Bank.* New York: Texere.

Hart, Keith. 2006. "Bureaucratic Form and the Informal Economy." In *Linking the Formal and Informal Economy: Concepts and Policies*, edited by Basudeb Guha-Khasnobis, Ravi Kanbur, and Elinor Ostromv, 21–35. Oxford: Oxford University Press.

Hashimzade, Nigar, and Chris Hedy. 2016. "Reflections on the Meaning and Measurement of Unobserved Economies: An Editorial Comment." *Journal of Tax Administration*, 2(2): 108.

Haugen, Heidi. O. 2012. "Nigerians in China: A Second State of Immobility." *International Migration*, 50(2): 65–80.

Havocscope. 2017. "Global Black Market Information." *Havocscope*, October 15, 2017. http://www.havocscope.com

Hay, Carter, and Walter Forrest. 2009. "The Implications of Family Poverty for a Pattern of Persistent Offending." In *The Development of Persistent Criminality*, edited by Joanne Savage, 54–70. Oxford: Oxford University Press.

Henry, Stuart, and Milovanovic Dragan. 1994. "The Constitution of Constitutive Criminology: A Postmodern Approach to Criminological Theory." In *The Future of Criminology*, edited by Nelken David. London: Routledge

Her Majesty's Government. 2013. *Serious and Organised Crime Strategy.* Her Majesty's Government, October 2013. https://assets.publishing.service.gov.uk

Herrera, Sascha C. 2012. "A History of Violence and Exclusion: Afro-Colombians from Slavery to Displacement." A Thesis submitted to the Faculty of The School of Continuing Studies and of The Graduate School of Arts and Sciences in partial fulfillment of the requirements for the degree of Master of Arts in Liberal Studies. Georgetown University Washington, DC. October 31, 2012. https://repository.l ibrary.georgetown.edu/bitstream/handle/10822/557698/Herrera_georgetown_0076 M_11964.pdf?sequence=1

Herschatter, Gail. 1997. *Dangerous Pleasures: Prostitution and Modernity in Twentieth-Century Shanghai.* The University of California Press.

Hicken, Allen. 2011. "Clientelism." *Annual Reviews of Political Science*, 14: 289–310.

Higuchi, Naoto. 2006. "Brazilian Migration to Japan Trends, Modalities and Impact." Expert Group Meeting on International Migration and Development in Latin America and the Caribbean. Population Division Department of Economic and Social Affairs. United Nations Secretariat Mexico City, 30 November–2 December 2005. UN/POP/EGM-MIG/2005/11 February 27, 2006. http://www.un .org

Hiil. 2018. "Justice Needs and Satisfaction in Nigeria. Legal Problems in Daily Life." *Hiil*, September 12, 2018. https://www.hiil.org/wp-content/uploads/2018/07/HiiL -Nigeria-JNS-report-web.pdf

Hirschfield, Katherine. 2015. *Gangster State. Organized Crime, kleptocracy and Political Collapse.* New York: Palgrave.

Ho, David Y. F. 1985. "Prejudice, Colonialism, and Interethnic Relations: An East-West Dialogue." *Journal of Asian and African Studies*, 20: 218–231.

Hobbes, Thomas. 1968. *The Leviathan.* Edited by Crawford B. Macpherson. Harmondsworth: Penguin, 1968. Print.

Hobbs, Dick. 1988. "Going Down the Glocal: The Local Context of Organised Crime." *The Howard Journal of Criminal Justice*, 37: 407–422.

Hobsbawm, Eric, and Terence Ranger, eds. 1983. *"The Invention of Tradition.* Cambridge: Cambridge University Press.

Hodgkinson, Peter, Lina Gyllensten, and Dianna Peel. 2010. "Capital Punishment Briefing Paper." *Centre for Capital Punishment Studies London.* https://studybest .com/db/files/images/pdf/1/1829_1151551.pdfhttps://studybest.com/db/files/imag es/pdf/1/1829_1151551.pdf

Hoffmann, Leena K., and Raj N. Patel. 2017. "Collective Action on Corruption in Nigeria: A Social Norms Approach to Connecting Society and Institutions." *Chatham House Report*, May 17, 2017. https://www.chathamhouse.org/publication /collective-action-corruption-nigeria-social-norms

Holloway, Richard. 2008. "Corruption and Civil Society Organisations in Indonesia." *Unpan1.un.org.*, April 25, 2018. http://www.richardholloway.org/wp-content/upl oads/2014/04/CSOs-and-Corruption-in-Indonesia.pdf

Holloway, Thomas. 1993. *Policing Rio de Janeiro: Repression and Resistance in a Nineteenth Century City.* Stanford, CA: Stanford University Press.

Home Office. 2016. *Drug Misuse: Findings from the 2015/16 Crime Survey for England and Wales Second Edition.* Edited by Deborah Lader. National Statistic. Statistical Bulletin 07/16. Home Office, July 2016. https://assets.publishing.serv ice.gov.uk/government/uploads/system/uploads/attachment_data/file/564760/drug -misuse-1516.pdf

Hopkins, Anthony G. 1973. *An Economic History of West Africa.* London: Longman.

Hristowa, Bobby. 2019. "Canada Ranks Second in the World for Cocaine Use (but Feels Conflicted About It): Report." *National Post.com*, May 16 2019. https:// nationalpost.com

Huggins, Robert, and Piers Thompson. 2014. "Culture, Entrepreneurship and Uneven Development: A Spatial Analysis, Entrepreneurship & Regional Development." *An International Journal*, 26(9–10): 726–752.

Hughes, Caitlin E., and Alex Stevens. 2010. "What Can We Learn from the Portuguese Decriminalization of Illicit Drugs?" *British Journal of Criminology*, 50(6): 999–1022.

Huguet, Clarisa, and Ilona Szabó de Carvalho. 2008. "Violence in the Brazilian Favelas and the Role of the Police." *New Directions for Youth Development*, 119 (Fall 2008): 93–109.

HRW (Human Rights Watch). 2004. "IV. Human Rights Abuses and the War on Drugs." *HRW*, April 15, 2020. https://www.hrw.org/reports/2004/thailand0704/4 .htm

HRW (Human Rights Watch). 2018. "Brazil: Police Killings at Record High in Rio. Unlawful Actions Undermine Public Security." *HRW*, December 19, 2018. https:// www.hrw.org/news/2018/12/19/brazil-police-killings-record-high-rio#

HRW (Human Rights Watch). 2019. "World Report 2019. Brazil Events of 2018."
HRW. https://www.hrw.org/world-report/2019/country-chapters/brazil#709451

Hutton, Will. 1995. *The State We're In*. London: Cape.

Ibagere, Eniwoke. 2000. "Drugs: The Nigerian Connection." *BBC*, June 6, 2000.
http://news.bbc.co.uk/2/hi/778299.stm

Ifemesia, Chieka. 1979. *Traditional Humane Living among the Igbo: As Historical Perspective*. Enugu: Fourth Dimension Press.

Igwe, Austine U. 2015. "Zik of Africa: An Appraisal of the Contributions of Dr. Nnamdi Azikiwe to African Socio-Political and Economic Growth in the Twentieth Century." *Global Journal of Arts Humanities and Social Sciences*, 3(4) (April): 14–27.

Igwe, Paul A., Amarachi N. Amaugo, Oyedele M. Ogundana, Odafe Martin Egere, and Juliana Amarachi Anigbo. 2018. "Factors Affecting the Investment Climate, SMEs Productivity and Entrepreneurship in Nigeria." *European Journal of Sustainable Development*, 7(1): 182–200.

Igwe, Wilson C., Ngozi Ojinnaka, S. O. Ejiofor, G. O. Emechebe, and B. C. Ibe. 2009. "Socio-Demographic Correlates of Psychoactive Substance Abuse Among Secondary School Students in Enugu, Nigeria." *European Journal of Social Science*, 12(2) (Dec): 277–283.

Ikoh, Moses U. 2013. "Organised Crime in the Gulf of Guinea with a Focus on Nigeria." In *The Impact of Organised Crime in West Africa*, edited by Etannibi E. O. Alemika, 20–30. Abuja: Friedrich-Ebert Stiftung.

Imouokhome, Aize O. 1989 "Identification of Cultural Variables in the Undisclosing Nigerian Counselling Clients." *Nigerian Journal of Counseling and Development*, 4: 77–89.

Index Mundi 2018. "Palm Oil Production by Country in 1000 MT." *Index Mundi*, March 27, 2020. https://www.indexmundi.com/agriculture/?commodity= palm-oil

Indonesia Investments. 2016. "Corruption in Indonesia: Suryadharma Ali Found Guilty by Jakarta Corruption Court." *Indonesia Investments*, January 12, 2016. https://www.indonesia-investments.com/news/news-columns/corruption-in-indon esia-suryadharma-ali-found-guilty/item6367

IANS (Institute for Applied Network Security) Jakarta. 2016. "Indonesia Executes Four Drug Convicts; Indian Not Among Them." *Business Standard*, July 29, 2016. https://www.business-standard.com/article/news-ians/indonesia-executes-four -drug-convicts-indian-not-among-them-116072900120_1.html

Institute for Criminal Policy Research. (n.d.). "World Prisons Brief Data Nigeria." *Prison Studies.org*, November 27, 2019. http://www.prisonstudies.org/country/nigeria

IARD (International Alliance for Responsible Drinking). 2015. "Responsible Service of Alcohol: A Server's Guide." *IARD*. Washington, DC. http://www.iard.org/wp -content/uploads/2016/01/TK-Servers-Guide.pdf

IBA (International Bar Association). 2010. "One in Five: The Crisis in Brazil's Prisons and Criminal Justice System. Human Rights Institute Report." *IBA*, February 2010. http://penselivre.org.br/wp-content/uploads/2014/01/Brazil_report _February-2010.pdf

International Commission of Jurists. 2012. *Access to Justice: Human Rights Abuses Involving Corporations—Federal Republic of Nigeria*. Geneva Switzerland: International Commission of Jurists. https://www.business-humanrights.org/sites/ default/files/media/documents/icj-report-access-to-justice-nigeria-22-feb-2012.pdf

ILO (International Labour Organization). 2016. *World Employment and Social Outlook: Trends 2016*. Geneva: ILO. https://www.ilo.org/wcmsp5/groups/public /---dgreports/---dcomm/---publ/documents/publication/wcms_443480.pdf

IMF (International Monetary Fund). 2017. *Nigeria Selected Issues. IMF Country Report No 17(81)*. Washington, DC: IMF. http://www.imf.org

INCB (International Narcotics Control Board). 2017. "INCB Annual Report 2017." *INCB*, March 1, 2018. https://www.incb.org/documents/Publications/AnnualRepor ts/AR2017/Annual_Report/E_2017_AR_ebook.pdf

INCSR (International Narcotics Control Strategy Report). 2014. *INCSR Volume 1 Drug and Chemical Control 2014*. United States Department of States. Bureau of International Narcotics and Law Enforcement Affairs. Washington, DC. March 2014. https://www.state.gov/documents/organization/222881.pdf

INCSR (International Narcotics Control Strategy Report). 2016. *Countries/ Jurisdictions of Primary Concern Nigeria*. U.S. Department of States, INCSR Bureau of African Affairs, March 2016. https://www.globalsecurity.org/security/ library/report/2016/2016-narcotics-control-strategy-report_vol1.pdf

INCSR (International Narcotics Control Strategy Report). 2017. *INCSR Volume 1 Drug and Chemical Control March 2017*. US Department of State, Bureau for International Narcotics and Law Enforcement Affairs. Washington, DC, March 2017. https://www.state.gov/wp-content/uploads/2019/04/2017-INCSR-Vol.-I.pdf

INCSR (International Narcotics Control Strategy Report). 2018. *INCSR Volume Drug and Chemical Control March 2018*. U.S. Department of State. Bureau of International Narcotics and Law Enforcement Affairs, March 2017. March 2018. https://www.state.gov/wp-content/uploads/2019/04/2018-INCSR-Vol.-I.pdf

INCSR (International Narcotics Control Strategy Report). 2019. *INCSR 2019 Volume 1 Drug and Chemical Control March 2019*. United States Department of State. Bureau for International Narcotics and Law Enforcement Affairs. INCSR. March 2019. https://www.state.gov/wp-content/uploads/2019/04/INCSR-Vol-IN CSR-Vol.-I-1.pdf

Iroanusi, Queen E. 2017. "Over 1000 Nigerian Youth Languishing in Thai Jails— Ambassador." *Premium Times Nigeria*, October 20, 2017. https://www.premiumt imesng.com/news/headlines/246707-1000-nigerian-youth-languishing-thai-jails -ambassador.html

Izugbara, Chimaraoke, Latifat Ibisomi, Alex C. Ezeh, and Mairo Mandara. 2010. "Gendered Interests and Poor Spousal Contraceptive Communication in Islamic Northern Nigeria." *JFam Plann Reprod Health Care*, 36(4): 219–224.

Jaguaribe, Beatriz. 2009. "Hijacked by Realism." *Public Culture*, 21(2): 219–227.

Jamalmanesh, Arash, Ali A. N. Meidani, and Mahdi M. K. Mashhadi. 2014. "Government Effectiveness, Rule of Law and Informal Economy in Asian Developing Countries." *International Journal of Economy, Management and Social Sciences*, 3(10): 551–555.

James, Cyril L. R. 1989. *The Black Jacobins: Toussaint l'Ouverture and the San Domingo Revolution*. Knopf Doubleday Publishing Group.

Jennings, Allyson. 2018. "How to Deal with the Police in Thailand." *World Nomads*, June 4, 2018. https://www.worldnomads.com/travel-safety/southeast-asia/thailand/police-what-you-need-to-know

Jiang, Shanhe, Deping Xiang, Qi Chen, Hengxiang Huang, Shengyong Yang, Dawei Zhang, and Anna Zhao. 2014. "Community Corrections in China: Development and Challenges." *The Prison Journal*, 94(1): 75–96.

Jiang, Shanhe, Jin Wang, and Eric Lambert. 2010. "Correlates of Formal and Informal Control in Guangzhou, China Neighborhood." *Journal of Criminal Justice, Elsevier*, 38(4) (July): 460–469.

Jiao, Allen Y. 2001. "Police and Culture: A Comparison Between China and the United States." *Police Quarterly*, 4(2): 156–185.

Joseph, Richard. 2013. "Prebendalism and Dysfunctionality in Nigeria." *Africaplus*, July 26, 2013. https://africaplus.wordpress.com/2013/07/26/prebendalism-and-dysfunctionality-in-nigeria/

Kail, Tony M. 2008. *Magico-Religious Groups and Ritualistic Activities: A Guide for First Responders*. Boca Raton, FL: CRC Press, Taylor & Francis Group.

Kalama, John, Charity E. Etebu, Charles A. Martha, and Sophia M. John. 2012. "Legislator's Jumbo Pay, Cost of Governance and the State of Education in Nigeria: Issues and Contradictions." *Journal of Educational and Social Research*, 2(4): 73–77.

Kanato, Manop, Poonrut Leyatikul, and Chuanpit Choomwattana, 2017. "ASEAN Drug Monitoring Report 2016." *ASEAN Narcotics Cooperation Center- ASEAN-NACO*, August 2017. https://asean.org/wp-content/uploads/2016/10/Doc6-ADM-Report-2016-as-of-15-November-2017-FINAL.pdf

Katz, Jack. 1988. *The Seductions of Crime*. New York: Basic Books.

Katzenbach, Nicholas deB. 1967. "The Challenge of Crime in a Free Society: A Report by the President's Commission on Law Enforcement and Administration of Justice." United States Government Printing Office Washington, DC, February 1967. Accessed February 28, 2022. https://www.ojp.gov/sites/g/files/xyckuh241/files/archives/ncjrs/42.pdf

Kauzlarich, David, and Kramer C. Ronald. 1998. *Crimes of the American Nuclear State: At Home and Abroad*. Boston: Northeastern University Press.

Kawachi, Ichiro, Bruce P. Kennedy, and Richard G. Wilkinson. 1999. "Crime: Social Disorganization and Relative Deprivation." *Social Science & Medicine*, 48(6): 719–731.

Kazeem, Yomi. 2017. "Only One in Four Nigerians Applying to University Will Get a Spot." *Quartz Africa*, February 22, 2017. https://qz.com/africa/915618/only-one-in-four-nigerians-applying-to-university-will-get-a-spot/

Kempton, Nicole, and Richardson Nan, eds. 2009. *Laogai: The Machinery of Repression in China*. Brooklyn, NY: Umbrage Editions.

Khapoya, Vincent B. 2010. *The African Experience: An Introduction*, 3rd edition. Longman.

Kibble, Steve. 1998. *Drugs and Development in South Africa*. London: Catholic Institute for International Affairs.

Kilmer, Beau, and Greg Midgette. 2017. "Mixed Messages: Is Cocaine Consumption in the U.S. Going Up or Down?" *Brookings*, April 28, 2017. https://www.bro okings.edu/opinions/mixed-messages-is-cocaine-consumption-in-the-u-s-going-up -or-down/

Kilmer, Beau, Susan Everingham, Jonathan Caulkins, Gregory Midgette, Rosalie Pacula, Peter Reuter, Rachel Burns, Bing Han, and Russell Lundberg. 2014. "What America's Users Spend on Illegal Drugs: 2000–2010." *RAND Corporation*, February 2014. https://www.ncjrs.gov/App/Publications/abstract.aspx?ID=267458

King, Gary, Robert Keohane, and Sidney Verba. 1994. *Designing Social Inquiry: Scientific Inference in Qualitative Research*. Princeton: Princeton University Press.

Kitschelt, Herbert, and Steven I. Wilkinson. 2007. *Patrons, Clients, and Policies: Patterns of Democratic Accountability and Political Competition*. Cambridge: Cambridge University Press.

Kiye, Mikano E. 2015. "The Repugnancy and Incompatibility Tests and Customary Law in Anglophone Cameroon." *African Studies Quarterly*, 15(2) (March 2015): 86–106.

Klantschnig, Gernot. 2014. "Histories of Cannabis Use and Control in Nigeria, 1927–67." In *Drugs in Africa: History and Ethnographies of Use, Trade and Control*, edited by Klantschnig, Gernot, Neil Carrier and Charles Ambler, 69–88. New York: Palgrave.

Klantschnig, Gernot. 2015. "The Politics of Drug Control in Nigeria: Exclusion, Repression and Obstacles to Policy Change." *International Journal of Drug Policy*, 30 (April 2016):132–139.

Klantschnig, Gernot, Margarita Dimova, and Hannah Cross. 2016. "Africa and the Drugs Trade Revisited." *Review of African Political Economy*, 43(148): 167–173.

Klein, Axel. 1994. "Trapped in the Traffick: Growing Problems of Drug Consumption in Lagos." *The Journal of Modern African Studies*, 32(4): 657–677.

Klein, Axel 1999a. "Nigeria & the Drug War." In *"Africa and the Drug Trade."*, edited by Allen Chris, and Jan Burgess. *Review of African Political Economy*, 79: 51–73.

Klein, Axel 1999b. "The Barracuda's Tale: Trawlers, the Informal Sector and a State of Classificatory Disorder Off the Nigerian Coast." *Africa: Journal of the International African Institute*, 69(4): 555–575.

Klingeren, Bert van, and Ten Ham, M. 1976. "Antibacterial Activity of Δ9-Tetrahydrocannabinol and Cannabidiol. *Antonie van Leeuwenhoek*, 42(1–2): 9–12.

Klitgaard, Robert. 2010. "Addressing Corruption in Haiti." The American Enterprise Institute Working Paper Series on Development Policy Number 2, April 2010. https://www.monroecollege.edu/uploadedFiles/_Site_Assets/PDF/addressing-sys temic-corruption-in-haiti-version-2.pdf

Korf, Dirk. 1995. "Dutch Treat: Formal Control and Illicit Drug Use in the Netherlands." Thela Thesis, Amsterdam.

Kosten, Dan. 2018. "Immigrants as Economic Contributors: Immigrant Entrepreneurs." *International Immigration Forum*, July 11, 2018. https://immigra

tionforum.org/article/immigrants-as-economic-contributors-immigrant-entrepr
eneurs/

Kouwagam, Santy. 2013. "Is the Indonesian Constitutional Court Corrupt?" *Leiden Law Blog*, October 11, 2013. http://leidenlawblog.nl/articles/is-the-indonesian -constitutional-court-corrupt

Kruisbergen, Edwin W., Henk G. van de Bunt., and Kleemans R. Edward. 2012. *Georganiseerde criminaliteit in Nederland: Vierde Rapportage op Basis van de Monitor Georganiseerde Criminaliteit.* Den Haag: Boom Juridische Uitgevers.

Labrousse, Alain. 2001. "The War Against Drugs and the Interests of Governments: Sub-Sahara Africa Facing the Challenge of Drugs." Senate of Canada, Accessed March 28, 2020. https://sencanada.ca/content/sen/committee/371/ille/presentation/ labrousse1-e.htm

Lambo, Thomas A. 1965. "Medical and Social Problems of Drug Addiction in West Africa." *Bulletin on Narcotics*, 27(1): 3–13.

Lan, Shanshan. 2017. *Mapping the New African Diaspora in China: Race and the Cultural Politics of Belonging.* New York; London: Routledge.

Lawal, Iyabo. 2018. "Cesspool of Corruption at Nigerian Universities." *The Guardian*, April 12, 2018. https://guardian.ng/features/cesspool-of-corruption-at- nigerian-universities

LeCompte, Margaret D., and Judith P. Goetz. 1982. "Problems of Reliability and Validity in Ethnographic Research." *Review of Educational Research Spring*, 52(1): 31–60.

Leechaianan, Yingyos, and Longmire, Dennis R. 2013. "The Use of the Death Penalty for Drug Trafficking in the United States, Singapore, Malaysia, Indonesia and Thailand: A Comparative Legal Analysis." *Laws, 2013* 2(2):115–149.

Leeds, Elizabeth. 1996. "Cocaine and Parallel Polities in the Brazilian Urban Periphery: Constraints on Local-Level Democratization." *Latin American Research Review*, 31(3): 47–83.

Lefkowitz, Melissa. 2013. "Strike Hard against Immigration: China's New Exit-Entry Law." *China Brief*, 13(23). The Jamestone Foundation, November 22, 2013. https ://jamestown.org/program/strike-hard-against-immigration-chinas-new-exit-entry -law/

Leiman, Jeffrey, and Paul Leighton. 2017. *The Rich Get Richer and the Poor Get Prison: Ideology, Class and Criminal Justice.* New York; London: Routledge.

Lemert, Edwin M. 1951. *Social Pathology: Systematic Approaches to the Study of Sociopathic Behavior.* New York: McGraw-Hill.

Leuw, Ed. 1991. "Drugs and Drug Policy in the Netherlands." In *Crime and Justice: A Review of Research*, edited by Michael Tonry, vol. 14, 229–276. Chicago: University of Chicago Press.

Leuw, Ed, and Ineke Haen-Marshall. 1994. *Between Prohibition and Legalization the Dutch Experiment in Drug policy.* Amsterdam; New York: Kugler Publications.

Levine, Harry. G. 2002. "The Secret of Worldwide Drug Prohibition the Varieties and Uses of Drug Prohibition." *The Independent Review*, VII(2) (Fall 2002): 165–180.

Li, Enshen. 2010. "Chinese Administrative Justice System: Its Malpractice and Possible Reform." *Frontiers of Law in China,* 5(4): 548–579.

Li, Spencer D., Xiaohua Zhang, Wei Tang, and Yiwei Xia. 2017. "Predictors and Implications of Synthetic Drug Use Among Adolescents in the Gambling Capital of China." *SAGE Open*, October–December 2017: 1–12.

Li, Wei. 1998. "Anatomy of a New Ethnic Settlement: The Chinese Ethnoburb in Los Angeles." *Urban Studies*, 35(3): 479–501.

Liberty Writers Africa. 2019. "How China's Prisons Harvest the Organs of Nigerians/ Africans and Kills Them." *Liberty Writers Africa*, June 25, 2019. https://libertywrit ersafrica.com

Lie, Jiang. 2015. "China Grows More Popular for Foreigners, Finds Report." *Global Times*, March 20, 2015. http://www.globaltimes.cn/content/913109.shtml

Lines, Rick. 2007. "The Death Penalty for Drug Offences: A Violation of International Human Rights." *International Harm Reduction Association*, January 2007. https://www.researchgate.net/publication/237484349_The_Death _Penalty_for_Drug_Offences_A_Violation_of_International_Human_Rights_L aw

Lissardy, Gerardo. 2013. "Itaí, la Torre de Babel de las Prisiones en Brasil." *BBC Mondo*, October 15, 2013. https://www.bbc.com/mundo/noticias/2013/10/131002_ brasil_carcel_il

Little, Peter D. 2003. *Somalia: Economy Without State*. Oxford: International African Institute in Association with James Currey.

Liu Si-Yu, Wen-Jing Yu, Yi-Ru Wang, Xue-Ting Shao, and De-Gao Wang. 2021. "Tracing Consumption Patterns of Stimulants, Opioids, and Ketamine in China by Wastewater-Based Epidemiology." *Environmental Science and Pollution Research (international)*, January 4, 202. Doi: 10.1007/s11356-020-12035-w.

Lo, Clifford. 2021. "Hong Kong Customs Officers Seize HK$126 Million of Cocaine Hidden in Grape Shipment from Peru." *SCMP*, February26, 2021. https://www .scmp.com/news/hong-kong/law-and-crime/article/3123236/hong-kong-customs-o fficers-seize-hk126-million-cocaine

Lo, Wing T. 2002. *The Map of Triad Juvenile Gangs*. Hong Kong: Youth Studies Net, City University of Hong Kong. http://www.cityu.edu.hk/prj/YSNet/gangwo rk/01/index.htm

Lo, Wing T. 2010. "Beyond Social Capital: Triad Organized Crime in Hong Kong and China." *British Journal of Criminology*, 50: 851–872.

Lo, Wing T., and Sharon I. Kwok. 2012. "Traditional Organized Crime in the Modern World: How Triad Societies Respond to Socioeconomic Change." In *Traditional Organized Crime in the Modern World: Responses to Socioeconomic Change*, edited by Dina Siegel, and Henk van de Bunt, 67–89. New York: Spring.

Lofland, John. 1969. *Deviancy and Identity*. Englewood Cliffs, NJ: Prentice-Hall.

Lomax, John N. 2015. "Louisiana "Witch Doctor" Jailed for Aiding Texas Cocaine Cartels." *Texas Monthly*, May 1, 2015. https://www.texasmonthly.com/the-daily-p ost/louisiana-witch-doctor-jailed-for-aiding-texas-cocaine-cartels

Lombroso, Cesare. 2006. *Criminal Man*. Translator(s): Mary Gibson, Nicole H. Rafter. Duke University Press.

Londoño, Ernesto, and Andreoni, Manuela. 2019. "'They Came to Kill.' Almost 5 Die Daily at Hands of Rio Police." *The New York Times*, May 26, 2019. https://ww w.nytimes.com/2019/05/26/world/americas/brazil-rio-police-kill.html

Loseke, Donileen R. 1999. *Thinking About Social Problems: An Introduction to Constructionist Perspectives*. New York: Aldine de Gruyter.

Lozano, André. 1997. "Preso Nigeriano Acusado de Chefiar Tráfico." *Folha De S. Paulo*, March 28, 1997. https://www1.folha.uol.com.br/fsp/1997/3/28/cotidiano/3 3.html

Lupsha, Peter A. 1996. "Transnational Organized Crime Versus the Nation-State." *Transnational Organized Crime*, 2(1): 21–48. London: Frank Case.

Lyman, Michael D. 2017. *Drugs in Society: Causes, Concepts, and Control*, 8th edition. New York; London: Routledge.

Lyng, Stephen. 2004. *Crime, Edgework and Corporeal Transaction*. Theoretical Criminology. London: Sage Publications.

Madaki, Maikano, Aminu M. Dukku. 2017. "The Influence of Substance Abuse on Youths' Prospects in Nigeria and the Way Forward." *Advances in Psychology and Neuroscience*, 2(2/1): 15–20.

Main, Gill, and Jonathan Bradshaw. 2016. "Child Poverty in the UK: Measures, Prevalence and Intra-Household Sharing." *Critical Social Policy*, 36(1): 38–61.

Manja, Abraham D., Hendrien L. Kaal, and Peter D. A. Cohen. 2003. *Licit and Illicit Drug Use in Amsterdam, 1987–2001: Development of Drug Use in Amsterdam, as Measured in Five Population Surveys Between 1987 and 2001*. Amsterdam: CEDRO/Mets & Schilt.

Marchal, Roland. 2012. "Boko Haram and the Resilience of Militant Islam in Northern Nigeria." *Norwegian Peacebuilding Resource Centre* Report, June 2012. https://www.files.ethz.ch/isn/147775/dc58a110fb362470133354efb8fe e228.pdf

Marcus, Caroline. 2011. "Australian Boy Arrested in Bali for Drugs Urges Other Teenagers to Heed the Warning." *The Daily Telegraph*, December 5, 2011. https:/ /www.dailytelegraph.com.au/australian-boy-arrested-in-bali-for-drugs-urges-other -teenagers-to-heed-the-warning/news-story/ad264404d5299841ea06740cfbe42aa0 ?sv=2a2f163a1241dc5940ab64c9d216529d

Martin, Anderson, and Anette Kjellgren. 2016. "Aspects of Substance Displacement– from Illicit Drugs to Novel Psychoactive Substances." *Journal of Addiction Research & Therapy*, 7(3):1–3.

Marx, Karl, 1848. *The Communist Manifesto*. Moscow: Progress Publishers.

Marx, Karl. [1867] 1976. *Capital*. Volume 1. New York: Penguin Books; Marx, K. [1894] 1981 *Capital*. Volume 3. New York: Penguin Books; Marx, K. 1971. *Theories of Surplus Value*. Volume 3. Moscow: Progress Publisher.

Masih, Abul M. M., and Rumi Masih. 1996. "Temporal Causality and the Dynamics of Different Categories of Crime and Their Socio-Economic Determinants: Evidence from Australia." *Applied Economics*, 28: 1093–1104.

Massey, Douglas S., Rafael Alarcon, Jorge Durand, and Humberto González. 1987. *Return to Aztlan: The Social Processes of International Migration from Western Mexico*. Berkeley: University of California Press.

Mathews, Gordon. 2015. "Foreign Lives in a Globalising City: Africans in Guangzhou." *Journal of Current Chinese Affairs*, 44(4): 7–15.

Mathews, Gordon. 2018. "Low-End Globalization: How China is Developing the Developed World." *Asia Global Online*, May 24, 2018. https://www.asiaglobalonl ine.hku.hk/low-end-globalization-china-developing-world

Mathews, Gordon, and Yang Yang. 2012. "How Africans Pursue Low-End Globalization in Hong Kong and Mainland China." *Journal of Current Chinese Affairs*, 41(2): 95–120.

Mathews, Gordon, Linessa D. Lin, and Yang Yany. 2017. *The World in Guangzhou: Africans and Other Foreigners in South China's Global Marketplace*. Chicago; London: The University of Chicago Press.

Matza, David. 1969. *Becoming Deviant*. Englewood Cliffs, NJ: Prentice Hall.

Maynard, James E. 1992. "The Influence of the Soft State on the Performance of Development Finance Institutions." PhD diss., Napier University in Collaboration with the University of Edinburgh and the Institute of Development Studies at the University of Sussex. June 1992. https://www.napier.ac.uk/~/media/worktribe/ou tput-292320/maynardpdf.pdf

McFarlane, John. 2000. "Corruption and the Financial Sector: The Strategic Impact." *Penn State International Law Review*, 19, 1(3): 47–76.

McCoy, Alfred W. 1991. *The Politics of Heroin: CIA Complicity in the Global Drug Trade*. New York: Lawrence Hill Books.

McGranahan, Gordon, and Martine, George, ed. 2014. *Urban Growth in Emerging Economies: Lessons from the BRICS*. London: Routledge.

McLaughlin, Eugene, and John Muncie, ed. 2005. *The Sage Dictionary of Criminology*, 2nd edition. London: Sage Publishing.

Meagher, Kate. 2010. *African Issues: Identity Economics: Social Networks and the Informal Economy in Nigeria*. Oxford: Boydell & Brewer, James Currey.

Medard, Jean-Francois. 1991. "L'État Néo-Patrimonial en Afrique Noire." In *États d'Afrique Noire: Formation, Mécanismes et Crises*, edited by Jean-Francois Médard, 232–353. Paris: Karthala Joanne.

Medina, Leandro, Andrew Jonelis, and Mehmet Cangul. 2017. "The Informal Economy in Sub-Saharan Africa: Size and determinants." Working Paper WP/17/156, International Monetary Fund, July 2017. https://www.imf.org

Mejía, Daniel, and Csete, Joanne. 2016. "The Economics of the Drug War: Unaccounted Costs, Lost Lives, Missed Opportunities." *Open Society Foundation*, March 29, 2020. https://www.opensocietyfoundations.org/uploads/cbed29ba-dbad -4c95-93f8-c501b8d4c0eb/economics-drug-war-20160928.pdf

Merton, Robert K. 1938. "Social Structure and Anomie." *American Sociological Review*, 3(5): 672–682.

Metz, Helen C. 1992. *Nigeria: A Country Study*. Washington, DC: Federal Research Division, Library of Congress, June 1991. http://cdn.loc.gov/master/frd/frdcstdy/n i/nigeriacountryst00metz_0/nigeriacountryst00metz_0_djvu.txt

Mhuentoe, Tanongsak. 2013. "Corruption: Governance Problem of Thailand." In *Governance in Afro Asian Countries: Challenges and Approaches*, edited by Smita Srivastava, and Somesh Srivastava, 215–233. http://www.academia.edu

MWCA (Midwest Writing Centers Association). 2007. "Applying for the MWCA Scholarship & Travel Grants, 2007." *MWCA*, 28(1): Fall 2007. http://www.midw estwritingcenters.org/newsletter/MWCA28.1.FA07.pdf

Miller, Seumas. 2016. *Corruption and Anti-Corruption in Policing—Philosophical and Ethical Issues.* Springer Briefs in Ethics. Springer.

Mincer, Jacob. 1978. "Family Migration Decisions." *Journal of Political Economy*, 86(5): 749–773.

Mingardi, Guaracy. 2001. "Money and the International Drug Trade in São Paulo." *International Social Science Journal*, 53: 379–386.

Mingardi, Guaracy. 2007. "O Trabalho da Inteligencia no Controle do Crime Organizado." *Estudos Avançados*, 21(61): 51–69.

Minteh, Binneh S. 2013. "The Perils of Drugs in West Africa: Implications on Governance, Economic Development and Transnational Terrorism." Presentation at the American Political Science Association 2013 Annual Conference Palmer House Hilton Chicago August 29. https://www.academia.edu/4415338/Perils_of _Drugs_in_West_Africa_Implications_on_Governance_Economic_Development_ and_Transnational_Terrorism

Miroff, Nick. 2017. "American Cocaine Use is Way Up: Colombia's Coca Boom Might be Why." *Washington Post*, March 4, 2017. https://www.washingtonpos t.com/news/worldviews/wp/2017/03/04/colombias-coca-boom-is-showing-up-on -u-s-streets/

Miron, Jeffrey. 2018. "The Budgetary Effects of Ending Drug Prohibition." *CATO Institute Tax and Budget Bulletin* No. 83, July 23, 2018. https://www.cato.org/publ ications/tax-budget-bulletin/budgetary-effects-ending-drug-prohibition

Miron, Jeffrey, and Katherine Waldock. 2010. "The Budgetary Implications of Ending Drug Prohibition." *CATO Institute White Paper*, September 27, 2010. http: //www.antoniocasella.eu/archila/Miron_ending_prohibition_2010.pdf

Misse, Michel. 2017. "The Social Accumulation of Violence in Brazil: Some Remarks." *Sociology International Journal*, 1(2): 71–77.

Mitchell, David. 2019. "Teaching English in China Salary: How Much Can You Make in 2019?" *Work and Live in China*, March 31, 2019. https://www.workandl iveinchina.com/teaching-english-in-china-salary/

Modern Ghana. 2013. "Nigerian Lawmakers Are Highest Paid Globally." *Modern Ghana*, July 25, 2013. https://www.modernghana.com/news/477551/nigerian-l awmakers-are-highest-paid-globally.html

Monks, Kieron. 2017. "Nigeria Announces $5.8 Billion Deal for Record-Breaking Power Project." *CNN*, September 14, 2017. https://www.cnn.com/2017/09/14/afri ca/nigeria-china-hydropower/index.html

Montgomery, James. D. 1991. "Social Networks and Labor-Market Outcomes: Toward an Economic Analysis." *American Economic Review*, 81(5) (December 1991): 1408–1418.

Morais, Isabel. 2009. "(Re)Inventing "Realities" in China. "China Wahala": The Tribulations of Nigerian "Bushfallers" in a Chinese territory." *Transtext (e)s Transcultures Journal of Global Cultural Studies* 5/2009: Varia.

Morreale, Joseph C., Anna Shostya, and Mariana Villada. 2018. "China's Rising Middle Class: A Case Study of Shanghai College Students." *Journal of International Studies*, 11(2): 9–22.

Mortelmans, Dimitri. 2010. "Het Kwalitatief Onderzoeksdesign." In *Kwalitatieve methoden en technieken in de criminologie*, 2nd edition, edited by Tom Decorte, and Damián Zaitch, 75–118. Leuven & Den Haag: Acco.

Moser, Caroline O. N. 1998. "The Asset Vulnerability Framework: Reassessing Urban Poverty Reduction Strategies." *World Development*, 26(1):1–19.

Muggah, Robert, and Ilona Szabo de Carvalho. 2014. "Behind Bars in Brazil Is no Place You Want to Be." *Los Angeles Times*, January 22, 2014." https://www.lat imes.com/opinion/op-ed/la-oe-muggah-brazil-prisons-20140122-story.html

Murray, Lisa, and Angus Grigg. 2013. "Qantas Named as Forced Labour in Chinese Prisons Exposed." *The Australian Financial Review*, June 26, 2013. http://www.afr.com/news/policy/foreign-affairs/qantas-named-as-forced-labou r-in-chinese-

Murray, Nicholas A. A. 2007. "The Theory and Practice of Field Fortification from 1877–1914." Presented for the D.Phil. in Modern History. St. Antony's College University of Oxford. https://www.academia.edu/2064808/FIELD_FORTIFICATI ON_THEORY_AND_PRACTICE_1877_1914_COPYRIGHT_BELONG_TO _THE_ORIGINAL_AUTHORS_

Mustapha, Abdul R. 2002. "Coping with Diversity: The Nigerian State in Historical Perspective." In *The African State: Reconsiderations*, edited by Samatar, Abdi I., Ahmed I. Samatar and Abdul R. Mustapha. Portsmouth: Heinemann.

Myrdal, Gunnar. 1968. *Asian Drama*. London: Allen Lane.

Nadelmann, Ethan. A. 1991. "Drug Prohibition in the United States: Costs, Consequences, and Alternatives." *Notre Dame Journal of Law, Ethics & Public Policy*, 5(3): 783–808.

Naím, Moisés. 2012. "Mafia States: Organized Crime Takes Office." *In Foreign Affairs*, 91(3) (May/June 2012): 110–111. London: Council on Foreign Relations.

Narayan, Deepa. 1999. "Bonds and Bridges: Social Capital and Poverty (English)." Policy, Research Working Paper; No. WPS 2167. Washington, DC: World Bank. http://documents.worldbank.org/curated/en/989601468766526606/Bonds-and -bridges-social-and-poverty

Narcotic Laws of Thailand. 2007. "Third Published B.E. 2550." Office of the Narcotics Control Board. Bangkok. Ministry of Justice. http://forum.awd.ru/files /30/10/3215_3ba952d6997dea64e40c07bbc4b18cbc.pdf

NAFDAC (National Agency for Food and Drug Administration and Control). 2000. "The Role of NAFDAC in the Prevention and Control of Drug in Nigeria, Its Relationship and Expectation from Community/NGOs/CBOs." Paper presented at conference organized by Youth Society for the Prevention of Infectious Diseases and Social Vices. October 5, 2000. Kano.

National Assembly Press, Abuja. 2016. "Senate of The Federal Republic of Nigeria Order Paper." *First Session, No127, 292–299*, February 25, 2016. Abuja. National Assembly. http://nass.gov.ng/document/download/7899

NBS (National Bureau of Statistics). 2015. "Statistical Report on Women and Men in Nigeria 2015." *NBS*, October 09, 2017. www.nigerianstat.gov.ng/download/491

NBS (National Bureau of Statistics). 2017. "Key Indicators Unemployment/ Underemployment, Q4 2016." *NBS* Website, October 09, 2017. http://nigerianstat .gov.ng

NBS (National Bureau of Statistics) 2018a. "2017 Demographic Statistics Bulletin." *NBS*, May 2018. https://nigerianstat.gov.ng/download/775

NBS (National Bureau of Statistics) 2018b. "Labor Force Statistics - Volume I: Unemployment and Underemployment Report (Q4 2017-Q3 2018)." *NBS*. December 2018. www.nigerianstat.gov.ng

NDCMP (National Drug Control Master Plan). 2015. "The National Drug Control Master Plan 2015–2019." *National Coordinating Unit, NDLEA*, June 2015. https ://www.unodc.org/documents/nigeria/publications/National_Drug_Control_Maste r_Plan_2015-2019.pdf

NDLEA (National Drug Law Enforcement Agency) Decree 1989. "Decree No 84. Supplement to Official Gazette Extraordinary No. 75, Vol 76, Part A." *NDLEA*, December 29, 1989. https://gazettes.africa/archive/ng/1989/ng-government-gazett e-supplement-dated-1989-12-29-no-75-part-a.pdf

NDLEA (National Drug Law Enforcement Agency). "2010. Annual Report." *NDLEA*. Unpublished.

NDLEA (National Drug Law Enforcement Agency). 2016/2017. "Annual Report 2016/2017." *NDLEA*, March 29, 2020. https://drive.google.com/file/d/1LaeCI5-B _oQnRs19KyknpmWfTuYRRuTl/view

NDLEA (National Drug Law Enforcement Agency). 2017. "NDLEA Seizes Tons Drugs Six Months." *NDLEA*, December 9, Press Release. https://www.ndlea.gov .ng/annual-reports/

NDLEA (National Drug Law Enforcement Agency) 2018a. "Germany Donates Six Sniffer Dogs and a Bus to NDLEA." *NDLEA*. Accessed March 29, 2020. https://nd lea.gov.ng/new-and-event/germany-donates-six-sniffer-dogs-and-a-bus-to-ndlea/

NDLEA (National Drug Law Enforcement Agency). 2018b. "US Supports NDLEA Operations." *NDLEA*. Accessed March 29, 2020. https://ndlea.gov.ng/new-and-e vent/us-donates-11-vehicles-to-ndlea/

NDLEA (National Drug Law Enforcement Agency). 2021. "UNODC Assures NDLEA More Support, Hails Marwa's Appointment." *NDLEA*, February 2, 2021. http://ndlea.gov.ng/unodc-assures-ndlea-of-more-support-hails-marwas-appoin tment/

NPE (National Policy on Education). 2013. *National Policy on Education,* 6th edition. Nigerian Educational Research and Development Council. Lagos: NERDC Press, February 22, 2016. https://educatetolead.wordpress.com/2016/02/22/nat ional-policy-on-education-6th-edition-2013/

Neubauer, Ian L. 2017. "How Tourists are Getting Inside Bali's Kerobokan Prison." *News.com.au.*, August 28, 2017. https://www.news.com.au/travel/travel-updates/ travel-stories/how-tourists-are-getting-inside-balis-kerobokan-prison/news-story/0 b3fee19bed8f9d7714170f13f1b821d

Newburn, Tim., and Web Barry, ed. 1999. "Understanding and Preventing Police Corruption: Lessons from the Literature." Police Research Paper Series 110. London: Home Office. http://citeseerx.ist.psu.edu/

Newburn, Tim, ed. 2004. *Policing: Key Readings*. Cullompton: Willan Publishing.

Newman, Edward. 2007. "Weak States, State Failure, and Terrorism." *Terrorism and Political Violence*, 19(4): 463–488. DOI: 10.1080/09546550701590636.

News 24 Archives. 2005. "Nigerian Prince Jailed in UK." *News 24*, October 25, 2005. http://www.news24.com/World/News/Nigerian-prince-jailed-in-UK-20051025

Newswatch. 1987. "Drug-Running: How it Works (Cover Story)." *Newswatch*, May 12, 1987, 14–22. Citied in Isidore. S. Obot. 2004. "Assessing Nigeria's Drug Control Policy, 1994–2000." *International Journal of Drug Policy*, 15: 17–26.

Ngomba, Teke. 2007. "We Are Just Trying to Do Something Good: Contending Perspectives on Contemporary Sino-African Relations." *AfricaFiles AT Issue ezine*. http://www.africafiles.org/atissueezine.asp?issue=issue6#art2

Nigeria Curiosity. 2009. "Nigeria's Punishment Problem." *Nigeria Curiosity*, April 17, 2009. http://www.nigeriancuriosity.com/2009/04/nigeria.html

Nigerian Labour Act. 1971. *Labour Act Chapter 198. Laws of the Federation of Nigeria 1990*, August 1, 1971. https://www.ilo.org/wcmsp5/groups/public/---ed _protect/---protrav/---ilo_aids/documents/legaldocument/wcms_127565.pdf

Nikiforov, Alexander S. 1993. "Organized Crime in the West and in the Former USSR: An Attempted Comparison." *International Journal of Offender Therapy and Comparative Criminology*, 37(1): 5–15.

Nixon, Richard. 1971. "Remarks About an Intensified Program for Drugs Abuse Prevention and Control." *The American Presidency Project*, June 17, 1971. https://www.presidency.ucsb.edu/documents/remarks-about-int

Noaks, Lesley, and Wincup, Emma. 2004. *Criminological Research: Understanding Qualitative Methods*. London: Sage Publications.

Nordstrom, Joseph. 2013. "Nigeria's Trade with China Grows 700%." *Biz Wire BONTV*, Beijing, July 8, 2013. https://www.youtube.com/watch?v=7zixXVv-Q1o

Nwannennaya, Chukwunyere, and Temitope F. Abiodun. 2017. "Illicit drug Trafficking in Nigeria: Obstacle to National Development and Security." *Journal of Political Sciences & Public Affairs*, 5:1.

Nwogugu, Edwin. I. 2014. *Family Law in Nigeria*. 3rd edition. Ibadan: HEBN Publishers Plc.

Nzeka, Uche. 2020. "Grain and Feed Update." *USDA*, NI2020–0002, September 16, 2020. https://apps.fas.usda.gov/newgainapi/api/Report/DownloadReportByFileNa me?fileName=Grain

Obayan, Aize. O. I. 1995. "Changing Perspectives in the Extended Family System in Nigeria: Implications for Family Dynamics and Counselling." *Counselling Psychology Quarterly*, 8(3): 253–257.

Oberhuber, Florian, and Michal Krzyzanowski. 2008. "Discourse Analysis and Ethnography." In *Qualitative Discourse Analysis in the Social Sciences*, edited by Ruth Wodak, and Michal Krzyzanowski, 182–203. Houndmills, Basingstoke & New York: Palgrave Macmillan.

Obia, Vincent. 2016. "On the Low Rating of Nigerian Universities." *This Day*. https://www.thisdaylive.com/index.php/2016/12/11/on-the-low-rating-of-nigerian-univer sities/

Obilade, Akintunde O. 1979. *The Nigeria Legal System*. London: Sweet and Maxwell.

Oboh, Jude R. 2011. "Cocaine Strikers: The Role of Nigerians in International Cocaine Trafficking." MA Thesis. Utrecht. Willem Pompe Institute for Criminal Law and Criminology, University of Utrecht, The Netherlands.

Oboh, Jude R. 2016. "Cocaine Hoppers: The Nigerians Involvement in the Global Cocaine Trade." PhD diss., Willem Pompe Institute for Criminal Law and Criminology, University of Utrecht, The Netherlands.

Oboh, Jude R., and Schoenmakers, Yvette M. 2010. "Nigerian Advance Fee Fraud in Transnational Perspective." In *Policing Multiple Communities*, edited by Fank Bovenkerk, Marleen Easton, Lodewijk G. Moor, and Paul Ponsaers, 235–254. Antwerpen, Apeldoorn & Portland: Maklu.

Obot, Isidore S. 2004. "Assessing Nigeria's Drug Control Policy, 1994–2000." *International Journal of Drug Policy*, 15:17–26.

Odita Sunday. 2017. "NDLEA Arrests Man Who Hid Cocaine in Shoe Soles." *The Guardian*, January 3, 2017. https://guardian.ng/news/ndlea-arrests-man-who-hid -cocaine-in-shoe-soles/

Oduh, Moese O. 2012. "The Dynamics of Poverty and Income Distribution: Is The Nigerian Middle Class Statistically Or Economically Growing?" *Developing Country Studies, 2(7)*:84–94.

ONCB (Office of the Narcotics Control Board). 2015. *Thailand Narcotics Control Annual Report 2015*. Office of the Narcotics Control Board Ministry of Justice. https://aseannarco.oncb.go.th/download/article/article_20171124182948.pdf

Ogbaa, Kalu. 2003. *The Nigerian Americans*. Westport, CT: Greenwood Press.

Ogundipe, Samuel. 2016. "Nigeria Publishes Details of Recovered Assets, Withholds Names of Looters." *Premium Times*, June 4, 2016. https://www.premiumtimesng .com/news/headlines/204676-nigeria-publishes-details-of-recovered-assets-withho lds-names-of-looters.html

Oguntoke, Olusegun, and Adeyemi Adeoye. 2016. "Degradation of Urban Environment and Human Health by Emissions from Fossil-Fuel Combusting Electricity Generators in Abeokuta Metropolis, Nigeria." *Indoor and Built Environment* (February 2016):1–15.

Okoh, Lize. 2018. "How Nigeria is Preserving the Legacy of Its Slave Ports." *Culture Tripe*, May 24, 2018. https://theculturetrip.com/africa/nigeria/articles/how-nigeria -is-preserving-the-legacy-of-its-slave-ports/

Oladimeji, Ramon. 2016. "Nigerians in Chinese Prisons Allege Mysterious Deaths, Organ Harvesting." *Punch Nigeria*, March 10, 2016. http://punchng.com/nigerians -in-chinese-prisons-allege-mysterious-deaths-organ-harvesting/

Olinto, Antonio. 1970. *The Water House*. New York: Carroll and Graf.

Olurounbi, Ruth. 2020. "Nigeria Dangerously Exposed to Oil Crash." *Petroleum Economist*, March 24, 2020. https://www.petroleum-economist.com/articles/polit ics-economics/africa/2020/nigeria-dangerously-exposed-to-oil-crash

Olurounbi, Ruth. 2020. "Nigerian Inflation Rate Rises More Than Expected on Food Costs." *Bloomberg,* October 15, 2020. https://www.bloomberg.com/news /articles/2020-10-15/nigerian-inflation-rate-rises-more-than-expected-on-food -costs

Olusegun, Abejide. 2011. *IBB-Smart but Foolish: The Fall of a Goliath.* Trafford Publishing.

Olutayo, Olanrewaju A. 1999. "The Igbo Entrepreneur in the Political Economy of Nigeria." *African Study Monographs,* 20(3) (September 1999): 147–174.

Oluyede, Peter. 1989. *Modern Nigerian Land Law.* Ibadan: Evans Brothers.

O'Malley, Pat and Stephen Mugford. 1994. "Crime, Excitement and Modernity." In *Varieties of Criminology,* edited by Gregg Brarak, 189–211. Westport, CT: Praeger.

Omonobi, Kingsley. 2018. "We Murdered Oriade, OOU Student, Girlfriend for Sponsoring Rival Group—Suspected Cultists." *Vanguard,* June 24, 2018. https ://www.vanguardngr.com/2018/06/murdered-oriade-olabisi-onabanjo-university-student-girlfriend-sponsoring-rival-group-suspected-cultists/

Oni, Babatunde. 2014. "Discriminatory Property Inheritance Rights Under the Yoruba and Igbo Customary Law in Nigeria: The Need for Reforms." *IOSR Journal of Humanities and Social Science,* 19(2), Ver. IV (Feb. 2014): 30–43.

Onifade, Peter O., Edward B. Somoye, Olorunfemi O. Ogunwobi, Akinwande O. Akinhanmi, and Taiwo A. Adamson. 2011. "A Descriptive Survey of Types, Spread and Characteristics of Substance Abuse Treatment Centers in Nigeria." *Substance Abuse Treatment, Prevention, and Policy,* 6: 25.

Onunwa, Udobata. 1990. *Studies in Igbo Traditional Religion.* Obosi: Pacific Publishers.

Onuoha, Chima B. 2013. "Wealth Creation, Retirement and Succession Planning of Entrepreneurs in South-East, Nigeria." *International Business and Management,* 7(1): 99–105.

Onuoha, Freedom C., and Ezirim, Gerald E. 2013. "Terrorism" and Transnational Organised Crime in West Africa." *Aljazeera Center for Studies,* June 24, 2013. https://studies.aljazeera.net/en/reports/2013/06/2013624102946689517.html

Onwuameze, Nkechi C. 2013. "Educational Opportunity and Inequality in Nigeria: Assessing Social Background, Gender and Regional Effects." PhD diss., University of Iowa, 2013. https://doi.org/10.17077/etd.bs85au87

Onyekwere, Joseph. 2017. "LEDAP Creates Database of Nigerians on Death Row in Asia." *The Guardian,* October 31, 2017. https://guardian.ng/features/ledap-creates -database-of-nigerians-on-death-row-in-asia

Opejobi, Seun. 2018. "Okorocha to Imo Youths: It is Better to be an Armed Robber Than to Smoke Weed." *Daily Post,* January 26, 2018. https://dailypost.ng/2018/01 /26/okorocha-imo-youths-better-armed-robber-smoke-weed-video/

Ooyen-Houben, Marianne van, and Edward Kleemans. 2015. "Drug Policy: The 'Dutch Model'." *Crime and Justice,* July 2015. DOI: 10.1086/681551]

OECD (Organisation for Economic Cooperation and Development). 2018. *"Brazil", in Financing SMEs and Entrepreneurs 2018: An OECD Scoreboard.* OECD Publishing, Paris. https://doi.org/10.1787/fin_sme_ent-2018-16-en

Othman, Shehu. 1989. "Nigeria: Power for Profit - Class, Corporatism, and Factionalism in the Military." In *Contemporary West African States,* edited by Donal Cruise O'Brien, John Dunn, and Richard Rathbone. Cambridge: Cambridge University Press.

Ottenberg, Simon 1959. "Ibo Receptivity to Change." In *Continuity and Change in African Cultures,* edited by William R. Bascom and Melville J. Herskovits, 130–143. The University of Chicago Press, Chicago and London.

Otu, Smart E. 2013. "The 'War on Drugs' in Nigeria: How Effective and Beneficial is it in Dealing with the Problem." *African Journal of Drug and Alcohol Studies,* 12(2): 120–135.

Otu, Sorochi M. 2015. "Analysis of the Causes and Effects of Recidivism in the Nigerian Prison System." *International Journal of Development and Management Review,* 10 (June 2015): 136–145.

OSAC (Overseas Security Advisory Council). 2019. *Brazil 2019 Crime & Safety Report: São Paulo.* OSAC. Bureau of Diplomatic Security. U.S. Department of State Washington, DC, April 14, 2020. https://www.osac.gov/Country/Brazil/Cont ent/Detail/Report/88e4a26a-4eef-4ce1-a89b-15f4aecc5e1e

Oxfam (Oxford Committee for Famine Relief). 2017. "Inequality in Nigeria. Exploring the Drivers." *Oxfam International,* May 2017. https://www-cdn.oxfam .org/s3fs-public/file_attachments/cr-inequality-in-nigeria-170517-en.pdf

Pachico, Elyssa. 2013. "Four Nigerians Arrested for Drug Trafficking in Venezuela." *The Christian Science Monitor,* January 3, 2013. https://www.csmonitor.com/Worl d/Americas/Latin-America-Monitor/2013/0103/Four-Nigerians-arrested-for-drug -trafficking-in-Venezuela

Packer, Herbert L. 1968. *The Limits of the Criminal Sanction.* Stanford University Press.

Pantoja, Enrique. 2000. "Exploring the Concept of Social Capital and Its Relevance for Community-Based Development: The Case of Coal Mining Areas in Orissa, India." Working Paper No. 18, The World Bank Social Capital Initiative, March 2000. http://siteresources.worldbank.org

Papastergiadis, Nikos. 2000. *The Turbulence of Migration: Globalization, Deterritorialization and Hybridity.* New York: Wiley.

Payne, Richard, and Cassandra R. Veney. 1998. "China's Post-Cold War African Policy." *Asian Survey,* 38(9): 867–879.

Pearl, Betsy. 2018. "Ending the War on Drugs: By the Numbers." *Center for American Progress,* June 27, 2018. https://www.americanprogress.org/issues/crimi nal-justice/reports/2018/06/27/452819/ending-war-drugs-numbers/

Pearson, Geoffrey, Richard W. Hobbs, Steve Jones, John Tierney, and Jenifer E.F. Ward. 2001. *Middle Market Drug Distribution.* Home Office Research Study 224. London, England: Home Office.

Peattie, Lisa. 1987. "An Idea in Good Currency and how it Grew - The Informal Sector." *World Development,* 15(7): 851–860.

Penal Reform International. 2018. *Global Prison Trends 2018. Special Focus Pull-Out Section: The Rehabilitation and Reintegration of Offenders in the Era of Sustainable Development.* Penal Reform International, May 2018. https://cd

n.penalreform.org/wp-content/uploads/2018/04/PRI_Global-Prison-Trends-2018_EN_WEB.pdf

Peláez, Vicky. 2019. "The Prison Industry in the United States: Big Business or a New Form of Slavery?" *Global Research*, December 5, 2019. https://www.globalre search.ca/the-prison-industry-in-the-united-states-big-business-or-a-new-form-of -slavery/8289

People's Republic of China. 1992. *Criminal Reform in China.* Information Office of the State Council of the People's Republic of China Beijing. Accessed March 30, 2020. http://www.chinaembassy.lt/eng/zt/zfbps/t125237.htm

Persson, Anna, Bo Rothstein, and Jan Teorell. 2010. "The Failure of Anti-Corruption Policies: A Theoretical Mischaracterization of the Problem." QoG Working Paper Series 2010:19. University of Gothenburg. https://www.qog.pol.gu.se/digitalAs sets/1350/1350163_2010_19_persson_rothstein_teorell.pdf

Petersilia, Joan. 2011. "Beyond the Prison Bubble." *Wilson Quarterly*, 35(52) (2011 January). Stanford Criminal Justice Center (SCJC).

Phillips, Dom. 2014. "Videos of Police Crimes Spur Brazilians to Confront a Longtime Problem." *The Washington Post*, August 4, 2014. https://www.was hingtonpost.com/world/videos-of-police-crimes-spur-brazilians-to-confront-a -long-time-problem/2014/08/03/cacab078-1825-11e4-9349-84d4a85be981_story .html

Phongpaichit, Pasuk, and Sungsidh Piriyarangsan.1999. *Corruption and Democracy in Thailand.* Silkworm Books.

Pitcher, Anne, Mary Moran, and Michael Johnston. 2009. "Rethinking Patrimonialism and Neopatrimonialism in Africa." *African Studies Review*, 52(1):125–156.

PM News. 2015. "$400 Billion Looted in 39 Years: UN Official Speaks on Negative Impact of Nigeria's Corruption." *PM News.* January 29, 2015. https://www.pmn ewsnigeria.com/2015/01/29/400-billion-looted-in-39-years-un-official-speaks-on -negative-impact-of-nigerias-corruption/

PM News. 2019. "Kashamu Smuggled 6.6kg of Heroin into USA: Court Papers." *PM News.* https://www.pmnewsnigeria.com/2019/06/21/kashamu-smuggled-6-6kg-of -heroin-into-usa-court-papers/

Politie. 2019. "Ondermijning." *Politie*, May 4, 2020. https://www.politie.nl/themas/ ondermijning.html

Pomeranz, Kenneth, and Steven Topik. 2006. *The World that Trade Created: Society, Culture, and the World Economy*, 1400 to Present, 2nd edition. Armonk, NY: M.E. Sharpe.

Portes, Alejandro, and Patricia Landolt. 2000. "Social Capital: Promise and Pitfalls of Its Role in Development." *Journal of Latin American Studies*, 32(2) (May 2000):529–547.

Portes, Alejandro, and William Haller. 2005. "The Informal Economy." In *The Handbook of Economic Sociology*, 2nd edition, edited by Niel. J. Smelser, and Richard Swedberg, 403–425. Princeton, NJ: Russell Sage Foundation; Princeton University Press.

Pratt, John. 2000. "Emotive and Ostentatious Punishment: Its Decline and Resurgence in Modern Society." *Punishment and Society*, 2(4): 417–439.

Pratt, Travis C., and Francis T. Cullen. 2005. "Assessing Macro-Level Predictors and Theories of Crime: A Meta-Analysis." *Crime and Justice*, 32: 412–413.

Premium Times. 2012. "457 Nigerians in Brazilian Prisons Over Drug Trafficking—Reps." *Premium Times*, April 4, 2012. https://www.premiumtimesng.com/regional/nnorth-east/4522-457_nigerians_in_brazilian_prisons_over_drug_trafficking_-_reps.html

Premium Times. 2017. "36,000 Nigerians Crossed Mediterranean to Italy in 2016." *Premium Times*, January 11, 2017. https://www.premiumtimesng.com/news/top-news/220197-36000-nigerians-crossed-mediterranean-italy-2016.html

Premium Times. 2020. "Police Arrest 69 Suspected Kidnappers, Armed Robbers in Adamawa." *Premium Times*, June 1, 2020. https://www.premiumtimesng.com/news/395604-police-arrest-69-suspected-kidnappers-armed-robbers-in-adamawa.html

Prohibition Partners. 2019. "Key Insights from the Global Cannabis Report." *Prohibition Partners*, November 7, 2019. https://prohibitionpartners.com/2019/11/07/key-insights-from-the-global-cannabis-report/

Pryor, William H. Jr., Rachel E. Barko W, Charles R. Breyer, Danny C. Reeves, Patricia J. W. Smoot, Zachary Bolitho, and Kenneth P. Cohen. 2017. "Mandatory Minimum Penalties for Drug offenses in the Federal Criminal Justice system." *U.S. Sentencing Commission*, October, 2017. https://www.ussc.gov/sites/default/files/pdf/research-and-publications/research-publications/2017/20171025_Drug-Mand-Min.pdf

Pulse.ng. 2015. "'229 Drug Trafficking Nigerians Deported'—NDLEA." *Pulse.ng*., January 15, 2015. http://www.pulse.ng/gist/bad-guys-229-drug-trafficking-nigerians-deported-ndlea-id3409927.html

Pulse.ng. 2018. "7 Corruption Allegations that Will Frustrate Saraki's Presidential Ambition—APC." *Pulse.ng*., August 20, 2018. https://www.pulse.ng/news/local/2019-election-7-corruption-allegations-that-will-frustrate-sarakis-presidential/7337dm6

Putnam, Robert D. 1993. "Social Capital and Public Affairs." *Bulletin of the American Academy of Arts and Sciences* 47(8) (May 1994): 5–19.

Quantson, Kofi B. 2002. *Travelling and Seeing: Johnny Just Come*. Accra: NAPASVIL Ventures.

Quirino, João de Deus F, Modesto, L. R. Neto, and Vânia B. do Nascimento. 2020. "Incarcerated People in Prisons: A Public Health Priority in Resource-Poor Settings." *Forensic Science International: Mind and Law*, 1: 100007. Elsevier.

Rabuy, Bernadette, and Daniel Kopf. 2015. "Prisons of Poverty: Uncovering the Pre-incarceration Income of the Imprisoned." *Prison Policy Initiative*, July 9 2015. https://www.prisonpolicy.org/reports/income.html

Ramírez, Julio. 2017. "Fifteen Years of Plan Colombia (2001–2016): The Recovery of a Weak State and the Submission of Narco-Terrorist Groups?" *Analecta Politica*, 7(13): 315–332.

Reich, Michael, David M. Gordon and Richard C. Edwards. 1973. "Dual Labor Markets: A Theory of Labor Market Segmentation." *American Economic Review*, 63(2): 359–365.

Reid, Sue T. 1976. *Crime and Criminology*. New York: Holt, Rinehart, and Winston.

Reiman, Jeffrey, and Paul Leighton. 2017. *The Rich Get Richer and the Poor get Prison: Ideology, Class and Criminal Justice.* New York; London: Routledge.

Reiss, Suzanna. 2014. *We Sell Drugs: The Alchemy of US Empire.* Oakland: University of California Press.

Ren, Xin. 1997. *Tradition of the Law and Law of the Tradition.* Westport, CT: Greenwood.

Renard, Ronald D. 1996. *The Burmese Connection. Illegal Drugs and the Making of the Golden Triangle- Studies on the Impact of the Illegal Drug Trade,* Vol. 6. Boulder; London: Lynne Rienner Publishers.

Reuters 2017a. "Indonesian President Orders Officers to Shoot Drug Traffickers." *Reuters,* July 22, 2017. https://www.reuters.com/article/us-indonesia-drugs/indo nesian-president-orders-officers-to-shoot-drug-traffickers-idUSKBN1A708P

Reuters 2017b. "Indonesia Ombudsman Finds Rights Violations in Execution of Nigerian." *Reuters,* July 28, 2017. https://www.reuters.com/article/us-indonesia-execution-idUSKBN1AD10O

Reuters. 2019. "Update2-Nigeria's Buhari Approves Record 2020 Budget, on Time for His First Time." *Reuters,* December 17, 2019. https://www.reuters.com/article /nigeria-budget-idUSL8N28R4N4

Richmond, Matthew A. 2019. "The Pacification of Brazil's Urban Margins: How Police and Traffickers Co-Produce Insecurity. *LSC,* October 03, 2019. https://bl ogs.lse.ac.uk/latamcaribbean/2019/10/03/the-pacification-of-brazils-urban-margin s-how-police-and-traffickers-co-produce-insecurity/

Riemer, Jeffrey. 1981. "Deviance as Fun." *Adolescence,* 16(61): 39–43. Spr 1981.

Robinson, James A., and Thiery Verdier. 2013. "The Political Economy of Clientelism." *Scandinavian Journal of Economics,* 115(2): 260–291.

RAD (Rockefeller Foundation-Aspen Institute Diaspora Program). 2015. *The Nigerian Diaspora in the United States.* Immigration Policy Institute, RAD Diaspora Profile, June 2015 Revised. https://www.migrationpolicy.org

Rodney, Walter. 1973. *How Europe Underdeveloped Africa.* Translated by Joaquin Arriola. London; Dar-Es-Salaam: Bogle L'Ouverture.

Rodney, Walter. 1981. *A History of the Guyanese Working People, 1881–1905.* Baltimore: Johns Hopkins University Press.

Rolles, Stephen, and Danny Kushlick. 2014. "Prohibition Is a Key Driver of the New Psychoactive Substances (NPS) phenomenon." *Addiction,* 109(10): 1589–1590.

Rolles, Steve., George Murkin, Martin Powell, Danny Kushlick, and Jane Slater. 2012. "The Alternative World Drug Report: Counting the Costs of the War on Drugs." *Count the Costs,* June 26, 2012. https://www.opensocietyfoundations.org/uploads /640e45e3-1413-4f19-b18d-c12303bbe9fc/alternative-drug-report-20120626.pdf

Room, Graham. 2016. *New Poverty' in the European Community.* Palgrave Macmillan.

Rosenzweig, Mark R. 1988. "Risk, Implicit Contracts and the Family in Rural Areas of Low-Income Countries." *The Economic Journal,* 98(93): 1148–1170.

Ross, Michael L. 2001. "Does Oil Hinder Democracy?" *World Politics,* 53(3) (April 2001): 325–361. Cambridge University Press. http://www.jstor.org/stable /25054153

Ross, Michael L. 2012. *The Oil Curse: How Petroleum Wealth Shapes the Development of Nations*. Princeton University Press.

Rotberg, Robert I. 2003. *Failed States, Collapsed States, Weak States: Causes and Indicators*. Cambridge, MA; Washington, DC: Brookings Institution Press; World Peace Foundation.

Roth, Mitchel P. 2017. *Global Organized Crime: A 21st Century Approach*, 2nd edition. Oxon; New York: Routledge.

Ruggiero, Vincenzo. 1993. "Organized Crime in Italy: Testing Alternative Definitions." *Social & Legal Studies*, 2(2): 131–148.

Ruggiero, Vincenzo. 1996. *Organized and Corporate Crime in Europe*. Hampshire: Dartmouth Publishing Company.

Ruggiero, Vincenzo, and Khan, Kazim. 2006. "British South Asian Communities and Drug Supply Networks in the UK: A Qualitative Study." *International Journal of Drug Policy,* 17: 473–483. December 2006.

Sabiu, Ibrahim T., Fakhrul A. Zainol, and Mohammed S. Abdullahi. 2018. "Hausa People of Northern Nigeria and their Development." *Asian People Journal*, 1(1): 179–189. www.uniszajournals.com/apj

Said, Edward W. 1993. *Culture and Imperialism*. London: Chatto and Windus.

Salary Explorer. 2020. "Police Officer Average Salary in Brazil 2020." *Salary Explorer*. Accessed April 14, 2020. http://www.salaryexplorer.com/salary-survey .php?loc=30&loctype=1&job=504&jobtype=3

Schiraldi, Vincent. 2002. "Spend More Money on Education, Not Prison." *Newsweek*, August 29, 2002, A39.

Schmitz, Hubert, and Khalid Nadvi. 1999. "Clustering and Industrialization: Introduction." *World Development,* 27(9): 1503–1514. September 1999.

Schneider, Friedrich and Domink Enste. 2000. "Shadow Economies Around the World: Size, Cause and Consequences." International Monetary Fund Working Paper, WP/00/26. https://www.imf.org/en/Publications/WP/Issues/2016/12/30/Sha dow-Economies-Around-the-World-Size-Causes-and-Consequences-3435

Schneidera, Friedrich, Andreas Buehnb, and Claudio E. Montenegroc. 2010. "New Estimates for the Shadow Economies all over the World." *International Economic Journal*, 24(4): 443–461.

Shareef, Mohammad A. A. 1998. "The Islamic Slave Revolts of Bahia, Brazil: A Continuity of the 19th Century Jihaad Movements of Western Sudan." *Sank ore' Institute of Islamic - African Studies*. Pittsburg, PA. http://arks.princeton.edu/ark: /88435/dsp01gh93h198f

Shaw, Mark. 2003. "Crime as Business, Business as Crime: West African Criminal Networks in Southern Africa." *SAIIA*, July 2003. Johannesburg: Jan Smuts House.

Shepherd, Jean. 1991. *In God We Trust: All Others Pay Cash*. Broadway Books.

Shiu-Hing Lo, Sonny. 2009. *The Politics of Cross-Border Crime in Greater China: Case Study of Mainland China, Hong Kong, and Macao*. Armonk: M. E. Sharpe [EastGate].

Shivji, Issa G. 1982. "Semi-Proletarian Labour and the Use of Penal Sanctions in the Labour Law of Colonial Tanganyika 1920–38." In *Crime, Justice and Underdevelopment*, edited by Colin Sumner. Supra

Siddle, John. 2013. "Anatomy of Cocky's Crime Empire: Curtis Warren and His '£200m World- Wide Web'." *Liverpool Echo*, October 23, 2013. http://www.liverpoolecho. co.uk/news/liver- pool-news/anatomy-cockys-crime-empire-cur- tis-6225546

Siegel, Dina. 2011. "Secrecy, Betrayal and Crime." *Utrecht Law Review*, 7(3):107–119.

Siegel, Dina, and Frank Bovenkerk. 2001. "Crime and Manipulation of Identity Among Russian- Speaking Immigrants in the Netherlands." *Journal of Contemporary Criminal Justice*, 16(4): 424–444. November 2000.

Siegel, Dina, and Henk van de Bunt, ed. 2012. *Traditional Organized Crime in the Modern World: Responses to Socioeconomic Change*. New York: Spring.

Silvestrini, Elena. 2014. "Injection, Ingestion, & Misconception: Drug Use & Rehabilitation in Indonesia." *Independent Study Project (ISP)* Collection Paper 1794, (Spring). http://digitalcollections.sit.edu/isp_collection/1794

Simandjuntak, Deasy. 2015. "Perspective. Spectacle of the Scaffold? The Politics of Death Penalty in Indonesia." *ISEAS Yosuf Ishak Institute*, 46: 1–8.

Simpson, Sally S. eds. 2000. *Of Crime & Criminality. The Use of Theory in Everyday Life*. Pine Forge Press.

Sinha, Surya P. 1996. *Legal Polycentricity and International Law*. Carolina Academic Press.

Smith, Daniel J. 2008. *A Culture of Corruption: Everyday Deception and Popular Discontent in Nigeria*. Princeton, NJ: Princeton University Press.

Smith, David. 2010. "Wikileaks Cable: Shell's Grip on Nigerian State Revealed." *The Guardian*, December 8, 2010. https://www.theguardian.com/business/2010/dec/08 /wikileaks-cables-shell-nigeria-spying

Smith, David. 2015. "Switzerland to Return Sani Abacha 'Loot' Money to Nigeria." *The Guardian*, March 18, 205. https://www.theguardian.com/world/2015/mar/18/ switzerland-to-return-sani-abacha-loot-money-to-nigeria

Smith, Dawn W. 2016. "Black History Month. Hallowed Grounds: Sites of African American Memories." *Defense Equal Opportunity Management Institute*, Patrick Air Force Base, Florida. February 2016. https://dod.defense.gov/Portals/1/featur es/2016/0216_aahm/images/BLACK_HISTORY_MONTH_2016_ODMEO_fina l.pdf

Smith-Spark, Laura, Claudia Rebaza, and Jason Hanna. 2014. "UK Soldier's Killers Sentenced." *CNN*, February 26, 2014. http://edition.cnn.com/2014/02/26/world/ europe/uk-soldier-killing-sentencing/index.html

Soyinka, Wole. 1988. "This Past Must Address its Present." In *The 1986 Nobel Lecture. Occasional Paper of the Phelps-Stokes Fund*, vol. 3, edited by Ronald A. Wells. New York: Phelps-Stokes Fund.

Soyinka, Wole. 2006. *You Must Set Forth at Dawn: A Memoir*. New York: Random House.

Spiteri, Stephen C. 2016. "Baroque Routes." *Baroque Routes Issue*, 11, 2016. https ://web.archive.org/web/20160828161039/https://www.um.edu.mt/__data/assets/pd f_file/0005/284756/BaroqueRoutes_2016_lowresforwebsite.pdf

Spohn, Cassia C. 2000. "Thirty Years of Sentencing Reform: The Quest for a Racially Neutral Sentencing Process." *Criminal Justice*, 3: 427–501. https://www.ncjrs.gov/ criminal_justice2000/vol_3/03i.pdf

Standard Chartered Bank Nigeria. 2020. "Credit Interest Rates Table." *Standard Chartered Bank Nigeria*, March 26, 2020. https://www.sc.com/ng/download/en/_pdf/current-interest-rates.pdf

Statistics Solutions. 2019. "Theoretical Sampling in Grounded Theory." *Statistics Solutions*, March 30, 2020. https://www.statisticssolutions.com/theoretical-sampling-in-grounded-theory/

Steinberg, Michelle. 1982. "An Anglo-American Intelligence Project: The Mafia and Sicily's Separatism." *Executive Intelligence Review*, 9(15) (April 20, 1982). https://larouchepub.com/eiw/public/1982/eirv09n15-19820420/eirv09n15-19820420_025-an_anglo_american_intelligence_p.pdf

Stone, Hanna. 2011. "Brazil Arrests Point to Southern Africa Cocaine Trade." *In Sight Crime*, August 3, 2011. https://www.insightcrime.org/news/analysis/brazil-arrests-point-to-southern-africa-cocaine-trade/

Stratfor Global Intelligence. 2008. "Organized Crime in China." *Stratfor Global Intelligence*, August 19, 2008. https://worldview.stratfor.com/article/organized-crime-china

Street Journal 2011a. "Two Foreigners Jailed for Importing Cocaine into Nigeria." *The Street Journal*, July 8, 2011. https://thestreetjournal.org/2011/07/two-foreigners-jailed-for-importing-cocaine-into-nigeria/

Street Journal 2011b. "Appeal Court Upturns Former NDLEA Chairman Lafiaji's Conviction." *The Street Journal*, November 22, 2011. /https://thestreetjournal.org/2011/11/appeal-court-upturns-former-ndlea-chairman-lafiaji's-conviction

Strom, Kay M. 2014. "The Slave Ship Jesus." *Kaystrom*, March 31, 2014. http://www.kaystrom.com/blog/the-slave-ship-jesus

Suiming, Pan. 2018. "The Truth About China's Unknown Millions of Drug Users. Survey on Drug Taking Reveal Much More Users Than Official Estimates- And We Should Adjust Our Policies Accordingly." *Sixth Tone*, January 23, 2018. http://www.sixthtone.com/news/1001599/the-truth-about-chinas-unknown-millions-of-drug-users

Sullum Jacob. 2011. "Bummer: Barack Obama Turns Out to be Just Another Drug Warrior." *Reason,* October 2011. https://reason.com/2011/09/12/bummer/

Sutherland, Ewin H. 1947. *Principles of Criminology*, 4th edition. Philadelphia: Lippincott.

Suzhou Industrial Park Administrative Committee. 2004. "New Mode of International Cooperation, Opens A New Chapter in Reform and Opening-Up." *Suzhou Industrial Park Administrative Committee*, 2004. http://www.sipac.gov.cn/english/zhuanti/fnotpoc/fnotpoc_nmoic/

Svrluga, Susan. 2016. "Descendants of Slaves Sold to Benefit Georgetown Call for a $1 Billion Foundation for Reconciliation." *Washington Post*, September 9, 2016. https://www.washingtonpost.com/news/grade-point/wp/2016/09/08/descendants-of-slaves-sold-

Sykes, Gresham M., and David Matza. 1957. "Techniques of Neutralization: A Theory of Delinquency." *American Sociological Review*, 22(6) (December 1957): 664–670.

Syvertsen, Jennifer L., Kawango Agotc, Spala Ohagac, and Angela Robertson B. 2019. "You Can't Do this Job When You are Sober: Heroin Use Among Female

Sex Workers and the Need for Comprehensive Drug Treatment Programming in Kenya." *Drug and Alcohol Dependence*, 194:495–499.

Syvertsen, Jennifer L., Spala Ohaga, Kawango Agot, Magarita Dimova, Andy Guise, Tim Rhodes, and Karla D. Wagner. 2016. "An Ethnographic Exploration of Drug Markets in Kisumu, Kenya." *International Journal of Drug Policy*, 30, 82–90.

Tanner, Murray S., and Eric Green. 2007. "Principals and Secret Agents: Central Versus Local Control Over Policing and Obstacles to 'Rule of Law' in China." *The China Quarterly*, 191 (September 2007): 644–670.

Tarus, Isaac K. 2004. "A History of the Direct Taxation of the African People of Kenya, 1895–1973." Thesis Submitted in Fulfilment of the Requirements for the Degree of Doctor of Philosophy. Rhodes University, February 2004. https://core.ac .uk/download/pdf/145055296.pdf

Taylor, Erin B. 2009. "Poverty as Danger: Fear of Crime in Santo Domingo." *International Journal of Cultural Studies*, 12(22): 131–148.

Taylor, Ian R., Paul Walton, and Young Jock. 1973. *The New Criminology: For a Social Theory of Deviance*. Routledge.

Teeuwen, Dirk. 2009. "Gold Coast's Elmina Castle, a Dutch-Ghanaian monument Text and photographs." *Rendez-vous Batavia—The Netherlands*. http://www.indo nesia-dutchcolonialheritage.nl/historicalsitessouthafrica/ghanaheritage/Elmina, %20Dutch%20heritage.pdf

Tengpongsthorn, Wuthichai. 2017. "Factors Affecting the Effectiveness of Police Performance in Metropolitan Police Bureau." *Kasetsart Journal of Social Sciences*, 38: 39–44.

Thai BPS (Thai Public Broadcasting Service). 2018. "Three Nigerians Arrested for Recruiting Thai Women to Smuggle Drugs to Japan." *Thai BPS*, January 27, 2018. http://englishnews.thaipbs.or.th/three-nigerians-arrested-recruiting-thai-women-smuggle-drugs-japan/

The Cable. 2019. "NDLEA Destroys 3,900 Hectares Cannabis Farm in Ondo—Despite Akeredolu's Call for Legalization." *The Cable*, May 21, 2019. https://ww w.thecable.ng/ndlea-akeredolu-destroy-3900-hectares-cannabis-farm-ondo

The Economic Times. 2010. "China to Frame Its First Immigration Law to Attract Foreigners." *The Economic Times,* May 23, 2010. https://economictimes.indiatim es.com/news/international/china-to-frame-its-first-immigration-law-to-attract-fo reigners/articleshow/5966111.cms

The Economist. 2016. "Chinese Society: The New Class War. Special Report." *The Economist*. July 9, 2016. http://www.economist.com/sites/default/files/sr_china_m ailout_09.07.16.pdf

The Guardian. 2018. "Why Many Nigerians Are in Chinese Prisons—Envoy." *The Guardian Nigeria,* February 26, 2018. https://guardian.ng/news/why-many-nigeri ans-are-in-chinese-prisons-envoy/

The Guardian. 2021. "NDLEA Arrests Two for Cocaine Trafficking at Lagos Airport." *The Guardia,* January 13, 2021. https://guardian.ng/business-services/nd lea-arrests-two-for-cocaine-trafficking-at-lagos-airport/

The Jakarta Post. 2013. "Akil Mochtar Assaults Journalist." *The Jakarta Post*, October 4, 2013. https://www.thejakartapost.com/news/2013/10/04/akil-mochtar-assaults-journalist.html

The Jakarta Post. 2018. "Compromise Reached on Death Penalty." *The Jakarta Post*, January 11, 2018. http://www.thejakartapost.com/news/2018/01/11/compromise-reached-death-penalty.html

The Migration Observatory. 2017. "Migrants in the UK: An Overview." *Migration Observatory*, February 21, 2017. http://www.migrationobservatory.ox.ac.uk/resources/briefings/migrants-in-the-uk-an-overview

The Nation. 2017. "SMEs Contribute About 48% to GDP." *The Nation*, October 8, 2017. https://thenationonlineng.net/smes-contribute-48-gdp/

The Sentencing Project. 2017. *Fact Sheet: Trends in U.S. Corrections. U.S. State and Federal Prison Population, 1925–2017.* 2017: 1,439,808. The Sentencing Project. Accessed March 31, 2020. https://www.sentencingproject.org/publications/trends-in-u-s-corrections/

The Straits Times. 2016. "Malaysia Smashes 30 Major Drug Rings." *The Straits Times*, February 13, 2016. https://www.straitstimes.com/asia/se-asia/malaysia-smashes-30-major-drug-rings

The Sun. 2018. "The Nigeria/China Prisoners' Swap Deal." *The Sun,* August 11, 2018. Accessed January 28, 2019. https://www.sunnewsonline.com/nigeria-china-prisoners-swap-deal

The Sun Daily. 2017. "Nigerian Student Among 9 Detained in Major Drug Bust." *The Sun Daily,* August 24, 2017). http://www.thesundaily.my/news/2017/08/24/nigerian-student-among-9-detained-major-drug-bust

Theobald, Robin. 1990. *Corruption, Development and Underdevelopment.* London: MacMillan.

This Day. 2017. "Is NDLEA Winning the War against Illicit Drugs?" *This Day*, December 8, 2017. https://www.thisdaylive.com/index.php/2017/12/08/is-ndlea-winning-the-war-against-illicit-drugs/

Thomas, Charlie. 2012. "HSBC Settles $1.9bn For Aiding Drug Lords, Terrorists and Rogue States." *Huffington Post*, December 12, 2012. https://www.huffingtonpost.co.uk/2012/12/11/hsbc-settles-2bn-for-drug-lords-dealings_n_2275157.html

Tibke, Patrick. 2017. "Drug Dependence Treatment in China: A Policy Analysis." *International Drug Policy Consortium* Briefing Paper, February 2017. London. http://fileserver.idpc.net/library/IDPC-briefing-paper_China-drug-treatment.pdf

Toit, Brain M du. 1975. "Dagga: The History and Ethnographic Setting of Cannabis Sativa in Southern Africa." In *Cannabis and Culture*, edited by Vera Rubin, 51–62. Chicago: Mouton Publishers.

Tomlinson, John. 1999. *Globalization and Culture.* Chicago: University of Chicago Press.

Tonry, Michael. 1999. "Why Are U.S. Incarceration Rates So High?" *Crime and Delinquency*, 45(4): 419–437.

Trading Economics. 2020. "Nigeria National Minimum Wage." *Trading Economics.* Accessed, March 31, 2020. https://tradingeconomics.com/nigeria/minimum-wages

TNI (Transnational Institute). 2015. *"About Drug Law Reform in Brazil."* *TNI*, June 30, 2015. https://www.tni.org/en/publication/about-drug-law-reform-in-brazil

Transparency International-Malaysia. 2017. "The 2017 Global Corruption Barometer (GCB)—Asia Pacific Region." *Transparency International-Malaysia*, February 28, 2017. https://transparency.org.my/pages/what-we-do/indexes/global-corru ption-barometer-asia-pacific-2017

Travis, Jeremy, Bruce Western, and Steve Redburn. eds. 2014. *The Growth of Incarceration in the United States: Exploring Causes and Consequences.* Washington: The National Academy Press.

TV People. 2011. "Reportage Nigerian Cocaine Trafficker." *TV People,* February 2, 2011. Accessed, March 19, 2015. http://tv.people.com.cn/GB/166419/13864060.htm

Tyessi, Kuni. 2017. "UNICAL VC Blows Whistle on Ex-Bursar Over N200m Fraud." *This Day*, March 1, 201. https://www.thisdaylive.com/index.php/2017/03 /01/unical-vc-blows-whistle-on-ex-bursar-over-n200m-fraud

Ucha, Chimobi. 2010. "Poverty in Nigeria: Some Dimensions and Contributing Factors." *Global Majority E-Journal,* 1(1): 46–56. June 2010.

Uchendu, Victor C. 1995. "Ezi-Na-Ulo: The Extended Family in Igbo Civilization." The 1995 Ahiajoku Lecture. Owerri: Ministry of Information and Culture. *Igbo Net.* Accessed March 31, 2020. http://ahiajoku.igbonet.com/1995/

Udama, Rawlings. A. 2013. "The National Drug Law Enforcement Agency." *The Journal of International Social Research*, 6(24). http://www.sosyalarastirmalar. com/cilt6/cilt6sayi24_pdf/udama_akonbede.pdf

Ugwummadu, Somuadila. 2017. "Ozubulu Massacre: The Hidden Truth Revealed." *Elombah News*, August 10, 2017. https://elombah.com/index.php/analysis/ozubulu -massacre-the-hidden-truth-revealed-by-somuadila-ugwummadu

Ujumadu, Vincent. 2018. "Ozubulu Massacre: Widows Protest Threat to Witnesses." *Vanguard,* March 15, 2018. https://www.vanguardngr.com/2018/03/ozubulu-m assacre-widows-protest-threat-witnesses

UN (United Nations). 1996. *Report of the World Summit for Social Development Copenhagen, 6–12 March 1995.* New York: United Nations. https://www.un.org/d evelopment/desa/dspd/world-summit-for-social-development-1995.html

UN (United Nations). 2020. *Rising Inequality, Exclusion Still Threaten Global Well-Being despite Impressive Gains in Poverty Reduction, Speakers Tell Social Development Commission.* Economic and Social Council, Commission for Social Development 4the& 5the Meetings. SOC/4885 February 11, 2020. UN Meeting and Press Release. https://www.un.org/press/en/2020/soc4885.doc.htm

UN (United Nations) Commission on Narcotic Drugs. 2018. *Report on the Sixty-First Session (8 December 2017 and 12–16 March 2018). Economic and Social Council Official Records, 2018 Supplement No. 8.* New York: United Nations. https:// www.unodc.org/documents/commissions/CND/CND_Sessions/CND_61/E2018_2 8_advance_unedited.pdf

UNCOVA. 2017. "95% of Nigerians Indulge in Bribery—NBS." *UNCOVA*, August 17, 2017. https://uncova.com/95-of-nigerians-indulge-in-bribery--nbs

UNDP (United Nations Development Programme). 1977. *Human Development Report 1997.* New York: Oxford University Press.

UNECA (United Nation Economic Commission for Africa). 2016. *Country Profile Nigeria,* March 2015. Addis Ababa: UNECA. https://repository.uneca.org/handle /10855/23709

UNECA (United Nation Economic Commission for Africa). 2017. *Country Profile Nigeria,* March 2016. Addis Ababa: UNECA. https://www.uneca.org/sites/default/ files/uploaded-documents/CountryProfiles/2017/nigeria_cp_eng.pdf

UN General Assembly. 1998. *20th Special Session of the UN General Assembly: World Drug Problem (8–10 June 1998).* New York: United Nations. https://www .un.org/en/events/pastevents/GA_drugs_1998.shtml

UNHRC (United Nations Human Rights Council). 2010. *Report of the Special Rapporteur on Extrajudicial, Summary or Arbitrary Executions. Follow-Up to Country Recommendations—Brazil.* Philip Alston. Addendum. UN A/HRC/14/24/ Add.4. UNHRC, May 28, 2010. https://www2.ohchr.org/english/bodies/hrcouncil/ docs/14session/A.HRC.14.24.pdf

UNHRC (United Nations Human Rights Council). 2014. *Report of the Working Group on Arbitrary Detention Addendum Mission to Brazil.* UN A/HRC/27/48/ Add.3. UNHRC, June 30, 2014. https://www.refworld.org/docid/53eb2e9e4.html

UNODC (United Nations Office on Drugs and Crime). 2007. *Anti-Corruption Climate Change: It Started in Nigeria. 6th National Seminar on Economic Crime.* Vienna: UNODC, November 13, 2007. https://www.unodc.org/unodc/en/about -unodc/speeches/2007-11-13.html

UNODC (United Nations Office on Drugs and Crime) 2008a *West Africa Under Attack. Drug Trafficking is a Security Threat ECOWAS High-level Conference on Drug Trafficking as a Security Threat in West Africa.* Praia, Cape Verde: UNODC, October 28, 2008. https://www.unodc.org/unodc/en/about-unodc/speeches/2008 -28-10.html

UNODC (United Nations Office on Drugs and Crime) 2008b. *Drug Trafficking in West Africa As a Security Threat in West Africa.* Vienna: UNODC, November 2008. https://www.unodc.org/documents/data-and-analysis/Studies/Drug-Traffic king-WestAfrica-English.pdf

UNODC (United Nations Office on Drugs and Crime). 2011. *World Drug Report 2011.* Vienna: UNODC, May 2011. https://www.unodc.org/documents/data-and analysis/WDR2011/World_Drug_Report_2011_ebook.pdf

UNODC (United Nations Office on Drugs and Crime). 2013. *World Drug Report 2013.* Vienna: UNODC, May 2013. https://www.unodc.org/unodc/secured/wdr/ wdr2013/World_Drug_Report_2013.pdf

UNODC (United Nations Office on Drugs and Crime). 2016. *World Drug Report 2016.* Vienna: UNODC, May 2016. https://www.unodc.org/doc/wdr2016/W ORLD_DRUG_REPORT_2016_web.pdf

UNODC (United Nations Office on Drugs and Crime) 2017a. *World Drug Report 2017, 3. Market Analysis of Plant-Based Drugs. Opiates, Cocaine and Cannabis.* Vienna: UNODC, May 2017. https://www.unodc.org/wdr2017/field/Booklet_3 _Plantbased_drugs.pdf

UNODC (United Nations Office on Drugs and Crime) 2017b. *Corruption in Nigeria, Bribery: Public Experience and Response 2017.* Vienna: UNODC, July 2017. https

://www.unodc.org/documents/data-and-analysis/Crime-statistics/Nigeria/Corru ption_Nigeria_2017_07_31_web.pdf

UNODC (United Nations Office on Drugs and Crime) 2018a. *Drug Use in Nigeria 2018*. Vienna: UNODC. https://www.unodc.org/documents/data-and-analysis/stati stics/Drugs/Drug_Use_Survey_Nigeria_2019_BOOK.pdf

UNODC (United Nations Office on Drugs and Crime) 2018b. *World Drug Report 2018, 3. Analysis of Drug Markets Opiates, Cocaine, Cannabis, Synthetic Drugs.* Vienna: UNODC, 2018. https://www.unodc.org/wdr2018/prelaunch/WDR18_ Booklet_3_DRUG_MARKETS.pdf

UNODC (United Nations Office on Drugs and Crime) 2019a. *Massive Drug Operation by Cabo Verdean Authorities Successfully Seizes 9.5 tons of Cocaine in Praia.* Vienna: UNODC, February 5, 2019. https://www.unodc.org/westandcentra lafrica/en/2019-02-05-massive-cocaine-seizure-in-cabo-verde.html

UNODC (United Nations Office on Drugs and Crime) 2019b. *Bissau-Guinean Authorities Achieve largest ever Drug Seizure in the History of Guinea-Bissau.* Vienna: UNODC, March 9, 2019. https://www.unodc.org/westandcentralafrica/en /2019-03-15-seizure-guinea-bissau.html

UNODC (United Nations Office on Drugs and Crime) 2019c. *World Drug Report 2019, 1. Executive Summery Conclusions and Policy Implications*. United Nations publication, Sales No. E.19.XI.8. Vienna: UNODC, June 2019. www.unodc.org/ wdr2019

UNODC (United Nations Office on Drugs and Crime). 2021. *Development of the National Drug Control Master Plan 2021 to 2025: A Sustainable Policy that Responds to Drug Use and Illicit Trafficking and Related Organized Crime in Nigeria.* Vienna: UNODC, 2021. https://www.unodc.org/nigeria/en/ndcmp-2021-2025-a-sustainable -national-policy-for-nigerians-to-continue-fighting-against-drugs.html

United States Department of Justice, U.S. Attorney's Office, Eastern District of Virginia. 2019. For Immediate Release, November 5, 2019. "Nigerian Woman Pleads Guilty to Drug Trafficking and Fraud Schemes." U.S. Department of Justice. U.S. Attorney's Office, Eastern District of Virginia. https://www.justice.gov/usao -edva/pr/nigerian-woman-pleads-guilty-drug-trafficking-and-fraud-schemes

United States Department of Justice, U.S. Attorney's Office, Eastern District of Virginia. 2020. *For Immediate Release*, February 28, 2020. "Woman Sentenced for Cocaine Conspiracy and Multiple Fraud Schemes." U.S. Department of Justice. U.S. Attorney's Office, Eastern District of Virginia. https://www.justice.gov/usao -edva/pr/woman-sentenced-cocaine-conspiracy-and-multiple-fraud-schemes

United States Department of Justice. U.S. Attorney's Office Northern District of Georgia. 2020. "Dozens Charged in Atlanta-Based Money Laundering Operation That Funneled $30 Million in Proceeds from Computer Fraud Schemes, Romance Scams, and Retirement Account Fraud." *For Immediate Release*, March 13, 2020. U.S. Department of Justice. U.S. Attorney's Office Northern District of Georgia. https://www.justice.gov/usao-ndga/pr/dozens-charged-atlanta-based-money-lau ndering-operation-funneled-30-million-proceeds

United States Department of State. 2003. *Statement by the Press Secretary: Annual Presidential Determinations of Major Illicit Drug-Producing and Drug-Transit*

Countries. Washington, DC, January 31, 2003. U.S. Department of State Archive. Accessed March 7, 2020. https://2001-2009.state.gov/p/inl/rls/prsrl/ps /17092.htm

United States Department of State. 2016. *2015 Country Reports on Human Rights Practices- Nigeria*. Executive summary. Reworld UNHCR, April 13, 2016. https:/ /www.refworld.org/docid/5716122a15.html

United States Department of State. 2017. *Indonesia 2017 Human Rights Report. Executive Summary*. US Department of States, Bureau of Democracy, Human Rights and Labor. Accessed April 19, 2020. https://www.state.gov/wp-content/up loads/2018/04/Indonesia.pdf

United States Department of States DEA (Drug Enforcement Administration). 2017. *2017 National Drug Threat Assessment*. October, 2017. DEA-DCT-DIR-040-17. UNCLASSIFIED. Accessed April 12, 2020. https://www.dea.gov/sites/default/f iles/2018-07/DIR-040-17_2017-NDTA.pdf

United States Senate, Committee on Foreign Relations. 2000. *The Nigeria Transition and the Future of U.S. Policy. Hearing Before the Committee on Foreign Relations*. Senate Hearing 106–295. United States Senate, One Hundred Sixth Congress First Session. November 4, 1999. U.S. Senate, Committee on Foreign Relations, Washington, DC. U.S. Government Printing Office Washington: 2000. https://www.govinfo.gov/content/pkg/CHRG-106shrg61867/html/CHRG-106shr g61867.htm

United States Senate, Committee on Foreign Relations. 2001. *Review of the Anti-Drug Certification Process. Hearing Before the Committee on Foreign Relations*. Senate Hearing 107–18. United States Senate One Hundred Seventh Congress First Session. March 1, 2001. Certification decisions for 2001. Summary. Presidential Determination No. 2001–12. March 1, 2001. The White House, Washington. DC. Accessed April 19, 2020. https://www.govinfo.gov/content/pkg/CHRG-107shrg71 540/html/CHRG-107shrg71540.htm

Uphoff, Norman, and Chandrasekera Wijayaratna C. M. 2000. "Demonstrated Benefits from Social Capital: The Productivity of Farmer Organizations in Gal Oya, Sri Lanka." *World Development*, 28(11): 1875–1890.

Urevich, Robin. 2010. "Chasing the Ghosts of a Corrupt Regime: Gilbert Chagoury, Clinton Donor and Diplomat with a Checkered Past." *PBS*, January 8, 2010. http: //www.pbs.org/frontlineworld/stories/bribe/2010/01/nigeria-chasing-the-ghosts-of -a-corrupt-regime.html

Uwa, Osimen G., Patrick Chuke, and Micah E. Elton. 2016. "Youth Unemployment and Insecurity: Impediment of Nation-Building in Nigeria." *Research on Humanities and Social Sciences*, 6(12): 2016.

Uwameiye, Raymond, and Ede O. S. Iyamu. 2002. "Training Methodology Used by the Nigerian Indigenous Apprenticeship System." *Adult Education and Development* 59: 2002.

Uzuegbu-Wilson, Emmanuel. 2019. "Nigeria and Drug Cartel Links Close to the Summit of Power: A Critical Review." *Social Science Research Network*, November 6, 2019. http://dx.doi.org/10.2139/ssrn.3481710

Uzorma, Nathan. 2018. "Is Gov. Rochas Truly Corrupt?" *The Nigerian Voice*, January 22, 2018. https://www.thenigerianvoice.com/news/262442/is-gov-rochas -truly-corrupt.html

Vanguard. 2013. "Henry Okah Breaks Jail, Re-Arrested in S-Africa." *Vanguard*, February 11, 2013. https://www.vanguardngr.com/2014/02/henry-okah-breaks-jail -re-arrested-s-africa/

Vanguard. 2016. "NDLEA to Prosecute Four Mexicans Arrested Over 'Crystal Meth' Production." *Vanguard*, March 16, 2016. https://www.vanguardngr.com/2016/03/ ndlea-arrests-four-mexicans-producing-crystal-meth-in-asaba

Vanguard. 2018. "70,000 Nigerians Visit Chinese Province in One Year." *Vanguard*, February 5, 2018. https://www.vanguardngr.com/2018/02/70000-nigerians-visit -chinese-province-one-year/

Vanguard. 2021. "Drug Haul, as NDLEA Seizes N30bn Cocaine at Lagos Airport." *Vanguard*, January 30, 2021. https://www.vanguardngr.com/2021/01/drug-haul-as -ndlea-seizes-n30bn-cocaine-at-lagos-airport/

Vaughan, Jessica. 2017. "Immigration Multipliers Trends in Chain Migration." *Center for Immigration Studies*, September 2017. https://cis.org/sites/default/files /2017-09/vaughan-chain-migration_1.pdf

Vidal, John. 2010. "Nigeria's Agony Dwarfs the Gulf Oil Spill. The US and Europe Ignore It." *The Observer*, May 30, 2010. https://www.theguardian.com/world/2010 /may/30/oil-spills-nigeria-niger-delta-shell

Vieira, James B. 2013. "The Impact of Public Transparency in Fighting Corruption: A Study on Brazilian Municipalities E-government." *JeDEM- EJournal of EDemocracy and Open Government*, 5(1): 80–106.

VOA (Voice of America). 2018. "UN: In Nigeria More Than 13 Million School-Age Children Out of School." *VOA News Africa*, December 11, 2018. https://www .voanews.com/africa/un-nigeria-more-13-million-school-age-children-out-school

Von Lampe, Klaus, and Georgios A. Antonopoulos. 2018. "An Introduction to the Special Issue on 'Organised Crime and Illegal Markets in the UK and Ireland'." *Trends Organized Crime*, 21: 99–103.

Vulliamy, Ed. 2011. "How a Big US Bank Laundered Billions from Mexico's Murderous Drug Gangs." *The Guardian,* April 3, 2011. http://www.guardian.co.uk /world/2011/apr/03/us-bankmexico-drug-gangs

Wacquant, Loïc. 2004. "Decivilizing and Demonizing: The Remaking of the Black American Ghetto." In *The Sociology of Norbert Elias*, edited by Steven Loyal, and Stephen Quilley, 95–121. Cambridge University Press.

Wagner, Peter, and Bernadette Rabuy. 2017. "Following the Money of Mass Incarceration." *Prison Policy Initiative*, January 5, 2017. https://www.prisonpolicy. org/reports/money.html

Wagner, Peter, and Bernadette Rabuy. 2017. "Mass Incarceration: The Whole Pie 2016." *Prison Policy Initiative*, March 14, 2017. https://www.prisonpolicy.org/r eports/pie2017.html

Waller, Willard. 1936. "Social Problems and the Mores." *American Sociological Review*, 1(6): 922–933.

Wallerstein, Immanuel M. 1979. *The Capitalist World-Economy*. Cambridge: Cambridge University Press.

Wallerstein, Immanuel M. 2004. *World-Systems Analysis: An Introduction*. Durham: Duke UP.

Walmsley, Roy. 2018. "World Prison Population List." 12th edition. *World Prison Brief*, September, 2018. http://www.prisonstudies.org/sites/default/files/resources/downloads/wppl_12.pdf

Walt, Vivienne. 2019. "The Never-Ending $1.1 Billion Oil Scandal: Why a U.K. Court is Letting Nigeria Sue JPMorgan Chase." *Fortune*, October 11, 2019. https://fortune.com/2019/10/11/jpmorgan-eni-shell-nigeria-lawsuit-bribe/

Warsta, Matias. 2004. "Corruption in Thailand." *International Management: Asia Swiss Federal Institute of Technology Zurich*, Aril 22, 2004. http://aceproject.org/ero-en/regions/asia/TH/Corruption_in_Thailand.pdf

Wartna, Bouke S. J., Nikolaj Tollenaar, Suzan Verweij, Daphna L. Alberda, and Ad A.M. Essers. 2017. "2015 Recidivism Report. National Figures for the Reconviction Rates of Offenders Punished in the Period Between 2002 and 2012." *Factsheet 2016-1a*, June 2017. WODC (Research and Documentation Centre). https://english.wodc.nl/binaries/FS%202016-1a_tcm29-266946.pdf

Waterfeld, Bruno. 2011. "Maastricht Loses "£26 Million-a-year" After Drug Tourism Ban." *The Daily Telegraph*, November 3, 2011. http://www.telegraph.co.uk/news/worldnews/europe/netherlands/8867662/Maastricht-loses-26-million-a-yearafter-drug-tourism-ban.html

Watkins, Tannyr. 2018. "2018 Update on Prison Recidivism: A 9-Year Follow-Up Period (2005–2014) (NCJ 250975)." *Bureau of Justice Statistics*, May 23, 2018. https://www.bjs.gov/content/pub/press/18upr9yfup0514pr.cfm

Weber, Max. 1978. *Economy and Society*. Berkeley: University of California Press.

Webster, Colin, and Sarah Kingston. 2014. "Poverty and Crime Review: Anti-Poverty Strategies for the UK." *Joseph Rowntree Foundation*. London. https://eprints.lancs.ac.uk/id/eprint/71188/1/JRF_Final_Poverty_and_Crime_Review_May_2014.pdf

Wechsler, William. 2009. "Confronting Drug Trafficking in West Africa." U.S. Senate, Subcommittee on African Affairs, of the Committee on Foreign Relations. Senate Hearing 111–121. United States Senate One Hundred Eleventh Congress First Session. June 23, 2001. U.S. Government Printing Office. Washington: 2009. Accessed April 1, 2020. http://www.gpo.gov/fdsys/pkg/CHRG-111shrg52925/html/CHRG-111shrg52925.htm

Weingrod, Alex. 1968. "Patrons, Patronage and Political Parties." *Comparative Studies in Society and History*, 10(4): 377–400.

Weller Chris. 2017. "Dutch Prisons Are Closing Because the Country Is So Safe." *Independent*, May 31, 2017. https://www.independent.co.uk/news/world/europe/dutch-prisons-are-closing-because-the-country-is-so-safe-a7765521.html

West Africa Commission on Drugs. 2014. "Changing Drug Policy." *WACD*, June 23, 2014. https://www.kofiannanfoundation.org/changing-drug-policy/west-africa-commission-on-drugs/

West, Darrell M. 2011. "Creating a "Brain Gain" for U.S. Employers: The Role of Immigration." *Brookings Policy Brief* No. 178. January 12, 2011. https://www.bro

okings.edu/research/creating-a-brain-gain-for-u-s-employers-the-role-of-immigrat
ion/

Wike, Richard, and Bruce Stokes. 2016. "Chinese Public Sees More Powerful Role
in World, Names U.S. as Top Threat. Domestic Challenges Persist: Corruption,
Consumer Safety, Pollution." *Pew Research Centre*, October 5, 2016. https://ww
w.pewresearch.org/global/2016/10/05/chinese-public-sees-more-powerful-role-in
-world-names-u-s-as-top-threat/

Wikström, Per-Olf H., and Butterworth David A. 2006. *Adolescent Crime. Individual
Differences and Lifestyle.* Cullompton: Devon Willan.

Williams, Phil, and Godson Roy. 2002. "Anticipating Organized and Transnational
Crime." *Crime, Law and Social Change,* 37: 311–355.

Williams, Terry, Eloise Dunlap, Bruce D. Johnson, and Ansley Hamid. 1992.
"Personal Safety in Dangerous Places." *Journal of Contemporary Ethnography*,
21(3): 343–374.

Willis, Graham D. 2014. "Antagonistic Authorities and the Civil Police in São Paulo,
Brazil." *Latin American Research Review*, 49(1): 3–22.

Wilson, Laura, and Alex Stevens. 2017. "Understanding Drug Markets and How to
Influence Them." *Report 14 The Beckley Foundation.* http://www.beckleyfoundat
ion.org/pdf/report_14.pdf

Windle, James. 2015. "Drugs and Drug Policy in Thailand." *Foreign Policy at
Brookings*, August 26, 2015. https://www.researchgate.net/publication/281271815
_Drugs_and_Drug_Policy_in_Thailand

Winsor, Morgan. 2015. "Nigerian Senators Receive $2,500 or 506,000 Naira to
Spend on Clothes, Not $43 Million or 8.64 Million Naira, Senate President Says."
International Business Times, June 18, 2015. https://www.ibtimes.com/nigerian-se
nators-receive-2500-or-506000-naira-spend-clothes-not-43-million-or-864-1972843

Winstock, Adam R., Monica Barrette, Jason Ferris, and Larissa Maier. 2017. "Global
Drug Survey 2017. Global Overview and Highlights." *Global Drug Survey*, May
24, 20017. https://www.globaldrugsurvey.com/wp-content/themes/globaldrugsurv
ey/results/GDS2017_key-findings-report_final.pdf

Wolfgang, Marvin E., Arlene Kelly, and Hans C. Nolde. 1969. "Comparison of
the Executed and the Commuted Among Admissions to Death Row." *Journal of
Criminal Law and Criminology* 53(2) (3): 301–311.

Wolfgang, Marvin E., Robert M. Figlio, and Thorsten Sellin. 1972. *Delinquency in a
Birth Cohort.* Chicago: University of Chicago Press.

Wong Chen, Tuan Y. B. 2017. "Remedying Police Corruption: Candid Cops,
Not Corrupt Crooks." Office of Tuan YB Wong Chen, Member of Parliament
for Kelana Jaya. Accessed March 2, 2018. http://www.wongchen.com/wp-con
tent/uploads/2017/02/Remedying-Police-Corruption-Candid-Cops-not-Corrupt-Cr
ooks.pdf)

Woolcock, Michael, and Deepa Narayan. 2000. "Social Capital: Implications for
Development Theory, Research and Policy (English)." *The World Bank Research
Observer*, 15(2): 225–249.

Workman, Daniel. 2020. "Crude Oil Exports by Country." *World Top Exports*, March
8, 2020. http://www.worldstopexports.com/worlds-top-oil-exports-country/

Workpermit. 2020. "UK Tier 2 Shortage Occupation List." *Workpermit.com.* Accessed April 1, 2020. https://workpermit.com/immigration/united-kingdom/uk -tier-2-shortage-occupation-list

World Bank. 2013. *World Economic Forum: Insight Report: The Africa Competitiveness Report 2013.* World Bank. Washington, DC. http://www3.wef orum.org/docs/WEF_Africa_Competitiveness_Report_2013.pdf

World Bank. 2015. *Migration and Development Brief 25. Migration and Remittances: Recent Developments and Outlook.* October 13, 2015. World Bank. Washington, DC. http://pubdocs.worldbank.org/en/102761445353157305/MigrationandDe velopmentBrief25.pdf

World Bank 2019a. "Nigeria Economic Update Fall 2019. Jumpstarting Inclusive Growth: Unlocking the Productive Potential of Nigeria's People and Resource Endowments." *World Bank.* Washington, DC. Accessed February 18, 2021. http:/ /documents.worldbank.org/curated/en/394091575477674137/pdf/Jumpstarting-In clusive-Growth-Unlocking-the-Productive-Potential-of-Nigeria-s-People-and-R esource-Endowments.pdf

World Bank 2019b. "GDP Growth (Annual %). All Countries and Economies, Country, China." *World Bank.* Washington, DC, April 5, 2020. https://data.wo rldbank.org/indicator/NY.GDP.MKTP.KD.ZG

World Bank 2020. "Nigeria Releases New Report on Poverty and Inequality in Country." *World Bank*, May 28, 2020. Washington, DC. https://www.worldbank .org/en/programs/lsms/brief/nigeria-releases-new-report-on-poverty-and-inequali ty-in-country

WHO (World Health Organization). 2008. "Flawed but Fair: Brazil's Health System Reaches Out to the Poor." *Bulletin of the World Health Organization* 8(4) (April 2008): 241–320.

WHO (World Health Organization). 2015. "WHO Global Report on Trends in Tobacco Smoking 2000–2025." Geneva: WHO. Accessed February 15, 2021. 2019. https://www.who.int/tobacco/publications/surveillance/reportontrendstob accosmoking/en/

World Population Review. 2020. "São Paulo Population 2020." *World Population Review Website.* https://worldpopulationreview.com/world-cities/sao-paulo-pop ulation//

WPB (World Prison Brief). 2018. "Indonesia." *Data. WPB.* Accessed April 1, 2020. https://www.prisonstudies.org/country/indonesia

Write, Tim. 2014. "When Airliners Vanish." *Air and Space Magazine*, October 2014. https://www.airspacemag.com/flight-today/when-airliners-vanish-1809527 93/

Wu, Harry. 2010. "Not for Sale: Advertising Forced Labor Products for Illegal Export. Report on Laogai Enterprise Advertisements and Listings in English." *Laogai Research Foundation.* Accessed December 12, 2019. https://www.laogai.o rg/reports/not-sale-advertising-forced-labor-products-illegal-export

Wu, Harry, and Cole Goodrich. 2014. "A Jail by Any Other Name: Labor Camp Abolition in the Context of Arbitrary Detention in China." *Human Rights Brief*, 21(1): 2–8.

Wu, Harry, Jeffrey Fiedler, and Tienchi Martin-Liao. 2008. "Laogai Handbook 2007–2008." *Laogai Research Foundation*. Washington, DC 2006. Accessed December 12, 2019. https://laogairesearch.org/wp-content/uploads/2019/01/33-Laogai-Handbook-2007-08.pdf

Wu, Tiffany. 2012. "Media Narratives of Crime and the Fevelas of São Paulo and Rio de Janeiro." Bachelor of Arts Thesis. University of California Berkeley, May 2012. https://legalstudies.berkeley.edu/wp-content/uploads/2012/05/Wu-Thesis-Final.pdf

Wunyabari, Maloba O. 1993. *Mau Mau and Kenya: An Analysis of a Peasant Revolt*. Indiana University Press.

Wyman, James H. 1997. "Vengeance is Whose? Death Penalty and Cultural Relativism in International Law." *Jameswyman.com*. Accessed April 1, 2020. http://www.jameswyman.com/dp.html

Xinhua News. 2013. "3 Executed, 2 Sentenced to Death for Drug Trafficking." *Xinhua Net News*, June 25, 2013. Accessed April 05, 2018. From, http://en.people.cn/90882/8298951.html

Xinhua News. 2017. "Drug Addiction on the Rise in China: Report." *Xinhua News*, March 27, 2017. Accessed April 02, 2019. From, http://www.xinhuanet.com//english/2017-03/27/c_136161743.htm

Young Jock. 1999. *The Exclusive Society*. London: Sage.

Young Jock. 2007. *The Vertigo of Late Modernity*. London: Sage.

Zainal, Fatimah. 2018. "Anti-Drugs Agency Steps Up Op." *The Star Online*, Feb 20, 2018. https://www.thestar.com.my/news/nation/2018/02/20/antidrugs-agency-steps-up-op-we-aim-to-weed-out-substance-abuse-among-malaysians-says-dg/

Zaitch, Damián. 2002. *Trafficking Cocaine: Colombian Drug Entrepreneurs in the Netherlands*. The Hague: Kluwer Law International.

Zakaria, Fareed. 2008. *The Post-American World*. London: Allen Lane.

Zambito, Thomas. 2009. "Shell Oil Pays $15M to Nigerians on Eve of Manhattan Federal Court Trial." *Daily News*, June 8, 2009. https://www.nydailynews.com/news/world/shell-oil-pays-15m-nigerians-eve-manhattan-federal-court-trial-article-1.373298

Zhang, Sheldon X. and Ko-lin, Chin. 2016. "A People's War: China's Struggle to Contain its Illicit Drug Problem." *Foreign Policy at Brookings*. https://www.brookings.edu/wp-content/uploads/2016/07/a-peoples-war-final.pdf

Zhang, Xiaohan, Riheng Huang, Ping Li, Yuan Ren, Jianfa Gao, Jochen F. Mueller, and Phong K. Thai. 2019. "Temporal Profile of illicit Drug Consumption in Guangzhou, China Monitored by Wastewater-Based Epidemiology." *Environmental Science and Pollution Research (international)*, 26(23) (August 2019):23593–23602.

Zhou, Dan. 2017. "Talent Management for High-Quality Employee: Example of China." *International Journal of Trade, Economics and Finance*, 8(3):149–157 .

Zimmerman, Stan. 2006. *A History of Smuggling in Florida Rumrunners and Cocaine Cowboys*. Charleston: The History Press.

Index

14K, 179
"2019 Poverty and Inequality in Nigeria," 53

Abacha, Sani, 28, 29, 76, 79
Abada, 141
Aba market, 94
"Aba Women Riots." *See* "Women's War"
Abdulmutallab, Umar Farouk, 241
Abiodun, Temitope F., 18
Abubakar, Abdulsalami, 83
Achebe, Chinua, 60
Achema, Jona, 35
Action Group, 142
Adamu, Ali Bala, 126
Adebolajo, Michael, 241
Adebowale, Michael, 241
Adebukola, Mulikat, 102
Adekunle, Benjamin, 26
Adiele, Pius, 139
Administration of Criminal Justice Act (2016), 245
adulterants, 116
Afghanistan, 30, 226, 232
Afigbo, Adiele E., 48
Africa, 21, 22, 40, 42, 47, 49, 50, 52, 60, 66, 78, 86, 100, 111, 113, 117, 120, 134, 140, 244, 281

African(s): diaspora, 5, 8, 19, 24, 140, 143, 230, 232, 234; massacre, 21; slaves, 19–21
Afro-Colombian population, 22
Agnew, Robert, 97
Agozino, Biko, 7, 21, 22, 60, 167, 258
agricultural revolution, 89
agricultural sector, 63–64
Agudas, 141, 142
Aiye, 150
"AIYE." *See* Black Axe Confraternity
Ajaja, Patrick O., 59
Ajegunle, 107
Akçomak, Semih I., 81
Akyeampong, Emmanuel, 18
Alakija, Adeyemo, 142
Albanian groups, 238
alcohol, 40–42, 188, 268, 270, 272, 280
Alemika, Etannibi O., 18
Alison-Madueke, Diezani, 83
Al Jazeera, 111
al-Qaeda, 240
Alston, Philip, 161
Amazon, 238
"American Dream," 68, 73
American ghettos, 74
American legal system, 21
Amin, Samir, 77
"amnesty agreement," 214

amphetamines, 113, 186
amphetamine-type stimulants, 112
Amsterdam, 216, 238, 241
ANC, 27
Anderson, Martin, 255
anomie, 73
Ansaru, 50
"Antagonistic Authorities and the Civil
    Police in São Paulo" (Willis), 163
antidrug abuse campaign, 112
antidrug control agents/agency, 4, 134,
    165, 244, 246, 247
antidrug laws and measures, 278
Appadurai, Arjun, 214
Apple, 177
apprenticeships, 88, 103
Aradeon, David, 141
"area boys" syndrome, 70
Argentina, 109, 147, 151, 224, 229
Arhin, Kwame, 47
Article 1, UN Convention on the
    Elimination of All Forms of
    Discrimination Against Women, 97
Article 6(2), International Covenant on
    Civil and Political Rights (ICCPR), 256
Article 89, Indonesian House of
    Representatives, 259
Article 347, Criminal Law of the
    People's Republic of China, 199
Asia, 43, 104, 110, 115, 117, 124, 136,
    150, 159, 173, 176, 183, 281
"Asia Drama" (Myrdal), 51
Assunção, Marcolino, 142
Asuni, Tolani, 18
Atlantic slave trade, 20
Australia, 24, 194, 230, 270
Australian Financial Review, 208
"authoritarian populism," 60
Awosade, Hafsat, 153, 166
Ayortor, Eme Zuru, 80
Asia, Steve S., 45
Azikiwe, Nnamdi, 234

Babangida, Ibrahim Badamasi, 26
Babatunde, Murtala, 59

Bacrim, 263
Bagger, 178, 215
Bahia, 141, 143
Bamaiyi, Musa, 29, 31
Bamali, Nuhu, 230
Bangkok, 32, 228–30
Barry, Web, 227
Bashir, Jimoh Oladega, 102
Batey, Jesse, 20
battlefield approach, 130, 136
Baudrillard, Jean, 175
BCCI, 266
Becoming Deviant (Matza), 202
Beijing, 187, 188, 190, 195, 249
Belgium, 21, 228
Benin kingdom, 89
Best, Joel, 196
Biafra Civil War (1967–1970), 49
Biafra war, 26
Black Axe Confraternity, 59, 150, 179
black economy. *See* informal economy
Black Lives Matter movement, 39
"the Black Scorpion." *See* Adekunle,
    Benjamin
black slaves. *See* African(s), slaves
Blalock, Hubert M., Jr., 145
Bloomberg, 62
Blundy, Rachel, 179
BNN, antinarcotics agency, 255
boasting, 10
Bodomo, Adams, 197
body-packing, 188–90
Boko Haram, 33, 46, 50, 55, 60, 62, 63,
    66, 70, 93, 240, 241, 245, 263
Bolivia, 1, 149, 166
Bonife, 217
Borisovich, Roman, 82
Bourdieu, Pierre, 81
Bouze, Anthony, 265
Bovin, Rémi, 43, 78
Braithwaite, John, 218
Brazil, 1, 5, 6, 7, 8, 11, 30, 43, 104,
    108, 109, 118, 174, 180, 183, 204,
    210, 215, 226, 228, 240, 251, 270,
    274, 275, 278, 282

Brazil, Nigerian cocaine traffickers in: arbitrary arrest and denial of rights to progression, 166–69; Brazilian reaction, 153–58; combat, 160–63; communication in prison, 170–72; export methods, 150–53; historical context, 140–44; incursion, shops, and homes, 163–65; lack of good medical attention, 169–70; legislative measures, 158–59; police culture, 247–49; prisoners, 165–66; in São Paulo, 144–50

Brazilian descendants, 143–44

Brazilian Policia Federal, 145

Brazilian returnees' influence in Nigeria: economic influences, 142–43; knowledge and political influences, 142; sociocultural influences, 141–42

Briathwait, John, 67

bribes/bribery, 57–59, 75, 76, 78, 79, 119, 128, 160, 227, 247, 253, 258, 260

Britain, 47–49, 60, 115, 116, 123, 191, 271, 276. *See also* United Kingdom (UK)

British Broadcasting Corporation (BBC), 39, 69, 71

British colonialists, 17, 21, 108

Bubo Na Tchuto, José Américo, 33

Buhari, Muhammadu, 29, 39, 282, 283

Burduş, Eugen, 89

bureaucracy, 29, 49, 91, 249, 253

Burgess, Jan, 34

Bush Administration, 31

California Correctional Crisis, 167

Cambodia, 24

Canada, 40, 268, 270, 279

Candonbele, 141

cannabidiol (CBD), 40

cannabis, 33, 34, 39–42, 78, 112, 113, 241, 268, 280; farms, 28; market, 37, 40, 42, 272; production, 17, 35, 40; sale in Netherlands, 37; smoking, 18; in traditional medicinal practice, 19

capitalism, 65, 72, 77, 78, 103

capitalist production, 77

capital punishment, 15, 198, 199, 243, 244, 249, 255, 256, 259, 271

Cardoso, Fernando Henrique, 154

cargo and container packaging, 150–52

Caribbean, 19, 22, 140, 237, 244, 267

"Carnival Mirror," 5, 38

Carter, Jimmy, 262

CBD. *See* cannabidiol (CBD)

Celebrity Drug-Free Club, 112

Central Association of Nigerians, 234

Central Bank of Nigeria, 80, 92

Central Intelligence Agency (CIA), 26, 232

centralized Islamic system, 48

CFR. *See* Council on Foreign Relations (CFR)

Charles V (King), 20

Chase-Dunn, Christopher K., 78

Cheney, Dick, 79

Chibnall, Steve, 191, 192

child malnourishment, 54

China, 1, 6, 7, 8, 11, 30, 118, 166, 226, 230, 240, 274, 278, 282, 283

China, Nigerian cocaine traffickers in, 173–74, 176–78; chic parties and escorts, 187–89; Chinese reaction, 191–204; control, 249–55; old school and new generation influx, 178–80; "open talk" cocaine, 180–81; prison life, 205–10; recruitment, travel, control, and delivery, 181–86; survival strategy, 210–21; traders and drug addiction, 174–76

Chinese *ethnoburbs,* 178

Chinese Export-Import Bank, 83

Chinese People's Consultative Conference (2008), 195

"Chocolate Cities," 178

"chop money" syndrome, 75–79

Chris, Allen, 34

CIA. *See* Central Intelligence Agency (CIA)

Cinque, Joseph, 18

civil administrations, 76
civil wars, 50
CJS. *See* Criminal Justice System (CJS)
claims-makers. *See* moral entrepreneurs
clientelism, 48, 49, 81, 162
Clinton, William Jefferson, 30, 31
CNN, 74
cocaine, 224–26, 228, 229, 237–38, 240, 242, 248–49, 252, 268, 271, 272, 279, 281. *See also individual entries*
cocaine emergence in Nigeria, 43; decriminalize and regulate drugs, 34–42; *"na them wahala"* (it is their problem), 30–34; origins, 17–19; slavery and colonialism, 19–22; transit-transaction country, 22–27; war on drugs, 27–30
cocaine price and "cutting," 114–16
coca leaf, 271, 276
coca plantation, 17, 24, 112
codeine, 113, 114
Cohen, Corentin, 159, 179
Cohen, Stanley, 175, 192
Cold War, 27, 49
Colombia, 1, 151, 263
Colon, Cristobal, 140
colonialism, 19–22, 42, 47, 90, 91, 276
colonial taxation, 91
colonization, 17, 20, 45, 140
Columbia, 51, 111
Columbus, Christopher, 140
Commando Vermelho, 162
Communist Party, 253, 254
comprador classes, 47
Conectas Human Right Group, 167
"Confronting Drug Trafficking in West Africa" (Wechsler), 109
control theory, 200
Cooper, Robert, 61
corruption, 32, 33, 51, 53, 57–60, 65, 71, 72, 75, 77–79, 81–84, 111, 118–20, 122, 154, 163, 227–28, 231, 241, 245–47, 251–55, 259–61
Corruption and Democracy in Thailand (Phongpaichit and Piriyarangsan), 231

Corruption Eradication Commission (KPK), 260
Costa, Antonio Maria, 32, 59
Council on Foreign Relations (CFR), 160
counter-narcotics, 30, 37
Country Reports on Human Rights Practices, 244
Court of Appeals, Lagos, 247
Cox, Donald, 100
crack cocaine, 69, 114, 264
Crime, Edgework and Corporeal Transaction (Lyng), 201
Crime and Punishment in America (Currie), 159
crime news, 191–92
crime(s), 5, 7, 21, 25, 33, 38, 41–43, 45, 50, 58–61, 64–71, 73, 75, 78, 123, 159, 161, 166–67, 174, 176, 220–21, 268; corporate, 67, 78, 278; drug, 153, 154, 191, 192; economic, 275, 278; fabricated, 281; international, 225; organized, 34, 45–47, 76, 80, 87, 109, 118–20, 123, 132, 160, 162, 163, 227, 237, 238, 241, 252, 253, 278; street, 39, 67, 278; white-collar, 67
criminal activities, 3, 12, 50, 59, 64, 66, 70, 75, 81, 82, 107, 123, 132, 156, 167, 200, 201, 212, 278
criminalization, 22, 28, 159, 202, 276
criminal justice model, 38
Criminal Justice System (CJS), 4, 9, 10, 38, 39, 41, 71, 72, 159, 206, 239, 247, 258, 273, 278, 279
criminal law, 166, 167
Criminal Procedure Code, 158
criminogenic environments, 3, 7, 45, 47, 49, 50, 52, 71, 74, 76, 100, 109, 130, 274, 275, 277, 283
cross-border trade, 40
cross-ethnic partnerships, 237
Cullen, Francis T., 67
cultism and cult gangs, 215–17
cultural activism, 5

cultural capital, 10
cultural exchanges, 100
cultural factors and Nigerian cocaine
    trafficking, 85–105; excelling as
    traders, 103–4; extended family
    liabilities, 98–103; "*foo-foo (fufu)*"
    swallowing culture, 104–5; informal
    apprentices, 88–95; informal
    economy, 85–88; patrilineal culture
    of inheritance, 95–97
cultural networks, 147–48
cultural relativism, 259
cultural values, 72, 98, 100
culturocentrism, 196
Currie, Eliott, 159
Czech Republic, 24

Daily Post, 80
"Dangerous Drugs Ordinance" (1935),
    34
"dark numbers," 5
DEA. *See* U.S. Drug Enforcement
    Agency (DEA)
death penalty, 43, 182, 193, 204, 205,
    210, 224, 226, 230, 249, 250, 255–59
debt crisis, 42, 43, 86
de-civilizing process, 74, 75
decolonization, 22, 42
Decree 48 enactment (1989), 243
decriminalization, regulation and
    regularization of drugs, 17, 34–42,
    153, 154, 268, 269, 270, 271,
    279–81, 283; call for change, 37–38;
    cannabis, 39–42; chat with inmates,
    36–37; damage persists, 38–39
deficit, concept of, 118–19
democratic dictatorship, 206
democratic transition program, 31
Demographic Census 2010, 158
demonization, 74, 75, 157
Dengfeng, 180
Deng Xiaoping, 177–78
"Development of the National Drug
    Control Master Plan 2021 to 2025," 41
Deviance and Identity (Lofland), 202

deviant activities, 73, 79, 84, 98, 104,
    200
digital skills, 57
direct and indirect rule, 47, 48, 55, 142
discrimination, 22, 55, 97, 155, 197,
    265, 276
distrust, 10, 45, 49, 91
domestic drug consumption market,
    175, 179
domestic terrorism, 241
Dowdney, Luke, 157
Dred Scott decision (1857), 21
drug abuse, 35, 50, 112, 113
drug addiction, 175–76, 226
drug barons, 7, 17, 32, 35, 227, 262, 273
drug cartels, 7, 26, 50, 51, 112, 266, 280
drug control, 15, 17, 27, 28–32, 38, 45,
    51, 112
drug courier approach, 4, 111, 114,
    125–28, 152–53, 182–83
drug crops, 266, 267
Drug Data Collection Unit (1992), 36
"Drug Dependence Treatment in China"
    (Tibke), 175
drug enforcement activities, 230, 254
Drug Law (Law n.11.343/06, 2006), 153
"Drug Law: It's Time to Change"
    campaign, 159
drug offenses, 32, 35, 239, 240, 249,
    255
Drug Policy Research Center, 267
"Drug Policy: The 'Dutch Model'" (van
    Ooyen-Houben and Kleemans), 37
drug problems, 27, 31, 37, 268, 269
drug prohibition, 28, 67, 78, 263, 268–
    72, 279, 281
drug scan test, 128
drug trafficking/traffickers, 2–5, 9, 12,
    17, 18, 23–25, 29, 31–33, 35, 39, 43,
    46, 47, 50, 51, 72, 74, 76, 78, 80–82,
    85, 87, 92, 94, 99, 102–4, 108, 111,
    112, 117, 125, 132, 133, 144, 149,
    154, 156, 158–65, 168, 176, 179,
    191, 192, 214, 232, 233, 237, 266,
    267, 273, 278

drug wars, 4, 17, 22, 23, 27–30, 32, 35, 38, 41, 42, 154, 159, 226, 231, 233, 244, 261–63, 266, 267, 279, 281, 282

"Dual Labor Market," 65

The Duct Military Police Schiphol Airport Amsterdam, 129

Durkheim, Emile, 72, 73

"Dutch-Diseases," 62, 63

Dutch Opium Act, 37

Dutch West India Company, 20

A Dying Colonialism (Fanon), 21

Ebbe, Obi N. I., 21, 67, 248

Eboe-Osuji, Chile, 246

Economic and Financial Crime Act No. 20, 243

Economic and Financial Crimes Commission (EFCC), 75, 79, 82, 243

Economic Community of West African States, 46, 149

economic growth, 54, 61, 63, 68, 69, 78, 79, 83, 91, 97, 104, 144, 149, 158, 223, 277

economic liberalization, 61, 86, 146

economic mismanagement, 50, 60, 61, 86, 93, 123, 277

ecstasy, 113, 186, 228, 252, 260, 261

Ecuador, 151

edgework, 199, 201, 202, 215

education, 9, 13, 14, 23, 24, 36, 37, 42, 43, 46, 52–59

Edwards, Richard C., 65

EFCC. *See* Economic and Financial Crimes Commission (EFCC)

Eiye, 178, 215, 218

Ejike, Humphrey Jefferson, 257, 258

El Callao Port, 111

El Chapo, 236

Elechi, Oko, 246

election manipulations, 49

elites' self-centeredness, 60

Elizabeth I (Queen), 21

Ellis, Stephen, 23, 24

Elmina Castle, 20

embassy services, 206

embezzlement, 47, 58, 74, 75, 80, 252, 260

Embury-Dennis, Tom, 271

EMCDDA. *See* European Monitoring Centre for Drugs and Drug Addiction (EMCDDA)

Emerson, 208

emotional coping mechanisms, 199, 201, 215

employment, 39, 40, 65, 88, 146

endemic corruption, 46, 51, 58, 75, 111, 120, 227, 231, 249, 252, 258

England, 7, 9, 21, 62, 93, 116, 123, 132, 142, 233, 237, 269

Eni, 78

entrepreneurship, 88–90, 93, 95, 103, 104, 144

Enugu miner, 22, 90

environmental pollution, 79

equality/inequality, 20, 39, 52, 61, 62, 64, 66–69, 73, 75, 78, 156, 158, 159, 161, 221, 277

EU. *See* European Union (EU)

Europe, 2, 4, 23, 33, 40, 104, 110–12, 125, 136, 151, 162, 238, 241, 281

European Industrial Hemp Association, 40

European markets, 109, 110, 113, 137

European Monitoring Centre for Drugs and Drug Addiction (EMCDDA), 280

European Union (EU), 31, 39, 40, 194

examination malpractices, 58, 59

"executive lawlessness," 60

expediency principle, 269

exploitation, 19, 20, 22, 43, 47, 51, 61, 63, 66, 78, 90, 91, 95, 164, 207, 208, 224, 233, 276

extended family liabilities, 98–103; filling gaps, 100–103; social security pillar, 99–100

extensive network concepts, 147–49

extrajudicial killings, 71, 161, 230–31, 244

"extra-legality," 87

Eze Nri, 90

Fafchamps, Marcel, 99, 100
Fajnzylber, Pablo, 69
Familia Do Norte, 162
family planning, 53, 54
Fanon, Frantz, 21
FAO. *See* Food and Agriculture
  Organization (FAO)
Farah, Douglas, 109
FARC cartel, 111, 263
Federal Bureau of Investigation, 236
federal government scholarship scheme,
  145
federal laws, 168
female cocaine traffickers, 182, 185,
  224
FFAI. *See* Food for All International
  (FFAI)
"Financial Crimes: Money Laundering
  and Terrorism Workshop for
  Judges," 246
First Command of the Capital, 150, 162,
  172, 249
"Fixers, Super Fixers and Shadow
  Facilitators" (Farah), 109
Florida, 236
folk magic, 134
Food and Agriculture Organization
  (FAO), 13
Food for All International (FFAI), 36
food inflation, 62
"foo-foo (fufu)" swallowing culture,
  104–5
forced labor, 21, 206–8
foreign direct investment, 177
foreign exchange earnings, 64, 69, 123,
  234
foreign government sponsors, 38
foreign traffickers, 109–10
formal economy, 177
Foshan-Nanhai, 217–18
France, 137, 244, 276
The Fresh Toast, 154
"Fundamentals of Entrepreneurship"
  (Burduş), 89

funds/funding, 22, 26, 29, 36, 47, 50,
  53, 56, 58; embezzled, 75; public,
  75, 81, 144

Gaffey, Conor, 83
Galeria Presidente (Galeria De Sotto),
  156
GAN Business Anti-Corruption Portal,
  260
Garland, David, 212
GDP. *See* gross domestic product
  (GDP)
gender relations, 54
Geneva Opium Convention, 34
The Gentlemen's Club (Bruun et al.),
  270
geopolitical factors, 45
Georgetown University, 20
Germany, 7, 9, 137, 244, 270, 279
Ghana, 113, 114, 180
Ghanaian Narcotics Control Board
  (NACOB), 28, 149
Ghanaian Police, 28
Giade, Ahmadu, 112
Gilles, Angelo, 178
Gilman, Nils, 188
Giuliani, Rudy, 264
Giwa, Dele, 26
"Global Black Market Information,"
  115
Global Competitiveness Report, 57
Global Drug Survey, 116, 233
global economy, 61, 78, 93, 189
globalization of drug trade, 2, 14, 34,
  43, 75–79, 86, 100, 173, 176, 177,
  188–89, 225, 278
Global Regime for Transnational Crime,
  160
Golden Azalea, 175
Golden Crescent, 175
Golden Triangle (GT), 175
Goldman Sachs, 62, 65
Gonzalez, Luis, 111
"The Good Ship Jesus," 21

goof, 18

Gordon, David M., 65

Green, Penny, 123

green gold. *See* cannabis

Greer, Chris, 191

Grimes, Peter, 78

gross domestic product (GDP), 50, 56, 62, 64, 69, 76, 86, 103–4, 173

"group exonerations," 257–58

GT. *See* Golden Triangle (GT)

Guangzhou, Guangdong Province, 173, 174, 176–78, 185, 189–93, 195–97, 203, 204, 209, 211, 214–21, 282

guanxi, 253

Guardian, 25

Guinea-Bissau, 33, 51, 117

Guinness, Walter Edward (Lord Moyne), 91

Guyanese workers shooting (1905), 21

Habermas, Jürgen, 175

Hall, Stuart, 60, 175, 191, 192

Haller, William, 87

Halliburton, 79

Halliburton bribe scandal, 71

Hamilton, Joan, 42

"hard drugs," 37, 113, 114, 227, 269, 270

harm reduction concept, 17, 270, 271

Harris, Kamala, 42

Harris County, Texas, 239

Hart, Keith, 87

hashish, 269

Hausa/Fulani, 55, 90

Havocscope, 115

Hawkins, John, 21

HCI. *See* Human Capital Index (HCI)

health care, 54, 169, 170, 178

"Heinous Crimes Law" (1990), 153

"heretics and infidels," 20

heroin, 23–25, 30, 35, 78, 80, 109, 112, 113, 118, 176, 181, 186, 227–30, 232, 237, 240, 256, 258, 268, 272, 276, 279–81

Herzberg's two-factor theory, 231

high-end globalization, 177

Higuchi, Naoto, 146

"A History of the Direct Taxation of the African People of Kenya" (Tarus), 91

Ho, David, 196

Hobbes, Thomas, 49

Hobsbawm, Eric, 155

Holloway, Thomas, 165, 259

homicides, 26, 59, 79, 144, 154, 179, 192, 193, 213, 226, 240, 257, 258, 264, 268

Hommiprese, 81

Hong Kong, 7–8, 11, 14, 176, 179–80, 183, 188, 189, 191, 203, 274

Hooton, Albert, 264

Howard University, 234

How to Stop Crime (Bouze), 265

HSBC, 266

Huawei, 177

Human Capital Index (HCI), 56

humanitarian intervention, 27

human rights abuses, 38, 79, 167, 244, 246, 256, 281

human rights norms, 259, 271

Human Rights Report (2017), 261

human trafficking, 13, 66, 78, 225, 234, 235, 238, 275

Hung Mun, 179

"hut" taxes, 91

Hutton, Will, 145

Ibori, James, 71

ICCPR. *See* Article 6(2), International Covenant on Civil and Political Rights (ICCPR)

Idi Igi mode, 96

Idumota market, 94, 107, 121

Igbos, 55, 90, 96, 219

Ignatius of Loyola (1491–1556), 19

Ikechukwu, Kingsley, 144

Ikegwuonu, Aloysius, 133

Ikoh, Moses U., 34

illegal drugs, 17, 18, 22, 23, 27, 29, 46, 71, 78, 85, 90, 112, 115, 122, 123, 136, 230, 271, 280, 281
illegal economy. *See* informal economy
illicit drug trade, 86, 93, 97, 144–46, 149, 163, 180, 229, 248, 254, 255, 273, 275, 276
IMF. *See* International Monetary Fund (IMF)
immigration control, 22, 214
Immigration Office of Guangzhou, 212
immigration policy, 194
Imouokhome, Aize O., 98
imperialism, 21, 22, 42, 49, 61, 91, 276
income inequality, 68–69
INCSR. *See* International Narcotics Control Strategy Report (INCSR)
indenture, 93, 94
India, 18, 21, 23, 32, 174
Indian hemp. *See* cannabis
individualism, 72, 95
Indonesia, 30, 223, 240, 282
Indonesia, controlling cocaine hoppers in, 255–61; corruption, 259–61; death penalty, 256–59
Indonesian National Police, 260
Indonesia's Criminal Code, 260
industrialization, 72, 122
informal economy, 47, 85–88, 91, 92, 123, 146, 177
informal household enterprises, 86
informal loans, 99
informal sector apprenticeship system, 88–95; as communal spirit, 93; disappointed apprenticeship, 93–95; enterprising Nigeria, 89–93; untapped potential, 89
infrastructure, 9, 45, 52, 59, 65, 71, 74, 83, 104, 111, 150, 238, 241, 277
Innoson Vehicle Manufacturing, 93
Instituto Brasileiro de Geografia e Estatística, 156
insufficient governance, 60–61
intercropping, 39–40
internal colonialism, 22, 42, 276

international cocaine trafficking/ traffickers, 1, 2, 3, 9, 12, 15, 34, 45, 46, 52, 64, 69, 70, 73–75, 78, 82, 84, 107, 108, 110, 111, 120, 143, 144, 146, 147, 160, 173
"International Community Woos NDLEA," 29
international cooperation, 35
International Criminal Police Organization, 197
international drug trade, 1, 23, 25, 28, 40, 149
international law, 257, 259, 281
International Monetary Fund (IMF), 61, 62, 86, 87, 122
International Narcotics Control Board, 271
International Narcotics Control Strategy Report (INCSR), 2
International Programs, 267
Inter-University Centre for Terrorism Studies, 50
Intestate Customary Law, 95
Iran, 226
Iran-Contra Affair, 232
The Iran-Contra scandal, 26
"Is NDLEA Winning the War against Illicit Drugs?," 28
Itai prison, 32, 152, 156, 166, 167, 169
Italy, 7–9, 137, 174
Izomiwu, Sunny ("Sotto"), 156
Izugbara, Chimaraoke, 54

Jaguaribe, Beatriz, 156
Jaja (King), 21
Jakarta Post, 260
James, Cyril, 22
James, Devitt, 20
Jao Pho (godfather), 231
Japan, 109, 146, 223, 229, 271
Jefferson Dekker Juvenile Prison, 235
Jesuits. *See* Society of Jesus
John Paul II (Pope), 20
Johnson, Henry, 20
Jonathan, Goodluck, 4

Joseph, Richard, 119
JPMorgan Chase, 78
juju, 134
justice reinvestment, 220
"Just Stop Killing Us," 39

Kansas City, 233
karaoke bars, 186
Kashamu, Buruji, 80
Kauzlarich, David, 47
kele trafficking method, 105, 234
Kenya, 21, 40, 57, 80, 91, 113, 114, 146
Kenyatta, Jomo, 21
Kerobokan (Hotel K), 261
Kerry, John, 66
ketamine, 186, 189
khaki, 90, 92
khat, 40
kidnapping, 50, 59, 64, 65, 70, 71, 132,
    143, 154, 179, 213, 215
Kingston, Sarah, 67
KL. *See* Kuala Lumpur (KL)
Klantschnig, Gernot, 26, 38
Kleemans, R. Edward, 37
"Kleptocracy Tour," 82, 83
kleptocratic authoritarian regime, 76, 79
Klitgaard, Robert, 163
Kosoko, 142
KPK. *See* Corruption Eradication
    Commission (KPK)
Kuala Lumpur (KL), 188, 216, 224
Kuti, Fela, 142
Kwok, Sharon I., 179

labor force, 63, 64, 86, 91
labor markets, 65, 146
Lafiaji, Bello, 247
Lagos, 7, 107, 114, 115, 117, 121, 124,
    140, 142, 143, 179, 190, 216, 238
Lagos Island, 107, 115, 121, 126
Lagos State Judiciary 2017 Judges
    Retreat, 246
Lambo, Thomas A., 18
Lamorde, Ibrahim, 82
Landuji, Oshodi, 142

laogai (reform through labor), 206–8
Laogai Research Foundation, 207
laojiao (reeducation through labor),
    206, 210
Las Casas, Bartolomé de, 20
Latin America, 22, 33, 50, 86, 109, 117,
    118, 125, 134, 139, 142, 144, 149,
    183, 228, 237, 238, 244, 249, 254,
    267
Latin American traffickers, 111
law enforcement agency/agents, 5, 7, 9,
    13, 15, 24, 33, 51, 84, 111, 125, 129,
    140, 146, 174, 185, 192, 212, 216,
    217, 241, 247, 264, 269, 281
Law of Penal Execution, 159
Law of the People's Republic of China
    on Control of the Entry and Exit of
    Aliens (1985), 192
Law on Eradication of Criminal Acts of
    Corruption, 260
Lebanese traffickers, 24, 25, 108, 109
legal drugs, 272
legalization of drugs, 38, 269, 272, 280,
    281
legal reforms, 207
legitimacy, 51, 192, 195, 218, 263
Leighton, Paul, 38, 41, 67, 159, 167,
    220, 265
Leopold of Belgium (King), 21
"Let's Talk About a Revolution," 270
Leuw, Ed, 37
The Leviathan (Hobbes), 49
Liberty Writers Africa, 192
Lie, Jiang, 209
life sentences, 43, 210, 230, 239
Lo, Wing T., 179
"Looking Beyond Terrorism: Middle
    Eastern and African Criminal
    Enterprises Conference," 23
Los Angeles, 178, 233, 236, 240
Loseke, Donileen R., 196
Louisiana, 20
low-end globalization, 177
LSD, 35
Lula da Silva, Luiz Inácio, 249

Lund, Susan, 99
Luso-Brazilian Treaty of Friendship and Consultation (1953), 139

Macau, 183, 191
maconha (marijuana), 18, 26, 69, 114, 154, 186, 189, 226, 228, 230, 252, 260, 268–70
Macumba, 170
Maffiosi, 34
maiguan maiguan, 253
Malacca, 224
Malaysia, 7, 8, 14, 104, 128, 175, 183, 204, 251, 256, 274, 282
Malaysia, Nigerian drug traffickers in, 223–28; corruption, 227–28; female couriers, 224–26; societal reaction and government response, 226–27
Maloba, Wunyabari, 91
Mambila hydroelectric power project, 83
Mandela, Nelson, 27, 245
Mao Zedong, 206, 207, 253
marginalization, 22, 49, 53, 66, 74, 91, 156
Markis, 96
Marwa, Mohammed Buba, 29, 35
Marx, Karl, 65, 77
Maryland, 20
Maryland Society of Jesuits, 20
Masih, Abul M. M., 69
Masih, Rumi, 69
mass executions, 249
mass incarceration, 159, 244, 266, 281
master-apprentice relationships, 93, 94
materialism, 73
Mathews, Gordon, 177, 178
Matza, David, 30, 121, 217, 275
Mau Mau "Peasant Revolt," 91
Maynard, James E., 50
McLaughlin, Eugene, 73, 191
Meagher, Kate, 87, 94
Medicaid, 237
Medina, Leandro, 90, 91
Meliala, Adrianus, 261

MEND. *See* Movement for the Emancipation of the Niger Delta (MEND)
Meng Hongwei, 254
Merton, Robert K., 73, 120
methamphetamine, 3, 117, 189, 230, 260, 279
"Methodological Issues in Feminist Research" (Agozino), 7
Metropolitan Police Bureau, 231
Metz, Helen C., 48
Mexico, 5, 30, 51, 109, 267
Miami, 236
Michelle, Alexander, 265
middlemen minorities, 145
Midwest Writing Centers Association (MWCA), 212
military dictatorship, 86, 156
Mingardi, Guaracy, 162, 249
Ministry of Economic Relations and Foreign Trade, 209
Ministry of Health, 28
Ministry of Justice, China, 209
Ministry of Justice, Nigeria, 32
Ministry of Public Security, 180
Minteh, Binneh S., 18
Mitchell, Ofoyeju, 29
MMIA. *See* Murtala Mohammed International Airport (MMIA)
MNF. *See* Monkey No Fine (MNF)
Mochtar, Akil, 260
modern contraceptive methods, 54
money laundering, 30, 31, 71, 82, 83, 160, 179, 237, 248, 266
Money Laundering Act (1986), 266
Money Laundering Decree (1995), 35–36, 243
monkey-head, 18
Monkey No Fine (MNF), 146, 148, 248
moral entrepreneurs, 196
Morgan Stanley, 65
morphine, 113
Movement for the Emancipation of the Niger Delta (MEND), 66, 240
Mugford, Stephen, 203

Mujahidin rebels, 232
multinational companies/corporations,
    63, 69, 78, 123
Muncie, John, 73
Murtala Mohammed International
    Airport (MMIA), 4, 46, 102, 127,
    128
MWCA. *See* Midwest Writing Centers
    Association (MWCA)
Myrdal, Gunnar, 51, 72

NACOB. *See* Ghanaian Narcotics
    Control Board (NACOB)
Nadvi, Khalid, 148
NAFDAC. *See* National Agency for
    Food and Drug Administration and
    Control (NAFDAC)
Nana, Olomu, 21
narcoterrorism, 263
narcotic drugs, 4, 17, 25, 30, 37, 179,
    186, 226, 254
narcotics certification (decertification),
    30, 31, 34
The Nation, 103
National Academy of Sciences, 257,
    264, 265
National Agency for Food and Drug
    Administration and Control
    (NAFDAC), 122
National Anti-Drugs Agency, 226
National Board for Technical Education,
    88
National Bureau of Statistics (NBS),
    53, 57
National Council of Judges, 159
National Drug Control Master Plan
    2015–2019 (NDCMP), 1–2, 113, 243
National Drug Control Strategy Reports,
    262
National Drug Threat Assessment, 263
National Justice Council, 166
National Narcotics Control Commission,
    175
National Police Force, 248
National Policy on Education (NPE), 57

National Registry of Exonerations, 257
Nazis, 265
NBM. *See* Neo Black Movement
    (NBM)
NBS Demographic Statistic Bulletin, 53
NDCMP. *See* National Drug Control
    Master Plan 2015–2019 (NDCMP)
NDLEA. *See* Nigerian National Drug
    Law Enforcement Agency (NDLEA)
Ndrangheta, 280
Neo Black Movement (NBM), 150–51
neocolonialism, 21, 42, 91, 141
neoliberalism, 188
neopatrimonialism, 48
Netherlands, 5, 7–9, 28, 30, 40, 118,
    128, 137, 228, 238, 268–72, 274,
    276, 279; coffee shops, 37–38;
    Nigerian drug traffickers in, 241–42;
    tolerance policy in drug cases, 37
neutralization technique, 30, 122, 199,
    201, 204, 215, 217, 275
Newburn, Tim, 227, 233
The New Jim Crow (Michelle), 265
"The New Liberal Imperialism"
    (Cooper), 61
Newman, Edward, 51
news media, 4, 191, 192
Newswatch, 26
New York City, 233, 264
New Yorker, 65
New York Times, 196
New Zealand, 112, 270
Ngurah Rai International Airport, 258
Niger Delta, 36, 63, 66, 70, 77, 78, 240,
    241
Niger Delta militant groups, 33, 46, 63,
    70, 93, 263
Nigeria, 1–7, 8, 11, 12, 14, 204, 210,
    223, 226, 240, 273, 274, 277, 282,
    283; corrupt judiciary and antidrug
    enforcement, 245–47; deplorable
    prison conditions, 244–45; drug
    policy, 28, 30, 32, 38, 39; economy,
    35, 37, 51, 53, 61–64, 89, 119;
    ethnic groups, 2, 8, 45, 75, 81, 90,

95–96, 98; government, 29, 39, 45, 55, 74, 76, 77, 83, 87, 122, 178; military approach to drug control, 38; politics and politicians, 28, 75, 77, 81, 93, 119; role in global cocaine trade, 275–76; salary of lawmakers, 80; slums in, 74, 75, 158; universities, 56–57, 59. *See also* cocaine emergence in Nigeria
Nigeria National Assembly, 80
Nigerian civil war (1966–1970), 45
Nigerian cocaine traffickers, 1–3, 7, 9, 10, 12–15, 18, 23, 49, 64, 84, 93, 273; "big man" smugglers, 116–20, 275; chain of command, 131–33; cocaine consumption, 112–16; crowning, 110–11; early origins for modern network, 108–9; evade control, 128–30; foreign partners, 109–10; part-time couriers and freelance traffickers, 126–28, 275; problem of controlling, 243–47; resilient, 136–37; ritual priests and pastors, 134–35; small-scale traffickers, 120–23, 275; strikers, 10, 15, 27, 30, 31, 43, 92, 101, 124, 129, 132, 133, 182, 275, 276; "suicide birds" and couriers, 124–26, 275; widespread contacts, 131. *See also individual countries*
Nigerian cocaine trafficking, 1, 2, 3, 5–8, 7–11, 14, 17–18, 24, 26, 33–35, 43, 45–47, 52, 75, 78, 79, 82, 90, 109, 111, 143, 147, 152, 274. *See also* cultural factors and Nigerian cocaine trafficking
Nigerian Corruption Survey (2017), 57
"Nigerian Dream," 3, 46, 71–75, 120, 278
Nigerian Embassy, Beijing, 212
"Nigerian Inflation Rate Rises," 62
Nigerian Labour Act (1971, sect. 49–53, 59–60), 94
Nigerian National Drug Law Enforcement Agency (NDLEA), 1, 4, 17, 23, 28, 29, 31, 32, 34–37, 41,

102, 112, 115, 117, 118, 122, 126, 128, 235, 243–46
Nigerian Prison Correctional Service, 41
Nigerian(s), 1, 4–10, 11, 23, 25, 30–32, 74, 89, 119, 155; diaspora, 143, 230, 232, 234, 240, 282, 283; educated in US and UK, 234; fertility, 53, 54; living abroad, 43; Muslims, 67; "new generation" in São Paulo, 145–47; role in global cocaine trade, 275–79, 282, 283; traders and farmers, 92; youths, 39, 64–71, 101, 143
Nigerian "state crisis," 3, 5, 45–84, 86, 100, 122, 144, 146, 215; "chop money" syndrome and globalization, 75–79; historical influences, 47–50; nonstop looting, 82–84; permeable and ineffectual borders control, 46–47; rule of law and "Nigerian Dream," 71–75; soft state and weak state, 50–71; structurally underpinned economies, 79–82
night clubs, 186
Nixon, Richard Milhous, 4, 27
normalization policy, 268, 269
North, Oliver, 26
North Africa, 18, 33
"Not Just in Transit: Drugs the State and Society in West Africa," 13
NPE. *See* National Policy on Education (NPE)
Nwaliosa, Hansen A., 256
Nwannennaya, Chukwunyere, 18
Nwoko, Ginika, 133

Oakland, 233
Obasanjo, Olusegun, 220, 221
Observatory of Economic Complexity, 143
official corruption, 252, 254
Ogas, 101, 103, 107, 117, 275
OGD. *See* World Geopolitics of Drugs (OGD)
Ogoni tribe, 79
Ohafia, 96

oil boom, 27, 45, 123
oil industry, 64, 78, 79
oil prices decline, 61–62, 86
oil revenue, 60–63, 77, 277
oil thefts, 70
Ojukwu, Emmanuel Osita, 213, 214
Ojukwu, Ijeoma, 126
Okah, Henry, 240
Okolo Emenike Kingsley, 122
Okon, Gloria, 26
Okorocha, Rochas, 80–81
Okoye, Samuel I., 256
Okpala (Diokpa), 96
Olabisi Onabanjo University, 59
Olaiya, Temitope Ayoni, 236–37
Olateru-Olagbegi, Adegbenie, 116
Oloko, Wale, 193
Olorunkoya, Iyabo, 26
O'Malley, Pat, 203
Omigie, Christopher, 134, 135
ONCB. *See* Thai Office of the Narcotics
    Control Board (ONCB)
one-on-one crime, 38
Onunwa, Udobata, 100
Onwumere, Peter Christophe, 162
Operation Navara, 23, 33
Opium Act (1976), 269
Ori Ojori mode, 96
Ossy, Emma, 215
Otu, Smart E., 246
Outsiders (Becker), 196
Oxfam. *See* Oxford Committee for
    Famine Relief (Oxfam)
Oxford Committee for Famine Relief
    (Oxfam), 79
Oyibo JJC ("White Johnny Just
    Come"), 109, 117

Palermo Convention, 160
palm oil, 90, 92
Paraguay, 109, 151, 249
Paris Club, 31
parole, 36, 43, 166, 168, 169, 245
part-time couriers and freelance
    traffickers, 126–28, 188

patrilineal culture of inheritance, 95–97
patrimonialism, 48
Patriotic Citizen Initiatives, 192
Paul III (Pope), 19
peacekeeping (peace enforcement), 27
penal harm movement, 244
Penitenciária Feminina da Capital
    (PFC). *See* Women's Penitentiary of
    the Capital
People's Bank of China, 252
Pereira, Raimundo, 33
perfect-crime-as-no-crime thesis, 175
permanent residency permit, 195
Peru, 1, 30, 111, 149, 166, 271
Peru: The New Cocaine Kingdom, 111
pharmaceutical industry, 27
Philippines, 24, 189
Phillips, Dom, 161
Pius IX (Pope), 21
plural legal system, 95
police corruption, 233
policy decision-making, 28
political power, 76–78
Pomeranz, Kenneth, 78
"Poor Spousal Contraceptive
    Communication" (Izugbara et al.), 54
popular culture, 5
population growth, 43, 45, 46, 53, 54,
    59, 68
Portes, Alejandro, 87
Portugal, 21, 51, 270, 276, 279
postage method, 183–85, 228
poverty, 5, 39, 45, 52–54, 59–61, 64–
    71, 73, 79, 87, 111, 123, 125, 143,
    156, 158, 159, 221, 226, 240
"Poverty and Crime Review. Anti-
    Poverty Strategies for the UK"
    (Webster and Kingston), 66
Pratt, Travis C., 67
prebendalism, 119
predatory state, 45, 76
Premium Times, 166
"Preserving Judicial Independence in a
    Period of national Transformation,"
    246

Primeiro Comando da Capital (PCC).
See First Command of the Capital
primitive accumulation, 77
primogeniture, 96, 97
prison labor enterprises, 208
prison systems, 166, 168, 207, 236, 244,
    245, 261, 262, 264
private sector, 39, 64, 76, 77, 88, 95
private sector partnerships, 103, 104
prostitution, 69, 75, 78, 153, 235
PSB. *See* Public Security Bureau (PSB)
psychoactive substances, 30, 268
public sector, 52, 76, 77, 100, 146, 163
Public Security Bureau (PSB), 197, 214
Public Security Institute, 157
Pulse.ng, 82
Pure Third Command, 248
Putnam, Robert D., 81
Pyrrhic defeat theory, 5, 38, 42, 159, 281

qaf, 40
QSA. *See* Quota System of Admission
    (QSA)
quality education, 56, 57, 60, 277
Quota System of Admission (QSA), 56

race and class, 22
"Race and Wrongful Convictions in the
    United States" (Gross, Possley, and
    Stephens), 239
racism, 184, 196, 197, 257, 279
racist apartheid regime, 27
RAD. *See* Rockefeller Foundation-
    Aspen Institute Diaspora Program
    (RAD)
Ramkhamhaeng Road, 230
Ranger, Terence, 155
"Rank and Class Among the Asante and
    Fante in the Nineteenth Century"
    (Arhin), 47
rational choice theory, 200
Razak, Najib, 227
Razaq, Taiwo, 59
RCC. *See* Roman Catholic Church
    (RCC)

Reagan, Ronald, 26
recidivism, 208–10, 245
"The Reckoning is Real" (James), 20
recreational drugs, 114, 174
Red Command, 248
rehabilitation, 36, 208, 244, 254
Reich, Michael, 65
Reiman, Jeffrey, 38, 41, 67, 159, 167,
    220, 265
reintegrative shaming, 219
"Reissue of Regulations Prohibiting
    the Export of Products Made in a
    Reform-through-labor Programme,"
    209
relative deprivation, 67, 73, 122, 277
"rentier states," 63
Resident Labor Market Test, 194
Revenue Mobilization Allocation and
    Fiscal Commission, 80
reverse social capital, 3, 43, 46, 82, 84,
    116, 133
Ribadu, Nuhu, 82
Riemer, Jeffrey, 203
Rockefeller Foundation-Aspen Institute
    Diaspora Program (RAD), 232, 234
Rodrigo, E. K., 270
Rolles, Steve, 266
Roman Catholic Church (RCC), 17, 19,
    20, 276
Ronald, Kramer C., 47
Rosenzweig, Mark R., 99
Ross, Michael L., 62, 63
Rotterdam, 241, 242
routine activities theory, 200
Roy, Godson, 253
Royal Malaysian Police, 227
Royal Netherlands Marechaussee, 129
Royal Niger Company, 142
Ruggiero, Vincenzo, 45, 119, 278

Sabiu, Ibrahim T., 90
saidinha, 156–58
Samsung, 177
Santos, Juan Manuel, 154
Sanusi, Mallam Lamido, 80

Sanyuanli, 180
São Paulo (SP), 15, 93, 97, 100, 121, 127, 135, 136, 139, 144–50
SAP. *See* Structural Adjustment Program (SAP)
Saraki, Bukola, 82, 83
Saros, 141, 142
Saro-Wiwa, Ken, 79
Schiphol Airport, 241
Schmitz, Hubert, 148
Schneidera, Friedrich, 87
school dropouts, 59
secondhand smoke, 41
Second World War, 18, 19
Section 42(1) and Section 42(2), Constitution of the Federal Republic of Nigeria 1999, 97
The Seductions of Crime (Katz), 200
self-filling prophecy, 200
Service Delivery Indicator survey (2013), 56
SGBN. *See* Sociéte Generale Bank of Nigeria (SGBN)
shadow economy. *See* informal economy
Shagari regime (1979–1983), 123
shame management, 218–19
Shanghai, 187, 188
Sharia Law, 48
shark couriers, 118
Shaw, Mark, 123, 248
Shell Oil, 77–79
Shenzhen, 187
"Shila boys," 64
Shitta-Bey, Muhammad, 142
Shitta-Bey Mosque, 141
shotgun method, 130, 136
Sierra Leone, 18, 61, 141, 142
Sinaloa Cartel, 236
Singapore, 24, 173, 182, 256, 260
Sistema Único de Saúde, 169
skin color, 196
slavery, 17–22, 42, 91, 139–41, 143, 156, 276
slave trade, 1, 19–21, 108, 139–43, 276

Small and Medium Enterprises (SMEs), 103–4
Smart on Crime (Harris and Hamilton), 42
SMEs. *See* Small and Medium Enterprises (SMEs)
Smith, Daniel, 72
social capital, 81–82, 107, 131, 148, 167, 248
"Social Construction of Guangzhou as a Translocal Trading Place" (Gilles), 178
social exclusion, 52
socialization, 66, 98
social justice, 60
social mobility, 73, 82, 101
social networks, 3, 7, 9, 46, 81, 84, 148, 245
"Social Structure and Anomie" (Merton), 73
Sociéte Generale Bank of Nigeria (SGBN), 82
Society of Jesus, 19, 20
socioeconomic status, 67
"soft drugs," 37, 113, 185, 226–27
"sorting" and "half-baked/unbaked" graduates, 58–60
South America, 2, 47, 110, 115, 117, 140, 144, 149, 203, 273, 275
Southeast Asia, 3, 130, 223, 228, 229, 232, 255, 276
Southwest Asia, 23, 30
Soyinka, Wole, 48
Spain, 19, 121, 137, 174, 224, 225, 270, 276
spiritual beliefs and emotions, 54
Spohn, Cassia, 264
SSA. *See* Sub-Saharan Africa (SSA)
Standard Bank, 61
Standard Chartered Bank Nigeria, 92
standard of living, 67, 68, 83, 103
"State Collapse and Criminal Expansion" (Shaw), 123
State Crime Around the World (Ebbe), 21

State Department for Narcotics Investigations, 162
Stolpe, Oliver, 35
stop-and-search operations, 160
St. Philips Catholic Church, 133
strain theory, 97
street dealers and dealing, 114–16, 185–86, 190, 213–15, 252
Structural Adjustment Program (SAP), 86, 87, 122, 123
Sub-Saharan Africa (SSA), 56, 86, 92, 109, 110, 130, 134, 151, 195, 238, 249, 275
"suicide balls" (wrapped cocaine), 104, 105, 147, 234
Suiming, Pan, 175
Sukhumvit Road, 230
Sungai Buloh Prison, 32, 224
Sun Yee On, 179
supernatural protection, 134
sustainable agriculture, 39
Suzhou Industrial Park Administrative Committee, 177
Switzerland, 270, 271, 279
Sykes, Gresham M., 30, 121, 217, 275
syndicated plagiarism, 58
synthetic drugs, 13, 78, 112, 228, 241, 281

Tanzania, 182
Tarus, Issa, 91
TAST. *See* Trans-Atlantic Slave Trade (TAST)
tax burdens, 86, 90, 91, 120, 123
tax revenues, 17, 272, 280
Taylor, Erin B., 67
TBA. *See* Tri-Border Area (TBA)
Tengpongsthorn, Wuthichai, 231
terrorism, 50, 60, 68, 78, 238, 241, 277
ter Weel, Bas, 81
Thailand, 174, 183, 240, 256
Thailand, Nigerian drug traffickers in, 228–32; control, 230–32; couriers, 229–30

Thai Narcotics Act B.E. 2522 (1979), 230
Thai Office of the Narcotics Control Board (ONCB), 228, 231
Thalib, Iwan, 258
Thatcher, Margret, 60
Third National Human Rights Action plan, 231
Third Plenum, 18th Party Congress, 210
tiao-kuai system, 253
Tibke, Patrick, 175
Tin Can Port Lagos, 118
TNI. *See* The Transnational Institute (TNI)
tobacco use, 41
Topik, Steven, 78
Toumani, Jorge Rafaat, 249
tramadol, 113, 114
Trans-Atlantic Slave Trade (TAST), 19, 22
transnational black markets, 86
The Transnational Institute (TNI), 153
transnational mobility, 195, 214
Transparency International, 260
triad gangs, 179
Tri-Border Area (TBA), 109
Trump, Donald J., 60
"try your luck" method, 183–85
Tumorang, Raynov, 257
Turkey, 24
Tutu, 215
"two-track" policy, 269

UAC trading company, 90, 91
Ubiaja Prison, Edo State, 36
Ucha, Chimobi, 70
Udama, Rawlings. A., 247
Uganda, 56, 57, 113, 180, 187
UK Home Office, 233
ultimogeniture, 96, 97
underdevelopment, 50, 61, 62, 69, 119
UNECA. *See* United Nations Economic Commission for Africa (UNECA)
unemployment, 14, 33, 39, 53, 61–65, 68–70, 103, 120, 221, 226, 233, 277

UN General Assembly, 271, 279
UNHRC. *See* United Nations Human
 Rights Council (UNHRC)
UNHRC Working Group on Arbitration
 Detention, 168
UN International Conventions, 30, 243
UN International Day against Drug
 Abuse and Illicit Trafficking, 249,
 256
United Kingdom (UK), 8, 30, 40, 71,
 128, 137, 194, 270, 271, 279. *See
 also* Britain
United Nations, 40, 79, 155
United Nations Children Fund, 59
United Nations Convention Against
 Illicit Traffic in Narcotics Drugs and
 Psychotropic Substances, 3
United Nations Economic Commission
 for Africa (UNECA), 53
United Nations Human Rights Council
 (UNHRC), 165
United Nations International Drug
 Control Programme, 31
United Nations Office on Drugs and
 Crime (UNODC), 1, 2, 17, 24, 32,
 33, 35, 40, 59, 113, 114, 136, 159
United States, 8, 20, 23–28, 30, 31, 35,
 39–41, 50, 67, 71, 76, 103, 104, 112,
 120, 128, 134, 153, 162, 166, 173,
 174, 244, 269, 271, 272, 276, 281–83
United States and United Kingdom,
 cocaine strikers in, 232–33; African
 criminal groups, 236–38; cost of
 law enforcement, 261–67; labeling
 Nigerians, 234–36; Nigerian
 criminals and educated Nigerian
 professionals, 233–34, 283; Nigerian
 inmates, 238–41
United States Department of
 Agriculture, 62
universal primary education, 55
Universiti Utara Malaysia, 226
university education, 55–56
University of Chicago, 65
University of Ibadan (UI), 55, 57

The University System Study (2013), 57
The Unmaking of Tradition (Aradeon),
 141
UNODC. *See* United Nations Office on
 Drugs and Crime (UNODC)
UNODC Individual Drug Seizures, 43
UNODC World Drug, 112
unreported economy. *See* informal
 economy
UN World Drug Report, 115
urbanization, 61, 64
urban-rural migrations, 100, 158
Uruguay, 151, 268
U.S. Attorney's Office, Eastern District
 of Virginia, 237
U.S. Bureau of Justice, 221
U.S. Bureau of Justice Statistics, 262
U.S. Department of States, 24, 207, 244,
 261
U.S. Drug Enforcement Agency (DEA),
 28, 29, 120, 243, 263
U.S. embassy, 25
U.S. Supreme Court, 18, 21, 265
U.S. Uniform Crime Report (1974),
 264
Uyghur Human Rights Project, 207
Uzuegbu-Wilson, Emmanuel, 26

VAMP. *See* Victimization-As-Mere-
 Punishment (VAMP)
Vanguard, 133
van Ooyen-Houben, Marianne, 37
Venezuela, 151, 226, 249
victimization, 22, 30, 39, 42, 66
Victimization-As-Mere-Punishment
 (VAMP), 258, 276
Victimization-In-Punishment (VIP), 258
Vietnam War, 232
violence, 6, 11, 38, 51, 60, 68, 74–76,
 132, 154, 156, 157, 159, 162, 165,
 193, 215–17, 263, 268, 279
VIP. *See* Victimization-In-Punishment
 (VIP)
visa renewals, 201, 251
Vital National Interests Certification, 31

vocational education, 88
voodoo, 134, 169, 170

WACD. *See* West Africa Commission on Drugs (WACD)
Wachovia Bank, 266
Waller, Willard, 196
"Wall Street Profits Surge as Poverty Rises" (Cassidy), 65
war on crime, 5, 27
Waterfeld, Bruno, 272
The Water House (Olinto), 143
Waziri, Farida, 83
WCDDC. *See* White Cloud District Detention Centre (WCDDC)
"We Are Winning the Drug War," 29
Weber, Max, 49
Webster, Colin, 67
Wechsler, William, 109
wee-wee, 18
Wei Li, 178
West Africa, 2, 4, 5, 17, 18, 23, 24, 32, 33, 47, 51, 72, 108, 109–12, 117, 121, 136, 141, 249, 263, 267
West Africa Commission on Drugs (WACD), 13, 29
Western birth control methods, 53, 54
Western education, 55
Western values and beliefs, 100
White Cloud District Detention Centre (WCDDC), 181, 198, 206, 210
white market, 107, 121, 131, 132
"A Whole New Mind-set on Fighting Crime" (Covey), 212
Widodo, Joko, 256
"wife tax," 91
Williams, Phil, 253
Willis, Graham, 163

witchcraft, 134, 147, 169, 170
Women's Penitentiary of the Capital, 152, 167–71, 210
"Women's War," 90
Wong Chen, 227
Work and Life in China, 184
World Bank, 31, 47, 56, 57, 61, 69, 83, 86, 87
World Drug Day, 35
World Geopolitics of Drugs (OGD), 40
World Prison Brief (WPB), 261
World Summit on Social Development, 52
world systems theory, 78
The World University Rankings, 57
Wo Shing Wo, 179
WPB. *See* World Prison Brief (WPB)
The Wretched of the Earth (Fanon), 21

Xiamen University, 185
Xiaobei, 180
Xi Jinping, 252
Xinhua News, 195
Xin Ren, 209

Yang Yang, 177
Yardie gangs, 238, 280
Yoruba customary law, 96
Yorubas, 55, 141
You Must Set Forth at Dawn (Soyinka), 48
Young, Jock, 88, 146, 157
Yusuf, Musa Ahmed, 28

Zaitch, Damián, 127
Zhang Jijiao, 195
Zimbabwe, 182
Zuma, Jacob, 81

About the Author

As a son of a headmaster, Jude Roys Oboh was born and raised in Nigeria. Right from onset learning and studying were encouraged, also the Biafra civil war (1967–1970) influenced and motivated him to work hard. In 1977, his dream came true: he was selected by the Nigerian government to study in Italy. At the Istituto Professionale dell'Agricoltura he studied Agricultural Engineering. After graduation in Jesi (Ancona) he continued his education at the University of Florence, where he specialized himself in Tropical and Sub-Tropical Agriculture.

The author worked for several years through the Dutch Ministry of Foreign Affairs in The Hague for the FAO, in various agricultural projects in Africa, and in the South Pacific. These international commitments provided opportunities to live in various nations in the world and work with people from different backgrounds. It also gave him a possibility to learn several languages and develop insights into different cultures. This experiences and skills were paramount in the author's future career.

In the past 20 years, Jude Roys Oboh studied and worked in the Netherlands as a consultant for the Dutch Ministry of Justice. During his studies, Jude Roys became the best student in MA Global Criminology (2011) at the Utrecht University. He completed his PhD research in Global Criminology at the Willem Pompe Institute for Criminal Law and Criminology at the Utrecht University in the Netherlands (in 2016), and specialized in drug trafficking. The author's major areas are organized crime, crime/poverty and development in Africa, drug policies, environmental crimes, and qualitative research methods.

www.ingramcontent.com/pod-product-compliance
Lightning Source LLC
Chambersburg PA
CBHW050625280326
41932CB00015B/2532